Colorado & the Rockies For Dummies, 1st ~~Edition~~

BESTSELLING BOOK SERIES

Cheat!

Co_____ ___ Country

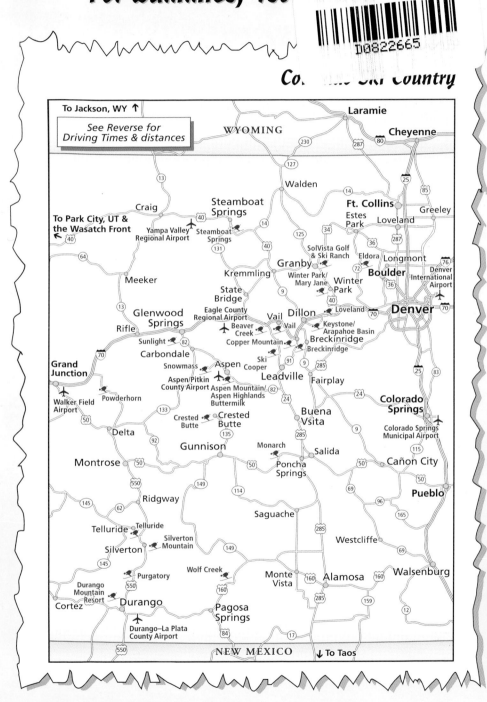

To Jackson, WY ↑

Laramie

See Reverse for Driving Times & distances

WYOMING

Cheyenne

For Dummies: Bestselling Book Series for Beginners

Colorado & the Rockies
For Dummies, 1st Edition

Cheat Sheet

Colorado Driving Times & Distances

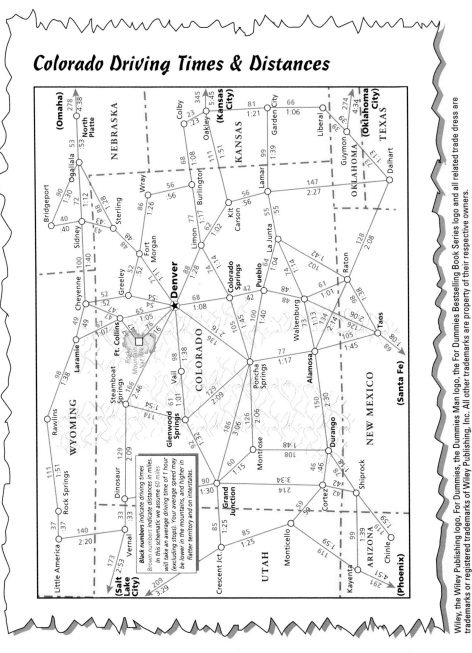

Copyright © 2003 Wiley Publishing, Inc.
All rights reserved.

Item 5492-1.

For more information about Wiley Publishing,
call 1-800-762-2974.

For Dummies: Bestselling Book Series for Beginners

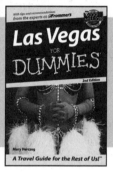

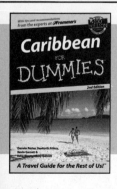
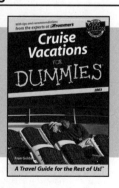

Colorado & the Rockies

FOR

DUMMIES®

1ST EDITION

by Alex Wells

Wiley Publishing, Inc.

Colorado & The Rockies For Dummies,® 1st Edition

Published by
Wiley Publishing, Inc.
909 Third Avenue
New York, NY 10022
www.wiley.com

Copyright © 2003 by Wiley Publishing, Inc., Indianapolis, Indiana

Published simultaneously in Canada

For general information on our other products and services or to obtain technical support, please contact our Customer Care Department within the U.S. at 800-762-2974, outside the U.S. at 317-572-3993, or fax 317-572-4002.

Wiley also publishes its books in a variety of electronic formats. Some content that appears in print may not be available in electronic books.

Library of Congress Cataloging-in-Publication Data:

Library of Congress Control Number: 2003101843

ISBN: 0-7645-5492-1

ISSN: 1541-6356

Manufactured in the United States of America

10 9 8 7 6 5 4 3 2 1

1B/QZ/QU/QT/IN

About the Author

Eighteen years ago, **Alex Wells** became transfixed by a Coors Light commercial and decided to drive west to Colorado to be a ski bum "for a year." He spent his first night shivering under a cotton blanket in the backseat of his Pontiac J-2000 at 8,000 feet in elevation, somewhere in Summit County. This experience taught him that the Rockies get frosty at night, even during the summer. A few years later, having already forgotten his first lesson, he rode his bicycle through Colorado during one of the wettest Mays in state history. On that trip, he discovered — on four separate occasions — that spring can be an atrocious time to pedal across the continental divide. A few years later, while checking into a famous luxury hotel in Denver on his first real business trip, he learned that his tattered old hockey-equipment bag was not suitable luggage for every Colorado accommodation.

For better or worse, Wells is still learning about Colorado every chance he gets. When not at his home in southern Utah, he regularly crosses the Colorado border to pedal the trails, soak in the hot springs, and ski the mountains. He still makes mistakes now and then, but the friendship, beauty, and joy that Colorado affords him more than compensate for his occasional misery.

A graduate of the Columbia School of Journalism, Wells is also the author of *Frommer's Grand Canyon National Park* and has written for publications such as *Men's Journal, Skiing, Condé Nast Traveler,* and *Backcountry.*

Author's Acknowledgments

Thanks to Kristin Rust of Colorado Ski Country U.S.A. for arranging a tour of Colorado's ski areas. What a blast!

Thanks to the following people in the following towns for setting up my visits: Jamie Hussman in Alamosa, Elizabeth Youngquist in Colorado Springs, Susan Ghysels in Steamboat Springs, Gaylene Ore in Grand County, Kayla Arnesen et al in Grand Junction, Ian Anderson et al in Vail, Dawn Ibis in Telluride, Rich Harter in Fort Collins, Rebecca Thompson in Crested Butte, Heidi Constock in Ridgway, Joy Kosenski in Boulder, Pat Richmond in Creede, Rich Grant and Jill Strunk in Denver, Lori Hogan and Tracey Walter in Glenwood Springs, Terry Hoffman in Evergreen, Sally Hameister in Pagosa Springs, Patti Zink in Durango, Jen Radueg in Breckenridge, Morene Scanlon in Leadville, Dixie Heyl in Carbondale, Rennie Ross in Ouray, and Lynn Dyer in Cortez. (Please forgive me if I omitted anyone.)

Thanks again to all the hoteliers, innkeepers, and restaurateurs — too numerous to name — who fed me, housed me, and then gently prodded me back on the road when it was time to go.

Thanks to the editors of this book, Naomi Kraus and Elizabeth Kuball.

And thanks, finally, to Dave at the Texaco near Cherry Creek, who plugged a nasty oil leak and made my truck purr even though it had 215,000 miles on it (and counting).

Publisher's Acknowledgments

We're proud of this book; please send us your comments through our Dummies online registration form located at www.dummies.com/register/.

Some of the people who helped bring this book to market include the following:

Editorial

Editors: Naomi P. Kraus and Elizabeth Kuball

Cartographer: Nicholas Trotter

Editorial Supervisor: Michelle Hacker

Editorial Assistant: Elizabeth Rea

Senior Photo Editor: Richard Fox

Cover Photos: Front Cover: Chris Marona/Viesti Collection, Inc.; Back Cover: Robert Mitchell/Viesti Collection, Inc.

Cartoons: Rich Tennant, www.the5thwave.com

Production

Project Coordinator: Ryan Steffen

Layout and Graphics: Joyce Haughey, Stephanie D. Jumper, Julie Trippetti, Jeremey Unger, Erin Zeltner

Proofreaders: John Greenough, Charles Spencer TECHBOOKS Production Services

Indexer: TECHBOOKS Production Services

Publishing and Editorial for Consumer Dummies

Diane Graves Steele, Vice President and Publisher, Consumer Dummies

Joyce Pepple, Acquisitions Director, Consumer Dummies

Kristin A. Cocks, Product Development Director, Consumer Dummies

Michael Spring, Vice President and Publisher, Travel

Brice Gosnell, Publishing Director, Travel

Suzanne Jannetta, Editorial Director, Travel

Publishing for Technology Dummies

Andy Cummings, Vice President and Publisher, Dummies Technology/General User

Composition Services

Gerry Fahey, Vice President of Production Services

Debbie Stailey, Director of Composition Services

Contents at a Glance

Maps at a Glance

Table of Contents

Introduction

● ●

*P*hotographs of purple mountain majesties, roaring rivers, and high alpine lakes don't even come close to capturing Colorado's essence. To do that, the photos would also have to deliver the sweet pungency of pine trees after a rainstorm, the coolness of snowflakes on your cheeks, and the half rustle, half rattle of aspen leaves in a fall breeze. They would have to re-create the weightless sensation that powder skiers experience in between turns and the icy splash of river water on a spring raft trip. Then they'd have to dish up a gourmet dinner of native game, a tasty microbrew, and the real-life smile of a friendly server. That's asking way too much of a photograph. And it's one big reason why you should travel to Colorado.

Unfortunately, like most things that are really sensational, Colorado involves a certain element of risk. While you absorb the mountain beauty, the mountain beauty can absorb you as well. If you're not careful, you can easily freeze, crash your car, get lost, or get swept away by snow. There are lesser risks, too: restaurants expensive enough to make Donald Trump blanch, motels with papier-mâché walls, servers who incessantly call you "dude," undersized beers, oversized bears, bad bands, boring boutiques, and black-and-white color televisions.

Luckily, you've done the right thing and bought this book, which will help you avoid any potential pitfalls that could mar your trip. In these pages, you'll find everything you need to know to freely enjoy the majestic mountains, rich history, and diverse cultures of the Rocky Mountain State.

About This Book

Guidebook writers like to think that readers page through their books from cover to cover as if the books were suspense thrillers or Harlequin romances. You're welcome to read *Colorado & The Rockies For Dummies* that way; I, for one, would appreciate your perseverance. Be forewarned, however, that nothing earthshaking will be consummated in the last chapter.

If you're pressed for time, you can read only the chapters or sections that interest you most because the book is set up to read like a reference book. In fact, the chapters on particular regions and cities are close to being guidebooks unto themselves. For example, if you plan to travel to Mesa Verde, you can go straight to Chapter 21, which covers Southwestern Colorado. It has the lowdown on the park, hotel and restaurant recommendations, maps, driving tips, area attractions, and curious facts that should inspire and delight you. If Rocky Mountain National Park is your destination, then Chapter 15 is the place to go.

Other parts of the book provide information that will help you *reach* your destination as efficiently as possible. For example, if you need to fly into Denver and then rent a car to drive to Mesa Verde, go to Chapter 6 for tips on traveling to Colorado. If you want to hit the slopes while you're in town, but you aren't sure when the flakes start flying, see Chapter 2 for suggestions on Colorado's seasonal offerings. Still other chapters offer tips that will make you a better traveler, no matter what your destination.

In order to make the region and city chapters self-contained, I do repeat myself some. For example, you'll find information on the Amtrak train that passes through Colorado in several destination chapters. I repeat this information not because of premature senility but because the train seemed to turn up nearly everywhere I visited. (It was almost creepy.)

Conventions Used in This Book

The hotel and restaurant recommendations in this book are split into two categories: my personal favorites and other places I feel comfortable recommending. Don't hesitate to visit any of the listed establishments. All are pleasant; the bad places have been relegated to other guidebooks. Sure, a little personal bias may have crept in to my selections, but I'm definitely not as bad as an Olympic figure skating judge. And I do try to clarify my reasoning, so you can factor in your own preferences.

I also provide some pricing information that you can use to help keep your trip on budget (or not). The number of dollar signs next to a hotel's name tells you roughly how much the hotel costs for a one-night stay for two people; the number of dollar signs next to a restaurant's name represents the general range of prices for dinner entrees (or, in some cases, fixed-price meals). Here's how to translate the dollar signs.

Dollar Signs	*Hotel*	*Restaurant*
$	$75 or less	$10 or less
$$	$76 to $125	$11 to $20
$$$	$126 to $175	$21 to $35
$$$$	$176 or more	$36 or more

After each review, you'll encounter a host of additional numbers, names, and abbreviations, which at first glance may seem confusing. These are how I condense key facts about the establishment. A few things to remember: Phone numbers are listed in bold alongside the telephone icon. Specific pricing information is also given. The hotel prices are usually the *rack rates* — that is, the double-occupancy rates before any discounts are given — for particular periods. (**Remember:** By using the tips in Chapter 8, you can often avoid paying the rack rate.) Unless otherwise noted, restaurant prices reflect the price range for dinner entrees.

I also use abbreviations for the credit cards accepted by the establishments I review in this book. I only kept track of the majors, so if your particular card isn't listed here, it may or may not be accepted. The abbreviations, and the credit cards represented by them, are as follows:

> AE: American Express
>
> DC: Diners Club
>
> DISC: Discover
>
> MC: MasterCard
>
> V: Visa

Foolish Assumptions

In writing this book, I made some assumptions about you and what you may need from a Colorado guidebook. Here's what I assumed:

- ✔ You may be a traveler who is new to Colorado, and you're trying to determine what to see and when to see it.

- ✔ You may have traveled through Colorado in the past, but now you have less time and want insider information that can help you plan the most efficient trip possible. Or you want to plan an adventure or two instead of just driving around looking at mountains.

- ✔ You don't want a book that lists every restaurant, bar, hotel, and attraction, no matter how bad. You just want accurate descriptions of the best places within a variety of price ranges.

If any of my foolish assumptions prove to be, in your case, not so foolish, you'll benefit from reading *Colorado & The Rockies For Dummies.*

How This Book Is Organized

In order to make this book more useful as a reference guide, I've broken it up into six logical sections, each one discussing a different aspect of your Colorado trip. Each section is further divided into a handful of quick, easy-to-read chapters. If a particular subject doesn't interest you, skip it and go straight to the chapter that has the information you need. You won't fail Colorado Vacation 101 just because you don't read the whole book. I'm too lazy to write an exam.

Part 1: Getting Started

This section identifies the state's treasures — both man-made and natural. It sums up the most interesting regions, from the red-rock canyons of the Four Corners area to the 14,000-foot summits of the southern Rockies. And it tells you the best times to go to the area of your choice. I also propose some itineraries, including ones for history buffs, for adventure-seekers, and for people traveling with children. And I offer Colorado-specific travel tips for those with special travel needs or interests, including families, seniors, people with disabilities, and gays and lesbians.

Part 11: Ironing Out the Details

If you have a question about trip-planning, this section more than answers it. Here you'll find tips on how to reach Colorado by plane, train, or automobile, and on how to get around Colorado after you cross the state line. I also discuss the various accommodations choices in Colorado. You'll discover when and why to choose different payment methods while traveling, and what to do when your wallet goes skittering down a mountainside (or is otherwise compromised), taking all those payment methods with it. I tell you which tickets and reservations you'll need to arrange in advance of your trip, and then share information on how to do it. There are even a few pointers on packing. By the time you finish Part II, you'll be ready to hit the road.

Part 111: Exploring the Big Cities

This part tells you everything you need to know in order to enjoy Colorado's two largest cities: Denver and Colorado Springs. In it, you'll get the lowdown on getting to them and, after you're there, getting around. I also direct you to the most exciting experiences and recommend the finest restaurants, the cushiest accommodations, the spiciest nightclubs, and the most intriguing neighborhoods. For those who want to spend most of their vacation in Denver or Colorado Springs, it also identifies fun side trips outside — but not too far outside — the city lights.

Part 1V: Northern Colorado

This section is a lot like the previous one, only with fewer people and more livestock. The four chapters in this part each cover a different region or national park inside Colorado. Although they do include some midsize cities (Boulder, for one), the regions consist mostly of small mountain towns (including some of Colorado's best ski spots) and open countryside. For each area I cover, I tell you how to get there and get around, and where to stay, play, party, shop, and eat. I also share some of my favorite natural settings to explore.

Part V: Southern Colorado

In addition to having many of the state's highest mountains, South Central and Southwestern Colorado are graced with smaller surprises such as hot springs, desert canyons, sand dunes, relaxed towns, and ancient Indian dwellings. In this part, I do everything possible to make sure you don't speed past the area's hidden wonders. And, of course, I also tell you where to stay and eat along the way.

Part VI: The Part of Tens

The Part of Tens is, in reality, far more lighthearted than its ominous-sounding title. Each chapter in this fun section showcases a roster of related items, much like one of David Letterman's Top Ten lists — only, in this case, each list pertains to Colorado, and I'm not half as funny.

Quick Concierge

Imagine a helpful concierge who is an all-around Colorado expert and has the recall of an elephant. The Quick Concierge section of this book is as close as you'll come to finding that person. It distills key information on subjects ranging from the American Automobile Association to weather. It also has contact numbers and Web sites for major airlines, rental-car agencies, and hotel chains; and it lists several outstanding sources for finding more information on current happenings in Colorado.

Icons Used in This Book

I use five different icons in this book to call your attention to different types of information. Here's what each means:

This icon means you're about to get some handy advice on how to budget your time and resources to make the most of an opportunity.

This icon stands for tourist traps, rip-offs, and other things to beware. Loosely translated, it means, "Don't do what the author did."

This one calls attention to restaurants, hotels, and attractions that are especially friendly to kids.

Whereas the Heads Up icon usually alerts you to great items for those with large trust funds and limitless bank accounts, the Bargain Alert icon identifies great deals for *you.*

Colorado is filled with magnificent scenery, and this icon highlights particularly noteworthy spots that showcase the state's natural beauty.

Where to Go from Here

Unlike most states, Colorado sprawls both horizontally and vertically. It has more 14,000-foot peaks (53) than any other state, not to mention grasslands, red-rock canyons, and high-desert mesas. This means your travels will involve not only significant distances, but also some major twists and turns. The beauty comes at you from a variety of angles, and there's never enough time to absorb it all. Nor is there time to experience all the activities that go with this turf — everything from hot springs to hiking.

You can smooth out your trip by considering ahead of time what attracts you most in Colorado, and then planning a trip around your interests. That way, fewer distractions will come into play, and you'll be able to concentrate on the magnificence of your surroundings. Be sure, however, to leave a few things to chance! Ideally, this book will help you straddle the divide between practicality and spontaneity; between security and adventure; and between a warm car and the call of the wild. So saddle up or strap on those skis and keep reading!

Part I
Getting Started

In this part . . .

So, you're thinking about visiting Colorado, but you aren't really sure where to start. Don't worry! This part tells you how to begin organizing your trip. After discussing the very best things in the state, it weighs the pros and cons of coming at different times, provides four great itineraries that will help you make the most of your time, and offers ideas on how to visit the state without exceeding your budget. It also provides travel tips for parents, gays and lesbians, people with disabilities, and seniors.

Chapter 1

Discovering the Best of Colorado

· ·

· ·

*I*f you've seen TV commercials showing images of mountain life in Colorado, you may wonder how much of what's on the screen is real and how much is the brainchild of copywriters on Madison Avenue.

On the truth side: Huge, silent, snowy mountains really do exist in the state, and they're even more awesome than those onscreen. Ranchers really do ride around on horses (and sometimes ATVs), mend fences, and then unwind over cheap beers. And, if you subtract a few emaciated female supermodels, the fun-loving young adults shown frolicking on television aren't much different from the ones you'll find in Colorado.

As for the myths: Well, Clydesdales cannot kick field goals, not even under the best conditions; bighorn sheep rarely butt heads with teenagers (though it may do some good); and SUVs do not make you invincible. Now that I've cleared up these popular misconceptions, I'll fill you in on the amazing things you'll find when you turn off the television and head to Colorado.

Tripping through History

During a noisy, wild, ambitious half-century from 1850 to 1900, recent arrivals to the southern Rocky Mountains homesteaded land, laid railroad track, cleared forests, erected towns, and dug up tons of precious ores. Their history would be fascinating even if they hadn't left such an obvious mark on the state. In Colorado, you'll not only hear their stories, you'll see the abandoned mines, Victorian homes, false-fronted Main Streets, broken rails, ghost towns, and dusty corrals. And the state's many museums help piece together the stories behind every landmark. Of these, my favorite is the **Ouray County Museum** (Chapter 21), which features a different exhibit in every room of a historic hospital building. But even when you step outside the museums, you'll still be surrounded by history.

Partly because they litter otherwise natural settings, the mines and mine tailings from the late 1800s are especially obvious. In **Willow Creek Canyon** (Chapter 19) above Creede, perfectly preserved wooden mine structures seem to cling to the sides of cliffs. The mining district around **Leadville** (Chapter 19) is so large, you can take three different hour-long driving tours of the area, passing tailings, town sites, and ramshackle buildings along the way. If you want an earful of Colorado's mining history, take a train ride a thousand feet into the cool darkness of **Old Hundred Gold Mine** near Silverton (Chapter 21), then hang on while your guide chatters away with the old drilling and mucking machinery.

The visitor centers of most towns offer brochures for self-guided walking tours. Grab a brochure, and then stroll past colorful Victorian homes and buildings that were once boarding houses, brothels, opera houses, saloons, general stores, railroad depots, and mills. Besides Leadville and Creede, you'll enjoy the historic mine towns of **Aspen** (Chapter 17), **Crested Butte** (Chapter 20), **Telluride** (Chapter 21), **Silverton** (Chapter 21), **Durango** (Chapter 21), **Lake City** (Chapter 20), and **Breckenridge** (Chapter 18), to name just a few spots.

The former boomtowns of **Cripple Creek, Central City,** and **Black Hawk** (Chapter 13) still showcase plenty of historic buildings despite being partially overrun by modern-day casinos. And don't miss **Redstone** (Chapter 17), where a coal-mining magnate built a Utopian community for his workforce in the early 1900s. An immense Tudor mansion, an Arts and Crafts–style lodge, and a handful of individually designed cottages remain from that grandiose but short-lived effort.

Railroads once snaked up river canyons and sliced across mountainsides near the mines. Because they were cheaper to build and could go through more rugged country, narrow-gauge rails often linked mines in the mountains to valley towns that were accessible by standard-gauge rails. Most of these narrow-gauge lines closed decades ago, but a handful remain in operation as tourist attractions. My favorite, the **Durango & Silverton Narrow Gauge Railroad** (Chapter 21), takes passengers through the San Juan mountains to the former mining town of **Silverton,** where you may feel as if you're disembarking in the past. There are other historic rail lines throughout the state, as well as several museums that specialize in trains.

Colorado

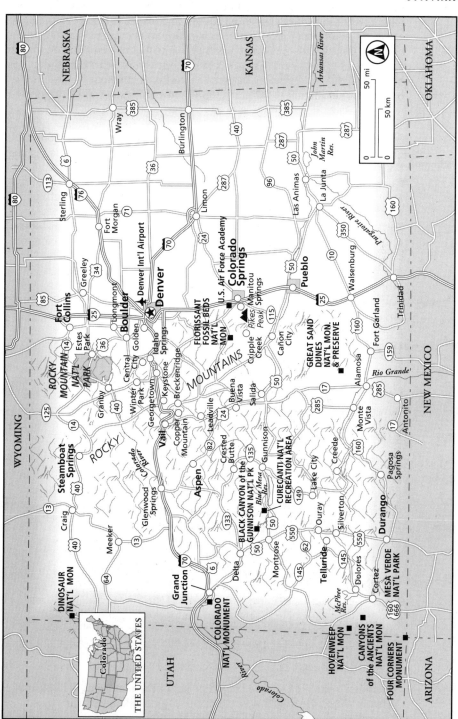

Unlike the old-time silver mines, ranching remains a living tradition, and you can discover a few things about Colorado's cowboy history by visiting working ranches in places such as **Steamboat Springs** (Chapter 17) and **Gunnison** (Chapter 20). In addition to the working ranches, a few old homesteads have also been preserved as they were a century ago. Of these, my favorite is the **Never Summer Ranch** in **Rocky Mountain National Park** (Chapter 15). Not only do most of the old buildings remain, nearly all the original furnishings and tools are here, too. It looks as if the family left only yesterday.

Because Colorado has so many historical sites from the late 1800s, it's easy to forget that the southern Rockies are the ancestral lands of the **Ute** tribe. You can learn about the tribe's art and history by visiting the **Ute Indian Museum** (Chapter 20) in Montrose or, better still, by going straight to the **Ute Mountain Ute Tribal Park** (Chapter 21) south of Cortez. The **Ancestral Puebloans,** precursors to the modern Hopi, Zuni, and Acoma tribes, lived in what is now Southwestern Colorado until the 13th century. At sites near Cortez, you can see their ancient pit houses, multistory cliff dwellings, and mesa-top pueblos. The cliff dwellings inside **Mesa Verde National Park** (Chapter 20) and the **Ute Mountain Tribal Park** look like a natural outgrowth of the earth. To me, these are the state's most stunning historical sites.

Checking Out the Scenery

In 1904, the view from atop **Pikes Peak** (Chapter 14) inspired Katherine Lee Bates to pen the words to "America the Beautiful," including the phrase "purple mountain majesties." Colorado's peaks aren't exactly the color of Barney, but they are sort of purplish, and they're definitely majestic. Uplifted by tectonic activity and sculpted by the creeping movements of glaciers during the Ice Age, vast peaks dominate much of the western half of the state. There are far more 14,000-foot peaks (53) in Colorado than in any other state.

If you want to get into mountain scenery without straining too hard, head for **Rocky Mountain National Park** (Chapter 15), home to 146 mountain lakes and 112 peaks over 10,000 feet. From Denver, you can drive into the park and up to tree line in just a few hours' time. Rocky Mountain National Park may hold the most popular mountains in the state, but they're not the highest. Along U.S. 24 between **Salida** and **Leadville** (Chapter 19), the fourteeners of the Sawatch Range stand, side by side, like particularly imposing football linemen. Anchoring them is the highest peak in Colorado and the second-highest peak in the lower 48 states (behind California's Mount Whitney), 14,433-foot **Mount Elbert.**

For sheer beauty, I love the jagged peaks of the **San Juan Mountains** between Telluride and Ouray (Chapter 21). Streaked by avalanche paths and drained by ribbon-like waterfalls, they take on curious hues in different light, perhaps because of their mostly volcanic rock. Speaking of color, check out the two conjoined pyramid-shaped peaks collectively known as **Maroon Bells** near Aspen. Even the eastern foothills of the Rockies can be glorious, especially in places such as **Red Rocks** (near Morrison; Chapter 13) and **Garden of the Gods** (in Colorado Springs; Chapter 14), where massive, tilting sandstone slabs seem to have only recently burst from the earth.

The mountains form the headwaters of rivers, which flow down onto the plains of Eastern Colorado and into the canyon country of Western Colorado. On the eastern slope of the continental divide, the **Arkansas, Rio Grande, South Platte,** and **Cache La Poudre** rivers brook no mercy for inept boaters. On the west, the **Gunnison, Colorado, Green, Yampa, Animas,** and **San Juan** rivers alternately thunder and drift downstream. As these immense rivers tumble down from the highlands, they sometimes carve canyons deep into the elevated earth.

The most awesome gorge is the **Black Canyon** (Chapter 20), where the Gunnison River slashed nearly straight down through 2,000 feet of some of the earth's oldest exposed rock. Farther west still, you can stop to see the serpentine paths of the **Green** and **Yampa** rivers inside **Dinosaur National Monument** (Chapter 20). And elsewhere in Colorado's plateau country, you can see where rivers and runoff have isolated mesas of colorful sedimentary rock. One great example of this is at **Colorado National Monument** (Chapter 20), near Grand Junction. And, of course, that's not all: The state also has sand dunes, grasslands, sagebrush desert, and high alpine lakes. Not to mention wheat fields, vineyards, and orchards.

Skiing the Slopes

The 23 major ski areas represented by **Colorado Ski Country USA** vary enormously in size, steepness, price, style, age, and location. If you shop around in advance, you can usually find a resort that suits your tastes. Or, if you're lucky, you can keep sampling the ski areas until you find a favorite. The best area? Depends what you're looking for.

My favorite place on a sunny late-spring day is **Loveland Ski Area** (Chapter 13). Loveland sits flush against the continental divide and has lots of wide-open, uncrowded terrain where you can really motor when conditions are right. The best small ski areas are **Monarch Ski and Snowboard Area** (near Salida; Chapter 19) and **Sunlight Mountain Resort** (near Glenwood Springs; Chapter 18). Monarch, which receives 360 inches of snow annually, would be my choice for a powder day; Sunlight has steeps and spunk. Factor in their low prices and relaxed atmosphere, and these are the places where I'd vacation.

For glade skiing, slip into the aspens at **Steamboat Ski Area** (Chapter 18). Steamboat's perfectly spaced trees seem to go on forever at just the right pitch, and the area gets the type of light powder that brings out their magic. Experts who crave serious steeps should go to **Crested Butte Mountain Resort** (Chapter 20). You don't *have* to scare yourself to ski here — there's lots of intermediate terrain — but you can if you want to. **Keystone Resort** (Chapter 18) is a prime spot for families, with user-friendly slopes and packages that include many off-slope activities.

The best moguls — and this is a tough choice, because Colorado has no shortage of them — are at **Telluride Ski Resort** (Chapter 21) and **Winter Park Resort** (Chapter 17). Both have an abundance of long fall-line bump runs. For a big-mountain descent that will make your brain sing, drop into **Highland Bowl** at **Aspen Highlands** (Chapter 17). My favorite vistas are atop **Aspen Highlands** and **Telluride,** each of which open onto immediate and breathtaking peaks. For a great all-around mountain that's easy to reach, try **Copper Mountain Resort** (Chapter 18). **Vail Mountain** (Chapter 18) deserves an award just for its enormity.

Taming the wild frontier

The big surprise for most Colorado visitors is how busy the state has become. Between 1990 and 2000 the state's population grew by 31% — about three times the national average. Most of the growth was along the Front Range — the area of the Rockies nearest to and encompassing Denver, Boulder, and Fort Collins — but newcomers are also moving into the state's remote areas.

It's also getting easier to live in Colorado's far-flung locales: Commuter jets now serve airports throughout the state, and most of the highways are passable in winter. Many recent arrivals are fairly wealthy or have information-age skills that they can use to earn money. The miners, loggers, and ranchers are still around, but if you're an urban professional traveling through the state for the first time, you may be surprised to find a lot of people just like you.

Despite the urban incursions, for a few more years at least, Colorado has the best of both worlds. Western traditions such as rodeos, 4H, county fairs, mountain-man contests, and even mule races are hanging on. Besides the rugged charm that lures visitors, the state now offers sophisticated new entertainment, paid for by locals and visitors alike. In Colorado, towns of 5,000 or less sometimes offer as much culture — including symphonies, theater, and music festivals — as cities of a quarter-million do in other states. And you can satisfy other expensive tastes: Microbrews are as easy to find as Budweiser. In some spots, espresso stands out-number diners, and nearly every town has an outstanding restaurant. And when you get tired of roughing it on the range, the good news is that everyone here has a friend who just graduated from massage school.

Seeing the Best Small Towns

Not only will you receive great service in Colorado's small towns, you'll get your rest, too. Another advantage to the little towns is that they're not as dressed up as the popular resorts. Their history feels authentic; their prices are fair. My favorite little town is **Fairplay** (Chapter 19). Located 30-some miles from Breckenridge, it seems to have dropped off the map despite being the inspiration for the bawdy *South Park* cartoon series, at one time the highest rated programming on cable television. Fairplay has a haunted hotel, a sleepy historic downtown, and a historical park named **South Park City,** where everyone in the county seems to have "donated" their old tools, machinery, and clothing. The big event here is an annual pack-mule race.

An excellent little town is **Lake City** (Chapter 20). It took an act of God — or, at least, a river-blocking earth slide — to give Lake City the body of water for which it's named. And it took a devilish act of cannibalism by **Alferd Packer** back in the 1870s to put this little mining town (briefly) on the national radar. Nowadays you can paddle around the lake or visit assorted Alferd Packer historical sites. When you're done, you can hike in wilderness, play miniature golf, or, if the golf gets too stressful, just flat-out relax.

Another blissfully non-famous community is **Mancos** (Chapter 21), located right where the mountains become the desert in Southwestern Colorado. During summer, Mancos always feels sedate and warm. The pavement turns to reddish dirt amid pinyon-juniper woodland right outside town. It's really peaceful. If you start thinking that you want to get even farther *out there,* try **Dinosaur** (Chapter 20). In Dinosaur, it feels as if the prevailing winds have blown away the rest of Colorado — and, for that matter, the world. Yet if you drive a few miles into **Dinosaur National Monument,** you'll be in some of the most colorful canyon country in the state.

Relaxing Resort Towns

Colorado's resort communities have a lot in common. They all know the hottest recipes, the most voguish decor, the latest treatments, and the most extravagant ways to pamper travelers. Yet they vary in other ways. If you like the idea of a pedestrian-friendly mountain village, try **Vail** or **Beaver Creek** (Chapter 18). Each has a European-style village that's largely free of automobiles. A former silver-mining hotbed, **Telluride** (Chapter 21) is in a particularly stunning alpine setting, in a box canyon that seems far-removed from the outside world. But it takes some extra work to get there. **Aspen** (Chapter 17) offers recreation, culture, history, and beauty, and it seems to be billing à la carte for every one of its attributes. **Breckenridge** (Chapter 18) and **Winter**

Park (Chapter 17) are the most convenient to Denver but have little in common: **Winter Park's** cool temperatures, deep snow pack, and surrounding pine forests make it feel as snug as an Alaskan village; Breckenridge feels like a spot that people reach in droves, and when they get there, they celebrate. **Colorado Springs** (Chapter 14) affords visitors a dozen prime attractions and a city of 350,000. Yet if you stay in accommodations near Pikes Peak, you may forget that the city even exists. In **Steamboat** (Chapter 18), you can earn your massage by helping cowboys herd cattle.

Buying Art in the Mountains

Nature has served as many an artist's muse and artists have migrated to Colorado from all over the country for a chance to absorb the state's beauty (and its residents' disposable income). My favorite art scene is in **Salida** (Chapter 19), where, years ago, painters, sculptors, and jewelry makers took over abandoned storefronts and set out to create art that moved them. A lot of those people are still there, selling their work out of storefront studios in what is now a revitalized, colorful downtown. But Salida is just a starting point. Denver's **LoDo** (Chapter 12) neighborhood has scores of galleries displaying art by masters and up-and-comers. Every ski town has talented artists. And if you're looking for great art — even masterpieces — you can find that, too, especially in affluent communities such as **Cherry Creek** (Chapter 12), **Aspen** (Chapter 17), and **Vail** (Chapter 18). For Native American art, head southwest to **Cortez** or even farther south onto the **Ute Mountain Ute reservation** (Chapter 21), where you can sometimes buy directly from the artists.

Chapter 2

Deciding When and Where to Go

*O*nce you decide to come to Colorado, your next major decision will involve deciding when and where to go. In this chapter, I introduce you to the top cities and the most tourist-friendly regions of the state, and I explain the pros and cons of traveling here at different times of year. I break down the weather by location and season and even provide a calendar of major Colorado events. Mind you, this isn't the part where I really dissect the destinations — you'll have to check out Chapters 11 through 21 for specific information on Colorado's most popular places.

I also have a confession to make: Not every place in Colorado is covered in this book. To cover every nook and cranny of Colorado, this book would need to be 20 times larger, and I'd need a stronger pair of legs, a new truck, a bigger paycheck, and a transplanted liver.

I don't even cover every single great spot. The state is *big* — it holds a lifetime's worth of secrets. Dozens of canyons and side canyons are etched into every vast mountainside, and every side canyon has a dozen more little hiding places that somebody somewhere dearly loves. Unfortunately, you may only have a week or two to see the state, so I boil down the best Colorado has to offer visitors with a limited amount of time on their hands. That means you won't read about Eastern Colorado — where the Great Plains gradually ascend to the base of the Rockies — even though it's definitely on the state map.

The places I do cover are the top cities and the major regions in the state. Within these locations, I fill you in on the best attractions to see and activities to do so that you don't waste a minute of your time going anywhere unworthy of your attention.

The Big Cities

Colorado's two largest cities, Denver and Colorado Springs, sit on the eastern slope of the Rocky Mountains near the center of Colorado. Denver is about 70 miles north of Colorado Springs. It's much larger and a few miles farther from the mountains. More than half of the state's 4.3 million people live in the Denver metropolitan area. Compared to Denver, parts of Colorado Springs feel like a sleepy little resort.

Denver

Denver has a thriving downtown and all the entertainment you'd expect of a major city: pro sports, gourmet restaurants, galleries, music, and museums. The town has a youngish, active, healthy population. When these people aren't off enjoying the nearby mountains, they're eating out, shopping, or watching their favorite pro team on television. The city is easy to tour — many of the major attractions are within a few miles of one another in the downtown, making it a good place for sightseeing. And the mountains start only about 14 miles west of town. I cover all the ins and outs of Denver, including some really cool side trips, in Chapters 11, 12, and 13.

Colorado Springs

With a native population of just 350,000 people, Colorado Springs is the proverbial big city with a small-town feel. The downtown area has spacious boulevards and a low skyline. A few miles southwest of the downtown, the resort community of Manitou Springs snuggles against the base of Pikes Peak. Because these towns have catered to tourists for over a century, they have a host of road-tested, family-friendly attractions, not to mention historic hotels such as **The Broadmoor** and the **Cliff House.** For in-depth information on Colorado Springs, turn to Chapter 14.

The Major Regions

All the regions I cover in this book offer stunning scenery and lively towns.

If you decide to go the regional route on your vacation, your best bet is to pick one of these regions and spend a week there. If you have more time, branch out and see more of the state.

Rocky Mountain National Park

Colorado's most popular national park makes seeing the mountains easy. Located within a few hours' drive of Denver, Rocky Mountain

National Park is traversed by **Trail Ridge Road,** which goes up and over the tree line, cresting at over 12,000 feet. After a day spent hiking some of the 300 miles of trails, camp inside the park or retreat to one of the gateway communities of Estes Park, Grand Lake, or Granby. I cover everything you need to know about the park in Chapter 15.

Boulder and Fort Collins

North of Denver along the eastern foothills of the Rockies are two lively college towns. Both have around 100,000 people; major universities with over 20,000 students; rivers and trails; lively downtowns; and locations convenient to the foothills. Yet their personalities are quite divergent: Boulder looks to the coasts and the stratosphere for inspiration, while Fort Collins stays more earthbound. For the inside scoop on these cities, see Chapter 16.

South Central Colorado (The Southern Rockies)

The highest peaks in the state tower above river valleys in this area just east of the continental divide. High in the mountains, the colorful mining towns of **Creede** and **Leadville** are virtual living museums, showing the life of Colorado 100 years ago. Downstream of Leadville, in a valley warmed by southerly winds, is the artsy, mellow town of **Salida.** And below Creede, the Rio Grande River has helped carve out the broad San Luis Valley, home to farms, geothermal springs, and **Great Sand Dunes National Monument and Preserve.** For detailed information on this region, see Chapter 19.

Northern Colorado High Country

This region is a skier's nirvana, with some of the best slopes in the state. The area includes the busy resort communities along and near the I-70 corridor west of the continental divide. Most of the state's best-known ski towns, including **Winter Park, Breckenridge, Aspen, Vail,** and **Steamboat Springs,** are here. So is the century-old resort town of **Glenwood Springs.** For the scoop on the best slopes in the state, see Chapters 17 and 18.

Black Canyon of the Gunnison and Western Colorado

This part of Western Colorado is home to the rugged Elk and San Juan mountain ranges, the mining towns of **Crested Butte** and **Lake City,** a ranching and college town **(Gunnison);** a stunning 2,000-foot-deep gorge **(Black Canyon),** and even some farmland. Farther west, near

Grand Junction, erosion has isolated the sandstone **Uncompahgre plateau** and the canyons of **Colorado National Monument.** I detail all the major highlights of this region in Chapter 20.

The San Juan Mountains, Mesa Verde, and the Four Corners Area

This area plummets from the 14,000-foot peaks of the San Juans to the canyon bottoms of the Four Corners area. The towns of **Telluride, Silverton,** and **Ouray** preserve a 100-year-old mining history in addition to offering abundant recreation. Other areas have ancient history. Near **Cortez** and **Durango**, you can explore the remnants of the Ancestral Puebloan culture, which flourished here until about A.D. 1300. For more on this historic region, see Chapter 21.

The Secrets of the Seasons

The single most important factor affecting Colorado weather is elevation. One general rule, subject to many exceptions, is that, for every 1,000 feet of elevation, the air temperature drops 3.5 degrees. When air cools, it condenses and forms precipitation that eventually comes down as rain or snow. So the higher up you go, the cooler — and snowier — it usually gets, no matter what the season. Mountain temperatures can be bitterly cold, especially if it's windy, but even at the higher elevations of some of the nation's top ski resorts, you'll find plenty of sunshine.

At 5,280 feet, Denver may be known as the Mile-High City, but it's much lower than the mountains to its west, 53 of which top 14,000 feet. (Locals refer to these peaks as *fourteeners.*) Whether you're in Denver or higher up in the Rockies, you'll probably notice the (relatively) cool, thin air. But like much of the state, Denver is a dry place that has more than 300 sunny days each year — more than Miami! — and it can get surprisingly warm here. Temperatures have been known to climb to 90 degrees and higher during the height of summer.

If you don't like the weather in Colorado, wait 10 minutes or, better yet, drive up or down. It's not uncommon for Coloradoans to ski and golf on the same day, simply by changing elevations. Still, you'll definitely want to come during the ideal season for pursuing your favorite activities. The only place you'll find snow in July is on the highest mountain peaks, so if you want to slalom, your best bet is to show up between late November and early April. But if you're a hiker or a biker, the trails are usually snowless and dry from late May through early October.

Unless you're traveling with children and are governed by their school schedules, the most convenient times to visit the state are during early spring and late fall. Not only will you avoid crowds, you'll also save money.

Along the Front Range, where Denver and Colorado Springs are
located, summer days are hot and dry, evenings pleasantly mild.
Relative humidity is low, and temperatures seldom rise above the 90s.
Evenings start to get cooler by mid-September, but even as late as
November the days are often warm. Surprisingly, winters here are
warmer and less snowy than those of the Great Lakes or New England.

Most of Colorado is considered semiarid, and overall the state has an
average of 296 sunny days a year — more sunshine than San Diego or
Miami Beach. The prairies average about 16 inches of precipitation
annually; the cities along the Front Range, 14 inches; the western slope,
only about 8 inches. Rain, when it falls, is commonly a short deluge —
a summer afternoon thunderstorm. However, if you want to see snow,
simply head to the mountains, where snowfall is measured in feet
rather than inches, and mountain peaks may still be white in July.

To get an idea of the average temperatures and precipitation you'll
encounter in some of Colorado's cities, see Tables 2-1 and 2-2.

In the following sections, I break down Colorado's seasonal score sheet.

Table 2-1	Denver's Average Temperatures (°F) and Total Precipitation (in.) by Month											
Month	*Jan*	*Feb*	*Mar*	*Apr*	*May*	*June*	*July*	*Aug*	*Sept*	*Oct*	*Nov*	*Dec*
High	43	46	52	61	70	81	88	85	76	66	52	44
Low	16	20	26	34	43	52	58	56	47	36	25	17
Precipitation	0.5	0.6	1.3	1.7	2.4	1.8	1.9	1.5	1.2	1.0	0.9	0.6

Table 2-2	Leadville's Average Temperatures (°F) and Total Precipitation (in.) by Month											
Month	*Jan*	*Feb*	*Mar*	*Apr*	*May*	*June*	*July*	*Aug*	*Sept*	*Oct*	*Nov*	*Dec*
High	29	31	35	42	53	64	70	68	61	51	38	30
Low	0	0	5	15	25	33	38	37	30	23	12	3
Precipitation	1.5	1.2	1.4	1.4	1.3	1.1	2.0	2.1	1.4	1.1	1.3	1.5

Spring

Depending on when you arrive and where you visit, spring in Colorado
can be either a beautiful blessing or a muddy nightmare. Here are some
of the season's pluses:

✔ By mid-May, Denver and the other Front Range towns have usually passed their freezing point. Flowers start blooming and the landscape is stunning.

✔ Rafting on mountain rivers, swollen by the winter snows and spring thaw, is an especially thrilling experience this time of year.

✔ No matter where you go in the state, you'll have many tourist destinations, including the national parks, nearly to yourself.

✔ Many resorts offer discounts and drop their rates.

But spring also has some serious downsides:

✔ Before all its flowers can bloom, the Front Range is often battered by thunderstorms caused by cold air sliding down from the mountains meeting sun-warmed, damp air surging northward from the Gulf of Mexico. On average, Denver receives 2.28 inches of precipitation during May, its wettest month.

✔ If you make a date with spring in the Rockies, you'll probably get stood up. The sun does shine sometimes, yet much of the high country remains snow-covered, and areas where the snow has melted can stay muddy into June.

✔ Temperatures in areas of high elevation remain cool. For example, in May, the average high temperature in Leadville is a not-so-balmy 53 degrees. So if you want to head up into the high country, this is not the time do it.

Summer

Colorado is very popular with visitors and outdoor enthusiasts in summer. The season sizzles because:

✔ Denver is usually sunny, warm, and mild.

✔ Summer is beautiful in the Rockies. Clusters of aspen trees bloom one by one, dabbing green across the hillsides. The mountains quickly become lush and fragrant, and when the snow in the high country melts (in mid-July), wildflowers such as penstemon, columbine, fireweed, and dwarf clover illuminate the meadows and tundra.

✔ Temperatures in the mountain regions climb blissfully into the 70s during the day.

✔ All the major attractions are up and running, and the going doesn't get much better in the hiking department.

But summer fizzles because:

✔ When the sun goes down, the mountainous areas in Colorado can get downright cold. Leadville's low temperature in July is a chilly

38 degrees and Aspen's nighttime low is a measly 47 degrees. Even cities at lower elevations, such as Denver, can get pretty cool at night. You'll need a jacket!

✔ Afternoon thunderstorms can flare up without warning in the Colorado Rockies, whose wettest months are July and August.

✔ The major parks can get uncomfortably crowded in summer, especially if you're unwilling or unable to head too far off the beaten path. Denver, too, buzzes with visitors.

✔ Your wallet will take a beating, because most resort and hotel rates climb as high as the Rockies.

Fall

Fall in Colorado starts off with a burst of color, but its end can be a little bleak. It's fabulous because:

✔ Denver is at its sunniest and dryest, and the temperature here remains pretty temperate — 60s in October, 50s in November. And the leaves first start turning colors in early October, so the foliage season lasts longer than in the mountains.

✔ Come September, the changing leaves in the mountains can be nearly as extraordinary as the late-summer wildflowers are. Rocky Mountain maple, Gambel oak, and quaking aspen spatter the hills with red, orange, and yellow, respectively, against a backdrop of evergreen trees.

✔ The start of the school year means fewer people in the parks and at the major attractions. You won't be alone, but you won't feel cramped either, especially not in late September and October.

✔ Prices drop from their stratospheric elevations to more reasonable levels.

On the other hand:

✔ Fall comes fast and early to the mountains, so the foliage show is over by early October. Miss it and the only leaves you'll see in the Rockies will be the ones on the ground.

✔ Temperatures drop, especially in the mountain zones. Snowstorms become an acute possibility in the Rockies — although they won't provide enough snow for good skiing — and it can get brutally cold. By late October, even Denver is pretty frosty.

Winter

Winter in Colorado brings most travelers visions of snow-covered mountains, and those visions are pretty true to life. This time of year is wonderful because:

✔ Snow falls, heavily at times, throughout the Rockies from October (and sometimes earlier) through May (and sometimes later). The amount of snowfall varies greatly from place to place and season to season, yet many towns average over 200 inches annually — even without the help of a ski-area marketing department. All that white stuff looks pretty, feels soft, absorbs sound, and is fun to slide around on.

✔ Because of their southern latitude, the Rockies warm up rapidly on sunny winter days, so you can stay relatively comfortable. Despite being perched at 10,046 feet, Leadville, has an average high temperature of 29 degrees during January.

✔ Storms coming from the west tend to lose moisture over the mountains, so Denver often stays dry in early winter. Denver's average high temperature in January is 43, and the skies are usually sunny. And a lot of the snow that falls during the rest of the winter here tends to melt quickly so you won't get snowed-in, but you can still take advantage of the city's proximity to good recreational opportunities.

But winter does have its downside. Consider the following:

✔ Nights in the moiuntain regions, when no clouds trap warm air in the atmosphere, are particularly frosty. Leadville's average low temperature in both January and February is 0 degrees. Towns in mountain valleys where cold air settles can be even more frigid. The communities of Gunnison and Fraser sometimes register the coldest temperatures in the continental United States!

✔ All that mountain snow may look beautiful, but it can wreak havoc on the roads and make life miserable for drivers.

✔ You won't be the only one basking in the beauty of the winter mountains. Crowds flock to all the major ski areas as soon as the snow gets deep enough for skiing.

✔ Hotel and resort rates skyrocket in the major ski towns during Christmas week and they don't start moving downhill until late March.

Frozen zones

The air temperature will not only affect how you feel when you visit Colorado, it will also affect the plant and animal species you'll see in a given area. Atop Colorado's highest peaks are zones of biological life comparable to ones found near sea level as far north as the Yukon. Meanwhile, the low-lying canyons in the southern part of the state bear species that flourish as far south as Mexico.

Colorado's Calendar of Events

Although I list Colorado's major annual events in the following sections, dozens of other local and regional events take place around the state every week. To find additional events on the dates you'll be visiting, check the Colorado Travel and Tourism Web site (www.colorado. com), the Colorado Festivals & Events Association Web site (www. coloradofestival.com), and the Web sites for individual towns and cities you'll be visiting.

January

National Western Stock Show and Rodeo: Denver (Chapters 11 and 12). Livestock buffs will enjoy this first-rate stock show, in which more than 15,000 hooved creatures are displayed and sold. Cowboys ride and rope some of the more cantankerous animals in 22 rodeo performances, including bull riding. The show is held mid-January. For more information, call ☎ 303-297-1166 or go to www.nationalwestern.com.

Gay and Lesbian Ski Week: Aspen (Chapter 18). One of the largest cold-weather gay happenings in the world, Gay and Lesbian Ski Week attracts upwards of 5,000 people to Aspen in late January. Attendees participate in ski clinics, costume parades, special shows, and parties. Call ☎ 800-367-8290 for more information or go to www.gayski week.com.

February

Steamboat Springs Winter Carnival: Steamboat Springs (Chapter 18). Hosted in mid-February by the Steamboat Springs Winter Sports Club, this 90-year-old tradition is the oldest annual Winter Carnival west of the Mississippi. Activities include ski racing, ski jumping, *ski joring* (in which snow skiers are towed, water-ski style, behind running horses), fireworks, and performances by the Steamboat Springs skiing band. Call ☎ 970-879-0880 for details, or visit www.steamboat-chamber.com.

March

St. Patrick's Day Parade: Denver (Chapters 11 and 12). Though not generally known as a hotbed of Irishness, on the Saturday before St. Patrick's Day, Denverites come out in force for this parade, which features floats, thousands of horses, and a Western spin. It's the second largest St. Patty's Day parade in the country. Call ☎ 303-321-7888 for details.

Denver March Powwow: Denver (Chapters 11 and 12). Representatives of over 70 tribes attend this annual three-day powwow, one of the largest in the nation. Activities include musical performances and competitions in dancing and drumming. Authentic Native American art and food is also sold. The event takes place in mid-March. Call ☎ 303-934-8045 or see www.denvermarchpowwow.org for details.

April

Easter Sunrise Services: Colorado Springs (Chapter 14). Easter sunrise services have been held in Garden of the Gods Park since the 1920s. For years they were broadcast live across America on CBS radio, and by the mid-1900s attendance had swelled to over 25,000. Today, interdenominational Easter services continue at the park, although the crowds are usually smaller. For more information, call ☎ 800-DO-VISIT or go to www.coloradospringstravel.com.

May

Cinco de Mayo: Denver (Chapters 11 and 12). America's largest Cinco de Mayo celebration takes place not in Albuquerque, El Paso, or Los Angeles but in downtown Denver. On May 5, upwards of 400,000 people flood this annual outdoor gathering in Civic Center Park. While performers ranging from mariachi bands to traditional Aztec dancers entertain the crowd from several stages, hundreds of booths sell Latino food, crafts, and art. Call ☎ 303-534-8342, ext. 106, for details.

Kinetic Conveyance Challenge: Boulder (Chapter 16). This crowd-pleasing event involving a race of imaginative human-powered vehicles is held every year in early May at Boulder Reservoir. Speed counts in this event, but so do costumes, color, creativity and all-around joie de vivre. Call ☎ 303-444-5600 for more information.

Boulder Bolder: Boulder (Chapter 16). Some of the world's fastest runners break away from a very large pack — upwards of 40,000 entrants — in this annual 10-kilometer run, the fourth largest running race in America. The event takes place on Memorial Day. Call ☎ 303-444-RACE or see www.bolderboulder.com for details.

June

Telluride Folk and Bluegrass Festival: Telluride (Chapter 20). Some of Telluride's lesser-known festivals are easier to endure and just as much fun as the one simply known as "Bluegrass," but this is the one everyone talks about. For four days in mid-June, the town hosts talented folk, bluegrass, and rock performers who share a fondness for acoustic music. Past performers have included the likes of Ani DiFranco, Lucinda Williams, Bela Fleck, David Grisman, and Peter Rowan. Call ☎ **800-624-2422** or check out either www.planetbluegrass.com or www.visittelluride.com for more information.

FIBArk Whitewater Festival: Salida (Chapter 17). A long-running celebration of whitewater rafting and paddling takes place on the Arkansas River near Salida in mid-June. Events include races, skills competitions, demonstrations, and live music. Call ☎ **877-772-5432** or visit www.fibark.net.

Pikes Peak International Hillclimb: Manitou Springs (Chapter 14). At 86 years and counting, this is America's second oldest automobile race. It's also the highest, reaching 14,000 feet in elevation at the finish line. The race is usually held on the final Saturday in June. For details, call ☎ **719-685-4400** or check out www.ppihc.com.

July

Cattlemen's Days: Gunnison (Chapter 19). Giddy up to this century-old Western celebration in downtown Gunnison. The bill for this mid-July event includes horse races, a parade, a PRCA rodeo, cowboy poetry readings, a carnival, a fashion show, and a country dance. For more information, call ☎ **970-641-1501.**

Cherry Creek Arts Festival: Denver (Chapters 11 and 12). Over a quarter million people attend this three-day arts festival, where 200 carefully selected artists display and sell works in media ranging from photography to glass. Musicians and dancers perform throughout the day on several stages. And area restaurants sell a variety of dishes from booths along "Culinary Row." It all happens in early July. For more information, call ☎ **303-355-2787** or head to www.cherryarts.org.

KBCO World Class Rock Fest: Winter Park Resort (Chapter 18). The biggest names in rock sometimes headline this two-day festival in mid-July, but the bands lower on the bill are often the most interesting. Backing up the superstars are some of Colorado's hottest up-and-coming players. For information, call ☎ **800-979-0332** or 970-726-5514, or go to www.skiwinterpark.com/attractions/events.html.

August

Palisade Peach Festival: Palisade (Chapter 19). Call it perfect. This timeless festival, held in mid-August in Western Colorado's orchard country, celebrates peach recipes, peach growers, and peach eating. There's also a street dance and an ice cream social. For more details, call ☎ **970-464-7458** or check out www.palisadepeachfest.com.

September

Telluride Blues & Brews Festival: Telluride (Chapter 20). Just when you thought the summer fun was over, Telluride brews up three days of blues (and, lately, jam band) music and beer tasting in Town Park. Past performers have included James Brown and Blues Traveler. Call ☎ **888-278-1746** or 970-728-8037 for more information or see www.visittelluride.com.

October

Great American Beer Festival: Denver (Chapters 11 and 12). Over 1,700 different beers compete for medals in the most prestigious beer festival in the United States. For a fee, you yourself can evaluate beers from throughout the nation, but your vote counts only for yourself. Be careful: If you have 1 ounce of all the competing brews, you'll end up drinking the equivalent of 108 12-ounce beers. The action takes place in mid-October. Call ☎ **303-447-0816** or check out www.beertown.org for information.

November

Lighting of Christmas Mountain U.S.A.: Salida (Chapter 17). On the day after Thanksgiving, Santa throws the switch that illuminates 10,000 bulbs on a mountainside overlooking the town. The bulbs, which are strung to form the outline of an enormous "tree," stay up until New Year's Day. On the day of the lighting, you can also enjoy refreshments and caroling.

December

World's Largest Christmas Lighting Display: Denver (Chapters 11 and 12). For the entire month of December, 40,000 lights illuminate Denver's City and County Building in one of the largest lighting displays in the nation.

Chapter 3

Four Great Itineraries

. . . .

In This Chapter

▶ Finding hot spots for history buffs

▶ Doing Colorado with youngsters

▶ Taking in amazing sights in Central and Western Colorado

. . . .

*I*tineraries that involve a lot of driving aren't for everyone. One of the best ways to enjoy Colorado is to rent a cabin for a week and then do a different outdoor activity or a new trail every day. But if you're the type of person who needs to see a lot on vacation, here are four itineraries designed to cover a string of highlights for people with specific interests. One is for history buffs. Another identifies family-friendly spots. The last two identify the most amazing sights in Western Central and far Western Colorado, respectively. If you want to travel Colorado for two weeks, just fuse together these two one-week itineraries.

Colorado for History Buffs

This tour is a hard-charging, weeklong romp across the state. It takes in some of the oddest and most unusual historical sites in the nation, but because of the extensive driving, it's really suitable only for avid drivers who have a strong historical bent.

Welcome to Colorado. If you're like most people who are flying into the state, you'll probably start out in Denver. Spend **Day 1** in **Denver** (Chapters 11 and 12). After settling in at your hotel, visit the **Molly Brown House** and then check out the Colorado history timeline at the **Colorado History Museum.** Have dinner alongside the taxidermy at the **Buckhorn Exchange,** the oldest restaurant in town. By the end of the day, a good night's sleep is in order, and I suggest you bed down at the ornate but friendly **Castle Marne Bed and Breakfast.**

On **Day 2,** ascend to **Leadville** (Chapter 19). Visit the **National Mining Hall of Fame and Museum,** and then take a driving tour of the historic mines around town. If you have a few minutes to spare, go hear the chilling story of Baby Doe Tabor at the **Matchless Mine.** Afterwards, walk the catacombs at the **Tabor Opera House.** Wind down your day with a beverage at one of Doc Holliday's old haunts, the **Silver Dollar Saloon,** before spending the night at the **Delaware Hotel.**

On **Day 3,** finish seeing any sights you missed in Leadville, then make the 253-mile drive to **Durango** (Chapter 21) and check into the **Strater Hotel.**

On **Day 4,** take the **Durango & Silverton Narrow Gauge Railroad** to the mountain town of **Silverton** (Chapter 21). If you have an extra day to spare, get a room at the **Wyman Hotel.** If you're sticking to the seven-day itinerary, return on the train to Durango that afternoon and stay another night at the Strater.

On **Day 5,** rise early, and then drive from Durango to **Mesa Verde National Park** (Chapter 21), and take an early morning tour of **CliffPalace.** Spend a few more hours at the park, and then head from Cortez to **Telluride** (Chapter 21). At twilight, walk Telluride's historic downtown. Spend the night at the **New Sheridan Hotel.**

On **Day 6,** drive from Telluride north to Delta. At Delta, cut off on Colorado 92 to Paonia, and then take Colorado 133 to **Redstone** (Chapter 17). Take an afternoon tour of **Redstone Castle,** built in the early 1900s by one of the richest men in America, John Osgood. Spend the night at the **Redstone Inn,** once part of Osgood's Utopian community for miners.

If you don't need to be in Denver on **Day 7,** drive an hour or so to **Glenwood Springs** (Chapter 17). Stay in the **Hotel Colorado** and soak in the **Hot Springs Pool.** If you need to be closer to Denver in order to catch a flight the next day, explore the mining towns of **Idaho Springs** and **Georgetown** (Chapter 13). Unwind by soaking at the historic **Indian Springs Resort** in Idaho Springs.

Touring Colorado with Kids

Most of the activities in this itinerary — designed for those traveling with kids — will work well for youths between the ages of 8 and 16. And they're fun for adults, too. What they aren't, however, is cheap. This trip impresses not just with natural splendor but also with spectacles bought and paid for with cash. If you're on a tight budget — or a tight schedule — you may need to cross off a few of the attractions listed here to save money, time, and energy.

Start **Day 1** in Denver (Chapters 11 and 12). If you arrived early in the morning and have at least a half-day, ride the roller coasters and water slides at **Six Flags Elitch Gardens Amusement Park.** If you only have a few hours, you'll have enough time to stroll past the aquariums and watch a simulated flash flood at **Ocean Journey.** Then drive south to **Manitou Springs** (Chapter 14) and spend the night there at the historic Broadmoor or one of the area's many family-friendly motels.

On the morning of **Day 2,** get up and take the **Pikes Peak Cog Railway** to the summit of Pikes Peak. In the afternoon, tour **Cave of the Winds,** or, if you'd prefer a free attraction, go hike among the immense sandstone slabs in **Garden of the Gods.** Come evening, enjoy the Skee-Ball, kiddy rides, and video games at **Arcade Amusements, Inc.,** in Manitou Springs (Chapter 14), where you should spend another night.

On **Day 3,** sleep late and then drive to the **Royal Gorge Bridge and Park,** near **Canon City** (Chapter 14). This is high-priced fun, but the bridge over the 1,000-foot-deep gorge is cool. Walk across it, walk back, take some rides, and then continue on to **Salida** (Chapter 19). After dinner in Salida, go swim and soak at the **Salida Hot Springs.** Spend the night in Salida at the Woodland Motel.

You'll spend most of **Day 4** taking a half-day **raft trip** on the Arkansas River. When you arrive back on dry land, drive north to **Breckenridge** (Chapter 18) and spend the night at the **Breckenridge Mountain Lodge,** which has a game room with a pool table, foosball, and video games.

On **Day 5,** let the kids go wild playing in the maze, on the climbing wall, and on the alpine slide at the **Peak 8 Fun Park** at **Breckenridge Mountain Resort.** Spend another night in Breckenridge.

On **Day 6,** drive a few miles to **Silver Plume** (Chapter 13). Take a ride on the **Georgetown Loop Railroad** and go for a mine tour midway through the ride. Spend the night in Georgetown (Chapter 13) at the **Georgetown Mountain Inn,** where the kids can cool off in the outdoor swimming pool.

On **Day 7,** return to **Denver.** Play around with the hands-on exhibits at the **Museum of Nature and Science** and then stroll through the **Denver Zoo.** Both attractions are within walking distance of one another at City Park.

Natural Wonders: Western Central Colorado

This scenic tour keeps you closer to the airport in Denver than a similar tour in far Western Colorado would. However, bear in mind that the areas nearest Denver often attract larger crowds than the ones farther west.

On **Day 1,** drive from Denver International Airport to **Estes Park** (Chapter 15). If you like historic hotels, stay at the **Stanley Hotel;** if you prefer a room with a view (of Longs Peak, no less) stay at the **Aspen Lodge.**

Get an early start on **Day 2** and hike near Bear Lake inside **Rocky Mountain National Park.** Then drive through the park on the **Trail Ridge Road,** ending the day at **Grand Lake Lodge** in Grand Lake (Chapter 15).

Begin **Day 3** by paddling a canoe on **Grand Lake,** Colorado's largest natural body of water. Then drive south to **Leadville** (Chapter 19) and spend the night there at the **Apple Blossom Inn.**

Rise before dawn on **Day 4** and climb **Mount Elbert,** Colorado's highest peak. Or, failing that, sleep in, rent bikes, and pedal around town on the paved **Mineral Belt Trail.** After you're done, make the short drive to **Salida** (Chapter 19), stopping en route to soak and swim at the **Mount Princeton Hot Springs.** Stay the night in one of the town's many B&Bs.

On **Day 5,** take a half-day raft trip on the **Arkansas River.** Then drive south to **Alamosa** (Chapter 19), where you can spend the night at a serene bed-and-breakfast, or choose among a number of chain hotels.

Start **Day 6** by visiting **Great Sand Dunes National Monument and Preserve.** See if you can't climb to the top of the dunes. After you're done, backtrack a few miles to Salida, then head east toward **Canon City** (Chapter 14). If you have time (and money), stop on the way and walk on the bridge above **Royal Gorge.** Drive to **Manitou Springs** (Chapter 14) and spend the night there.

On **Day 7,** ride to the top of **Pikes Peak** on the **Pikes Peak Cog Railway,** then visit **Garden of the Gods Park** and, if time permits, duck into the darkness at **Cave of the Winds** before heading off to the airport.

Desert Wonders: Western Colorado

You can choose between numerous small regional airports in Western Colorado, but because a lot of people end up renting cars in Denver and then driving west, this tour starts in Glenwood Springs. Glenwood is on I-70, 159 miles from Denver.

On **Day 1,** arrive in **Glenwood Springs** (Chapter 17) by midday, tour **Glenwood Caverns,** and then soak in the world-famous **Hot Springs Pool.** Spend the evening in the historic **Hotel Colorado.**

On **Day 2,** rise early and visit **Aspen** (Chapter 17). If time permits, hike the **Cathedral Lake Trail,** 15 miles southeast of town. Then drive over McClure Pass on Colorado 133 and make your way to **Redstone** (Chapter 17). Visit **Redstone Castle,** then spend the night at the **Redstone Inn.**

On Day 3, have a snack at Joe Cocker's **Mad Dog Café** in Crawford (Chapter 20) and then continue on to the north rim of **Black Canyon of**

the **Gunnison National Park** (Chapter 20). On the North Rim, hike the **North Vista Trail** to **Exclamation Point.** Spend the night in **Montrose** (Chapter 20) at the Lathrop House Bed & Breakfast or the Country Lodge.

On **Day 4,** drive to **Ouray** (Chapter 21), stopping en route to soak at the clothing-optional **Orvis Hot Springs** in Ridgway or at the city-owned pool in **Ouray.** Take a short hike to **Box Canyon Falls** or pick a longer trail if you feel like it. Spend the night in **Ouray** or **Silverton,** maybe at the **Wyman Hotel and Inn** or the **Box Canyon Lodge.**

On **Day 5,** backtrack a few miles to Ridgway. Then drive to Telluride and hike up to (and past) **Bridal Veil Falls.** Bunk down for the night in Telluride (Chapter 21), where you stay at a historic hotel with lots of character or a new hotel with every imaginable luxury.

On **Day 6,** top off your gas tank and drive to **Grand Junction** via seldom-traveled Colorado 141. Visit **Colorado National Monument,** and spend the night in Grand Junction (Chapter 20) at the **Adam's Mark** or the **Holiday Inn.**

On **Day 7,** tour a winery in **Palisade** (Chapter 20), then detour off of I-70 to the top of **Grand Mesa.** Rent a canoe and paddle around **Alexander Lake** or hike the **Crag Crest Trail.** Spend the night at **Alexander Lake Lodge.** From there, it's a quick jaunt back to I-70.

Chapter 4

Planning Your Budget

• •

In This Chapter

▶ Budgeting your trip costs

▶ Avoiding expensive surprises

▶ Cutting expenses

• •

Colorado may not be as expensive as, say, Manhattan, but it's not cheap either. If you're not careful during your travels, you may end up panning for gold in order to finance your bus ticket back home.

Adding Up the Elements

Making a budget for your trip ahead of time always pays, even if you won't necessarily stick to it after you arrive. You can use the budget worksheets in the back of this book to help you sort out your spending costs. Start by writing down the cost of transportation to and from the airport and continue adding anticipated costs until you've budgeted for every expense — even the smallest souvenirs you hope to buy. When you have your total, add another 15% for unexpected costs. As you complete the worksheet, you'll need to consider all the costs described in the following sections.

Tables 4-1 and 4-2 give you an idea of what things typically cost in Colorado, so you don't end up with sticker shock when you get there.

Table 4-1	What Things Cost in Denver
Item	*U.S. $*
Shuttle from Denver International Airport to downtown Denver (1 adult)	18
Double room Brown Palace Hotel (expensive)	225–275
Double room at Queen Anne Bed & Breakfast (moderate)	85–115
Lunch at Wynkoop Brewing Company (mod erate)	5.95–7.95
Dinner entrees at Gallagher's Steakhouse (expensive)	16–47
Adult admission to Denver Art Museum	6
Child (age 13–18) admission to Denver Art Museum	4.50
Denver Broncos ticket	30–311
Greens fees at City Park golf course	18
Adult ski-lift ticket at Loveland Ski Area	42

Table 4-2	What Things Cost in Vail
Item	*U.S. $*
Shuttle ride from Denver International Airport to Vail (1 adult)	62
Shuttle from Vail/Eagle County Airport to Vail (1 adult)	44
Room at Sonnenalp Lodge (expensive)	200–595
Room at Evergreen Hotel (moderate)	89–329
Lunch at Bully Ranch (moderate)	7.50–15.95
Dinner entrees at Sweet Basil (expensive)	23–28
Burrito at La Cantina (inexpensive)	3.75–6.95
Single adult admission to Colorado Ski Museum	1
Vail International Dance Festival tickets	15–85
Greens fees at Vail Golf Course	105–115
Adult ski-lift ticket at Vail	67

Totaling up your transportation

Transportation is one of the easiest categories to budget for ahead of time, because the airlines and rental-car companies will quote prices in advance. When you calculate your transportation costs, make sure you consider the taxes on both your rental car and your airfare, and don't overlook the cost of gas.

Some people prefer to avoid mountain driving — especially during winter, when roads can be treacherous — and instead fly closer to destinations such as Telluride, Crested Butte, and Aspen. This option is a pricey one, but it may let you get by without renting a car, because many ski towns have excellent, free shuttle systems.

For more on transportation costs, turn to Chapter 7, which has different options for flying inside Colorado and tips on how to keep your rental-car costs down.

Calculating lodging costs

Where and when you stay in Colorado will affect your accommodation expenses. The college towns, such as Boulder, are expensive in summer and during special university events (parents' weekends, football games, and so on) but are less expensive at other times. In resort communities such as Vail and Aspen, the price of a nice hotel room for even one night can rival the cost of airfare from the East Coast. If you want to stay in the fanciest hotels in the trendiest ski towns, be prepared to sell some stock. Downtown Denver is similarly pricey. You may be able to sell fewer shares if you stay in downtown Denver on weekends, and hit the ski towns in late April and early May (after the ski areas close) and November (before the ski areas open).

The good news is that a wide range of other options exists. People sometimes forget that the mountain West has not traditionally been a wealthy region; even today, you can often drive a half-hour from a resort town to a smaller ranching or mining community where lodging is available at a fraction of the price. Pleasant, spare, $50 motel rooms in pretty areas are hardly out of the question, especially during winter and spring.

Eating out

As with lodging, you can spend as much or as little as you want while dining in Colorado. You can eat pretty well for $30 to $40 a day per person if you skip the fanciest restaurants and don't load up on liquor.

The state has lots of charming but cheap small-town cafes that serve hearty meals for under $10. It also has more than its share of gourmet restaurants, most of them concentrated in the cities and resort communities, where a dinner entree can go for upwards of $20. At most good Colorado eateries, you can get a dinner entree for $8 to $20. Watch out for places that bill à la carte — your tab can add up quickly. If you decide to splurge, you can make up the difference by scrimping the next few days. Even in resort communities, you can often buy a tasty meal for $6 or $7 if you're willing to forgo table service.

If you're on a strict budget, know that many hotels offer a free continental breakfast as part of the room rate, so ask before you book a room. If a free breakfast is not offered at your hotel, you can usually save a few bucks by going to a local coffee shop or espresso bar instead of dining in the hotel restaurant. Not only will you save money, but you'll get a better feel for the town. And those traveling with children will be happy to know that many Colorado restaurants have special low-priced kids' menus.

Budgeting for attractions

Most Colorado attractions are fairly inexpensive — just make sure you stay around long enough to get to know them. In other words, if you go to four different attractions in a day, it's going to cost you. An adult ticket to the Denver Zoo during high season costs $8; in low season, it's $6. The national parks and monuments in Colorado are the state's best deals. For $15, a carload of people gets admitted to Rocky Mountain National Park for an entire week. Mesa Verde National Park costs just $10 per carload per week, and admission to Black Canyon of the Gunnison National Park runs a mere $7.

If you plan on visiting more than a few national parks and monuments, buy a Golden Eagle pass. For $50, the card admits you and others traveling with you to national parks and monuments for a year from the date of purchase.

Pricing activities and tours

Unlike parks and museums, recreation in Colorado can be dauntingly expensive. For example, ski-lift tickets at Colorado resorts can sell for $65 or more. These prices can really hurt your wallet, but most visitors manage to avoid paying them.

You can find discounted lift tickets — they let you ride the slope's chairlifts for a day — as part of travel packages or by coming during the off-season. You can also go to smaller ski areas that offer great skiing but less acreage and fewer amenities. If you plan your trip far enough in advance, you can save on lift tickets another way: season passes. Prices have dropped so low at the ski areas nearest Denver that season passes can be a bargain for visitors planning to spend a week at the same resort. The passes are cheapest early in fall and climb in price as you get closer to prime skiing season.

If you're a golfer, you can find discounts on late-afternoon tee times at many courses.

Shopping for Colorado goods

You can shop for fine art in galleries throughout Colorado. Like the land where they're located, prices at the hottest galleries start at mile-high and go up from there. A less expensive option is to browse the quirky crafts and homespun knickknacks in offbeat tourist shops, where you may find something you like for under $20.

Outdoor enthusiasts should watch for maverick companies producing clothing and gear. Although high-quality outdoor goods are pricey, you won't get fleeced if you buy directly from the source.

Another item that can cost a little — or a lot — is Native American art. If you know what you're doing, you can get the best deals by purchasing directly from the artist or from vendors on a reservation. If you don't know your Native American art, you're better off buying from a reputable trading post. I like the Cultural Center at 25 N. Market St. in Cortez (☎ **970-565-1151**), for one.

Controlling nightlife costs

The cost of a night on the town will vary widely depending on where you happen to be when the sun goes down. Most of the really expensive options are in Denver, where you can fork over $8 for a martini or up to $130 to take in an opera. But Denver also has some reasonably priced bars and clubs, and even the unreasonable ones offer drink specials and happy-hour deals.

Outside the cities, prices drop. In most ski towns, you can quaff a pint of Colorado microbrew for around $3.50 and hear live music for a cover charge of $8 or less. The really rural towns are even cheaper — a shot and a beer at a cowboy bar will dent your sobriety more than your pocketbook.

Keeping a Lid on Hidden Expenses

You're probably already aware that the price you're usually quoted for a hotel, rental car, or vacation package is never the price you actually pay for those items. Watch out for the following hidden charges and not-so-nice surprises when you're on vacation.

Getting tips on tipping

In Colorado, tip your server about as much as you would anywhere else in the States: 15% for average service, 18% to 20% for really attentive service. When dining with a group of four or more, make sure to double-check your bill to ensure that a gratuity has not already been added. Even seemingly ethical servers have been known to happily, silently dance in the kitchen after being double-tipped. The same holds true when you order room service.

Tipping the chambermaids after a multiple-night stay at a luxury hotel is courteous. Two dollars per night — more if the service included nightly turndowns and other amenities — should please the staff. You should also reward bellhops ($1 a bag), bartenders (15%), taxi and airport-shuttle drivers (15%), concierges ($5 for procuring rides or tickets), and ski instructors (bottles of Jagermeister).

Keeping your phone bills down

Hotels impose a variety of fees for telephone calls. Some allow free local calls; others charge 50¢ or more per call. If you need to make dozens of local calls, look for accommodations where you can make them for free.

No matter where you stay, never, ever direct-dial long distance from your room, where rates can top $2 per minute. And don't count on your cell phone working either, because signals can be weak in the mountains and roving charges often apply. If you expect to make long-distance calls while on the road, your best bet is to shop ahead of time for an inexpensive prepaid calling card. (The ones sold through Costco and Sam's Club cost around 4¢ per minute.) Make your calls via the toll-free number on the card. When calling from your room, you'll still have to pay any fees that apply to local calls, but your total cost will easily beat the tab for long distance. When using a prepaid calling card, remember that some hotels also start charging for calling-card (and other toll-free) calls after a given amount of time (usually about 20 minutes). If you're worried you'll go over the time limit, find a payphone and call from there.

Cutting Costs

The destination chapters in Parts III, IV, and V all include money-saving tips specific to those regions, but here's some additional free advice to help keep your money in your pocket:

✔ **Go in the off-season.** During nonpeak times, Colorado's hotel prices can be one-third of what they are during peak months. The ski areas slow down during the weeks preceding Christmas, the month of January (when the snow is often excellent), and April. If you simply want to visit the mountains but don't care when, consider going in mid- to late-September, when the leaves change and the rates start falling. In Denver, May and September are often uncrowded, and temperatures can be near-perfect.

✔ **Travel midweek.** If you can travel on a Tuesday, Wednesday, or Thursday, you may find cheaper flights to your destination. When you inquire about airfares, ask whether you can obtain a lower rate by flying on a different day.

✔ **Try a package tour.** For many destinations, you can book airfare, hotel, ground transportation, and even some sightseeing just by making one call to a travel agent, ski area, or packager, for a lot less than if you tried to put the trip together yourself. Skiers who sign up for packages often receive discounted or free lift tickets and meals along with their accommodations.

✔ **Reserve a room with a kitchen.** Lots of rooms in Colorado come with kitchens or kitchenettes. Doing your own cooking and dishes may not be your idea of a vacation, but you'll save a lot of money by not eating three meals a day in restaurants.

✔ **Drink the free coffee at your motel.** Down as much free coffee as possible before leaving your room. It tastes lousy, for sure, but it beats paying $4 for a cappuccino.

✔ **Mix drinks in your room before a night on the town.** This strategy allows you to minimize your bar tab when you finally go out.

✔ **Buy a big jug of water and refill it using the tap.** In the mountains you'll need to drink even more water than normal. If you spring for bottled water every time you're thirsty, your water bill will soon rival the one for your house. So keep a big jug and refill it in your motel room.

✔ **Load up on bulk food and beverages early in your trip.** Buy cereals, trail mix, snacks, and beverages in bulk at an inexpensive city grocery store before traveling out into the countryside.

✔ **Always inquire about discounts.** Membership in AAA, frequent-flier plans, trade unions, AARP, or other groups may qualify you for savings on car rentals, plane tickets, hotel rooms, even meals.

✔ **Ask if your kids can stay in the room with you.** A room with two double beds usually doesn't cost any more than one with a queen-size bed. And many hotels won't charge you the additional-person rate if the additional person is pint-sized and related to you. Even if you have to pay $10 or $15 extra for a rollaway bed, you'll save by not taking two rooms.

✔ **Try expensive restaurants at lunch instead of dinner.** At fine restaurants, lunch costs a lot less than dinner, and the menus often have many of the same specialties.

✔ **Get out of town.** Many Colorado resort communities are just a short drive from less trendy towns offering an abundance of inexpensive lodging.

✔ **Walk a lot.** By walking everywhere, you can avoid paying for taxis, get to know your destination more intimately, and spend less time in places that cost money.

✔ **Skip the souvenirs.** The most cost-effective souvenirs are the shampoos, soaps, and moisturizers from your favorite luxury hotel. Whenever you get nostalgic for a particular Colorado town, you can bathe and relive the whole experience. Another option is to bring along a disposable camera and take a few snapshots — you can capture your favorite vacation memories and scenic spots at little cost to you.

Chapter 5

Tips for Travelers with Special Interests

• •

In This Chapter

▶ Traveling with children

▶ Uncovering senior discounts

▶ Seeing Colorado if you have disabilities

▶ Navigating Colorado for gays and lesbians

• •

*W*hen I talk about "people with special interests," I don't mean opera buffs or model-airplane builders. I'm referring to people for whom travel presents some unique challenges. If this description fits you, read on.

Bringing Along the Family

Your family can have fun anywhere in the state, but if you want a little help with your kids now and then, the ski towns are among the best places to be. In the past 20 years, the ski areas have shifted their focus from attracting rowdy Baby Boomer partiers to luring responsible Baby Boomer families. All the resort areas offer reduced-price lift tickets for children, and many let small children ski and snowboard for free.

The ski zones have also expanded the family-friendly activities off the slopes. Most resort towns now have ice skating, tubing, and sleigh rides, among other options. And in summer, certain ski areas become full-on fun-centers for kids, replete with mazes, alpine slides, mountain-biking, horseback rides, and special trampolines. The ski towns also have strong support systems for families, such as learn-to-ski programs for small children, high-quality day care, and babysitting. None of it is cheap, but it is generally reliable.

Day care at a ski area usually costs around $80 per day (8:30 a.m. to 4:30 p.m.). All-day children's supervised skiing programs, including lessons and lift tickets, average around $80; add $20 or so for programs that include equipment.

People of all ages get dehydrated, sunburned, and tired much faster in the mountains. You'll feel the effects yourself if you don't drink enough water, wear sunscreen, and conserve energy. However, your kids are far more likely than you are to air their discontent. Here are some tips for keeping the kids happy when traveling in the mountains:

✔ To protect them from dehydration, give kids water bottles and make sure they drink a lot.

✔ Children burn far more easily than adults, so keep them slathered in sunscreen when you're spending any time outdoors, even in winter. Give them floppy hats and sunglasses with 100% UV protection — and encourage them to keep them on.

✔ Make sure your kids eat regularly when engaged in active pursuits. Pack healthy snacks such as fruits, vegetables, and trail mix.

✔ During cold weather, dress them in layers of synthetic fabrics such as polypropelene and polar fleece. Avoid cotton, which provides no insulation when wet.

✔ Set aside an hour or so in the afternoon for resting, whether it's in your room or at a scenic, quiet, natural setting.

✔ Let your kids pick many of the activitites your family will engage in. Because Colorado has so many activitites that are enjoyable for both parents and kids, this isn't as painful as it may sound.

✔ Plan a few Colorado-specific car activities. For example, buy a field guide and encourage your kids to check off animal species they see during the trip.

✔ Many of the national parks have kid-friendly activities and programs, so set aside some time to let your kids experience one of them.

The Web offers lots of information designed to make a trip with your kids easier on both you and them, so check out the following sites before you leave in order to have a stress-free family vacation.

✔ **Family Travel Network** (`www.familytravelnetwork.com`) offers travel tips and reviews of family-friendly destinations, vacation deals, and thoughtful features such as "What to Do When Your Kids Are Afraid to Travel" and "Kid-Style Camping."

✔ **Travel with Your Children** (`www.travelwithyourkids.com`) is a comprehensive site offering sound advice for traveling with children.

✔ **The Busy Person's Guide to Travel with Children** (`http://wz.com/travel/TravelingWithChildren.html`) offers a "45-second newsletter" where experts weigh in on the best Web sites and resources for tips for traveling with children.

Getting Travel Tips for Seniors

Many Colorado hotels offer discounts to seniors who are members of **AARP** (formerly known as the American Association of Retired Persons), 601 E St. NW, Washington, DC 20049 (☎ **800-424-3410** or 202-434-2277; Internet: www.aarp.org). AARP membership also entitles you to discounted airfares and car rentals, as well as a monthly newsletter and a subscription to *Modern Maturity* magazine. Anyone over 50 can join. (You need not be mature or retired.) Seniors can also save on their travel *to* Colorado: Many domestic airlines offer discount programs for senior travelers — be sure to ask whenever you book a flight. And Amtrak knocks 15% off its fares for people 62 and over.

Most Colorado attractions drop their prices for seniors, but the minimum age varies from place to place. Some of the best deals are at ski areas. Nearly all of them sharply reduce lift-ticket prices for seniors, and some stop charging altogether. (Again, the minimum age for discounts varies.)

If you look younger than your years, consider yourself blessed and always carry some form of photo ID so that you can take advantage of discounts wherever they're offered.

The National Park Service offers a Golden Age Passport that gives seniors 62 years or older lifetime entrance to U.S. national parks for a one-time processing fee of $10. You can buy a passport in person at any NPS facility that charges an entrance fee. Besides free entry, a Golden Age Passport also entitles the holder to a 50% discount on federal-use fees charged for such facilities as camping, swimming, parking, boat launching, and tours. For more information, check out www.nps.gov/fees_passes.htm or call ☎ **888-GO-PARKS.**

The Book of Deals, a collection of more than 1,000 senior discounts on airlines, lodging, tours, and attractions around the country, is available for $9.95 by calling ☎ **800-460-6676.** Another helpful publication is *101 Tips for the Mature Traveler,* available from Grand Circle Travel (☎ **800-221-2610** or 617-350-7500; Internet: www.gct.com).

Grand Circle Travel is one of the literally hundreds of travel agencies that specialize in vacations for seniors. But beware before you book a trip with one of these agencies: Many of their packages are of the tour-bus variety, with free trips thrown in for those who organize groups of 20 or more. Seniors seeking more-independent travel should probably consult a regular travel agent. **SAGA Holidays** (☎ **800-343-0273;** Internet: www.sagaholidays.com) offers inclusive tours and cruises for those 50 and older.

Elderhostel, 75 Federal St., Boston, MA 02110-1941 (☎ **877-426-8056;** Internet: www.elderhostel.org) offers educational programs for people over 55 (your spouse can be any age; a companion must be at least 50). Programs in Colorado include excursions to Steamboat Springs and Mesa Verde. The programs are generally a week long, and prices average $335 per person double, including room, classes, and in many cases meals.

Traveling without Barriers

A disability won't shut you out from enjoying the mountains, and if you want to, you can even learn to ski, rock climb, and run rivers. The **National Sports Center for the Disabled** (☎ **970-726-1540;** Internet www.nscd.org) in Winter Park has taught thousands of people with disabilities how to ski and pursue other recreation. Many athletes from the NSCD have competed and medalled in the Paralympics, and some have returned as coaches. Everyone's welcome.

Colorado's lodging establishments are usually equipped to handle people with disabilities. Even many of the historic hotels have at least a room or two that's been modified for use by guests with mobility impairments. Nevertheless, it's best to call ahead if you want to stay at a historic property to make sure it will be able to accommodate you.

Most Colorado attractions discount their rates for people with disabilities. Unfortunately, the rugged topography in Colorado can make it tricky for people in wheelchairs to get around. If you're hoping to enjoy the state's beauty away from your car, the best places to go are the national parks and monuments, most of which have wheelchair-accessible trails, overlooks, and facilities.

Some towns offer shuttles with lifts that can accommodate the mobility impaired, but others do not. Call ahead to the visitor information bureau of the town you'll be visiting to check.

Getting around Colorado

Many of the major car-rental companies now offer hand-controlled cars for disabled drivers. Avis can provide such a vehicle at any of its locations in the U.S. with 48-hour advance notice; Hertz requires between 24 and 72 hours of advance reservation at most of its locations.

Wheelchair Getaways (☎ **800-536-5518** or 606-873-4973; Internet: www.wheelchair-getaways.com) rents specialized vans with wheelchair lifts and other features for the disabled in more than 35 states, plus the District of Columbia and Puerto Rico.

Knowing about nationwide resources

The National Park Service offers a Golden Access Passport, good for free entrance for life to U.S. National Parks and Monuments, to people who can document that they are permanently disabled or blind. The passport entitles the holder a 50% discount on federal-use fees charged for camping, swimming, parking, boat launching, and tours at federally owned areas. For more information, surf the Web to www.nps.gov/ fees_passes.htm or call ☎ **888-GO-PARKS.**

Mobility International USA (☎ **541-343-1284;** Internet: www.miusa. org) publishes *A World of Options,* a 658-page book of resources, covering everything from biking trips to scuba outfitters, and a biannual newsletter, *Over the Rainbow.* Annual membership is $35. Another place to try is **Access-Able Travel Source** (www.access-able.com), a comprehensive database of travel agents who specialize in disabled travel; it's also a clearinghouse for information about accessible destinations around the world.

Travelers with disabilities may also want to consider joining a tour that caters specifically to them. One of the best operators is **Flying Wheels Travel,** P.O. Box 382, Owatonna, MN 55060 (☎ **800-535-6790;** Fax: 507-451-1685). It offers escorted tours and cruises that emphasize sports and private tours in minivans with lifts. **Access Adventures** (☎ **716-889-9096**), a Rochester, New York–based agency, offers customized itineraries for a variety of travelers with disabilities. And **Accessible Journeys** (☎ 800-TINGLES or 610-521-0339; Internet: www.disability travel.com) caters specifically to slow walkers and wheelchair travelers and their families and friends.

Vision-impaired travelers should contact the **American Foundation for the Blind,** 11 Penn Plaza, Suite 300, New York, NY 10001 (☎ **800-232-5463;** Internet: www.afb.org), for information on traveling with Seeing Eye dogs.

Tracking Down Tips for Gays and Lesbians

Two excellent resources are available to travelers seeking Colorado businesses that cater to gays and lesbians:

> ✔ **Damron's Guide** identifies gay- and lesbian-friendly bars, clubs, cafes, restaurants, bookstores, and shops throughout the world. You can order different guides or view listings online at www. damron.com. You'll need to pay a membership fee ($9.95 for three months) to access the online descriptions of certain clubs and

businesses, but even without joining you can jot down the names of gay-friendly establishments in each city.

✔ *Out Front Colorado,* a biweekly newspaper that serves Colorado's gay, lesbian, and transgender communities, can be found in many bookstores throughout the state and on the Internet at www.outfrontcolorado.com.

One useful national resource is **The International Gay & Lesbian Travel Association** (☎ **800-448-8550** or 954-776-2626; Internet: www.iglta.org), which links travelers up with gay-friendly hoteliers, tour operators, and airline and cruise-line representatives. The IGLTA offers monthly newsletters, marketing mailings, and a membership directory that's updated once a year. Membership is $200 yearly, plus a $100 administration fee for new members.

The biggest gay and lesbian happening in Colorado — and one of the biggest anywhere — is Aspen Gay and Lesbian Ski Week, held annually in late January. Most years, over 5,000 people attend some or all of the festivities, which include ski clinics, costume parades, special shows, and films addressing topics of particular importance to gays and lesbians. For more information call ☎ **800-367-8290** or go to www.gayski week.com on the Internet.

Part II
Ironing Out the Details

The 5th Wave — By Rich Tennant

"Okay—here they come. Remember, it's a lot like catching salmon, only spit out the poles."

In this part . . .

So you've decided to go to Colorado. Now you have to climb one small mountain before you embark on a relaxing vacation: trip-planning. This part deals with all the challenges you'll have to overcome in order to set up your adventure in Colorado. It goes over different ways to travel there (and how to find the best deals for each), transportation options for after you arrive, the types of accommodations that are available throughout the state, entertainment options that require some advance thought, and even last-minute details such as trip insurance and packing.

Chapter 6

Getting to Colorado

In This Chapter

▶ Finding a package that delivers

▶ Trawling for bargains using the Internet

▶ Deciding between plane, train, and automobile

*E*ver since the World Wide Web empowered travelers to search for the cheapest rates and fares, vacation planning has been a pain in the derriere. People often feel duty-bound to find the best deal, even if they grow old in the process. And there's a lot to think about. You can shop for the best airfares and room rates individually, seek the best package deals, or drop the mouse and hire a travel agent. Here are some tips that should help, no matter which course you choose.

Travel Agent: Friend or Foe

The best way to find a good travel agent is the same way you find a good plumber or mechanic or doctor — through word of mouth. Ask a friend who travels frequently if he or she has a favorite.

All travel agents can find bargain rental-car rates, accommodations, or airfares. Good travel agents stop you from choosing the wrong deal, even if it's cheap. The best travel agents can help you with all aspects of your vacation: arranging decent rental rates, budgeting your time, booking better hotels with comparable prices, finding cheap flights that don't require five connections, and recommending restaurants.

In the past, travel agents worked on commission. The airlines, resorts, and/or tour operators paid agents a percentage of the total cost of a booking, and agent services were free to travelers. But recently, many airlines and some resorts and cruise lines have started eliminating or limiting travel-agent commissions. Therefore, most travel agents have started charging customers for their services. According to the American Society of Travel Agents (ASTA), nearly 95% of their member- ship charges fees for some or all of their services, with the cost for issuing an airline ticket averaging about $27.

If you're dealing with a good agent, the money that he or she can save you on airfares, hotels, and car rentals — not to mention sparing you the hassle and time of making arrangements yourself — more than compensates for the fee you have to pay.

If you want to grade a travel agent, do a little homework. Read up on your destination (you've already made a sound decision by buying this book) and pick out some accommodations and attractions you think you like. If necessary, get a more comprehensive travel guide such as *Frommer's Colorado* (published by Wiley). If you have access to the Internet, check prices on the Web. (See "Getting the Best Deals on Airfare," later in this chapter.) You can then take your notes and ask a travel agent to make the arrangements for you. Because they have access to resources superior to even the most complete travel Web site, travel agents should be able to offer you a price that's better than one you can get yourself. Likewise, travel agents can issue your tickets or vouchers on the spot; if they can't get your number-one hotel, they can recommend an alternative, and you can look for an objective review in your guidebook right then and there.

Choosing a Package Tour

Package tours give you the opportunity to buy airfare, accommodations, and add-ons (if you choose) at the same time. I discuss the ins and outs of package deals in the following sections.

Why buy a package tour?

For popular Colorado destinations such as ski towns, package tours are the smart way to go. In many cases, a weeklong package trip that includes airfare, hotel, lift tickets, and transportation to and from the airport costs only slightly more than the hotel alone would cost if you booked it yourself. That's because packages are sold in bulk to tour operators, who resell them to the public. It's kind of like buying your garbage bags at Sam's Club — except the tour operator is the one buying the 1,000-count box of garbage bags and then reselling them 10 at a time at a cost that undercuts what you'd pay at your average neighborhood supermarket.

Package tours can vary in style and quality as much as those garbage bags, too. Some offer a better class of hotels than others. Some offer the same hotels for lower prices. Some offer flights on scheduled airlines; others book charters. In some packages, your choice of accommodations and travel days may be limited. Some let you choose between escorted vacations and independent vacations; others will allow you to add on just a few excursions or escorted day-trips (also at discounted prices) without booking an entirely escorted tour.

Where can I find package deals?

If you already know where you'd like to stay, go straight to the source and see what packages they offer. Many ski areas offer all-inclusive deals for lodging, airfare, lift tickets, and sometimes even meals.

If you haven't already decided on a package, check ads in the national travel magazines such as *Arthur Frommer's Budget Travel Magazine, Travel + Leisure, National Geographic Traveler,* and *Condé Nast Traveler.*

You can also shop around on any of several clearinghouses for package deals. Reputable package sources include the following:

✔ **Vacation Together, Inc.** (☎ **800-839-9851;** Internet: www.vacation together.com) allows you to search for and book packages offered by a number of tour operators and airlines.

✔ The **United States Tour Operators Association's** Web site (www.ustoa.com) lets you locate operators that offer packages to a specific destination. A number of Colorado companies are listed here. Travel packages are also listed in the travel section of your local Sunday newspaper.

✔ **Liberty Travel** (☎ **888-271-1584;** Internet: www.libertytravel.com), one of the biggest packagers in the Northeast, often runs full-page ads in Sunday papers.

Another valuable resource is the airlines themselves; they often package their flights together with accommodations. When you pick the airline, you should first consider ones that have frequent service to your hometown and ones on which you accumulate frequent-flier miles. If all airlines are the same to you, start your search with **United Vacations** (☎ **888-854-3899;** Internet: www.unitedvacations.com) because United Airlines has the most extensive service throughout Colorado. Other options include **American Airlines Vacations** (☎ **800-321-2121;** Internet: www.aavacations.com), **Continental Airlines Vacations** (☎ **800-301-3800;** Internet: www.coolvacations.com), and **Delta Vacations** (☎ **800-221-6666;** Internet: www.deltavacations.com).

Flying Into Colorado

More than 100,000 passengers pass through **Denver International Airport,** also known as DIA (☎ **800-AIR-2-DEN;** TDD 800-688-1333; Internet: www.flydenver.com) every day, but you can easily fly to Colorado without ever setting foot in DIA. Flights from outside Colorado land in or near Aspen, Colorado Springs, Durango, Grand Junction, Telluride, Montrose, Steamboat Springs, and Vail. Eight airlines, offering 100 flights daily, serve Colorado Springs alone.

During winter, the busiest mountain airport, **Vail/Eagle County Airport** (☎ **970-524-9490;** Internet: www.eagle-county.com/regional_ airport.cfm), has daily nonstop service to Dallas, Chicago, Minneapolis, Newark, and San Francisco, and weekend service to Detroit, Cincinnati, and Atlanta. If you do happen to land in Denver, you can take commuter flights to all the airports listed in the preceding paragraph as well as ones in Alamosa, Cortez, and Gunnison. Denver is, however, the only international airport in the state. In addition to serving 100 destinations in the United States, DIA offers nonstop service to 11 foreign destinations, including ones in Canada, Mexico, and Europe.

Major domestic and international carriers that fly into both Denver and Colorado Springs include America West, American, Continental, Delta, and United. Air Canada, ATA, British Airways, JetBlue, Lufthansa, Mexicana, Northwest, and U.S. Airways offer service to Denver only.

For phone numbers and Web sites of the major airlines, see the Appendix. Table 6-1 lists commuter airlines that service various cities in Colorado.

Table 6-1 Commuter and Regional Airlines Serving Colorado

Carrier	Phone	Web Site
Allegiant Air	☎ 877-202-6444	www.allegiantair.com
Big Sky Airlines	☎ 800-237-7788	www.bigskyair.com
Frontier	☎ 800-432-1359	www.flyfrontier.com
Great Lakes Aviation	☎ 800-241-6522	www.greatlakesav.com
Great Plains	☎ 866-929-8646	www.gpair.com
Mesa	☎ 800-637-2247	www.mesa-air.com
Rio Grande Air	☎ 877-435-9742	www.iflyrga.com

Getting the best deals on airfare

Airline ticket pricing is a great example of capitalism gone haywire. Competition among the major U.S. airlines has resulted in so many pricing schemes that the difference in price for a coach seat (where you'll be squeezed in tighter than a sardine, no matter what airline you fly) may be as much as $1,000 for a product with the same intrinsic value.

Business travelers and others who require refundable or adjustable tickets usually pay the full-fare price. Passengers who are able to book flights well in advance, don't mind staying over a Saturday night, or are willing to travel on a Tuesday, Wednesday, or Thursday, will usually pay a fraction of the full-fare price. Likewise, if you can fly on only a few days' notice, you can enjoy the benefits of cheaper airfare. On most flights, even the shortest hops, full-price fare is close to $1,000 or more, but a 7- or 14-day advance purchase ticket is closer to $200 to $300. Obviously, it pays to plan ahead.

Periodically, airlines lower prices on their most popular routes. Although these sale fares have date-of-travel restrictions and advance-purchase requirements, you can't beat buying a ticket for (usually) no more than $400 for a cross-country flight. To find these sales, watch for ads in your local newspaper, call the airlines, or check out the airlines' Web sites. (See the Appendix for Web addresses and phone numbers.) Keep in mind, however, that airline sales often take place during low travel-volume seasons. In fact, finding an airline sale around the holidays or around the peak summer vacation months of June, July, and August is rare.

Certain smaller carriers operating in Colorado are owned by larger airlines. For example, United Airlines owns United Express. If you need connecting service on a smaller airline to reach your destination, look for airlines that share ownership and do your best to get ticketed from your point of origin to your final destination through the same airline. This strategy can save you a lot of money, especially if you're continuing on from Denver to smaller Colorado towns such as Vail, Durango, Grand Junction, and Gunnison.

Utilizing consolidators

Consolidators, also known as bucket shops, can be a good place to find low fares. Consolidators buy seats in bulk and sell them to the public at prices below airline discount rates. Their small, boxed ads usually run in the Sunday Travel sections of major newspapers, at the bottom of the page. Before you pay, however, ask for a confirmation number from the consolidator and then call the airline to confirm your seat. Be prepared to book your ticket with a different consolidator — you'll find many to choose from — if the airline can't confirm your reservation.

Also, be aware that bucket-shop tickets are usually nonrefundable or rigged with stiff cancellation penalties, often as high as 50% to 75% of the ticket price. Protect yourself by paying with a credit card rather than cash. **STA Travel** (☎ 800-781-4040; Internet: www.statravel. com), which recently purchased rival Council Travel, caters especially to young travelers, but people of all ages can take advantage of their bargain-basement prices. **The TravelHub** (☎ 888-AIR-FARE; Internet: www.travelhub.com) represents nearly 1,000 travel agencies, many of whom offer consolidator and discount fares.

Other reliable consolidators include **1-800-FLY-CHEAP** (☎ 800-359-2432; Internet: www.1800flycheap.com) and **Cheap Tickets** (☎ 888-922-8849; Internet: www.cheaptickets.com), or *rebators,* such as

Travel Avenue (☎ **800-333-3335** or 312-876-1116; Internet: www.travel avenue.com), which rebate part of their commissions to you.

Booking your ticket online

Another way to find the cheapest fare is to scour the Internet. There are too many travel booking sites to mention, but a few of the better-respected (and more comprehensive) ones are **Travelocity** (www.travelocity.com), **Expedia** (www.expedia.com), and **Orbitz** (www.orbitz.com). Each has its own little quirks, but they all provide variations of the same service. Just enter the dates you want to fly and the cities you want to visit, and the computer looks for the lowest fares. Several other features have become standard to these sites: the ability to check flights at different times or dates in hopes of finding a cheaper fare, e-mail alerts when fares drop on a route you have specified, and a database of last-minute deals that advertises super-cheap vacation packages or airfares for those who can get away at a moment's notice.

Qixo (www.qixo.com) is a powerful search engine that allows you to search for deals on flights and hotel rooms on approximately 20 other travel-planning sites (such as Travelocity) at once. Qixo sorts results by price, after which you can book your travel directly through the site.

Great last-minute deals are also available directly from the airlines themselves. Most of these are announced each week on Tuesday or Wednesday and must be purchased online. They are only valid for travel that weekend, but some can be booked weeks or months in advance. Sign up for weekly e-mail alerts at airline Web sites or check mega-sites that compile comprehensive lists of last-minute specials, such as **Smarter Living** (www.smarterliving.com) or **WebFlyer** (www.webflyer.com).

Driving In

You can easily drive to Colorado via one of three interstate highways, all of which meet in Denver.

- ✔ **Interstate 70,** which stretches all the way from Baltimore, Maryland, to Southwestern Utah, is the primary east-west artery through Colorado.

- ✔ **Interstate 76** branches off of I-80 (which spans from Chicago to San Francisco) in Southwestern Nebraska and makes a 190-mile jaunt southwest to its terminus in Denver.

- ✔ **Interstate 25** links Denver with destinations in the north (Casper and Cheyenne, Wyoming) and the south (Albuquerque, New Mexico). As I-25 skirts the eastern slope of the Rockies, this heavily traveled freeway passes through major Colorado cities such as Fort Collins, Denver, Colorado Springs, and Pueblo.

Arriving by Rail

Amtrak's California Zephyr train traverses the entire width of Colorado en route from Chicago to Emeryville, California (near Oakland). Between Denver and Fort Collins it passes through some spectacular high country, crossing the continental divide just south of Rocky Mountain National Park and paralleling the Colorado River for long stretches in Western Colorado. The Zephyr doesn't exactly breeze down the tracks — it takes roughly 12 hours to cross the state — but its fares are fair: In February 2002, one-way coach tickets from Denver to Chicago, Salt Lake City, and Emeryville were $106, $72, and $108, respectively.

A second Amtrak train, the Southwest Chief, clips the southeast corner of Colorado on its way from Chicago to Los Angeles. For complete fare information and scheduling for both these routes, contact Amtrak (☎ **800-USA-RAIL;** Internet: www.amtrak.com).

Chapter 7

Getting Around Colorado

● ●

● ●

What's the best way to see Colorado? If you've got cash to spare, you may enjoy flying to an airport right near your favorite resort town, taking a cab into town, and then riding the free buses around the community. You can easily enjoy Colorado without ever getting behind the wheel of a car. If you're like most people, however, you'll eventually get behind the wheel, beginning your trip at either Denver International Airport or at points farther out.

Driving Around Colorado

The bicycle may be superior and the plane may be faster, but the car (or SUV) still moves most people around Colorado. Because you'll probably be driving in Colorado, here's some advice on getting around the state on four wheels.

Handling the highways

Mountains make for tricky driving. They lift and cool air, which releases rain and snow; they unloose rocks that roll onto roadbeds; and in spring, their snowmelt occasionally floods things. The condition of a Colorado highway often depends on whether the road crew or the mountain has mounted the most recent offensive. If the mountain happens to be winning while you're driving in the area, don't blame the road crew — they're plotting their next move over coffee as we speak!

Certain Colorado roads are especially vulnerable to mountain weather:

✔ **Interstate 70** east of Denver usually remains open during winter, but chains or four-wheel drive may be required during storms, and weekend traffic can slow to a near standstill.

✔ **Highway 550** between Ouray and Silverton serves up what is arguably the most frightening winter driving in the state. As it passes over 11,000-foot Red Mountain Pass, this two-lane highway edges across the tops of enormous cliffs yet offers little in the way of guardrails or shoulders for protection. It often closes during and after storms.

✔ Other roads close altogether. **Colorado 82** between Aspen and Leadville shuts down during winter due to heavy snows on 12,095-foot Independence Pass. **U.S. 34,** which crosses the continental divide at 12,183 feet inside Rocky Mountain National Park, also closes during winter.

For recorded updates on road conditions within two hours of Denver, call ☎ **303-639-1111.** For road conditions elsewhere in the state, dial ☎ **303-639-1234.**

Negotiating road hazards

Drivers in Colorado face a unique set of challenges that may phase visitors unused to the state's rugged terrain and weather. For a smooth ride, make certain you read this section, where I discuss climate and other related problems that may crop up while you're on the road.

Surviving snow and ice

Many Colorado highways traverse mountain passes that receive, on average, over 200 inches of snow annually. Most of us are ready for snow during winter, but it's easy to get fooled in spring and fall, when valley rains sometimes become snowstorms up high. If you're traveling in spring, fall, and winter, be ready for snowy and icy conditions in the mountains.

Here are some tips on how to prepare for a ride in the frozen stuff:

✔ Check your tires to make sure they have adequate tread and are properly inflated.

✔ If you don't have a four-wheel-drive vehicle with snow tires, carry chains.

✔ Make sure your brakes, wipers, defroster, and heater all work.

✔ Carry a small shovel, sand (for extra weight inside the car and traction under the tires), a window brush, and a scraper.

✔ Stow a sleeping bag in your vehicle, just in case you get stranded.

✔ Keep a powerful flashlight handy so you can signal other drivers in the event of an accident. You also may want to carry an emergency flare for the same reason.

✔ Watch the weather and try to imagine what may be happening high above. If you suspect bad weather and are ill-prepared, don't go.

✔ Clean and scrape all your windows so that you have maximum visibility. Shovel off the hood and roof as well, so snow doesn't blow onto your windshield and the cars around you.

✔ If you have four-wheel drive, make sure it is engaged.

✔ If you have rear-wheel drive, carry a set of chains.

When driving on snow and ice, use caution even if your vehicle has four-wheel drive. Sport-utility vehicles are great on snow, but on ice they're no better than your mother's Oldsmobile. Here are some more helpful tips for winter driving in Colorado:

✔ **Allow extra time for the trip.** Mountain driving takes longer, especially during winter.

✔ **Be especially cautious during descents.** There's less margin for error when gravity gives you an extra push from behind. Don't, however, ride the brakes. Carefully shift into a low gear and then let the car's engine limit your speed.

✔ **Watch for black ice on shadowy corners.** Certain stretches of mountain road receive almost no sunlight in mid-winter. When water trickles from sun-warmed areas onto these frigid, shadowy stretches, look out.

✔ **Beware of ice on bridges.** Without warm earth to heat them, bridges freeze sooner than the rest of the road when the temperature drops. Bridges that cross mountain streams may also gather condensation from the waters below.

✔ **Don't cut corners.** Although this holds true in all weather conditions, it is especially important during storms, when snowplows with enormous blades lurk.

Avoiding rockfall

Rockfall usually happens on warm days during late winter and early spring, when snowmelt permeates and loosens dirt that holds rock in place on hillsides. Other times, it happens when snowmelt seeps into cracks in cliffs, freezes, and then expands at night, wedging loose chunks of rock. The rocks careen downhill until they come to rest on relatively flat roads, where they wait around in hopes of destroying rental cars. Be particularly careful when low sunlight or shadows make it difficult for drivers to detect foreign objects on the road. Check the clearance on your vehicle before straddling anything big.

Eluding wildlife

Deer did not evolve to watch out for fast-moving automobiles; nor have they proved themselves quick studies in the century since Henry Ford invented the Model A. Roughly 7,000 of Colorado's half-million deer are hit by cars every year, causing $3 million in damage. The best way to avoid deer is to slow down considerably at night, when it's nearly impossible to detect their approach. (Deer are most active at dawn and dusk but can be encountered any time.) During winter, watch for groups of them browsing just below the snow line. If a deer crosses the road in front of you, always assume that a second one is trailing. Deer aren't the only animals to watch out for. At high elevations, you may encounter bighorn sheep and elk. Pronghorn antelope roam the grasslands and valleys. And, though most of the rangeland in Colorado is fenced, cows do sometimes shamble onto the pavement.

Getting the best deal on a rental car

Car-rental rates vary even more than airline fares. The price depends on the size of the car, the length of time you keep it, where and when you pick it up and drop it off, where you take it, and a host of other factors. Asking a few key questions can save you hundreds of dollars. Ask the following questions to help save money when renting a car:

- ✔ **Is the weekend rate lower than the weekday rate?** Ask whether the rate is the same for pickup Friday morning as it is Thursday night. If you're keeping the car five or more days, a weekly rate usually is cheaper than the daily rate.

- ✔ **Will I be charged a drop-off fee if I return the car to a location that's different from where it was rented?** Some companies may assess a drop-off charge, most notably National, although others do not. Ask whether the rate is cheaper if you pick up the car at the airport or a location in town.

- ✔ **May I have the price I saw advertised in my local newspaper?** Be sure to ask for that specific rate; otherwise, you may be charged the standard (higher) rate. Don't forget to mention membership in AAA, AARP, frequent-flier programs, and trade unions. These groups usually entitle you to discounts ranging from 5% to 30%. Ask your travel agent to check any and all of these rates.

And remember that most car rentals are worth at least 500 miles on your frequent-flier account!

Booking a rental car on the Internet

As with other aspects of planning your trip, using the Internet can make comparison shopping for a car rental much easier. All the major booking sites — **Travelocity** (www.travelocity.com), **Expedia** (www.expedia.com), **Orbitz** (www.orbitz.com), and **Cheap Tickets** (www.cheaptickets.com), for example — have search engines that can dig up discounted car-rental rates. Just enter the size of the car you want, the pickup and return dates, and the city where you want to rent, and the server returns a price. You can even make the reservation through these sites.

An excellent Web site, **BreezeNet's Guide to Airport Rental Cars** (www.bnm.com), offers tips and sample rates for car rentals at airports around the world. It also features destination-specific discount specials, including some for Denver.

If you want information about specific rental-car companies serving Colorado, see the Appendix at the back of this book.

Adding up the cost of renting a car

On top of the standard rental prices, other optional charges apply to most car rentals. The Collision Damage Waiver (CDW), which requires you to pay for damage to the car in a collision, is charged on rentals in most states, but it's covered by many credit-card companies. Check with your credit-card company before you go so that you can avoid paying this hefty fee (as much as $15 to $20 a day), if possible.

Car-rental companies also offer additional liability insurance (if you harm others in an accident), personal-accident insurance (if you harm yourself or your passengers), and personal-effects insurance (if your luggage is stolen from your car). If you have insurance on your car at home, you're probably covered for most of these unlikelihoods. If your own insurance doesn't cover you for rentals or if you don't have auto insurance, consider buying additional coverage. (Car-rental companies are liable for certain base amounts, depending on the state.) But weigh the likelihood of getting into an accident or losing your luggage against the cost of extra coverage (as much as $20 a day combined), which can significantly add to the price of your rental.

Some companies also offer refueling packages, in which you pay for an entire tank of gas up front. The price is usually fairly competitive with local gas prices, but you don't get credit for any gas remaining in the tank. If you reject this option, you pay only for the gas you use, but you have to return the vehicle with a full tank or face charges of $3 to $4 a gallon for any shortfall. If a stop at a gas station on the way to the airport will make you miss your plane, by all means take advantage of the fuel-purchase option. Otherwise, skip it.

Riding the rails

Amtrak's (☎800-USA-RAIL; Internet: www.amtrak.com) California Zephyr train works better as a way of getting *to* Colorado than as a way to get *around* it. The train stops in some intriguing locales, including downtown Denver's Union Station, Fraser (near the Winter Park Resort), Glenwood Springs, and Grand Junction. But if you want to keep your costs down, you'll probably have to choose a single destination when traveling by rail, and then drive or figure out another way to get around from there.

Winging it

Flying to airports in Western Colorado is an appealing option when mountain highways become snow-covered or crowded. Many small Colorado airports offer daily commuter service to and from Denver, and some have nonstop flights to and from destinations outside Colorado. The most active in-state carrier, **United Express** (☎ **800-241-6522;** Internet: www.ual.com) provides commuter service between Denver and Steamboat Springs, Durango, Telluride, Montrose, and Grand Junction.

The commuter service may be convenient, but it isn't necessarily cheap. Round-trip fares from Denver to Durango in the 2003 ski season averaged $230 per person.

If you fly all the way to one of Colorado's mountain towns, you may find that you don't need a car at all. Towns such as Aspen, Telluride, Winter Park, Vail, Crested Butte, and Steamboat all have free bus systems and are very pedestrian-friendly.

Taking the bus

Greyhound/Trailways (☎888-454-7277; Internet: www.greyhound.com) provides bus service to dozens of Colorado destinations — including, it seems, every possible city, town, burg, post office, gas station, bulletin board, and ranch exit. Greyhound also sells an **Ameripass** entitling users to unlimited bus travel in the U.S. for periods ranging from seven days (cost: $199) to 60 days (cost: $599). Pass holders can get off the bus and sightsee for a day, and then catch a bus passing through later. The passes can be bought through a travel agent or online at Greyhound's Web site.

Before splurging on an Ameripass, however, you should ask yourself two questions: First, given the comfort level, shouldn't they be paying *you* to ride the bus? And, given some of the tough neighborhoods where these buses tend to stop, are you sure want to get off?

Chapter 8

Booking Your Accommodations

- -

In This Chapter

▶ Choosing your lodgings

▶ Avoiding the rack rate

▶ Booking the best room

▶ Surfing the Internet to a better rate

- -

*T*he good news is that Colorado has a number of accommodations selections for you to choose from, no matter what your budget or interests. This chapter sums up a few of your lodging options in Colorado and then goes over a few different ways to save money when you're ready to book, no matter where you choose to stay.

Lining Up Your Lodging Choices

In Colorado, the accommodations you choose can set the tone for your vacation. You can have a Western experience at a ranch, simplify life at a mom-and-pop motel, luxuriate in one of the fancy hotels, or immerse yourself in history (and sometimes acquire a temporary family) at a B&B. Here's the lowdown on the major types of accommodations available to Colorado visitors.

Booking a B&B

Colorado has dozens of B&Bs, many of which offer surprisingly good value. If you take a room with a shared bath — and these are often great rooms — you can usually stay at a B&B for less than the price of a chain hotel. You'll stay in cozy (and often historic) surroundings, enjoy a full complimentary breakfast, and get to know your hosts and some fellow travelers. Some B&Bs have ultra-luxurious rooms and modern amenities such as steam showers, jetted baths, and TV/VCRs; others have hardly changed in a hundred years.

Not all B&Bs allow kids on the premises, so ask about this if you're planning your family vacation. You should also avoid B&Bs if you or your kids are rowdy, if you're on a tight schedule that means arriving late or leaving early, or if you simply want some downtime alone.

But if these exceptions aren't an issue, then bed-and-breakfasts are a great deal. Many of the state's B&Bs are written up in this book; others can be located through the **Bed & Breakfast Innkeepers of Colorado** (☎ **800-265-7696;** Internet: www.innsofcolorado.org).

Bunking down at a motel

The privately owned mom-and-pop motels in Colorado are often bright, clean, and reasonably priced. And they're only slightly less historic than the state's many Victorian B&Bs. Many Colorado motels date to the 1920s and 1930s, when car travel first became popular in the West. Because they're old, and because every owner is different, ask to see a room before settling in. After you're in, however, you can enjoy the solitude and convenience that a motel provides. Carry your bags a few yards from your trunk to your room, fetch some ice cubes and a soda, turn on the TV, and float downstream.

Staying at historic or luxury hotels

Colorado has two world-famous, historic luxury hotels. **The Brown Palace** in Denver and **The Broadmoor** in Colorado Springs have turned lodging into an art form. Elsewhere in Colorado are many less-expensive historic hotels that provide equally memorable experiences for travelers.

One caveat: At the most luxurious hotels, whether they're historic or not, you'll not only pay an expensive room rate, but you'll also have to tip for the many services provided. At some places, you can't even get ice cubes on your own, and you're discouraged from carrying your own bags. For people with bulging bank accounts, this can be paradise, but it may not feel that way if you're on a more modest budget.

Choosing a chain

Chain hotels are like your favorite pair of socks; they offer comfort with few surprises. If you've stayed often enough at a particular chain, then you'll probably know ahead of time what color scheme and amenities will be inside your room (although some chains do offer unique properties). In general, I like staying at chains. They wouldn't be such a popular option if their rooms weren't pleasant. And they're really great for control freaks. Yet, they do have their limitations. Colorado offers many other options that will color your experience in ways that chain hotels won't, and it would be a shame not to experience at least a few of these less-predictable properties. For the Web sites and phone numbers of the most popular chains in the U.S., see the Appendix.

Going to a guest ranch or dude ranch

With at least 40 officially recognized guest and dude ranches, you could say that Colorado has made a cottage industry of ranches. Other than their both being out in the sticks, guest ranches and dude ranches have little in common. Guest ranches tend to operate more like motels: You can often pay by the night, and few services are included in your room rate. Dude ranches are more likely to charge a set amount for an all-inclusive week that includes accommodations, meals, activities, and sometimes even your own horse. Some dude ranches are ultra-luxurious; others are rustic working ranches where you can help with roundups and other chores. For more information on dude and guest ranches in Colorado, contact the **Colorado Dude and Guest Ranch Association** (☎ **970-887-3128;** Internet: www.coloradoranch.com).

Camping out

Although I don't cover many Colorado campgrounds in this book, you should know that they're great options if you have the right gear. Campgrounds can be found in Colorado's national forests, national parks, state parks, and on private land. Most have drinking water and toilets; some have showers, too. You can make reservations for some, but most are first-come, first served. The going rate for a tent site at most campgrounds is $10 to $15, making this a fabulous option for those on a shoestring budget. You can also camp for free inside any of the national forests in Colorado, provided you follow a few simple regulations. Stop by any Forest Service office for details or surf the Internet to www.fs.fed.us.

Avoiding Rack Rates (and Why You Don't Have to Pay Them)

Rack rates are the standard, undiscounted rates that hotels charge for their rooms. If you call a hotel for a rate or walk into a hotel to get a room for the night, you're usually quoted the room's rack rate. Hotels also post their rack rates on the backs of room doors (unless the previous guests had one too many microbrews and swiped them as a souvenir).

You don't have to pay rack rates. In fact, hardly anyone does. Perhaps, the best way to avoid paying the rack rate is surprisingly simple: Ask for a cheaper or discounted rate. The answer may pleasantly surprise you.

In all but the smallest accommodations, the rate you pay for a room depends on many factors — chief among them being how you make your reservation. For example, a travel agent may be able to secure a better price with certain hotels than you can, because hotels sometimes give agents special discounts as a reward for bringing in an abundance of return business.

Please note that room prices are subject to change without notice, so even the rack rates quoted in this book may be different from the actual rate you receive when you make your reservation. And note that unless otherwise specified, all rates for accommodations in this book are the rack rate for a double room.

Getting the Best Room at the Best Rate

Finding the best hotel rate requires a bit of detective work. For example, reserving a room through the hotel's toll-free number may also result in a lower rate than if you called the hotel directly. On the other hand, the central reservations number may not know about discount rates at specific locations. For example, local franchises may offer a special group rate for a wedding or family reunion, but they may neglect to tell the central booking line. Your best bet is to call both the local number and the toll-free number and see which one gives you a better deal.

Room rates also change with the seasons, as occupancy rates rise and fall. If a hotel is close to full, it's less likely to extend discount rates; if it's close to empty, it may be willing to negotiate. Resorts are most crowded on weekends, and they usually offer discounted rates for midweek stays. The reverse is true for business hotels in downtown locations.

You can usually, but not always, get a room near your place of choice in Colorado. The busiest times in the ski towns are Christmas week, Presidents week, and spring break (mid- to late March). The next busiest time is July and early August. After the kids go back to school in late August, rooms start opening up. If you're coming during a busy time, try to book a spot a six months out. (At the hottest hotels during Christmas week, you may need to book a year or more out.) If you're flexible, however, you can sometimes wait and get a last-minute deal, especially during ski season.

Be sure to mention membership in AAA, AARP, frequent-flier programs, and any other corporate rewards programs when you make your reservation. You never know when your membership may be worth a few dollars off your room rate.

When you book a room, ask whether the hotel charges for parking. Also keep in mind that many hotels charge a fee just for dialing out on the phone in your room. Find out whether your hotel imposes a surcharge on local and long-distance calls. A pay phone, however inconvenient, may save you money, although many calling cards charge a fee when you use them on pay phones. Finally, ask about local taxes and service charges, which could increase the cost of a room by 25% or more.

Finding the right room

If you're looking for general guidelines for getting a great room, here are some strategies:

- ✔ **Always ask for a corner room.** They're usually larger, quieter, and sometimes closer to the elevator. Corner rooms have more windows and light than standard rooms, and they don't always cost more.

- ✔ **Steer clear of construction zones.** Be sure to ask if the hotel is renovating; if it is, request a room away from the renovation work. The noise and activity may be a bit more than you want to deal with on your vacation.

- ✔ **Request your smoking preference.** Be sure to ask for either a smoking or nonsmoking room, if you have a preference. Otherwise, you may get stuck with a room that doesn't meet your needs.

- ✔ **Inquire about the location of the restaurants, bars, and discos.** These areas of the hotel could all be a source of irritating noise. On the other hand, if you want to be close to the action, or if you have a disability that prohibits you from venturing too far very often, you may choose to be close to these amenities. (See Chapter 5 for more information about getting around if you have a disability.)

If you book your room through a travel agent, ask the agent to note your room preferences on your reservation. When you check in at your hotel, your preferences will pop up when the reception desk pulls your reservation. Special requests can't be guaranteed, but ask in advance anyway. If you aren't happy with your room when you arrive, talk to the front desk. If they have another room, they should be happy to accommodate you, within reason.

Surfing the Web for hotel deals

You may be better off dealing directly with the hotels, but if you don't like haggling, online reservation services can act like airline consolidators (see Chapter 6 for more information). They buy hotel rooms in bulk and sell them to consumers for less than the rack rates. The Internet also offers numerous sites that provide information on hotels or resorts in Colorado. The biggest advantage that you get from using the Internet is that you can see the hotel or resort before you book your trip. Plus, you can book online and save yourself the aggravation of listening to a slew of annoying automated voice systems.

Although the major travel booking sites (see Chapter 6 for details) offer hotel booking, your best bet is to use a site devoted primarily to lodging, because you may find properties that aren't listed on more-general online travel sites. Some lodging sites specialize in a particular type of accommodations, such as bed-and-breakfasts, which you won't find on the more-mainstream booking services. Other sites, such as **TravelWeb** (covered in the following list), offer weekend deals on major chain properties, which cater to business travelers and have more empty rooms on weekends.

Check out the following Web sites for hotel accommodations:

- ✔ Although the name **All Hotels on the Web** (www.all-hotels.com) is something of a misnomer, the site *does* have tens of thousands of listings throughout the world, including ones in many Colorado resort towns. Bear in mind each hotel has paid a small fee (of $25 and up) to be listed, so it's less an objective list and more like a book of online brochures.

- ✔ **hoteldiscount!com** (www.180096hotel.com) lists bargain room rates at hotels in more than 50 U.S. and international cities, including Denver. The cool thing is that hoteldiscount!com pre-books blocks of rooms in advance, so sometimes it has rooms — at discount rates — at hotels that are "sold out." The toll-free number is printed all over this site (☎ 800-96-HOTEL); call it if you want more options than those that are listed online.

- ✔ **Places to Stay** (www.placestostay.com) lists one-of-a-kind places in the U.S. and abroad that you may not find in other directories, with a focus on resort accommodations. This isn't a comprehensive directory, but it does have a broad selection of inns and hotels throughout Colorado.

- ✔ An excellent free program, **TravelAxe** (www.travelaxe.net), can help you search multiple hotel sites at once, even ones you may never have heard of. It allows you to compare prices (it even includes the hotel taxes) for a host of properties in Colorado.

- ✔ You can also book rooms in Denver through **Accommodations Express** (☎ 800-950-4685; Internet: www.accommodationsexpress.com) and **Quikbook** (☎ 800-789-9887, includes fax on demand service; Internet: www.quikbook.com).

- ✔ The Web site for **Frommer's** (www.frommers.com) has an extensive selection of mountain condominium properties.

Chapter 9

Money Matters

Maybe you've been brooding over how to pay for things in Colorado and how much cash to carry. If you have, this chapter's for you. If not, you can get away with skimming this chapter — at least, until you lose your wallet or someone swipes it.

Paper, Plastic, or Pocket Change

You can choose from a number of payment options for your vacation expenses, including meals, souvenirs, and so on. In this section, I explore the options to help you determine the one that's right for you.

Finding an ATM ASAP

Colorado, like most states, has an ample supply of 24-hour automated teller machines (ATMs) linked to national networks that almost always include your bank. **Cirrus** (☎ **800-424-7787;** Internet: www.mastercard.com) and **Plus** (☎ **800-843-7587;** Internet: www.visa.com) are the two most popular networks; check the back of your ATM card to see which network your bank belongs to. The toll-free numbers and Web sites will give you specific locations of ATMs where you can withdraw money while on vacation.

 Withdraw only as much cash as you need every couple of days. This strategy eliminates the insecurity (and the threat of pickpockets) that goes with carrying around a wad of cash.

 Many banks charge a fee ranging from 50¢ to $3 whenever a non-account-holder uses their ATMs. (In Colorado, the average is around $1 to $1.50.) Your own bank may also assess a fee for using an ATM that's not one of their branch locations. This means that, in some cases, you'll get charged *twice* just for using your ATM card when you're on vacation.

In addition, although an ATM card may be an amazing convenience when traveling in another country (put your card in the machine and out comes foreign currency), banks are also likely to slap you with a foreign currency transaction fee, just for making them do the conversion math. Given these sneaky tactics, if you're coming to the U.S. from another country, reverting to traveler's checks may just be cheaper (though certainly less convenient).

Toting traveler's checks

Traveler's checks are a throwback to the days before ATM machines gave you easy access to your money. Because you can replace traveler's checks if they're lost or stolen, they're a sound alternative to stuffing your wallet with cash. However, you may have trouble cashing them in some places.

You can get traveler's checks at almost any bank. **American Express** offers checks in denominations of $20, $50, $100, $500, and $1,000. You pay a service charge that ranges from 1% to 4% of the total value of the checks that you receive. Call American Express (☎ 800-221-7282) to purchase traveler's checks over the phone or visit its Web site at www. americanexpress.com.

Visa (☎ 800-732-1322; Internet: www.visa.com) also offers traveler's checks, available at Citibank locations and several other banks across the country. Call the toll-free number for a complete list of bank locations. Visa's checks come in denominations of $20, $50, $100, $500, and $1,000, with charges ranging from 1.5% to 2%. **MasterCard** also offers traveler's checks; call ☎ 800-223-9920 for a location near you.

AAA members can obtain traveler's checks without a fee at most AAA offices. Call your local office for details.

Charging up a storm

Traveling with credit cards is a safe alternative to carrying cash. Credit cards also provide you with a record of your vacation expenses, after you return home.

You can get cash advances from your credit cards at any bank. At most banks, you don't even need to go to a teller; you can get a cash advance at the ATM if you know your personal identification number (PIN). If you've forgotten your PIN or didn't even know you had one, call the phone number on the back of your credit card and ask the bank to send it to you. It usually takes between five and seven business days, though some banks will give you the number over the phone, if you tell them your mother's maiden name or pass some other security clearance.

Another hidden expense to contend with: Interest rates for cash advances are often significantly higher than rates for credit-card purchases. More importantly, you'll start paying interest on the advance *the moment you receive the cash.* On an airline-affiliated credit card, a cash advance does not earn frequent-flier miles.

What to Do if Your Wallet Is Missing (Besides Panic)

You just reached into your pocket for your wallet, only to find it's not there. Or perhaps some enterprising thief just made you his latest meal ticket. Colorado is a pretty safe place, but things happen.

In the unlikely event that you lose your wallet or it's stolen, be sure to report the situation and block charges against your account the minute you discover the loss. Then be sure to file a police report.

Almost every credit-card company has an emergency toll-free number to call if your card is stolen. The company may be able to wire you a cash advance off your credit card immediately, and in many places, it can deliver an emergency credit card in a day or two. The issuing bank's toll-free number is usually on the back of your credit card — though, of course, if your card has been stolen, that won't help you unless you wrote the number down and kept it elsewhere. Make sure you do so.

Citicorp Visa's U.S. emergency number is ☎ **800-336-8472.** American Express cardholders and traveler's check holders should call ☎ **800-221-7282.** MasterCard holders should call ☎ **800-307-7309.** If you have a different brand of card or traveler's check, call the toll-free number directory at ☎ **800-555-1212** to get the correct phone number.

If you opt to carry traveler's checks, be sure to keep a record of their serial numbers so you can handle just such an emergency.

Odds are that if your wallet is gone, you've seen the last of it, and the police aren't likely to recover it for you. However, it's still worth informing the authorities. You may need a police report number later, for credit-card or insurance purposes.

Chapter 10

Tying Up the Loose Ends

• •

• •

*T*his chapter deals with the little things that people tend to put off until the last minute before leaving on a trip, such as buying trip insurance, prepare for illnesses on the road, making reservations, and knowing what to pack (and how to pack it). I even give you the low-down on blending in with the locals.

Buying Travel and Medical Insurance

There are three primary kinds of travel insurance: trip-cancellation, lost-luggage, and medical. Trip-cancellation insurance is a good idea for some, but lost-luggage and additional medical insurance don't make sense for most travelers. Be sure to explore your options and consider the following advice before you leave home:

▶ **Trip-cancellation insurance:** Cancellation insurance is a good idea if you've paid a large portion of your vacation expenses up front. It also comes in handy if you've bought a package trip and a member of your party becomes ill or you experience a death in the family and aren't able to go on vacation.

▶ **Lost-luggage insurance:** Your homeowner's insurance should cover stolen luggage if your policy encompasses off-premises theft, so check your existing policies before you buy any additional coverage. Airlines are responsible for up to $2,500 on domestic flights (and $9.07 per pound, up to $640, on international flights) if they lose your luggage; if you plan to carry anything more valuable than that, stow it in your carry-on bag. but that may not be enough to cover your sharkskin suit.

✔ **Medical insurance:** Your existing health insurance should cover you if you get sick while on vacation. (However, if you belong to an HMO, check to see whether you're fully covered when away from home.)

Some credit cards (American Express and certain gold and platinum Visas and MasterCards, for example) offer automatic flight insurance against death or dismemberment in case of an airplane crash. If you still think you need more insurance, make sure that you don't pay for more than you need. For example, if you need only trip-cancellation insurance, don't purchase coverage for lost or stolen property. Trip-cancellation insurance costs approximately 6% to 8 % of your vacation's total value.

Keep in mind that in the aftermath of the World Trade Center attacks, a number of airlines, cruise lines, and tour operators are no longer covered by insurers. The bottom line: Always, always check the fine print before you sign on; more and more policies have built-in exclusions and restrictions that may leave you out in the cold if something does go awry.

Here's a list of some of the reputable issuers of travel insurance:

✔ **Access America,** 6600 W. Broad St., Richmond, VA 23230 (☎ **800-284-8300;** Fax: 800-346-9265; Internet: www.accessamerica.com)

✔ **Travelex Insurance Services,** 11717 Burt St., Suite 202, Omaha, NE 68154 (☎ **800-228-9792;** Fax: 800-867-9531; Internet: www.travelex-insurance.com)

✔ **Travel Guard International,** 1145 Clark St., Stevens Point, WI 54481 (☎ **800-826-1300;** Internet: www.travelguard.com)

✔ **Travel Insured International, Inc.,** P.O. Box 280568, 52-S Oakland Ave., East Hartford, CT 06128-0568 (☎ **800-243-3174;** Fax: 860-528-8005; Internet: www.travelinsured.com)

Although it doesn't really provide insurance, if you're planning on exploring the backcountry, spend $3 for a Colorado Outdoor Search and Rescue Card. The card guarantees that the local sheriff's departments will be reimbursed for search-and-rescue costs involving the card-holder. This may end up saving you a lot of money, because the sheriffs will have fewer costs to pass along if you need their services. Note, however, that not every conceivable rescue expense is covered. For example, if a medical helicopter flies you out of the mountains, you'll still end up paying. Cards are available at most Colorado State Parks, Division of Wildlife Offices, and private vendors. To locate a vendor near you, contact the **State of Colorado Department of Local Affairs** (☎ **970-248-7310;** Internet: www.state.co.us/searchandrescue).

Finding Medical Care on the Road

Getting sick on the road can ruin a vacation, and finding a doctor you trust or getting a prescription filled when you're out of town is no piece of cake either. So, here are some travel tips to help you avoid a medical dilemma while you're on vacation:

- ✔ If you have health insurance, carry your identification card in your wallet. Likewise, if you don't think your existing policy is sufficient, purchase medical insurance for more-comprehensive coverage.

- ✔ Bring all your medications with you as well as a prescription for more if you think you'll run out. And don't forget to bring over-the-counter medicines for common travelers' ailments, such as diarrhea or indigestion.

- ✔ Bring an extra pair of contact lenses or glasses in case you lose them.

- ✔ If you suffer from a chronic illness, talk to your doctor before taking your trip. For conditions such as epilepsy, diabetes, or a heart condition, wear a MedicAlert identification tag to immediately alert any doctor about your condition and give him or her access to your medical records through MedicAlert's 24-hour hotline. Participation in the MedicAlert program costs $35, with a $20 renewal fee. Contact the MedicAlert Foundation, 2323 Colorado Ave., Turlock, CA 95382 (☎ **888-633-4298;** Internet: www.medic alert.org) for more information.

If you do get sick, ask the concierge at your hotel to recommend a local doctor — even his or her own doctor if necessary. This is probably a better recommendation than any national consortium of doctors available through a toll-free number.

If you can't get a doctor to help you right away, try the emergency room at the local hospital. Many hospital emergency rooms have walk-in-clinics for emergency cases that aren't life-threatening. You may not get immediate attention, but you'll probably pay around $75 rather than the $300 minimum for just signing in at an emergency-room counter.

Making Reservations and Getting Tickets

The only thing you really need to book ahead of time in Colorado is your room. (For advice on when to book rooms, see Chapter 8.) After you have a place to bed down, you can usually get into the attractions and museums that most appeal to you (although calling a few days ahead of time to inquire about opening hours is still a good idea).

A handful of hot **restaurants** may require reservations more than a few days in advance. I identify these places in my reviews in Chapters 11 through 21. At most spots, however, you can get a table if you call a day or so in advance; and, if you're dining on a weeknight or during early or late evening, you can often get away with calling that day.

If you're coming from a town that's music-starved and you're rolling into a hotspot such as Denver or Boulder, you may want to find out ahead of time who's playing, just in case one of your favorite **rock, jazz, or blues performers** is going to be around. To find out what will be happening during your visit, check the calendar published by the alternative newsweekly *Westword* at www.westword.com.

For **dance, classical music, and theater,** surf to www.artstozoo.org or follow links from www.Denver.com. For information by phone, you can contact the **Denver Performing Arts Complex (☎ 303-640-PLEX;** Internet: www.denvercenter.org) or call the events hotline for the **Denver Center Theater Company (☎ 303-893-3272).**

If watching **pro sports** is your preferred entertainment, the two teams that regularly sell out in Colorado are football's Broncos and hockey's Avalanche. You'll need to plan ahead if you want to see these teams in person. **Ticketmaster (☎ 303-830-TIXS)** sells tickets for all five pro teams in town. It helps if, before calling, you identify the date of the contest you're hoping to see. You can view the team's schedules by checking their Web sites at www.denverbroncos.com and www.coloradoavalanche.com, respectively.

Gearing Up: Practical Packing Advice

Start packing for your trip by taking everything you think you'll need and laying it out on your bed. Then get rid of half of it.

It's not that the airlines won't let you take it all — they will, with some limits — but why would you want to lug half your house around with you? And remember, a wheeled suitcase doesn't roll so well when you're climbing uphill in the Rockies.

Bringing the basics

So what are the bare essentials for a trip to Colorado? During summer in Denver, you can usually get by with comfortable walking shoes, a camera, a sweater, a light jacket, a belt, toiletries and medications (pack these in your carry-on bag so you'll have them if the airline loses your luggage), and something to sleep in. Unless you'll be attending a board meeting, a funeral, or one of Denver's finest restaurants, you probably won't need a tie. You'll get more use out of a pair of jeans or khakis and a comfortable sweater — and you'll look a lot more like a local.

In the mountains, add a layer of light polypropylene long underwear and a wind-resistant, water-resistant jacket to the items described in the last paragraph. If you're planning to venture more than a few hundred yards from the safety and warmth of your car, throw in a warm hat, a polar fleece jacket, and some lightweight hiking boots (use heavier ones if you're backpacking as opposed to day-hiking). During winter you'll need a thicker outer shell as well as additional insulating layers, not to mention warm socks. You'll also want some gloves and winter boots.

 Colorado may not be a sun-worshipper's haven, but the state does get a lot of sun (300 sunny days a year in some spots) and the solar rays are more direct in the thinner atmosphere and cause sunburn more quickly. And the potential for skin damage increases when the sun reflects off snow or water. So make sure to pack a good sunblock, no matter what time of year you're traveling, as well as good-quality ultraviolet-blocking sunglasses. And remember that children need more protection than adults.

Know the limits on your carry-on luggage

Because lost-luggage rates have reached an all-time high, most people would rather bring their possessions onboard to try to divert disaster. Since the September 11, 2001, terrorist attacks on New York and Washington, the Transportation Security Administration (TSA), the government agency that now handles all aspects of airport security, has devised new restrictions for carry-on baggage. Passengers are now limited to bringing just one carry-on bag and one personal item (like a briefcase or a purse). For more information, go to the TSA's Web site (www.tsa.gov).

The agency has released a new list of items passengers are not allowed to carry onto an aircraft:

Not permitted: Knives and box cutters, corkscrews, straight razors, metal scissors, golf clubs, baseball bats, pool cues, hockey sticks, ski poles, and ice picks

Permitted: Nail clippers, nail files, tweezers, eyelash curlers, safety razors (including disposable razors), syringes (with documented proof of medical need), walking canes, and umbrellas (must be inspected first)

As for the size of carry-on bags, dimensions vary, but the strictest airlines say they must measure no more than 22 x 14 x 9 inches, including wheels and handles, and weigh no more than 40 pounds. The airline you fly may have additional restrictions on items you can and cannot carry on board. Call ahead to avoid problems.

Packing it all in

When packing, start with the biggest, hardest items (usually shoes) then fit smaller items in and around them. Pack breakable items in between several layers of clothes, or keep them in your carry-on bag. Put things that could leak, like shampoos, suntan lotions, and so on, in resealable plastic bags. Lock your suitcase with a small padlock (available at most luggage stores, if your bag doesn't already have one), and put a distinctive identification tag on the outside — some people tie brightly colored scarves onto their luggage handles — so your bag will be easy to spot on the carousel.

The tips of skis are very susceptible to damage during flight. If your ski bag lacks padding, wrap a T-shirt or two around your tips.

Your carry-on luggage should contain a book, any breakable items you don't want to put in your suitcase, a personal headphone stereo, water, a snack (in case you don't like peanuts), medications, any vital documents you don't want to lose in your luggage (like your return tickets, passport, wallet, and so on), and some empty space for the sweater or jacket that you won't want to be wearing while you're waiting for your luggage in an overheated terminal. (You will want to wear it on that often-chilly airplane, though.)

Dressing like a local

Visitors to Colorado who try to blend in often make the same mistake: Instead of dressing like the people who *live* in Colorado, they end up dressing like the people who used to *own* Colorado — that is, Texans. To avoid resembling a refugee from the Lone Star State, leave that full-length fur coat at home. Avoid attire that consists of a patchwork of animal skin and fur. Just because the stores in Aspen sell those clothes doesn't mean that Coloradoans actually buy them. And don't wear diamonds the size of street lamps (unless you really want to).

Before you can truly dress like a Colorado local, you first have to determine what constitutes one, and that's no easy task. Nearly a third of Colorado's 4.3 million residents arrived in the state in the last decade. It's safe to say that the true locals are the Navajo, Ute, Apache, Comanche, Cheyenne, Kiowa, and Arapaho tribes, who have occupied parts of the state since at least 1400.

The people with the next longest tenure, for the most part, are farmers and ranchers. To dress like a rancher, buy Wrangler jeans that are somewhat confining and then throw in some lace-up roper boots, a belt buckle the size of Toledo, a western shirt, and a Stetson hat. Among Colorado's more recent arrivals are snowboarders; to emulate them choose your pants size so you look exactly the opposite of how you would when impersonating a rancher.

The one thing that all these different locals have in common is a deep, abiding love for the Denver Broncos. So the single best way to dress like a Colorado local is probably to buy a hooded Denver Bronco sweatshirt and a Denver Bronco baseball cap or winter hat. Put those on, and you'll fit right in.

Part III
Exploring the Big Cities

The 5th Wave   By Rich Tennant

In this part . . .

When visiting Colorado, starting fairly low and working your way up is always a good idea. If you visit the cities of Denver and Colorado Springs, you'll have time to acclimate to the mile-high elevation before climbing even higher into the mountains. You can also find out more about the rest of the state by visiting the metropolitan museums. Best of all, you'll have all kinds of fun entertainment options to choose from.

This part tells you the best ways to reach the state's two largest cities — Denver and Colorado Springs — and gives you tips on where to stay and what to do after you arrive. I also throw in a few cool side trips to some of the state's former boomtowns, where you can still pan for gold, and some gambling zones, where you can also try to strike it rich.

Chapter 11

Settling Into Denver

● ●

In This Chapter

▶ Getting there without a hitch

▶ Moving around the city

▶ Finding a room that fits your budget

▶ Chowing down at the top restaurants

● ●

*W*ith its feet on the plains and its eyes on the mountains, Denver has always been a little restless. When a spur of the Transcontinental Railroad reached here in the 1880s, the town profited by smelting silver and gold from the nearby peaks, garnering enough wealth to build luxurious hotels, grand boulevards, and impressive edifices such as Union Station and the Tabor Opera House. During the mid-1900s Denver became a manufacturing center. And when the energy business boomed in the 1970s and early 1980s, a dozen or so skyscrapers etched an awesome skyline. By then, what had begun as a tiny mining camp had become a metropolis with a population of nearly a half million.

But Denver wasn't — and isn't — finished. During the past decade, amazing shapes have risen out of the old rail yards and runways of Denver's past. The silvery, open-ended Invesco Field at Mile High, home to the Denver Broncos football team, stands where a parking lot used to be. A short distance away, the roller coasters of Six Flags amusement park slither across the edge of downtown in what was once a dangerous flood plain. Coors Field, home to Major League Baseball's Colorado Rockies, has revitalized a blighted area of abandoned warehouses and vacant lots. Its clean, retro appearance mirrors the surrounding community, where Denver's gritty history has been scrubbed and packaged for mass consumption.

Development continues all around the city, in some of the fastest growing communities in America. Every day, thousands of people, most of them young and well educated, discover that the city and the nearby mountains afford limitless possibilities for recreation on weekends and holidays. The newcomers recharge the vitality of the area, even if they do contribute to its traffic and the bulldozing of the surrounding plains and foothills. Upon arriving in Denver, think about staying here for a day or two before going into the mountains. It will help you acclimate, you can discover more about the state by visiting some of Denver's many museums, and, above all, it's fun!

Arriving by Air

After a rocky beginning, **Denver International Airport** (☎ 800-AIR-2-DEN) — popularly referred to as **DIA** — now earns accolades for both efficiency and capacity. Located 23 miles northeast of downtown, the $4.3 billion airport has 94 gates and 5 runways on a 53-square-mile area. Twenty airlines fly into DIA, serving 105 domestic and 11 international destinations (see Chapter 6 for details). The airport's centerpiece is the 1.5-million-square-foot Jeppesen terminal, whose roof consists of 15 acres of a Teflon-coated, woven fiberglass that allows 10% of visible light to pass through it. From above, the terminal looks like a city of white tents. The terminal's interior, during daylight hours especially, feels light, spacious, and comfortable.

From Jeppesen terminal, passengers travel to three concourses, two of which are accessible only via an underground train. (Concourse A can also be reached by a pedestrian bridge that actually passes over the a runway.) The train runs every two minutes, and the longest ride lasts under five minutes. The train does, however, get crowded. And if you're late for a flight or trying to make a close connection, it can be disconcerting to take an escalator downstairs and then have to wait around on a platform.

When flying out of DIA, allow a little extra time both for the train and for the trip on foot — or via moving walkway — across one or more airport concourses, the longest of which is 3,300 feet. Also, if you get claustrophobic, bear in mind that the middle car on each train is usually less crowded than the end cars.

Despite having one of the world's most technologically advanced baggage-handling systems, DIA is simply too big for the airlines to instantly produce the baggage you check. You'll usually have to wait a bit at the carousels, which are located on Terminal Level 5. Immediately across from them are hotel and ground transportation information boards. If you're taking commercial transportation to your hotel, grab your bags and then head out the doors on Level 5 to the curbside pickup areas. If someone in a private vehicle is picking you up, go to Level 4.

Assistance is readily available and you should have no problems getting answers to questions while at the airport: In addition to DIA information booths in the main terminal and on all three concourses; the Denver Metro Convention and Visitors Bureau has its own information booths in the main terminal and on Concourse B.

For general airport information, call the **Denver International Airport Information Line** at ☎ **800-AIR-2-DEN,** 800-688-1333, or 303-342-2200. For **ground transportation,** the number is ☎ **303-342-4059.** When you have your bags and your bearings, you can choose from a number of options that will get you from DIA to your accommodations.

Renting a car

All the major rental-car companies are represented at DIA, so you're bound to find your favorite here. The list includes **Advantage, Alamo, Avis, Budget, Dollar, Enterprise, Hertz, National, Payless,** and **Thrifty.** For information on contacting individual car-rental agencies, see the Appendix.

To reach the downtown Denver area, exit the airport onto Trussville Street and go Southwest for 0.3 mile. Bear left onto Pena Boulevard and go southwest for another 10 miles. Continue on the ramp and go southwest for 1.3 miles. Take I-70 west for 9 miles, and take the exit that will bring you closest to your destination.

Taking shuttles or cabs

Three taxi companies are licensed to operate out of Denver International Airport: **Freedom Cab** (☎ **303-292-8900**), **Metro Taxi** (☎ **303-333-3333**), and **Yellow Cab** (☎ **303-777-7777**). All three charge a flat fee of $45.50 (including a $2.50 gate fee) to go from DIA to the downtown area. If you're traveling with a group of three to five people (the maximum that most companies will take), a cab affords you a per-person price second only to the skyRide public bus.

Dozens of private companies provide shuttle service from DIA to points throughout Colorado. One reliable service linking DIA with Denver's downtown area is **SuperShuttle** (☎ **800-525-3177** or 303-370-1300; Internet: www.supershuttle.com). You don't need a reservation to take SuperShuttle from the airport to your hotel. Simply go to the SuperShuttle desk near baggage claim and tell the representative that you'd like a ride. You'll probably have to wait 20 to 30 minutes, and the driver may drop off other passengers before you, but the per-person cost to most downtown hotels is a reasonable $18. For your return trip to the airport, make sure to call SuperShuttle for a reservation at least 24 hours in advance.

Hopping buses

The cheapest way to reach many destinations in Denver and Boulder is via a public **skyRide** bus (☎ **303-299-6000** and then speed dial **1-2-1**). Between 4 a.m. and midnight, skyRide buses — part of the city's public

Regional Transportation District (RTD) system — depart DIA's Level 6 (outside Door 613) at least once every hour. From DIA, the buses service 28 skyRide stops throughout the Denver metropolitan area, including 18 free park-and-ride lots, and provide links to other RTD buses and light rail.

At a cost of $6 to $10, skyRide may work for you if you're on a tight budget, have time to spare, and are traveling light. (At DIA, skyRide drivers may assist you with luggage; but don't count on this service if you transfer to another RTD bus.) If you're considering using RTD, you can get more information by visiting the skyRide counter in the ground-transportation area of Level 5, or by going to the RTD's Web site at www.rtd-denver.com. If you do decide to take skyRide, bring plenty of small bills and quarters, because drivers cannot make change.

Arriving by Car

Interstate 70, which passes within a few miles of Denver International Airport, is the principal east-west corridor through both Denver and Colorado. En route from St. Louis to southern Utah, it passes a few miles north of Denver's downtown and then climbs into the Colorado high country, passing through the towns of Vail, Glenwood Springs, and Grand Junction, among others, before crossing the Utah border. I-25, which slices through the west side of the city, travels north and south between New Mexico and Wyoming. Take I-25 to reach Denver from the major Front Range cities of Colorado Springs and Fort Collins. To get to Denver from Boulder, you'll need to head southeast to I-70 on U.S. 36. U.S. 285 goes northeast to Denver from Salida.

Riding In (No, Not on Horseback)

With more than 60 daily arrivals and departures at its Denver terminal at 19th and Arapahoe streets, **Greyhound** (☎ **800-231-2222**) provides a variety of options for reaching destinations both inside and outside Colorado. This terminal, located in the Central Business District, is convenient to city bus and light rail service. You'll also find taxis readily available outside the station.

If you choose to come into Denver via train, Amtrak runs two routes — both go from Chicago to various destinations in California — that pass through Denver. The Amtrak trains stop at historic Union Station, at 17th and Wynkoop streets (☎ **800-USA-RAIL** or 303-825-2583; Internet: www.amtrak.com) in the lower downtown area.

Orienting Yourself in Denver: The Neighborhoods

If you get lost in Denver, look for the Rocky Mountains, visible 14 miles west of town. As long as some of the city's taller buildings don't block your view, you should always be able to figure out which way is west. Had the city's founders initially created a north-south grid to go with the obvious north-south mountain range, Denver would be as easy to navigate as that paragon of sensible roads, Salt Lake City. Unfortunately, Denver's first grid paralleled not the Rocky Mountains but the South Platte River, which flows northeast through the present downtown area (and isn't even navigable). That's why the grid that covers the Lower Downtown and Central Business District neighborhoods runs northeast and northwest. To complicate matters, Denver's next generation surrounded this grid with roads on a traditional north-south grid. When you see roads connecting at unusual angles, you've probably reached an interface between the two grids.

Historic areas such as the **Central Business District** and the **Lower Downtown** (locally referred to as **LoDo**) neighborhoods are on this older grid. The **Five Points** area is situated on the old grid's northeast corner. And part of the **Uptown** neighborhood occupies its southeast corner. The west side of Denver's central downtown is bordered by Speer Boulevard, which parallels Cherry Creek (the actual creek not the neighborhood). Many other intriguing neighborhoods are located just south of the downtown, on the newer, north-south grid. Heading south from downtown, zigzagging slightly to the east and west, you'll pass through the **Capitol Hill, Cherry Creek,** and **Washington Park** neighborhoods, each with its own unique personality. The neighborhoods don't have perfect dividing lines, and Denverites sometimes disagree as to where one begins and another one ends. Still, the descriptions I provide below should give you some idea where you're going, and what to expect when you get there.

Central Business District

To find this area, head for the skyscrapers on 16th, 17th, and 18th streets between Broadway and Lawrence. Built primarily in the 1970s and 1980s, these tall buildings define the Denver skyline and make it easy to forget that this is also one of the oldest parts of town. Be sure to see the district's remaining 19th-century buildings, including the Brown Palace Hotel and the Trinity Methodist Church, as you tour the area.

On weekends, business travelers vacate the area's many luxury hotels, only to be replaced by tourists arriving for shows in The Plex, shopping in the 16th Street Marketplace, and games at Coors Field, all of which are within walking distance of this section of town. In spite of the tourist influx, the area becomes less crowded and more relaxed on weekends.

Lower Downtown (LoDo)

Once a blighted area of abandoned factories and warehouses, LoDo's modern heyday began soon after Coors Field was completed, at a cost of $215 million, in 1995. Parking for this redbrick, state-of-the-art ballpark was scattered throughout the LoDo area, so fans of the Colorado Rockies baseball team began wandering through the neighborhood, pausing for food, drink, and entertainment along the way. LoDo, which runs from Speer Boulevard northeast to 20th Street and from Market Street northwest to Wynkoop Street, is the center of the city's nightlife and now houses dozens of bars, brewpubs, restaurants, and galleries. Many of these businesses occupy restored brick warehouses with high ceilings, hardwood floors, and (sometimes) rooftop seating. The area has 127 historic structures, including Union Station. Many date back to the 1870s, when the railroad first reached Denver.

Uptown

The highlights of this neighborhood, stretching from Broadway east to York Street and from 23rd Street south to Colfax, are its lovely homes. Before the price of silver crashed in 1888, the city's first millionaires built ornate Victorian and Queen Anne–style homes in this area west of Denver. The area became run down in the 1950s, but today many of its houses have been lovingly restored. New restaurants, bars, and coffee shops have popped up to serve this recently gentrified area, particularly along 17th Street. The west side of Uptown borders City Park, home to the Denver Zoo and Denver Museum of Nature and Science. The southern border of this neighborhood is a gritty but interesting strip of Colfax Avenue, where you can get tattooed, buy vinyl records, load up on your incense, and learn Kung Fu.

Capitol Hill

Capitol Hill, which spans from Broadway east to York Avenue and from Colfax Avenue south to Sixth Avenue, has impressive Victorian homes like the ones in the Uptown neighborhood to its north. It also is home to some of Denver's best-known landmarks, including the State Capitol, whose gold dome is visible for miles around, and the expansive Civic Center Park, which has a symmetrical, European-style design. Along the park's edges are the Denver Public Library, the Denver Art Museum, and the Colorado History Museum. The U.S. Mint, recently closed to tourists because of security issues, is a block away from the park.

Denver Neighborhoods

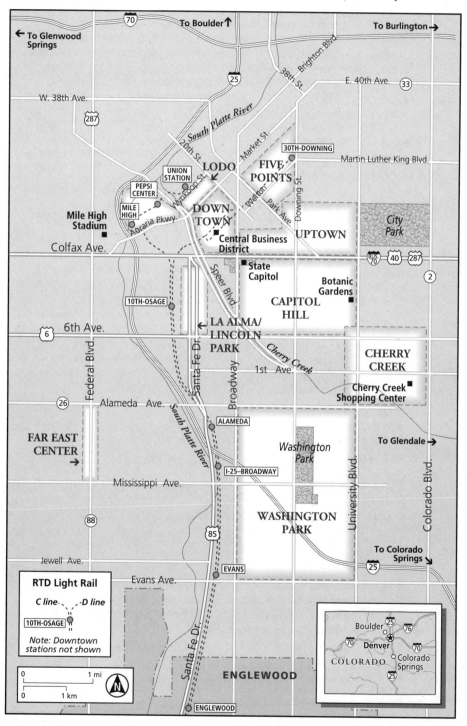

To Boulder↑   To Burlington→

← To Glenwood Springs

W. 38th Ave.   E. 40th Ave. 33

LODO   FIVE POINTS

PEPSI CENTER   UNION STATION   30TH-DOWNING   Martin Luther King Blvd.

Mile High Stadium   MILE HIGH   DOWN-TOWN   UPTOWN   City Park

Colfax Ave.   Central Business District

State Capitol   Botanic Gardens

10TH-OSAGE   CAPITOL HILL

6th Ave.   LA ALMA/ LINCOLN PARK   CHERRY CREEK

Alameda Ave.   1st Ave.   Cherry Creek Shopping Center

FAR EAST CENTER →   ALAMEDA   To Glendale →

Mississippi Ave.   Washington Park   I-25–BROADWAY

WASHINGTON PARK   To Colorado Springs ↘

Jewell Ave.   Evans Ave.   EVANS

RTD Light Rail
C line ⋯ D line
10TH-OSAGE
Note: Downtown stations not shown

0   1 mi
0   1 km

ENGLEWOOD   ENGLEWOOD

Boulder   25   76
70   Denver   70
COLORADO   Colorado Springs
25

Cherry Creek

Fifty years ago few people would have foreseen Cherry Creek, which runs from East First Avenue north to East Eighth Avenue and from Downing Street east to Colorado Street, encompassing Denver's wealthiest neighborhoods. Located near the city dump, it was the place where returning World War II veterans built bungalows and quietly raised families. Today, many of those bungalows have been replaced by glitzy mansions; the Denver Country Club, which counts some of the city's financial elite among its members, is located here; and the chic stores in the Cherry Creek Mall attract shoppers from throughout the region. Just north of the mall, in Cherry Creek North, you'll find tree-lined streets with expensive galleries, boutiques, spas, and restaurants.

South Platte Valley

A decade ago there was little reason to visit the broad, dusty flood plain of the South Platte River west of downtown. Then new dikes and dams stabilized the river flow, and the city of Denver built new bike paths and cleaned up the river corridor. Some of Denver's biggest attractions have sprouted alongside the river in an area loosely defined by Speer Boulevard on the northeast, I-25 on the west, and Auraria Parkway on the south. New additions include the Pepsi Center, a 20,000-seat arena for the city's pro hockey and basketball teams; Invesco Field at Mile High, a 76,000-seat football stadium for the Denver Broncos (which is just west of I-25); the Six Flags Elitch Gardens Amusement Park; and Colorado's Ocean Journey, a $93 million aquarium.

Other Denver neighborhoods

The neighborhoods described in the preceding sections tend to attract the most attention from tourists, but they're just a few of the many intriguing downtown spots. Here are some others that merit attention:

- **Far East Center,** a strip of Federal Boulevard between West Alameda and West Mississippi avenues, has a large Asian-American population and some fine Vietnamese and Thai restaurants.

- **Five Points,** which runs west from Park Avenue to Downing Street and southeast from 38th to 23rd streets, is a center for Denver's African-American population and home to the Black American West Museum and Heritage Center.

- Denver's Latino population operates many shops, restaurants and stores in the **La Alma Lincoln Park Area,** on Santa Fe Drive between West Colfax and West Sixth avenues.

✔ The **Washington Park** area is alive with the young professionals of all ethnicities who have bought homes around Denver's largest park. The area, known to locals as "Wash Park," spans from Broadway east to University Boulevard, and from Alameda Avenue south to Evans Avenue.

Getting Information After You Arrive

The best source for area information is the **Denver Metro Convention and Visitors Bureau,** 1668 Larimer St., half a block south of the 16th Street Marketplace (☎ **303-892-1112;** Internet: www.denver.org). It's open Monday through Friday from 8 a.m. to 5 p.m. and on Saturday from 9 a.m. to 1 p.m.

The Visitors Bureau also operates information booths in the main terminal and in Concourse B at Denver International Airport. A small information booth operates weekdays from 10 a.m. to 4 p.m. at **Larimer Square,** on Larimer Street between 15th and 14th streets (☎ **303-893-0740**). You can also get information during business hours inside the **State Capitol** (☎ **303-866-2604**), at the corner of Broadway and Colfax. The public entrance to the capitol is at street level on the building's south (14th Street) side.

If, for some reason, you lose your bearings at **Cherry Creek Mall,** 3000 E. First Ave. (☎ **303-388-3900**), you can stop at an information booth there.

Getting Around

No matter how you choose to travel, you'll find Denver to be a fairly user-friendly city. Of course, there are always a few tie-ups in any major city. Whether you're traveling by car, bus, train, or even on foot, here's how to avoid the ones in Denver.

By mass transit

An immense bus and light rail system known as **Regional Transportation District (RTD)** serves Denver, Boulder, and other communities.

With 179 bus routes going to 41 municipalities, the system can be tricky to figure out if you're using it for the first time. You can try using the route planner on the RTD's Web site (www.rtd-denver.com), but you stand a better chance of sorting things out if you talk to a warm-blooded information specialist at the RTD hotline (☎ **800-366-7433**).

Printed bus and rail schedules are available at **Market Street Station,** on the corner of Market and 16th Street; **Civic Center Station,** on the corner of Broadway and 16th Street; and at many area King Soopers and Safeway stores.

While in Denver, take advantage of the free bus system that runs the length of the 16th Street Mall, from near Civic Center Park to Union Station. During peak hours, you seldom have to wait more than a minute or two for a bus; at off hours, the wait can be a little longer. By using these buses, which run from 6 a.m. to 1 a.m. daily, you can shorten walks to many of the prime attractions in the downtown area while sparing yourself parking headaches.

Also worth trying is the new light-rail train into the Platte Valley. From Union Station, you can take the train to stations at Invesco Field at Mile High, the Pepsi Center, Six Flags Elitch Gardens, and Colorado's Ocean Journey. This new line makes nearly all the major downtown attractions easily accessible, via mass transit, from downtown hotels. In general, the light rail is easier to grasp than the bus lines. The color-coded routes are posted at the stops, and they're relatively easy to decipher.

The cost for local light rail or bus routes is $1.10 for adults, 55¢ for seniors and youths ages 6 to 18. Express routes cost $2.50 for adults, $1.25 for seniors and youths. Regional buses are $3.50 for adults, $1.75 for seniors and youths. If you're taking the train, bring plenty of quarters and $1 bills for the ticket machines at each stop. The machines provide no more than $1 in change.

After buying your ticket, you'll need to validate it before getting on the train. If you're taking the bus, put your exact fare into the box next to the driver, and ask for a free transfer slip if you need to change buses. The light rail lines operate from about 6 a.m. to midnight, depending on where you board the last train.

If you're planning to rapidly take in cultural attractions throughout the downtown area, pay $16 for a daylong pass on the **Cultural Connection Trolley** (☎ **303-289-2841;** Internet: www.grayline.com). Every hour between 8:30 a.m. and 5:30p.m., the Grayline-operated trolley stops at Denver's prime tourist attractions, including Cherry Creek Shopping Center, Ocean's Journey, Union Station, Larimer Square, and Coors Field. The trolley operates only from Memorial Day through Labor Day.

Although the Trolley technically runs until 5:30 p.m., a full loop of the tour takes two hours and the last trolley leaves Cherry Creek Shopping Center at 3:30 p.m.

By taxi

Taxi drivers in Denver charge an initial drop-flag fee of $1.60, plus $1.60 per mile. You're allowed to hail a cab in Denver, but unless you're downtown and have some luck, the attempt could be a Hail Mary. This is especially true on weekends, after the bars have shut down for the night. Most of the time, you're probably better off calling for a cab or going to the taxi stand at your hotel. Companies with large fleets are **Freedom Cab** (☎ 303-292-8900), **Metro Taxi** (☎ 303-333-3333), **Yellow Cab** (☎ 303-777-7777), and **Zone Cab** (☎ 303-444-8888).

By car

You can walk and use mass transit to reach the major attractions in the downtown area — indeed, it's much cheaper and easier for you to do so — but you need a car if you hope to take in all the sights in the out-lying communities and the mountains.

Driving is surprisingly manageable in LoDo and the Central Business District, which are on Denver's oldest grid. This grid consists of num-bered streets running northwest and southeast, intersected at right angles by named arteries such as **Market Street** (one-way northeast), **Lawrence Street** (one-way northeast), and **Larimer** (one-way south-west). Traffic usually moves well, especially on weekends.

Most streets in downtown are one-way, so you may have to go around the block in order to get to your destination.

The drawback to driving downtown is trying to find inexpensive park-ing. Daily parking usually costs $5 to $10, with hourly rates sometimes running $2.50 or more. Some hotels charge upwards of $15 per night for valet parking. If you manage to find a parking space on the street, the meter will usually cost 25¢ for every 15 minutes, with a two-hour maximum in effect.

If you're going to park downtown, bring quarters for meters and small bills for the self-pay lots.

You'll have an easier time parking, but you can expect to encounter more intense traffic as you leave the downtown area and move from the old grid to the new grid. The new grid consists of numbered avenues that run east and west, intersected by named streets and boulevards that run north and south.

If an address is on a numbered road, check to see whether the road is a street or an avenue, so you know which grid it's on. Numbered streets are on the old grid; numbered avenues are on the new one. Some of the main streets on the new grid, such as Colorado Avenue and Colfax Avenue, get clogged during rush hour. And, as in most major cities, freeway traffic can slow dramatically during rush hour.

A highway construction project known as T-Rex will slow traffic on I-25 until 2006. Traveling south on I-25 from the Central Downtown to the Tech Center area can be particularly agonizing during peak periods.

On foot

By and large, Denver is a great place to walk. Hundreds of miles of bike and walking paths wend their way through the city, with the majority of these in the parks and on old rail grades paralleling the city's waterways. If you're walking for pleasure only, the trails along the South Platte River and Cherry Creek are especially nice. They're mostly below street level, along rivers that, except for the occasional bobbing vodka bottle or half-submerged shopping cart, are remarkably clean. If transportation is your goal, you can easily reach the popular tourist destinations in the Central Business District, LoDo, and Capitol Hill areas on foot, especially if you occasionally jump on a free bus on the 16th Street Mall to shorten the distances. However, you'll need a car to reach most other areas in and around the city.

As for problem areas, don't go too far east on Colfax Avenue — but don't shun Colfax, either. The stretch between Broadway and University has some lively music venues (including the revamped Fillmore Theater) and restaurants, and it passes between the Capitol Hill and Uptown neighborhoods, which boast many of the city's historic homes. The crime-riddled spots on Colfax are east of Colorado Street, where there are few tourist attractions.

Where to Stay

As in most major cities, staying in downtown Denver on a weeknight is expensive. The Central Business District and LoDo areas are long on luxury hotels for business travelers and short on budget accommodations for families. Weeknight prices often run $175 to $225, including parking. On Friday and Saturday nights, however, business travelers vacate the Central Business District and you can usually find a luxurious room for under $100. The lower end of the rack rates I list in this section tend to be weekend rates, while the higher end is what you'll pay on a weekday.

If you have to be in downtown Denver on a weeknight, look for a small room at one of the area's bed-and-breakfasts. These often cost under $100 and include free breakfast. Plus, they're nice. Prices for rooms drop as you move farther from downtown. Accommodations in the Cherry Creek area, roughly ten minutes from downtown by car, cost about $20 to $30 dollars less than downtown and have free parking. If you need a motel or hotel room in the $70 range, your best bet may be to surf the Internet for deals at the many chain hotels in the suburbs. (See Chapter 8 for more information on getting good hotel deals.)

The top hotels

Brown Palace Hotel
$$$$ Central Business District

The Brown Palace has always been *the* place to stay in Denver, attracting everyone from Dwight Eisenhower to the Beatles. The atrium inside the 101-year-old hotel is one of those rare architectural masterpieces that are nearly as breathtaking as a natural wonder. A skylight illuminates eight stories of balconies with cast-iron grillwork; floors and columns of white Onyx; and a tea area, where a piano player or lutist plays daily. The hotel is shaped like a triangle, and it's old, so the rooms come in a variety of shapes and sizes. That said, the rooms are quite comfortable and decorated in either a Victorian or Art Deco style. The hotel promotes itself not only to wealthy and expense-account travelers but to regular people hoping to create their own memories, and a number of weekend package deals do bring the hotel's prices into the lower reaches of the earth's atmosphere. But even if you can't stay here, definitely peek inside at the lobby.

321 17th St. ☎ *800-321-2599 or 303-297-3111. Fax: 303-312-5900. Internet:* www. brownpalace.com. *$22 valet parking. Rack rates: $225–$275, suites $325–$1,275. Valet parking, $22 per night. AE, DC, DISC, MC, V.*

Castle Marne Bed and Breakfast
$$–$$$ Uptown

One of Denver's most famous architects, William Lang, designed this 1889 stone mansion, which looks and feels like a living museum (it's a registered National Landmark). Everywhere you look, you'll find something stunning, whether it's the circular stained-glass window on the stairs, wainscoting of Honduran mahogany, floors of quarter-sawn oak, or the specially textured walls in the dining room (which are protected by the U.S. Department of the Interior). The guest rooms are equally beautiful and several rooms have private balconies with hot tubs. Fortunately for the guests, all the beauty doesn't make things seem stuffy or tense — innkeepers Jim and Diane Peiker somehow keep things down to earth, making this a winning experience in every way. ***Note:*** The inn is entirely nonsmoking, so if you like to light up, look elsewhere.

Children age 10 and under are not permitted on the premises, making this a lousy choice for families but a great one for couples looking for a more sedate atmosphere.

1572 Race St., at 16th Avenue. ☎ *303-331-0621. Fax: 303-331-0623. Internet:* www. castlemarne.com. *Rack rates: $105–$170 double; $200–$255 suite. Rates include full breakfast and afternoon tea. Children under 10 not permitted. AE, DC, DISC, MC, V.*

Downtown Denver Accommodations and Dining

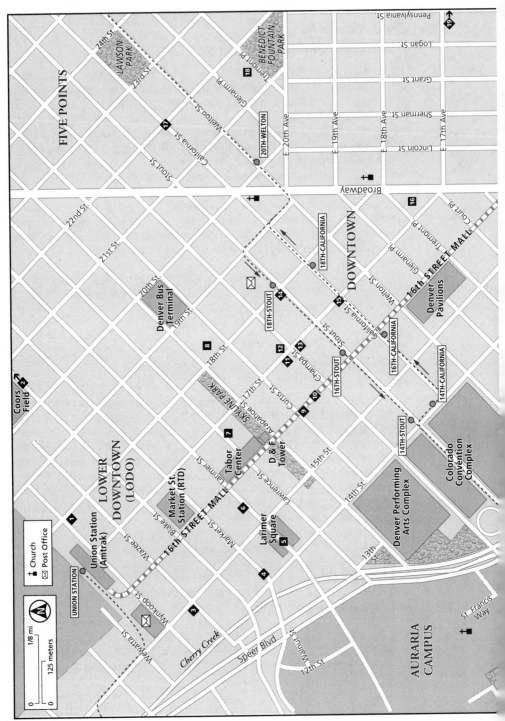

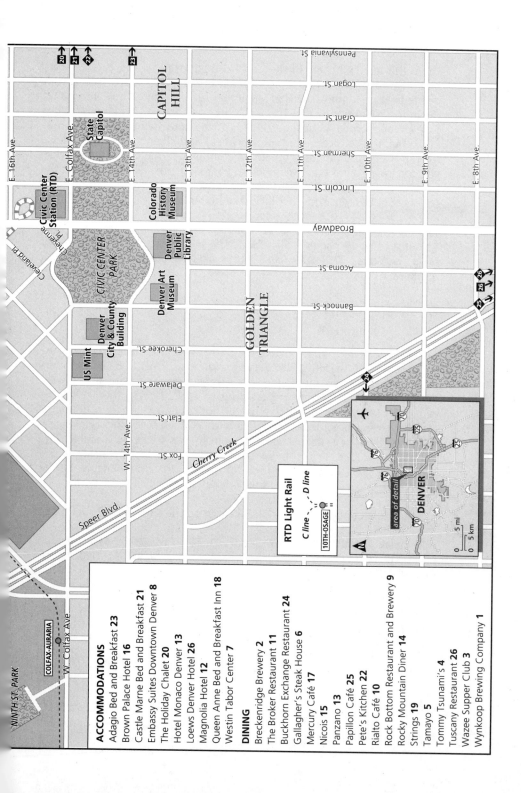

ACCOMMODATIONS
Adagio Bed and Breakfast **23**
Brown Palace Hotel **16**
Castle Marne Bed and Breakfast **21**
Embassy Suites Downtown Denver **8**
The Holiday Chalet **20**
Hotel Monaco Denver **13**
Loews Denver Hotel **26**
Magnolia Hotel **12**
Queen Anne Bed and Breakfast Inn **18**
Westin Tabor Center **7**

DINING
Breckenridge Brewery **2**
The Broker Restaurant **11**
Buckhorn Exchange Restaurant **24**
Gallagher's Steak House **6**
Mercury Café **17**
Nicois **15**
Panzano **13**
Papillon Café **25**
Pete's Kitchen **22**
Rialto Café **10**
Rock Bottom Restaurant and Brewery **9**
Rocky Mountain Diner **14**
Strings **19**
Tamayo **5**
Tommy Tsunami's **4**
Tuscany Restaurant **26**
Wazee Supper Club **3**
Wynkoop Brewing Company **1**

Embassy Suites Downtown Denver

$$$–$$$$ **Central Business District**

Of all the luxury hotels in the Central Business District, this 19-story building, located just two blocks from the 16th Street Marketplace, may be the best for families. Kids in particular seem to enjoy the suite rooms, the in-room Nintendo games, and the pool and spa. All accommodations here are one- or two-bedroom suites, with separate living areas (with pull-out sofas, refrigerators, and microwaves) and sleeping areas. Because the hotel's complimentary breakfast combines buffet and table service, you can locate a few favorite items for your kids, then leave the rest of the work to a professional server. For an extra $10 you can use the 65,000-square-foot Denver Athletic Club, attached to the hotel.

1881 Curtis St., at 18th Street. ☎ *303-297-8888. Fax: 303-298-1103. Internet:* www.esdendt.com. *Parking $19 Sun–Thurs; $15 Fri–Sat. Valet only. No RVs or roof racks. Rack rates: $139–$259. Rates include full breakfast and evening cocktail reception. AE, DC, DISC, MC, V.*

The Holiday Chalet

$$–$$$ **Capitol Hill**

This oasis of Victorian propriety amid the neon on Colfax Avenue is one of the best deals in Denver. Built as a mansion in 1896, the B&B now offers 12 comfortable and family-friendly mini-suites. The mini-suites were added in the 1950s and are starting to feel historic themselves — especially the kitchens, which have tile floors and gas stoves. The rooms also have antiques, desks, and TVs with VCRs; a few rooms have sunrooms and two have fireplaces. Ice cream socials are held in summer and barbecue grills are available for guest's use. If you plan to stay a while, bring your pet (for an extra $5 a day), your kids (baby-sitting can be arranged), and your food, and take advantage of a $500 weekly rate.

If traffic noise bothers you, ask for a room on the side away from Colfax.

1820 Colfax Ave. ☎ *800-626-4497 or 303-321-9975. Fax: 303-377-6556. Internet:* bbonline.com/co/holiday. *Free street parking. Rates: $94–$160. AE, DC, DISC, MC, V.*

Loews Denver Hotel

$$–$$$ **Cherry Creek/Glendale**

Robert Redford, President Gerald Ford, and the New York Giants have all stayed at this sleek member of the upscale Loews hotel group (though the first two were probably more welcome than the latter in Bronco land). Leave it to Loews to supply an art guide explaining a hotel's decor, which is styled after an Italian villa. The lobby boasts faux-marble columns, ornate antiques, and a mural of the view from a Palladian country home. In the halls are paintings of cherubs and roman goddesses. The decor carries over into the sumptuous guest rooms, which have glass-topped coffee tables, marble-topped desks and vanities, and ornate lamps. Most importantly, they're comfortable and quiet, and the service — especially the hotel's Gold Key concierge — is dandy. You wouldn't expect a place like this to be pet-friendly, but the Loews not only welcomes dogs, it pampers them to the same degree as its two-legged guests.

4150 E. Mississippi Ave. ☎ ***303-782-9300.*** *Fax: 303-758-0283. Internet:* www.loews hotels.com. *Free parking. Rack rates: $99–$199, suites $199–$299. Children under 18 stay free in parents' room. AE, DC, DISC, MC, V.*

The runner-up hotels

Adagio Bed and Breakfast
$$–$$$ **Capitol Hill** Housed in an 1882 Victorian mansion, this B&B offers rooms — each named for a classical composer — featuring both antiques and modern amenities such as TVs with VCRs. *1430 Race St.* ☎ ***800-533-3241*** *or 303-370-6911. Fax: 303-377-5968. Internet:* www.adagiobb.com.

Hotel Monaco Denver
$$$$ **Central Business District** This hotel, which oozes 1960s excess, sports lavishly decorated rooms, whose amenities include CD stereos, terrycloth robes, and Starbucks coffee. And if you're lonely, the hotel will send up a free "companion goldfish," although at these rates, they should send a dolphin. *1717 Champa, at 17th Street.* ☎ ***800-397-5380*** *or 303-296-1717. Fax: 303-296-1818. Internet:* www.Monaco-denver.com.

Magnolia Hotel
$$–$$$ **Central Business District** If the European-inspired guest rooms here seem small, maybe it's because of the oversized bathtubs and expansive views of downtown Denver. The suites may also seem smallish when you see their kitchens, which are large enough for a home. *818 17th St., at Stout Street.* ☎ ***888-915-1110*** *or 303-607-9000. Internet:* www.the magnoliahotel.com.

Queen Anne Bed and Breakfast Inn
$$ **Clements Historic District** This award-winning bed-and-breakfast, which occupies adjacent 19th-century Victorian homes laden with art and antiques, offers excellent service with a personal touch. Some rooms offer canopy beds, jet tubs, and TVs; all of the accommodations have air conditioning. *2147–51 Tremont Place.* ☎ ***800-432-4667*** *or 303-296-6666. Fax: 303-296-2151. Internet:* www.queenannebnb.com.

Westin Hotel
$$$$ **Central Business District** This cool, business-oriented hotel has one of the best locations in downtown and features large guest rooms

beautifully appointed with modern European-style furnishings. Drift upstairs to the indoor-outdoor swimming pool on a fourth floor deck. *1672 Lawrence St.* ☎ *303-572-9100. Fax 303-572-7288. Internet:* www.westin.com.

Where to Dine

Denver has a burgeoning dining scene to go along with its ever-expanding population. Eating at every single restaurant in town — all 2,000 of them — would be an impossible task, but I've eaten at enough places to know that the food in Denver is delicious and varied, and that you can eat well at restaurants in a variety of price ranges.

The scene is most interesting downtown, where expensive restaurants come and go like the seasons, and where high-profile chefs such as Kevin Taylor and Richard Sandoval vie for the same fickle audience. The new downtown restaurants tend to have striking decor, and they often serve European-, South American–, or Asian-influenced fare, not to mention some traditional American comfort food. Dinner entrees are usually in the $15 to $25 range, with salads costing extra. It's expensive; yet not as exorbitant (not for the moment anyway) as comparable fare in other major U.S. cities.

Besides the trendy new restaurants, there are some old standbys serving Colorado native game such as elk, rattlesnake, buffalo, and quail. The Fort and The Buckhorn Exchange were each doing business long before most Denverites were born, and both have unforgettable interiors and good food. Although they do well with native meats, these restaurants may not serve the best steaks in town. If you're looking for beef, try a franchise house such as Gallagher's or Ruth's Chris and be ready for a hefty bill: Prime beef in Denver usually goes for $30 or more.

For less expensive fare, try one of the many area brewpubs, where dinner entrees usually cost $8 to $14. Gone are the years when these pubs assaulted customers with battered foods. Today, they serve as many bean sprouts as bratwursts, and the beers are smoother than ever.

The top restaurants

Breckenridge Brewery
$–$$ LoDo   **AMERICAN**

My favorite servers in Denver are here. They gladly share their views on beer and baseball if you come here when the place isn't packed with Rockies fans. The restaurant, in a warehouse that's kitty-corner to Coors field, nicely complements the park. Old baseball photos hang on the walls, and large-screen TVs make sure you won't miss a pitch. Breckenridge also brews some of the state's hottest-selling micro-beers.

Menu offerings include fajitas, sandwiches, salads, pub fare, and entrees such as grilled salmon and homemade pork tamales.

2220 Blake St. ☎ *303-297-3644. Reservations accepted. Main courses: $10.95– $16.95. AE, DISC, MC, V. Open: Lunch and dinner daily.*

Buckhorn Exchange Restaurant

$$$–$$$$ **Central Business District   STEAKS/GAME**

For an unforgettable experience, hop on Denver's light rail system and ride to the Buckhorn (it's at the Osage station), which stands — barely, it seems — right next to the train tracks in a forgotten area near Denver's downtown. The oldest restaurant in Colorado, the Buckhorn was founded by one Henry H. Zietz, who befriended Chief Sitting Bull, hunted with Teddy Roosevelt, and accepted the sword of the vanquished General George Custer from the Blackfeet Sioux. You'll believe these seemingly far-fetched tales when you peek inside the restaurant, at the 500-odd pieces of taxidermy on the walls and — in the spaces where nothing stares back at you — at the historic photos and antique guns. The restaurant serves items that would have been available in Colorado when it opened in 1883, such as elk, steaks, pheasant, grouse, and buffalo. Vegetarians should definitely head elsewhere.

1000 Osage St., at 10th. ☎ *303-534-9505. Internet:* www.buckhorn.com. *Reservations strongly recommended. Main courses: $18–$42. AE, DC, DISC, MC, V. Open: Weekdays lunch and dinner; weekends, dinner only. Bar open all day.*

The Fort

$$$$ **Morrison   COLORADO GAME**

Don't come to The Fort to eat the usual steak and potatoes while sitting in a 1962 adobe reproduction of Historic Bent's Fort (a trading post in southeast Colorado), even though you can. And don't come here for the panoramic views of southeast Denver, even though the place does have them. Come here for the restauran't's native game dishes such as braised buffalo leg in oatmeal stout gravy; elk bone marrow; and farm-raised rattlesnake. There is a filet mignon on the menu, but your server may discourage you from ordering it. After 40 years here, the people at this sprawling, 350-seat restaurant know their strengths, and they want you to experience them.

Located in Morrison on Colorado 8, just north of Highway 285. ☎ *303-697-4771. Reservations accepted. Main courses: $20–$45. AE, DC, MC, V. Open: Dinner daily. Call for special holiday hours.*

Panzano

$$ **Central Business District   NORTHERN ITALIAN**

Tucked inside the Hotel Monaco and popular with the power-lunch crowd, Panzano features a densely decorated dining room with a busy open kitchen. Among the menu highlights are personal pizzas with such toppings as black mission fig compote, gorgonzola, prosciutto, and arugula. You can also choose from pasta dishes laden with aged cheeses, seafood, and other Mediterranean ingredients, as well as assorted meaty entrees. If you're hungry for fish, don't overlook the *Osso Buco di Pesce* (pan-braised monkfish wrapped in Pancetta, creamy mascarpone polenta, roasted vegetables, and sherry vinegar sauce). And make sure to save room for the yummy tiramisu as dessert.

909 17th St., in the Hotel Monaco. ☎ *303-296-3525. Reservations recommended. Main courses: $7–$16 lunch, $12–$23 dinner. AE, DC, DIS, MC, V. Open: Breakfast, lunch, and dinner on weekdays; brunch and dinner on weekends. Closed Thanksgiving, Dec 25.*

Papillon Café
$$ Cherry Creek   NORTH FRENCH/ASIAN FUSION

If you're browsing the chic stores in Denver's Cherry Creek North, plan on coming to this upscale restaurant to experience the colorful creations of chef Radek R. Cerny, who likes adding Asian oils, curries, and spices to what might otherwise be French food. Cerny's lobster ravioli has been earning raves for years, but the best items are sometimes the daily specials, which may include tuna with sesame, wasabi, and soy. You'll eat in a stylish dining room graced with a long bank of windows and huge planters of fresh-cut flowers. Make sure to reserve your spot in advance. After seven years here, Cerny is still packing in the well-to-do of Denver.

250 Josephine St. ☎ *303-333-7166. Reservations recommended. Main courses: $9–$12 lunch, $14–$22 dinner. AE, DC, DISC, MC, V. Open: Mon–Fri, lunch and dinner; Sat–Sun dinner only.*

Rialto Café
$$ Central Business District   NEW AMERICAN

A streamlined, Art-Deco appearance, strong coffee, and a staff with a sunny outlook are just a few reasons to have Sunday brunch at the Rialto Café. But the best reasons are the four "Mile High" egg dishes, each consisting of herb potatoes, eggs, meats, and/or vegetables, and either hollandaise or béarnaise sauce. The chefs layer the ingredients like geological strata, mold them into a cylinder, and stack them to an improbable height. The lunch and dinner menu blends elements of Continental cuisine, comfort food, and Asian cuisine. Try the Asian grilled ahi with wasabi mashed potatoes.

934 Sixteenth St., in the 16th Street Marketplace. ☎ *303-893-2233. Reservations accepted. Main courses: $5–$13.95 lunch; $11.95–$21.95 dinner. AE, DC, DISC, MC, V. Open: Breakfast, lunch, and dinner daily.*

Strings

$$ Uptown Contemporary AMERICAN

Splashy and colorful, Strings would more likely attract Michael Jackson than George W. Bush. Seventies music plays over the stereo; an exhaust duct over the open kitchen has been painted to resemble a giant guitar; and the floor looks slick enough to break-dance on. As for the menu, it's as hard to figure out as the Gloved One. For example, the black pepper linguini has grapefruit segments for an ingredient. The cashew-crusted sea bass includes cranberry catsup. And the porcini-dusted salmon is enhanced, somehow, by golden beet emulsion. No matter how strange it looks on paper, it works well enough in practice and this is one of my favorite restaurants in Denver.

1700 Humboldt, at 17th Avenue. ☎ *303-831-7310. Reservations accepted. Main courses: $9.50–$14 lunch; $13–$26 dinner. AE, DC, DISC, MC, V. Open: Mon–Sat lunch and dinner; Sun dinner only.*

Tamayo

$$–$$$ Larimer Square CONTEMORARY MEXICAN

Tamayo's owner, Richard Sandoval, learned to cook seafood as a child at his family's restaurant in Acapulco. In New York City, he made a name for himself by reinterpreting traditional Mexican cooking at his popular restaurant, Maya. These days, you can savor Sandoval's cutting-edge Mexican recipes at Tamayo in Larimer Square. Entrees include *Salmon Tolteca* (pan-seared salmon medallion served with chive-plantain cous cous, black bean reduction and roasted tomato-chile pasilla vinaigrette) and *Puerco Tamayo* (roasted pork loin with roasted garlic mashed potatoes, vanilla bean corn, and chile jalapeno barbeque sauce). My favorite is the *mole poblano* (grilled chicken breast served with cilantro rice, mole poblano sauce, and sweet chunks of plantain).

On theater nights, wait until the pre-show crowd disperses at 8 p.m. before coming.

1400 Larimer St. ☎ *720-946-1433. Reservations accepted. Main courses: $10.95–$14.95 lunch, $17.50–$25.95 dinner. AE, MC, V. Open: Lunch and dinner on weekdays; dinner only on weekends.*

Tommy Tsunami's

$$–$$$ LoDo SUSHI

This restaurant takes its name and its theme from a mythical Hawaiian surfer who went on to become a rich Tokyo stockbroker, lost his moral compass, and then returned to the simple life of surfing. The legend comes close to explaining the decor, which blends dissonant elements like stock-market tickers, ads for Levi's and Coke, and surfboards. It also nearly explains why the restaurant's food, including noodle bowls, sashimi, sushi, and traditional rolls, is prepared and served less formally than at a Japanese-style sushi bar. Even if it doesn't quite make sense, the legend of Tommy Tsunami allows you to roll in casually like a Hawaiian and munch on sushi that's very nearly as succulent as in Japan.

1432 Market St. ☎ 303-534-5050. Reservations welcome. Main courses: $10–$25; $3.50–$16 sushi. AE, DC, DISC, MC, V. Open: Dinner and late-night sushi daily.

Tuscany Restaurant
$$–$$$ Cherry Creek   ITALIAN

Located inside the Loews Denver Hotel, the Tuscany Restaurant has been accurately pegged by the media as the ideal place both for power breakfasts (*USA Today*) and romantic dinners (Denver's *Westword* newspaper). The elegant dining room is decorated with polished marble, fresh-cut flowers, and fine art; the mostly Italian fare should impress anyone who needs impressing. At lunchtime, you can choose between salads, gourmet personal pizzas, sandwiches, and entrees such as *papardelle* (spicy grilled chicken breast tossed with limoncello pomodoro) and porcini mushroom ravioli. A number of beef and seafood dishes are also available. The fare is similar at dinner, only without the pizzas and sandwiches.

4150 E. Mississippi Ave., off Colorado Street. ☎ 303-782-9300. Reservations accepted. Main courses: $6–$19.50 lunch, $15.50–$33 dinner. AE, DC, DISC, MC, V. Open: Breakfast, lunch, and dinner daily.

The runner-up restaurants

The Broker Restaurant
$$$$ Central Business District   This restaurant in the basement of a 1903 bank building is the place to go to reduce your holdings. All meals start with a huge, complimentary platter of Gulf shrimp in the shell. If you're still hungry after that, choose between steaks, chicken, lamb, and seafood, washed down with any of 820 wines (the real treasure here now). *821 17th St., at Champa. ☎ 303-292-5065. Internet:* www.broker restaurant.com.

Gallagher's Steak House
$$$$ LoDo   Modeled after New York's first-ever steakhouse, this place will give you nothing but a steak if you order a steak — side dishes are à la carte. And you'd better believe that the dry-aged beef, broiled over hickory charcoal, is going to satisfy. *1480 Arapahoe St. ☎ 303-293-6555.*

Mercury Café

$ **Central Business District**   This artsy, bustling cafe has performance spaces upstairs and two large dining areas downstairs. Upstairs, you can take in shows ranging from poetry slams to belly dancing, usually for a fee; downstairs, you can hear free live music while tasting food that's made with mostly organic ingredients. The best selections on the eclectic menu are probably the pasta dishes. *2199 California St.* ☎ *303-294-9258 (reservations) or 303-294-9281 (information).*

Nicois

$$ **Central Business District**   Run by one of Denver's hottest chef's, Kevin Taylor, Nicois presents rustic fare inspired by the Mediterranean regions of Europe in a beautiful atrium setting. If you want to experience a variety of flavors, choose from any of 15 tapas (Spanish appetizers), each costing $3.50. *815 17th St.* ☎ *303-293-2322.*

Pete's Kitchen

$ **Capitol Hill**   If you find yourself dimly wandering Colfax Avenue late at night after leaving one of the many area bars, head towards the big neon cook flipping pancakes. You'll soon be inside a 1942 diner where the food gets better as you get worse. It's very popular with the bar crowd and the service is fast. Try the Greek-style chicken kabobs. *1962 E. Colfax Ave.* ☎ *303-321-3139.*

Rock Bottom Restaurant and Brewery

$ **16th Street Marketplace**   With as many as 18 handcrafted beers on tap, this is a beer lover's paradise. But even if you don't love beer, you'll enjoy the salads, brick-oven pizzas, burgers, and pastas, especially after working up an appetite by walking the adjacent 16th Street Mall. *1001 16th St.* ☎ *303-534-7616. Internet:* www.rockbottom.com.

Rocky Mountain Diner

$ **Central Business District**   Like a 1940s diner, this restaurant has vinyl booths, long counters, and an open kitchen, but the paintings on the walls are splashy and modern. The menu, like the decor, blends traditional and modern elements, and features items ranging from chicken fried steak to duck enchiladas (a real treat). 800 18th St., at Stout. ☎ *303-293-8383. Internet:* www.rockymountaindiner.com.

Wazee Supper Club

$ **LoDo**   This funky little supper club in a former plumbing supply store claims to cater to "people of good character from around the globe." If this means you, and if you happen to love great pizza, you'll be happy here. *1600 15th Street, at Wazee.* ☎ *303-623-9518.*

Wynkoop Brewing Company

$–$$ **LoDo**   Colorado's first brewpub helped revitalize LoDo, and is housed in a likable, renovated warehouse (circa 1899) across from Union Station. The food, perhaps the best of Denver's brewpubs, includes traditional pub fare as well as fancier entrees such as elk medallions, and — best of all — grilled portobello mushroom caps. And it also brews great beer, including the Mile High Malt and Boxcar Kolsch. *1634 18th St.* ☎ *303-297-2700. Internet:* www.wynkoop.com.

Chapter 12

Seeing the Best of Denver

- -

In This Chapter

▶ Visiting must-see attractions and sights

▶ Finding the perfect pub

▶ Tackling the city's best activities

▶ Planning touring itineraries for Denver

- -

A s Colorado's state capitol and the gateway city to the mountain West, Denver offers an abundance of world-class attractions — and a few small treasures that are all too easy to miss if you don't have someone to tell you about them. Luckily, you do. In this chapter, I visit the biggest and the best first and then burn off some energy discussing all the neat outdoor and recreational opportunities. And if your idea of exercise involves charging up your credit card or dancing the night away, I give you tips on the best stores and nightlife in Denver.

Exploring Denver

Whether it's a museum of miniatures or a mile-high football stadium, you can find an attraction that interests you in Denver. The city's many top sights are conveniently clustered, so you can see a lot of them in a few short days. This section tells you which ones are worth seeing.

The best things to see and do

Colorado History Museum
Capitol Hill

Even if the mere idea of a diorama makes you drowsy, you should check out the ones at this museum. Using paper, cardboard, matchsticks, and wood veneers, artists in a Depression-era work relief program created tiny, meticulously detailed renderings from Colorado's history, which are displayed today in this museum. You can also view exhibits on pioneers, miners, ranchers, and Native Americans, and read a timeline tracing the

Downtown Denver Attractions

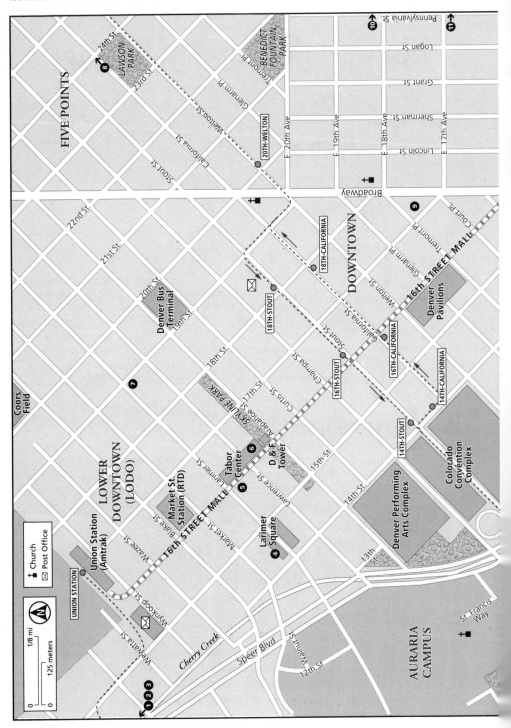

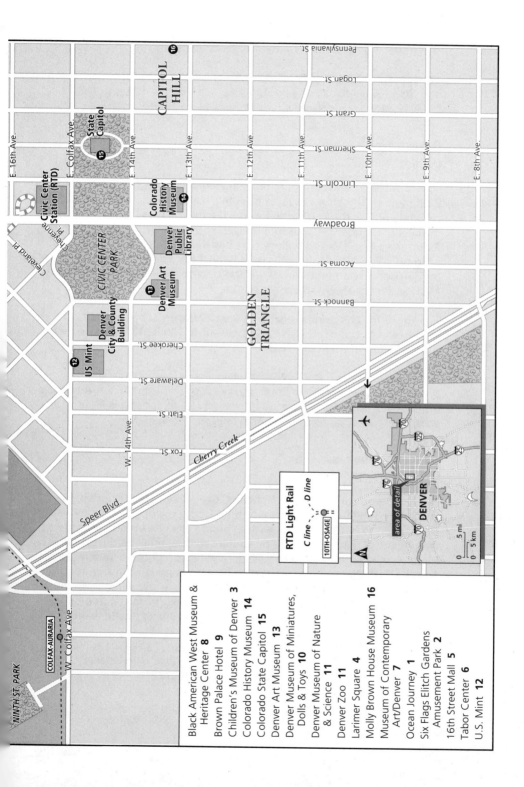

RTD Light Rail
C line — D line
10TH-OSAGE

DENVER
area of detail
0   5 mi
0   5 km

Black American West Museum & Heritage Center **8**
Brown Palace Hotel **9**
Children's Museum of Denver **3**
Colorado History Museum **14**
Colorado State Capitol **15**
Denver Art Museum **13**
Denver Museum of Miniatures, Dolls & Toys **10**
Denver Museum of Nature & Science **11**
Denver Zoo **11**
Larimer Square **4**
Molly Brown House Museum **16**
Museum of Contemporary Art/Denver **7**
Ocean Journey **1**
Six Flags Elitch Gardens Amusement Park **2**
16th Street Mall **5**
Tabor Center **6**
U.S. Mint **12**

major events of the past 150 years in the state's history. Memorabilia of a more recent vintage is also on display, including a gondola car from Steamboat Ski Area and a Denver Nuggets warm-up suit.

13th Street and Broadway. ☎ *303-866-3682. Internet:* www.coloradohistory. org. *Open: Mon–Sat 10:00 a.m.–4:30 p.m., Sun noon to 4:30 p.m. Admission: $5 adults, $4.50 seniors 65 and up and students 13–18, $3.50 children 6–12.*

Denver Art Museum
Capitol Hill

One of America's premier art museums sits right next to Civic Center Park in a startling, fortress-like building. The building's architecture is certainly fitting; the Geo Ponti–designed museum is the protective home of many treasures. The museum houses an immense collection of Native American art; a Western gallery that has Remingtons and Russells; and pre- and post-Colombian works from Latin America. If the European masters intrigue you most, you won't be disappointed. Works by Degas, Matisse, Picasso, and others are on display.

The museum has a kids' corner where children can make art, and it schedules special kids' activities, too. Call ☎**720-913-KIDS** to see what will be on tap during your visit.

13th Street and Acoma. ☎ *720-865-5000. Internet:* www.denverartmuseum.org. *Open: Tues–Sat 10 a.m.–5 p.m., Wed 10 a.m.–9 p.m., Sun noon to 5 p.m. Admission to permanent collection: $6 adults, $4.50 seniors over 65 and youths 13–18, 12 and under free. Free admission for Colorado residents on Saturdays.*

Denver Botanic Gardens
Cherry Creek

On the 23 acres of the Denver Botanic Gardens, scientists nourish, breed, and study 15,000 plant species from around the world, including many threatened varieties. The individual plants are like brush strokes on a living canvas; each of the 30 or so gardens qualifies as a work of art. Highlights include a Japanese garden replete with pools, carefully placed granite, and aggressively pruned trees; an alpine garden that features high-alpine species from around the world; and a water garden with more than 400 types of aquatic plants. There's also a warm, misty, tropical conservatory, where you can forge through the fronds of jungle plants.

1005 York St. ☎ *303-331-4000. Internet:* www.botanicgardens.org. *Open: May–Sept Wed–Fri 9 a.m.–5 p.m., Sat–Tues 9 a.m.–8 p.m.; Oct–April daily 9 a.m.– 5 p.m. Admission: $5.50 adults 16 and over, $3.50 seniors 64 and over; $3 students and youths 4–15.*

Denver Museum of Nature and Science
City Park

The fourth largest natural history museum in the United States, this museum has dioramas of wildlife from around the globe; mounted butterflies and insects; mummies; gems and minerals; and dinosaur skeletons. But the place is hardly musty. Almost everywhere you turn, you can try an interactive activity, whether it's prospecting for mineral pockets inside a simulated mine, comparing the densities of rocks, or smelling the odor that attracts a doe to a buck (not as bad as you'd expect). A new space-themed permanent exhibit and the state-of-the-art Gates Planetarium will open sometime in 2003. The museum also has a large hall that houses popular touring exhibits; a recent space-themed one featured the spacecraft in which Gus Grissom orbited the earth in 1961.

If you'd like to take in a very large movie at the adjoining IMAX Theater, you can buy combination tickets for both the museum and the show at a considerable discount — only a few dollars more than the price of museum admission.

2001 Colorado Blvd. ☎ ***303-370-6357.*** *Internet:* www.dmnh.org. *Open: Daily 9 a.m.–5 p.m. Closed December 25. Museum admission: $8 adults, $5.50 seniors 60 and over and kids 3–12. Museum and IMAX combination tickets: $12 adults, $8 seniors and kids 3–12.*

Denver Zoo
City Park

The nation's fourth most popular zoo and Colorado's number-one cultural attraction, the zoo has a marvelous array of critters, including rhinos (one of whom paints — I kid you not) and hippos; lions, tigers, and jaguars; a large bird population that includes a rare Andean condor; a group of rare Komodo dragons; and 29 species of primates, including Brazilian monkeys that wander freely through the zoo (with zoo employees close behind). Not only do the 3,500 animals appear healthy, the zoo also seems determined to teach visitors about the destruction of animal habitats around the planet. Numerous information panels discuss threats to animals and explain how zoos protect endangered species through conservation and breeding programs.

The zoo offers eight free admission days annually. The dates change, so call before you go to find out if a free day will occur during your visit. Keep in mind, though, that the zoo tends to be *very* crowded on these days.

23rd Avenue between Colorado and York. ☎ ***303-376-4800.*** *Internet:* www.denverzoo.org. *Open: April–Sept daily 9 a.m.–6 p.m. (gates close at 5 p.m.); Oct–March daily 10 a.m.–5 p.m. (gates close at 4 p.m.). Admission: $9 adults summer, $7 adults winter; $7 seniors 62 and over summer, $6 seniors winter;*

$5 children 4–12 (accompanied by an adult) summer, $4 children winter; free for children under 4.

Ocean Journey
Platte River Valley

Two distinct journeys are offered at this $93 million aquarium. One traces a river as it flows from an Indonesian rain forest to the Pacific Ocean; the other follows the Colorado River from the Rockies to the Sea of Cortez. Each journey features aquariums housing the plant and animal species that the river would have at different points. For example, the first tanks in the Colorado River journey show trout and other species that may inhabit a mountain brook; the last show seahorses, eels, and puffer fish (among many other species) in the Sea of Cortez, below the river's delta. Watching the Pacific Ocean tanks, where sharks and colorful reef fish swim all around you, even underfoot and overhead, is the most fun. The most breathtaking display, however, is a simulated flash flood in the red rock desert of Utah. The price of admission is steep, but you'll enjoy what you get, even if it only lasts a few hours.

As of press time, Ocean Journey had filed for bankruptcy and its long-term propsects looked shaky. Call before you go to make sure it's still operating.

*700 Water St. ☎ **303-561-4450**. Internet:* www.oceanjourney.org. *Daily 10 a.m.–6 p.m. Admission: $14.95 adults, $12.95 youths 13–17 and seniors 65 and up, $6.95 children 4–12, free for children under 4.*

Six Flags Elitch Gardens Amusement Park
Platte River Valley

This Six Flags–owned amusement park, which opened in the Platte Valley in 1996, takes its name from an 1889 theme park in another, leafier part of town. With 48 thrill rides on the premises, the newer incarnation is more about defying gravity than gardening. Highlights include Boomerang, which drops you 125 feet, throws you for a few twists and flips, and then replays the whole ordeal in reverse; and Mind Eraser, a suspended roller coaster that hits speeds over 60 mph. The park also has gentler rides for kids too little and adults too big to enjoy nausea. Admission to Island Kingdom Water Park, which has a wave pool and giant waterslides, is included in the price.

*2000 Elitch Circle. ☎ **303-455-4771**. Internet:* www.sixflags.com. *Open: Daily 10 a.m.–10 p.m. during summer. Usually open 10 a.m.2nd8 p.m. on weekends during May, Sept, and Oct. (Call for low-season hours.) Admission: $33 for people over 48 inches tall; $20 for people under 48 inches tall, seniors 55–69, and the disabled; free for children under 4 and seniors over 69.*

Touring historical sites

Built over the course of 30 years beginning in 1886, the **Colorado State Capitol Building** can't help but command attention. It has 4-foot-thick granite walls, immense pillars, and a 272-foot-high, gold-coated dome visible from miles away. Inside, the capitol has wainscoting of rare Colorado onyx, stained-glass windows, murals, paintings, chandeliers, and an 80-foot rotunda. Free 40-minute tours depart every half hour from 9:00 a.m. to 3:30 p.m. during summer and every 45 minutes from 9:00 a.m. to 2:30 p.m. the rest of the year. The tour guides are thorough — and then some. If you're short on time, pick up a free guide to the capitol at the tour desk and walk around on your own. And don't worry about doing something wrong — if you're about to violate protocol, a very large guard will let you know. For more information on tours, call ☎ **303-866-2604.** The capitol is at the corner of Broadway and Colfax Avenue. The public entrance is at street level on the building's south (14th Street) side.

Molly Brown not only survived the *Titanic* disaster, she was also a philanthropist, suffragist, fashion plate, activist, mother, social matron, and sometime yodeler who lived in Denver's Capitol Hill neighborhood. You can almost sense Brown's unsinkable presence at the **Molly Brown House Museum,** 1340 Pennsylvania St. (☎ **303-832-4092**), an 1888 Victorian mansion where Brown lived in the early 1900s. Some of Brown's personal effects are here, including alabaster sculptures, a Tiffany lamp, and a Mother of Pearl tray from Japan. And the house itself has been lovingly restored. The only way you can go inside is on a 45-minute tour, offered from 10:00 a.m. to 3:30 p.m. Tuesday through Saturday, noon to 4:30 p.m. on Sunday. (During summer, tours are also offered from 10:00 a.m. to 3:30 p.m. on Monday.) Cost is $6.50 for adults, $4.50 for children ages 6 to 12, and $4.50 for ages 65 and up.

The free walk-in tours of the **U. S. Mint,** located at West Colfax Avenue and Cherokee Street, were suspended after the terrorist attacks of September 11, 2001. At press time, visitors couldn't enter the mint unless they prearranged a visit through their congressman. To check on the status of the tours, call ☎ **303-405-4761.**

Other things to see and do

Like a lot of cities, Denver brims with small, diverse attractions that can momentarily (and sometimes permanently) change your perspective. Around Denver, you can

> ✔ **Look closely at small things.** The **Denver Museum of Miniatures, Dolls, and Toys,** 1880 Gaylord St. (☎ **303-322-1053**), exhibits miniatures, including some tiny, highly detailed dollhouses; dolls from around the globe; and toys ranging from 17th-century antiques to modern action figures. It's in the 1899 Pearce-McAllister Cottage.

Open: Tuesday through Saturday 10 a.m. to 4 p.m., Sunday 1 to 4 p.m. Admission: $5 adults, $4 seniors and children 2 to 16.

✔ **Shrink your art world.** There's no reason to run through the 3,500-square-foot **Museum of Contemporary Art,** 1275 19th Street, in Sakura Square (☎ **303-298-7554;** Internet: www.mcartdenver.org). Go slowly and absorb the full impact of the paintings, sculptures, and installations, because the space is small, the concepts are thought-provoking, and the art will never be here again. (There is no permanent collection; the exhibitions change every few months.) If you're a film buff, call and inquire about experimental film nights, which showcase works from the Modern Art Library in New York. Open: Tuesday throgh Saturday 11:00 a.m. to 5:30 p.m. Admission: $5 adults, $3 students and seniors, free for children 12 and under.

✔ **Recognize long-overlooked cowboys.** As many as a third of the cowboys on the great cattle drives of the 19th century were African American. The **Black American West Museum and Heritage Center,** 3091 California St., at 31st Street (☎ **303-292-2566**), celebrates their often-overlooked role in pioneering and settling the American West. It also tells the stories of other early black settlers, including physicians, legislators, miners, and teachers. Open since 1971, the museum is in the three-story, 1,800-square-foot home of Justina Ford, the first African American female doctor in Denver. It's right across from the Downing Street light rail stop. Hours: May through September daily 10 a.m. to 5 p.m.; October through April Wednesday through Friday 10 a.m. to 2 p.m. and Saturday and Sunday 10 a.m. to 5 p.m. Admission: $6 adults, $5.50 seniors 65 and over, $4 children 5 to 12.

✔ **Chase butterflies.** The main attraction at the **Butterfly Pavilion and Insect Center,** 6252 W. 104th Ave., at U.S. 36 in Westminster (☎ **303-469-5441;** Internet: www.butterflies.org), is a conservatory housing 1,200 butterflies from around the world. If you're used to visiting museums where displays are fixed in place, you'll need to get used to this place, where butterflies flutter all around you and sometimes disappear altogether. When you get in the habit of scanning the tropical vegetation for resting butterflies, however, you'll be able to admire more of them up close, and you may even come to enjoy the search. In the museum's Crawl-A-See-Um, kids can pet a tarantula and examine other creepy-crawlers such as giant centipedes, black widows, and cockroaches. If they still feel like eating afterward, there's a snack shop, too. Open: Daily 9 a.m. to 5 p.m. (until 6 p.m. in summer). Admission: $6.95 ages 13 to 61, $4.95 seniors 62 and up, $3.95 children 4 to 12.

✔ **Get small.** About 30 miles west of Denver, brake fast and you'll find yourself at **Tiny Town,** 6429 S. Turkey Creek Rd., off U.S. 285 5 miles west of C470 (☎ **303-697-6829;** Internet: www.tinytown railroad.com). All 100 buildings in this historic Wild West town are to ⅙ scale — even the windows, doorknobs, and doorways. The buildings are too small for adults or anyone else who is not to ⅙ scale, but small kids fit inside and adults will appreciate the detail work. A miniature steam locomotive circles a ⅝-mile track through the grounds (cost: $1). Built by a father for his daughter in the early 1920s, Tiny Town became a popular tourist attraction in the late '20s, but after a flood made it a tiny disaster area, it became a tiny ghost town in the early '70s. In the late 1980s, the owners restored the site and it's now a great place for kids. There's also an open-air playground, snack bar, picnic area, and gift shop. Open: 10 a.m. to 5 p.m. on weekends in May, September, and October; daily 10 a.m. to 5 p.m. from Memorial Day through Labor Day. Admission: $3 ages 12 and up, $2 children 2 to 12.

Staying Active

Denver residents are an active bunch — statistically the thinnest city dwellers in the United States. When they get serious about exercising, they often make a beeline for the mountains surrounding the city. But there is plenty to do around town as well. While you're in Denver, you can take a break from sightseeing to:

✔ **Bike:** Denver's extensive trail system makes this a fun place to ride a bike. You can't go everywhere on a bike (safely), but you can pedal and run on over 400 miles of paved designated trails. My favorite places for biking are the trails alongside **Cherry Creek** and the **South Platte River.** You can access these trails at many downtown locations. For more information, contact **Bicycle Colorado** (☎ **303-417-1544;** Internet: www.bicyclecolo.org).

✔ **Go boating/rafting:** At the confluence of Cherry Creek and the South Platte River, there's a short stretch of whitewater in a man-made park where you can practice your kayaking during peak flows. The park is near **R.E.I.,** 1416 Platte St. (☎ **303-756-3100**). Use the designated parking area near the park, or else feed one of the meters on the street.

✔ **Golf:** The City of Denver operates seven public golf courses, and there are many more in the suburbs. The one most conven-ient to downtown is at **City Park,** E. 25th Ave. at York Street (☎ **303-295-4420**). Greens fees are $18 for 18 holes, $11 for 9 holes. You can't reserve a tee time until the day you want to play.

✔ **Hike:** If you're interested in hiking (as opposed to walking), head for **Denver's Mountain Parks,** a system of 31 parks totaling 14,000 acres in the foothills and mountains west of town. One favorite for short hikes is **Red Rocks Park,** on Colorado 74 between Evergreen and Morrison. For more on the mountain parks, surf the Internet to www.denver.org or call ☎ **303-697-4545.**

✔ **Run:** You can run in any number of Denver City parks. **Cheesman Park,** at Eighth Avenue and Franklin Street, has a lengthy trail around its perimeter, partly shaded by hardwood trees.

✔ **Play tennis:** The Denver Department of Parks and Recreation
(☎ **303-964-2500**) manages or owns close to 150 tennis courts,
more than a third of them lit for night play. For $3 an hour, you can
rent one of the 12 courts at **City Park,** E. 25th Avenue at York
Street. Go to the **Denver Parks and Recreation Permitting Office,**
2300 15th St. (☎ **303-964-2522**), to purchase some court time.

Pro Sports

Anyone who has seen Denver Broncos fans smeared with orange and
blue body paint knows that the town takes its sports nearly as seriously
as Cleveland. It's a big-league city, with pro teams in Major League
Baseball, the National Football League, the National Basketball
Association, the National Hockey League, and Major League Soccer.
All of these teams sell tickets through **Ticketmaster (☎ 303-830-TIXS**).
Here's the roster that spur the city's sport-minded faithful:

✔ **Colorado Avalanche:** To the chagrin of the Quebequois — and the
delight of Denverites —, the Colorado Avalanche (☎ **303-893-
6700**) captured the National Hockey League's Stanley Cup in 1996,
the first season after they moved to Denver from Quebec City. The
team won the championship again in 2001 and has challenged for
the Cup most years since then. Winning early and often helped
them develop an ultra-passionate following that continues to
show up in force for their contests at the **Pepsi Center** (corner of
Speer Boulevard and Auraria Parkway). Tickets to Avalanche
games are the second most difficult to obtain in Denver (behind
Broncos tickets), and season tickets are completely sold out. Even
if you can find a seat at face value, it won't come cheap. Prices
range from $22 for the upper-end balconies to $193 for the front
row behind the glass.

✔ **Colorado Rockies:** Because of the thin air in Denver, baseballs that
are walloped at **Coors Field** (in Denver's LoDo section) tend to
carry out of the park easily. The atmosphere is such a nightmare
for pitchers, that the Colorado Rockies (☎ **800-388-7625** or 303-
762-5347) have a hard time attracting talented hurlers, so they tend
to sign sluggers instead. All this adds up to runs and action galore,
which may be one reason why they regularly sell most of their
50,000 seats. The retro-style park is clean, has great sight lines, and
is easy to negotiate. A handful of Rockies games completely sell
out, but most of the time you can obtain a ticket without having to
go to a scalper.

Prices range from $4 to $41, with the leftover cheap seats, in an
area known as the Rockpile, going for $1 and $4 on gameday —
one of the best deals in baseball.

✔ **Denver Broncos:** The Denver Broncos (☎ 720-258-3333) play their home National Football League games at **Invesco Field at Mile High,** a $360 million, 76,000-seat stadium that was completed in 2001. The silvery stadium near the South Platte River has 530 TV monitors, a 96-foot video board and, oversized seats with great sightlines. Played from September through December, the eight regular-season home games always sell out, but if you order your tickets right after they go on sale in early summer, you should be able to obtain seats. Prices range from $30 to $311. The team's box office, at 1701 Bryant St., is open on weekdays from 8 a.m. to 5 p.m., on Saturdays before home games from 9 a.m. to 1 p.m., and on game days, too.

✔ **Denver Nuggets:** The Denver Nuggets have been popular whipping boys during most of their time in the NBA. They do, however, play at the striking new **Pepsi Center** (☎ 303-405-1100), at the corner of Speer Boulevard and Auraria Parkway. If you attend a game, you can watch opposing teams dunk on the stadium's state-of-the-art, four-sided video scoreboard or wander out into the two grand six-story atrium entranceways. The place could conceivably seat up to 19,309 Nuggets fans, if the fans had something to show up for. The season runs from late October through mid-April. Tickets range in price from $10 to $262. The Pepsi Center box office is open weekdays from 10 a.m. to 6 p.m. and Saturdays from 10 a.m. to 3 p.m.

✔ **Colorado Rapids:** The Colorado Rapids (☎ 800-844-7777 or 303-299-1599) compete in Major League Soccer from late March through early September at **Invesco Field at Mile High.** Tickets cost $14 to $40.

Guided Tours

If Denver seems like too much of a load for you to tackle alone, you can choose from a number of guided walking, bus, and trolley tours. Here are a few good options.

Faux trolley tours

During summer, the **Cultural Connection Trolley** (☎ 303-289-2841), which strongly resembles a bus, makes hourly stops at each of Denver's prime tourist attractions, including Cherry Creek Shopping Center, Ocean Journey, Union Station, Larimer Square, and Coors Field. Most major hotels have brochures with the trolley's schedule. Just pay the driver $16 per person (MasterCard and Visa are accepted) upon boarding, and you can ride between 8:00 a.m. and 5:30 p.m. A recording triggered by a global positioning system highlights the major sights you pass, and you can get on and off at any of the stops and catch the next bus, er, trolley.

Real trolley tours

The **Platte Valley Trolley** (☎ 303-458-6255) parallels a scenic stretch of the Platte River while passing Invesco Field at Mile High, the Six Flags Amusement Park, and Ocean Journey Aquarium. Unlike the Cultural Connection Trolley, this trolley actually travels on tracks. It operates from May 25 through September 8, daily from 11 a.m. to 4 p.m. Cost for the half-hour ride is $2 for adults, $1 for seniors and children. To get there take I-25 to 23rd Avenue (Exit 211). Turn east onto Water Street and follow the signs.

Guided tours

Half- and full-day bus tours of Denver and the nearby Rockies are offered by the ubiquitous **Gray Line** (☎ 800-348-6877 for information only, 303-289-2841 for reservations and information; Internet: www.coloradograyline.com). Prices include entry fees but usually no food; children 12 and under pay half the adult price. Tours depart the Cherry Creek Shopping Center at First Avenue and Milwaukee Street, as well as local hotels and hostels on a reservation basis.

Another company offering guided tours in and around Denver is **The Colorado Sightseer**, 6780 W. 84th Circle, Suite 60 (☎ 303-423-8200; Internet: www.coloradosightseer.com).

The **LoDo District** (☎ 303-628-5484; Internet: www.lodo.org) offers guided walking tours of the historic area. Tours depart from Union Station (17th and Wynkoop streets) on Saturday at 10 a.m.; the cost is $5 per person. Two certified paranormal investigators conduct a variety of tours given by **Gunslingers, Ghosts & Gold** (☎ 800-275-8802; Internet: www.denverhauntedhistory.com). As the name implies, the emphasis is on haunted houses and history, with some humor thrown in. Tours costs around $10 to $15 per person.

One-, Two-, and Three-Day Itineraries

If you don't add a trip to a remote destination, the sightseeing in Denver breaks down neatly into a three-day itinerary. None of the daylong itineraries is clearly superior to the others. If you're only in town for a day or so, you'll just have to choose which itinerary you (or your kids) like best. If you have a few extra hours in the evening, LoDo and the 16th Street Malls are always fun options.

On **Day 1,** concentrate on the **Capitol Hill** area. Take in some of the works at the **Denver Art Museum.** From there, look at the tiny dioramas at the **Colorado History Museum.** In the afternoon, tour the **Molly Brown House.** If you're hungry for lunch, stop at one of the cafes near

13th and Pearl Street. Allow a little extra time to stroll past the historic homes near the Molly Brown House, and then accompany a group through the **State Capitol Building.** Finish by cruising three blocks north on Broadway to the ornate **Brown Palace Hotel** for a cold beverage.

The art museum has taken pains to make itself kid-friendly, but children still may not enjoy this day as much as Days 2 and 3, so if you have young children, you may want to skip this plan and go straight to Day 2.

Start **Day 2** by venturing a few miles west of the downtown to **City Park.** Visit the **Denver Museum of Nature and Science,** then walk across the park to the **Denver Zoo.** After observing the animals, make the short drive to the **Cherry Creek North** area. Have a late lunch, and then browse the shops and galleries there. In the soft light of late afternoon, wind down with a stroll in the **Denver Botanic Gardens.** If you're heading back into the downtown from here, detour past some of the historic homes in the **Uptown** neighborhood. Consider dining at one of the fine restaurants on 17th Avenue.

On **Day 3,** drive or take a light rail train into the **Platte River Valley** and visit **Ocean's Journey.** Lunch at **Zang Brewing Co.,** 2301 Seventh St. (☎ **303-455-2500**), a historic brewery that now houses a popular sports bar and restaurant. Then head for **Six Flags Elitch Gardens Amusement Park.** You can kill the better part of a day at the park, but you may want to save some time and energy to really visit LoDo on your way back downtown. If you're taking the light rail into town, stop at or near **Union Station** and stroll the galleries in **LoDo.** Use the free buses on 16th Street to take in other parts of the 16th Street Mall. Enjoy dinner at one of the dozens of restaurants in this area.

Shopping

Store hours in Denver tend to vary from place to place. Generally, stores are open Monday through Saturday, with many open on Sunday, too; department stores usually stay open until 9 p.m. at least one evening a week. Discount stores and supermarkets are often open later than other stores, and some supermarkets are open 24 hours a day.

The best shopping areas

Denver's most lively shopping district is the **16th Street Mall,** a downtown street that's been converted into a pedestrian-only walkway and has free bus service running its entire mile-long length. The mall's clientele includes everyone from office workers to tourists, and the businesses are as diverse as the shoppers. Nestled into the mall between Welton and Tremont streets is the glittery new, $100 million **Denver Pavilions,** home to trendy chains such as NikeTown, Wolfgang Puck's Café, and Virgin MegaStore. Besides the big stores, the 16th

Street Mall features discount outlets such as T.J. Maxx and Ross Dress for Less as well as dozens of locally owned shops, T-shirt stores, brewpubs, and cafes. During warm weather, you can sit at one of many sidewalk cafes, people-watch, and soak in the colors from some of the 25,000 flowers planted annually. Also located on the mall is the **Tabor Center,** home to ESPN Zone and other restaurants. Business at the Tabor Center hasn't taken off as anticipated, but more store openings are expected in the near future.

When you're walking the 16th Street Mall, make sure to detour south two blocks on Larimer Avenue. Follow the street as it takes you past **Writer Square,** 1512 Larimer (☎ **303-628-9056**), a block of jewelry stores, gift shops, galleries, and restaurants, and on to **Larimer Square** (☎ **303-534-2367**), where quirky businesses are tucked into nooks and crannies of historic Victorian buildings. If you tire of shopping, walk over to the Larimer Square information booth and get a free brochure describing a walking tour of the area. And if you feel like wandering the galleries of **LoDo,** venture in either direction off of 16th Street onto Wynkoop, Wazee, or Blake streets.

Don't come to **Cherry Creek Mall,** 3000 E. First Ave. (☎ **303-388-3900**), for bargain hunting. Located 3 miles west of downtown, this thriving, upscale mall is one of the largest and most popular attractions in Denver, and the prices reflect the high demand. Premium retailers such as Saks Fifth Avenue, Nieman Marcus, Lord & Taylor, and Foleys anchor the 160 shops and restaurants. Parking is free and usually easy. If it isn't, you can valet park for $7 for the first three hours, $1 for each additional hour. The mall is open Monday through Friday from 10 a.m. to 9 p.m., Saturday from 10 a.m. to 8 p.m., and Sunday from 11 a.m. to 6 p.m.

Across the street from Cherry Creek Mall, along First, Second, and Third avenues between University Boulevard and Steele Street, you'll find the leafy suburban shopping district of **Cherry Creek North** (☎ **303-394-2903**), home to 330 shops, 50 spas and salons, and 25 high-end art galleries. Around here, it's easier to find a large gem than a polished rock and much easier to find a priceless antique than cool junk. Even if you're not buying, come here to admire the galleries, many of which feature museum-quality work. Plan on staying for a meal — some of the city's finest restaurants are in this area. Most stores are open Monday through Saturday from 10 a.m. to 6 p.m., Sunday from noon to 5 p.m.

What to look for and where to find it

You can find everything from A to Z in Denver, provided you have enough time for all the letters. Here are some places with character where you can start your Denver-area shopping.

Art

Earthzone Mineral and Fossil Gallery, 1411 Larimer St. (☎ **303-572-8198**), offers art, jewelry, home decorations, and gifts made partly or entirely of fossils and minerals. The stones aren't as precious as gems or diamonds, but they're nearly as pretty after the gallery's featured artists finish with them. If you want to find that perfect oil painting of a cowboy at sunset, start your search at **Mudhead Gallery** at the Hyatt Regency, 555 17th St. (☎ **303-293-0007**). As one of Denver's main trading posts for Southwestern and Western Art, Mudhead offers paintings and bronze sculptures by Western artists, as well as Native American pottery, baskets, fetishes, and rugs. The **Camera Obscura Gallery,** 13th Avenue and Bannock Street (☎ **303-623-4059**), is the place to go for great photography, past and present. **David Cook/Fine American Art,** 1637 Wazee St. (☎ **303-623-4817**), specializes in Native American art and trades for premium items.

Books

If it starts raining during your visit, head for either of two **Tattered Cover Bookstores.** The employees at these stores actually want you to sit around and read. You can settle into an overstuffed chair near a reading lamp, then leaf through a magazine or book without worrying about whether the pages become dog-eared. Eventually, as payment, you should consider purchasing one of the more than 150,000 available titles or at least get some coffee to stay alert. The older and larger store is in Cherry Creek, at the corner of First Avenue and Milwaukee Street (☎ **303-322-7727;** Internet: `www.tatteredcover.com`); the other occupies a historic mercantile building at corner of 16th and Wynkoop streets (☎ **303-436-1070**) in the 16th Street Mall.

Imports

For clothes by the hottest designers from New York, Rome, and Paris, shop the big stores and boutiques at **Cherry Creek Mall,** 3000 E. First Ave. (☎ **303-388-3900**). For clothes by the hottest designers in Nepal, Tibet, and India, go to **Mount Everest Import,** 707 16th St. (☎ **303-573-8451**), in the 16th Street Mall. The shop also carries fabrics, weavings, and musical instruments.

Maps

Mapsco Map and Travel Center, 800 Lincoln St. (☎ **800-456-8703** or 303-830-2373), has maps of Colorado and the Southwest, globes showing the whole planet, and GPS systems that will help you find your way even if you happen to lose your globe.

Music

If you like the sound of music on vinyl, **Jerry's Records,** 312 E. Colfax (☎ **303-830-2336**), is the place for you. It has thousands of LPs in stock.

Sports equipment/gear

Denver's **R.E.I. Flagship,** 1416 Platte St. (☎ 303-756-3100), occupies a parklike setting near the confluence of Cherry Creek and the South Platte River. The gargantuan store features a climbing wall, an outdoor bike-testing area, and a "cold room" to try out outerwear and sleeping bags. You can load up on the gear of your dreams, then go running or bicycling on paved paths alongside the river or, better still, kayak in a nearby whitewater park on the South Platte River.

The **Gart Sports** store at Tenth and Broadway (☎ 303-861-1122; Internet: www.gartsports.com) was the outdoor retailer's first huge Sportscastle and is the largest sporting goods store in the country. Since then, Gart has opened another 17 Denver-area stores. Unlike R.E.I., which concentrates more intensely on backcountry endeavors, Gart covers a wider variety of sports, including old standbys such as basketball, baseball, and football. The store's five stories feature a range of fun activities for the sports-minded, including a driving cage for golfers and ball courts on the roof.

Gart Sports's annual Sniagrab (that's *bargains* spelled backwards), offers rock-bottom prices on ski equipment every Labor Day Weekend.

Nightlife

Denver has some 30 theaters, more than 100 cinemas, and dozens of concert halls, nightclubs, discos, and bars. Clubs offer country-and-western music, jazz, rock, and comedy. A good online resource for local music is www.coloradomusic.org.

Current entertainment listings appear in special Friday-morning sections of the two daily newspapers, the *Denver Post* and *Rocky Mountain News. Westword,* a weekly newspaper distributed free throughout the city every Wednesday, has perhaps the best listings: It focuses on the arts, entertainment, and local politics. *The Denver Post* (☎ 303-777-FILM; Internet: www.777film.com) provides information on movie showtimes and theaters.

Hitting the local clubs

It may not be renowned for its underground, but Denver has an active club scene and you usually won't have to go far to find a place that will suit your taste. There are lounges, dance halls, music clubs, and even a few genuine dives. Here's a sampling of the best clubs around town.

Country

Touring country acts sometimes park their buses at the **Grizzly Rose Saloon and Dance Emporium,** 5450 N. Valley Hwy. (☎ 303-295-2353).

Downtown on Thursday and Saturday nights, the place to be is **Skylark Lounge,** 58 Broadway (☎ 303-722-7844), which hosts some talented, unorthodox country musicians.

Dance

The most popular dance club in town, as of this minute, is **The Alley Cat** (☎ 303-571-4545), located at 1222 Glenarm Place behind the Diamond Cabaret strip club. On weekends it has a $15 cover charge, gets thronged with young people who are half-dressed to the nines, and features cage dancers who look as if they just got off work next door. There's a main chamber where DJs spin music and a smaller lounge with trance music. If salsa is more to your liking, head for **La Rumba,** 99 West Ninth St. (☎ 303-572-8006).

Jazz

Jazz enthusiasts should not miss **El Chapultepec,** 1962 Market St. (☎ 303-295-9126). This small club has offered free nightly jazz since the 1950s. One long wall is covered with photos of jazz legends who have played this tiny room, including Tony Bennett, Ella Fitzgerald, and Frank Sinatra. Despite having such an illustrious past, the bar still charges no cover and has just a one-drink minimum per set. Just make sure you get here early.

Rock, funk, and R&B

Herb's Hideout, 2057 Larimer St. (☎ 303-299-9555), books some high-energy R&B, jazz, and funk outfits on weekends. It's particularly popular with young professionals. If you like your rock 'n' roll loud, check out the lineup at the **15th Street Tavern,** 623 15th St. (☎ 303-572-0822), or, for an aggressive metal sound, go to **Sports Field Roxx,** 8501 E. Colfax (☎ 303-377-0200).

For the past 20 years, **Herman's Hideaway,** 1578 S. Broadway (☎ 303-7777-5840), has helped launch the careers of Colorado's up and coming bands. Herman's keeps its prices reasonable even when the most popular acts are playing: $4 on most weekend nights, and $7 on most Fridays and Saturdays. Area jam bands and Grateful Dead cover bands like to play **Quixote's True Blue,** 7 S. Broadway (☎ 720-570-8249).

If you want to catch a national touring act, check the listings at two theatres on Colfax: **Bluebird Theater,** 3317 E. Colfax (☎ 303-322-2308), and the larger **Fillmore Auditorium,** 1510 Clarkson, at Colfax (☎ 303-837-1482), an all-ages ballroom that has limited seating and a large dance floor.

Drinking up

More beer is brewed in Denver than in any other U.S. city, and foamy, frothy beverages flow liberally at establishments throughout town. No matter what your preferred poison — be it a Bond-style martini or a microbrew — you're sure to find a place that serves it.

Lounges/martini bars

The bartenders at the **Purple Martini,** 1448 Market St. (☎ **303-820-0575**), can make over 80 kinds of martinis, even at one in the morning — this, in addition to dispensing single-malt scotches and premium cigars. The bar has free live jazz Sundays through Wednesdays, and there's never a cover. Another popular martini bar is **Blue 67,** 1475 Lawrence St. (☎ **970-260-7505**).

Brewpubs

Wynkoop Brewing Co., 1634 18th St. (☎ **303-297-2700**), gave birth to the modern American brewpub, and many still consider it Denver's best. Along with its great beer, Wynkoop may serve the tastiest food of the area brewpubs, and an added attraction is a large upstairs pool hall, which generally attracts a more party-hearty crowd than the bar.

Breckenridge Brewery, 2220 Blake St. (☎ **303-297-3644**), has a convenient location kitty-corner to Coors Field and boasts some of the hottest selling microbrews in the west. **Rock Bottom Restaurant and Brewery,** 1001 16th St. (☎ **303-534-7616**), usually has around 18 beers on tap, including one named for the brewery's cat, Splatz. It's a popular stopping point for shoppers in the 16th Street Mall, especially when its large patio is open. And the Coors-owned **Sandlot Brewing Company,** inside Coors Field, sells handcrafted beers with baseball-inspired names. It doesn't open onto the field, but you can hear the crowd while watching the games on TV.

Many local brewpubs — including Breckenridge and Rock Bottom — offer free tours of the brewing process. Call ahead if you're interested.

Sports bars

Denver being one of America's premier sports cities, it hardly lacks for sports bars. The biggest and best known of them is **ESPN Zone,** 1187 16th Street (☎ **303-595-3776**), a place with more television sets (130) than many underdeveloped nations. ESPN often does live feeds from the bar during sporting events. The Zone also has food and lots of games that simulate athleticism.

The performing arts

Denver may be best known as a sports town, but its performing-arts scene is pretty active and has a loyal following. A Tony-winning theater company, a symphony orchestra, a ballet, and a modern dance company, among other groups can all be found in town. And when the big Broadway productions go on tour, they always come out to Denver, attracting theatergoers from throughout the Midwest and the mountains.

The Red Menace

Unless you're from Michigan, think twice before setting foot in **Tin Lizzie**, 1410 Market St. (☎ **720-932-0181**). As the official home to displaced Detroit Red Wings fans, this sports bar is as repulsive as a leper colony to most Denverites. It's an especially loathsome place when the Red Wings defeat their archrivals, the Colorado Avalanche.

Tickets to some of the big shows are available through Ticketmaster (☎ 303-830-TIXS). The Denver Center for the Performing Arts box office (☎ **800-641-1222** or 303-893-4100; Internet: www.denvercenter. org) handles other attractions.

Arts venues

The hub of Denver's arts community is the **Denver Performing Arts Complex,** 14th and Curtis streets (☎ **303-640-PLEX;** Internet: www. denvercenter.org). Also known as "The Plex," the Performing Arts Complex covers four city blocks and has nine theaters totaling 10,000 seats. A walkway under a giant glass arch connects the four theater buildings, which range in age from 11 to 94 years.

The oldest venue, **The Auditorium Theatre,** hosted the 1908 Democratic National Convention and is now home to the Colorado Ballet and touring Broadway musicals. Completed in 1978, **Boettcher Concert Hall** was the nation's first in-the-round symphony hall, with seating for 2,750. The Colorado Symphony Orchestra and other performers take advantage of the superb acoustics, which are adjusted by moving discs suspended from the ceiling. The 2,800-seat **Temple Buell Theater** is the stomping (and leaping) grounds of the Colorado ballet. And the **Helen Bonfils Theatre Complex** houses five small performance venues, the smallest being the 200-seat Source Theatre. A wide variety of productions are staged in the complex each year.

Ballet

The **Colorado Ballet** (☎ 303-837-8888; Internet: www.coloradoballet. com) leaps into action from October through May. Tickets range from $19 for rear balcony seating to $101 for the prime spots.

Modern dance

The **Cleo Parker Robinson Dance Company** (☎ 303-295-1759), a multicultural dance ensemble, celebrates "the universal language of movement" in productions in fall, winter, and spring. It also has a year-round dance school and outreach programs, including an intervention program for troubled kids. They perform at both the Auditorium Theatre and the Space Theater at the Plex. Tickets are $15 to $38.

Opera

Founded in 1981, **Opera Colorado** (☎ **303-778-1500;** Internet: www.
operacolorado.org) performs three operas between February and
May every year. World-class performers often assume the leading roles.
Tickets range from $25 to $130.

Symphony

The Colorado Symphony Orchestra (☎303-893-4100; Internet:
www.coloradosymphony.com) performs over 100 concerts a year,
including classical, pops, and family concerts. From September
through June, they usually play at the Boettcher Theater in Denver.
Tickets cost $15 to $70.

Theater

The **Denver Center Theater Company** (☎303-893-3272 events line,
800-641-1222 or 303-893-4100 for tickets) won the 1998 Tony for best
regional theater company. It's a very active company, staging 11 plays
between October and June every year. Offerings run the gamut from
Shakespeare to world premieres. Tickets cost $29 to $34.

Fast Facts: Denver

Area Code

Denver's area codes are **303** and **720.** You
must dial all ten digits of a phone number
even when making local calls.

American Express

The American Express office at 555 17th St.
(☎ 303-383-5050) is open weekdays from
8 a.m. to 5 p.m. Call ☎ 800-528-4800 if you've
lost your American Express card or ☎ 800-
221-7282 if you've lost your traveler's checks.

Emergencies

Dial **911.**

Hospitals

St. Joseph Hospital, 1835 Franklin St. (☎ 303-
837-7111), and Children's Hospital, 1056 E.
19th Ave. (☎ 303-861-8888), each provide
24-hour emergency care.

Internet Access and Cybercafes

Many downtown hotels offer business
centers for guests and Internet access from

guest rooms. At Common Ground Coffee
Shop, 17th Street and Wazee (☎ 303-296-
9248), you can get online for 10¢ a minute.

Maps

Mapsco Map and Travel Center, 800 Lincoln
St. (☎ 800-456-8703 or 303-623-4299), has
USGS maps, state maps, globes, and other
navigational aids.

Newspapers/Magazines

Denver has two daily papers, *The Denver
Post* and *The Rocky Mountain News,* and an
alternative newsweekly, *Westword.* National
papers such as *The New York Times* and *The
Wall Street Journal* are also available.

Pharmacies

Two chain drugstores — Walgreens (☎ 800-
WALGREENS or 800-289-2273; Internet: www.
walgreens.com) and Longs (☎ 800-865-
6647; Internet: www.longs.com) — have a
strong presence in Denver. Call to find the
local branch nearest to your location.

Police

Dial ☎ **911.**

Smoking

Denver prohibits smoking in restaurants that don't have separate, well-ventilated areas for smokers, and it limits smoking to designated areas in public venues such as airports and sports arenas.

Weather and Road Updates

Call ☎ 303-337-2500 for recorded weather forecasts and ☎ 303-639-1111 for road conditions.

Chapter 13

Side Trips from Denver

In This Chapter

▶ Touring a trio of boomtowns

▶ Finding a slot machine you can call your own

▶ Escaping to Evergreen

*J*ust a few miles west of Denver, the terrain becomes rugged and the towns are steeped in mining history. Even if you feel most comfortable in a big city, don't pass up the chance to day-trip into the foothills of the Rockies and beyond.

Riding through the Golden Circle

Golden, Idaho Springs, and Georgetown — collectively known as the "Golden Circle" — boomed during Colorado's first gold rush in 1859. Since then, Golden has grown into a small city of 13,000, thanks in part to the Coors Brewing Company, which operates the world's largest brewery there. Golden works hard to retain a Western flair, partly in honor of "Buffalo Bill" Cody, who is buried outside the town. Idaho Springs has flourished as a tourist hub, capitalizing on its mining past, its historical hot springs, and its prime location on I-70 west of Denver. Georgetown is the quietest town of the three, but it's also fun. It has a neighborhood of well-preserved Victorian homes, a slow-paced but colorful downtown, and, during the summer months, a historic railroad.

Getting there

Golden is 15 miles west of downtown Denver. You can get there by exiting off I-70 onto either U.S. 6 or Colorado 58. Idaho Springs is 32 miles west of Denver on I-70, and Georgetown is 13 miles west of Idaho Springs on I-70.

Side Trips from Denver

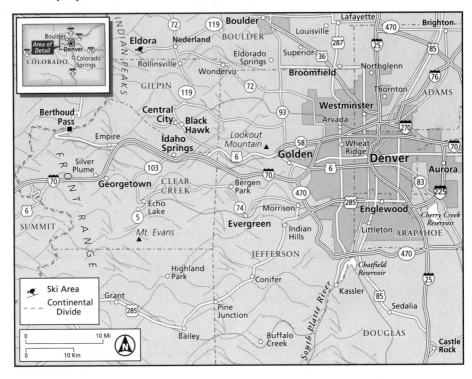

Exploring Golden, Idaho Springs, and Georgetown

The grave of William "Buffalo Bill" Cody — the long-haired Pony Express rider, buffalo hunter, soldier, and showman — sits atop the aptly named **Lookout Mountain** (I-70, Exit 256), between Interstate 70 (to the south) and Golden (to the north). After paying your respects at the grave and absorbing the views of Denver and the Plains, walk a few steps to the **Buffalo Bill Memorial Museum,** 987½ E. Lookout Mountain Rd. (☎ **303-526-0747**). Established soon after Cody's death in 1917, it's loaded with colorful memorabilia from Cody's famous Wild West Show. There's also a short video about the show, which traveled the country for nearly 30 years before closing in 1913. The museum is open Tuesday through Sunday from 9 a.m. to 4 p.m. Admission is $3 adults 16 and over, $2 seniors 65 and over, and $1 for children ages 6 to 15.

Also atop Lookout Mountain is **Boettcher Mansion** (☎ **303-526-0855**). Built in 1917 as a hunting lodge by the Denver millionaire Charles Boettcher, the 10,000-square-foot mansion displays the gables, clipped roofs, turrets, and cupolas associated with the Arts and Crafts style. The inside is used for weddings and doesn't look much like it did in the old days. Unless you're in a wedding party, you're probably better off staying outside.

The **Colorado Railroad Museum,** 17155 W. 44th Ave. in Golden (☎ 800-365-6263 or 303-279-4591; Internet: www.crm.org), exhibits thousands of historic photos and documents relating to Colorado's past and present railroads. If need be, you can rest your eyes by looking at larger antiques from Colorado's railroads or by clambering around on some of the 60 historic locomotives and rail cars outside. Downstairs, put a quarter in the slot and watch a large, painstakingly decorated model railroad in action. It's fun to see, even if you're not a model-train buff. The museum is open daily from 9 a.m. to 5 p.m. (6 p.m. in summer); admission is $6 adults, $5 seniors over 60, $3 for youths under 16, and $14.50 per family.

The **Georgetown Loop Railroad,** 1106 Rose St. in Georgetown (☎ 800-691-4386 or 303-569-2403; Internet: www.georgetownloop.com), follows tracks that are as interesting as the steam engine pulling the cars. In 1877, a railroad company wanted to extend an existing narrow gauge (3-foot-wide) rail line 2 miles from Georgetown to Silver Plume, 600 feet higher than Georgetown but just 2 miles away. To keep the grades manageable, the engineers needed to add as much distance as possible to the line, so they built a 100-foot-high, 300-foot-long trestle where the track finishes an ascending circle by crossing over itself. Today, the train completes the 9-mile round-trip in an hour and ten minutes. Rides are offered daily from mid-May through mid-September. You can catch the train in either Georgetown or Silver Plume, 2 miles west of Georgetown on I-70. If you depart from Silver Plume, you can also take a 70-minute mine tour as part of the package. Trains depart every 80 minutes, daily from late May to early October. Tickets for the train ride only cost $14.50 adults, $9.50 for children ages 3 to 15. The train and mine tour package costs $20.50 adults, $13.50 children.

Indian Springs Resort, 302 Soda Creek Rd. in Idaho Springs (☎ 303-989-6666), has indoor private baths, a swimming pool, outdoor Jacuzzis, and mud baths, but what sets the place apart are its geothermal caves. Segregated by sex, each cave has its own pools fed by geothermal hot springs. The pools are an intense 104 to 112 degrees, and the air temperature inside the caves is in the 90s, so you can really roast yourself. Built in 1905, the main resort building looks its age, and the men's changing area resembles a high-school locker room, but the caves make it worthwhile. If you're too zapped to go anywhere after getting out of the caves, rent a rustic room in the lodge or a room in newer buildings across the street. The caves are open 7:30 a.m. to 10:30 p.m. daily; admission (you must be at least 14) costs $15 on weekdays, $17 on weekends. Rooms at the resort cost $57 to $88 double.

Taking a tour

If the wait isn't too long, the free **Coors Brewery Tour** (☎ 303-277-BEER) is a winner: Just follow the signs to the parking area at 13th and Ford streets in downtown Golden. Shuttles will pick you up and take you to the brewery entrance. Inside, you can look at displays on the history of Coors; watch dewy commercials starring the company chairman, Pete Coors; go on a 40-minute brewery tour; and then quaff 24 ounces of free beer. Oddly enough, the tour is most interesting for what is *not* going on. The brewery, the world's largest, is so thoroughly mechanized that few employees are visible and almost nothing moves until you reach the packaging area. The wait can be long on summer afternoons, and it may not always be worth it.

If your main goal is to down a couple free beers, tell the people in front that you want to go on a "short tour" or beer tasting. They'll point you to the taps. Tours run Monday through Saturday from 10 a.m. to 4 p.m. Admission is free.

The **Phoenix Mine Tour** (☎ 303-567-0422; Internet: www.phoenixmine. com) is a small operation just outside Idaho Springs on Trail Creek Road (off Stanley Road). As part of the tour, you get a hard hat and then accompany a real miner on foot into a working gold mine. Afterward, you can pan for gold in a nearby creek; you can keep whatever you find. The cost is $9 for adults, $8 for seniors, and $5 for children under 12. It's open 10 a.m. to 6 p.m. daily, when the road is passable. To reach the mine, follow Colorado Boulevard west through town, go under the bridge and follow the signs.

Hitting the slopes

Travelers heading west from Denver on I-70 may catch a glimpse of a few runs near the base of **Loveland Ski Area** just before disappearing into Eisenhower tunnel, which crosses the continental divide by going directly *under* the hill. What they don't see is a beautiful ski area, particularly when the weather is calm and fair. Much of the skiable terrain is above the tree line, in a vast, horseshoe-shaped basin that sits flush against the east side of the continental divide. Loveland allows skiers of all ability levels to sample the joy of skiing at high elevations, on open faces where the air is so thin and fresh it seems to hum. The best skiing is off Lift 9, the highest four-person chairlift in North America, which unloads you atop the continental divide at 12,700 feet in elevation. From there, you can head in either direction, eventually dropping in wherever the terrain intrigues you. Lift lines here are usually short, and the base area, which has ample parking, tends to be relaxed. The main drawback to this mountain is its potentially ferocious storms. But that same weather contributes to the 400-inch annual snowfall here, which allows the resort to stay open into May.

For $32, Loveland offers a four-hour lift ticket that goes into effect the moment it is sold, no matter what time of day it is. Buy this $32 ticket and ski four hours straight, then call it a day. You'll save money, enjoy a great day of skiing, and quit before your legs get too tired.

For all of the vital facts and figures on Loveland Ski Area, see Table 13-1.

Table 13-1	Ski Report: Loveland Ski Area
Location: 56 miles west of Denver on I-70 (Exit 216)	
Trails: 70	
17% beginner	
42% intermediate	
41% advanced	
Base elevation: 10,600 feet	
Summit elevation: 13,010 feet	
Vertical drop: 2,410 feet	
Skiable terrain: 1,265 acres	
Lifts: 8	
Average annual snowfall: 400 inches	
Information: ☎ 800-736-3SKI	
Snow report: ☎ 303-571-5554	
Internet: www.skiloveland.com	
2002–2003 peak-season adult lift ticket: $43	

Where to stay and dine

Each of the 72 rooms at the faux-adobe **Table Mountain Inn,** 1310 Washington Ave. in Golden (☎ **800-762-9898** or 303-277-9898; Internet: www.tablemountaininn.com), has its own, unique Southwestern decor, and most have private decks with views of the town and the surrounding hills. The location at the edge of Golden's historic downtown is even better; and the prices are best of all. The rates — $115 to $194 double — are fixed year-round, so what seems like a fair price on a fall weekday becomes a steal on a summer weekend. During peak season, the inn often sells out a month or more in advance, so be sure to book early.

The **Georgetown Mountain Inn,** 1100 Rose St. in Georgetown (☎ **303-569-3201;** Internet: www.georgetownmountaininn.com), is just 11 miles from the Loveland Ski Area and has some of the most reasonable rooms near Denver. All have ceiling fans and tables, and the upgraded rooms have log furniture, wood-paneled walls, refrigerators, microwaves, and oversized bathrooms. In-season rates run from $56 to $95. For an extra $8, it's worth getting an upgraded room. The inn also has an outdoor swimming pool and hot tub, and offers free coffee and pastries every morning.

Make your dinner reservations early for **Hilltop Café,** 1518 Washington Ave. in Golden (☎ **303-279-8151**), because it sometimes fills up days in advance. Perched in a historic home near Golden's downtown, Hilltop Café happily dishes up traditional dishes that have been enhanced for the new millennium. The chef, Ian Kleinman, changes the menu regularly to use the freshest ingredients and is known for his ever-evolving soups. The room, with large windows and widely spaced tables, is as pleasing as the fare. Main courses at dinnertime will set you back $13 to $22.

A fellow traveler informed me that the food at this historic **Red Ram & Rathskeller,** 606 Sixth St. in Georgetown (☎ **303-569-2300**), was "very good, and normal" — with a strong emphasis on the "normal." She was right — the menu consisted entirely of normal dinner fare such as burgers, fried chicken, and steaks, not to mention oversized (but still normal) salads and a handful of Mexican dishes. What makes this restaurant noteworthy is its atmosphere — a historic 1876 building replete with vintage signs, photos of old Georgetown, and a hand-carved bar that is said to have been dragged here by horse and buggy from Oregon. A dinner entree at the restaurant costs between $5.95 and $14.95.

Gambling in Central City and Black Hawk

People returning to Central City and Black Hawk for the first time in a decade or so are in for a jolt. Fueled by the losses of day-tripping gamblers from Denver, a small Las Vegas has erupted around the southern edge of these two adjoining, 19th-century mill towns. At the south end of Black Hawk, casinos as high as eight stories now obscure the town's historic brick buildings. The change began in 1990, when a statewide referendum legalized gambling in Black Hawk, Central City, and Cripple Creek (west of Pikes Peak). At the time, Black Hawk and Central City were dilapidated remnants of what was once one of the richest mining districts in the state. Today, a few casinos have moved into the historic brick buildings in downtown Black Hawk and Central City, and other buildings have been revamped and repaired.

Getting there

Central City and Black Hawk are 34 miles west of Denver. Take I-70 west to Colorado 119, then follow Colorado 119 north to Black Hawk. You can self-park in the lots at some of the casinos; others require valet parking. Free 24-hour shuttles regularly run between the two towns. Some of the casinos also run buses to Denver. If you take a casino bus, you'll usually get your fare back in vouchers for free food and drink and gambling tokens.

Exploring Black Hawk and Central City

These towns pack as much history as anywhere in the state, but most people just gamble. When you're here, you have every right to:

- ✔ **Wager, wager, and wager.** A Black Hawk city employee told me there was nothing to do in town but gamble. A closer look revealed that there were, in fact, many activities: You can also eat, drink, smoke, stare, walk around, and, if you're lucky enough to get a room, sleep. The town's 24 casinos range from small rooms to sprawling, multistory complexes. Some offer poker and blackjack tables; others have only slot and video machines. Most provide free cocktails if you're playing, and some have even exhumed Las Vegas lounge acts such as Tony Orlando and Sha Na Na. The **Black Hawk Casino by Hyatt,** 111 Richman St. (☎ **303-567-1234**), boasts the most impressive room. It's decorated in the Colorado Rustic motif, replete with antler lamps, fake logs, lamps that resemble rawhide, and murals of mountain scenes — only, in this case, the rustic look is accompanied by dazzling lights and a bar with televisions the size of drive-in movie screens. Don't ask for a room at the Hyatt — the hotel part hasn't been built yet. If a tropical motif is more to your liking, go to **Isle of Capri Casino,** 401 Main St. (☎ **800-THE-ISLE**). It has a real, live tropical bird, a three-story waterfall, and fake palm trees — as well as the most rooms in town.

- ✔ **Walk around and look at historic buildings.** This is my favorite year-round activity here by far, which isn't saying much. Historic shacks, sheds, homes, and mine buildings are all crammed into the most improbable places in Central City. The precarious perches of certain buildings hint at the area's once-dense population. Walking around and looking at them is fun. The brick buildings postdate a catastrophic fire that destroyed much of the town in 1874. Some of the other structures are even older.

Where to stay and dine

For years, Black Hawk and Central City attracted few overnight visitors. Most drove up from Denver to gamble for a few hours, and then returned home. More people are spending the night these days, and the town's 400 rooms often sell out. With 237 Caribbean-style rooms, **Isle of Capri Casino and Hotel,** 401 Main St. (☎ **800-THE ISLE;** Internet: www.isleofcapricasino.com/Black_Hawk) accounts for more than half of the town's lodging and is the only one to have used lime-green in its decor. The hotel's Cabana rooms, decorated in a bright tropical motif, cost $114 on weekdays, $135 to $165 on weekends.

None of the buffets in town clearly transcends the others. If you're hungry for both American and international fare, go to the **World's Fare Buffet** ($15 for dinner) at the **Riviera Black Hawk Casino,** 444 Main St. in Black Hawk (☎ **303-582-1000**). For upscale dining with full table service, try **Farraddays' Restaurant** ($14 to $28 for an entree), open for dinner nightly inside the **Isle of Capri Casino.** Farraddays' serves mostly seafood and steaks.

The coupon page inside the free *Colorado Gambler* newspaper — distributed in both Central City and Black Hawk — sometimes has two-for-one deals on weekday meals at area casinos.

Cooling Off in Evergreen

At 7,500 feet in elevation, Evergreen is the place to go for a quick cool-down from Denver. It's only 29 miles west of the city, but it feels more remote than the mountain communities along the I-70 corridor. On the hillsides around town, ponderosa pines shade granite boulders flecked with green and orange lichens. Elk graze in meadows around upper Bear Creek, which flows down from Mount Evans and goes right through town.

Because of its beauty, Evergreen has attracted vacationers since at least the 1920s, when movie stars and millionaires gathered at a resort known as Troutdale-in-the-Pines. These days the town is a suburb, but there are a few attractions and some nice places to dine and stay that make this a worthwhile stop.

Getting there

To reach Evergreen from downtown Denver, take U.S. 6 to I-70 West. Exit I-70 at Colorado 74 East (Evergreen Parkway). Follow Colorado 74 East to Evergreen.

Exploring Evergreen

Between Evergreen and Morrison on Colorado 74, stop and check out the world famous **Red Rocks Amphitheater,** 16351 Country Road 93, Morrison. Part of Denver's mountain parks system, the amphitheatre is on a hillside between two 300-foot sandstone slabs and has views up to

60 miles out onto the plains. Even the stage and seating area are on red rock. The amphitheater and surrounding grounds are open to the public. When no concerts are scheduled you can walk the same stage where U2, the Grateful Dead, and the Beatles have performed. For more on the mountain parks, call ☎ **303-697-8935.** The park closes at 4 p.m. on event days.

While in Evergreen, history buffs should visit the **Hiwan Homestead Museum,** 4208 S. Timbervale Dr. (☎ **303-674-6262**). This 17-room log lodge was built in installments beginning in 1890. If you ever wondered who thought up Colorado Rustic decor, look no further than this place. Right from the get-go, the people who lived here collected Indian art, animal pelts, and hand-carved furniture, much of which is still on display. Shoe-horned between ponderosa pine trees, the house has seven fireplaces, seven staircases, two towers, and a chapel. To go inside, you have to join one of the free 45-minute tours. The museum is open Tuesday through Sunday from noon to 5 p.m. (11 a.m. to 5 p.m. in summer).

To smooth out the rough spots in your life (and maybe your complexion), visit **TallGrass Spa,** 997 Upper Bear Creek Rd. in Evergreen (☎ **303-670-4444**), for a body polish or a purifying sea herbal body masque. En route to the spa, you'll pass immense summer homes and lodges built by Denver's wealthiest families in the late 1800s and early 1900s.

In downtown Evergreen, **Creekside Cellars,** 28036 Hwy. 74 (☎ **303-674-5460**), provides free samples of the wines bottled here. When you're ready for a glass ($4.50 to $7) or bottle ($6 to $20), you can enjoy it at a table on the deck above Bear Creek while nibbling from an antipasto tray ($7.95 per person) or munching a gourmet sandwich ($6 or less). In summer, the cellars are open Tuesday through Sunday from 11 a.m. to 5 p.m. The rest of the year, they're open Wednesday through Sunday from 11 a.m. to 5 p.m.

Where to stay and dine

At **Highland Haven Creekside Inn,** 4395 Independence Trail (☎ **800-459-2406** or 303-674-3577; Internet: www.highlandhaven.com), you'll be shaded by ponderosa pines, serenaded by a nearby creek, and stuffed with a rich breakfast in an 1884 log cabin. Accommodations, in restored 1920s and 1930s cottages, are both private and luxurious. All have mountain-rustic furnishings, televisions, and VCRs, and many have fireplaces. There are also motel rooms in the main lodge. Rates run from $90 for a single room in low season to $275 for a cottage in high season.

The Bistro, 6830 Colorado 73 (☎ **303-674-7670**), merges the ruggedness of the mountains with the sophistication of an urban bistro. The dining area is in a log cabin with a flagstone fireplace, hardwood floors, and unpeeled log beams, but the food consists mostly of European-style tapas, pastas, and meat dishes. A main course at dinner costs $10 to $28. The **Tivoli Deer,** 26300 Hilltop Dr. in Kittredge (☎ **303-670-0941**), serves a prix-fixe menu, including wine, for $44 per person.

Where to get your kicks

For years, famous musicians such as Leon Russell, Dave Mason, Greg Allman, and Jerry Jeff Walker have played the **Little Bear Saloon,** 28075 Colorado 74 (☎ **303-674-9991;** Internet: www.littlebearsaloon.com), in downtown Evergreen. No one knows exactly why. The place isn't that big and it's 35 miles from the city. As for the decor, if it hasn't broken yet, it probably won't. The advantages seem to be an intimate setting, pitchers of cold beer, and lingerie hanging from the ceiling.

Chapter 14

Colorado Springs

- -

In This Chapter

▶ Staying at Colorado's grandest resort

▶ Pikes Peak or bust for family fun

▶ Visiting a divine, red-rock garden

- -

*I*f you like orderly, clean-cut, traditional towns, you'll enjoy Colorado Springs. The Air Force Academy is nearby, along with several military installations. The international Christian organization Focus on the Family has its headquarters in town, and the first U.S. Olympic Training Center still conditions athletes here. Even the town's layout feels disciplined — a neat grid centered around a wide boulevard known as Pikes Peak Avenue. Within that grid, the downtown buildings barely obstruct the mountain views. The town and county have 158 nicely maintained parks, including the spectacular Garden of the Gods, where red sandstone slabs seem to have erupted out of the earth at the base of the mountains.

Colorado Springs has been a resort since the 1870s (though many early "guests" were tubercular people, who came here for the fresh air). Flush with mining profits from nearby Cripple Creek, millionaires built several grand hotels in and around Colorado Springs in the early 1900s. Visitors flocked here not only for the weather and the mountain views, but for attractions such as the Pikes Peak Cog railway, the Garden of the Gods, Cave of the Winds, and later, the Pikes Peak Highway. These same attractions still lure throngs of visitors to the area. Colorado Springs isn't too expensive for most families, yet a certain formality remains: This is one of a handful of places in the state where men need a jacket and tie to dine in the finest restaurants.

Getting There

Eight commercial airlines together offer about 100 flights daily to **Colorado Springs Airport (CSA).** The airport has only three runways and a small terminal, so negotiating it is easy. You can get your bearings quickly by stopping at the **ground transportation booth (☎ 719-550-1930)** on the terminal's lower level, open from 7 a.m. to midnight daily. **Avis, Dollar, Hertz,** and **National** all have desks and return areas at the airport. Other companies, including **Advantage, Budget, Enterprise,** and **Thrifty** do business nearby in Colorado Springs. For information on contacting individual airlines and car-rental agencies, see the Appendix.

Downtown Colorado Springs is 12 miles from the airport. Coming from the airport, go right (north) on Powers Boulevard, and then take a left (west) onto Colorado 24 (Platte Avenue). Follow Platte Avenue into the downtown area.

A few hotels offer free shuttle services for guests. If yours doesn't, call one of three taxi companies — **Express Airport Taxi** (☎ 719-634-3111), **Fremont County Cab** (☎ 719-784-2222), or **Yellow Cab** (☎ 719-634-5000) — for a ride into town. The cheapest company, Express Airport Taxi, bills $2 plus $1.50 per mile. The trip downtown usually costs around $18.

You can drive into Colorado Springs via Interstate 25, which crosses the west side of town between Denver (70 miles north) and Pueblo (40 miles south). If you're heading west on I-70 and shooting for Colorado Springs, you'll need to exit onto U.S. 24 in Limon, and then follow that highway southwest for 70 miles into the city. If you're heading east on I-70, take Colorado 9 south for 53 miles to U.S. 24, then follow U.S. 24 east for 66 miles into Colorado Springs.

Getting Around

Colorado Springs is a pedestrian-friendly city. Even so, you'll need a car to reach many of the most popular attractions, because they're scattered around town and in the mountains.

U.S. 24 borders the south edge of the downtown, while **I-25** skirts the west side. The major north-south arteries in the downtown are **Nevada Avenue** and **Cascade Avenue.** The main east-west roads are **Colorado Avenue** and **Platte Avenue** (U.S. 24). The intersection of east-west Pikes Peak Avenue and Nevada Avenue marks the center of town. Street addresses prefaced with *North* or *South* indicate their location relative to Pikes Peak Avenue; ones prefaced with *East* or *West* describe their location relative to Nevada Avenue.

If you follow Colorado Avenue northwest out of the downtown, you'll quickly pass through **Old Colorado City,** between 21st and 31st streets The oldest part of Colorado Springs, Old Colorado City was a supply stop for gold miners heading west in the late 1850s. It became Colorado's first territorial capitol in 1861 but degenerated into a saloon and red-light district. Run-down in the 1970s, much of it has since been restored into a quaint redbrick shopping area. Farther west, Colorado Avenue becomes Manitou Avenue and enters **Manitou Springs,** where some of the first resort hotels were built. Manitou Springs has a large historic district, including many Victorian homes. It's closer to the mountains, more compact, and more colorful than Colorado Springs. The Pikes Peak Cog Railway has its depot at the edge of town. West of town, Manitou Avenue joins U.S. 24, which continues west into the mountains.

Parking can be challenging in Manitou Springs. When you find a parking spot, you can take advantage of the **Manitou Trolley** (☎ **719-385-RIDE**), which provides free transportation around the town every half hour from Memorial Day through September 8 and again between Thanksgiving and New Year's Day. Two trolley buses each make one-hour loops to major tourist destinations (including Garden of the Gods), and you can get on and off as you please. By calling the trolley number, you can also find out about Colorado Springs's citywide bus service, **Springs Transit** (cost: $1.25 adults, 60¢ seniors and kids 6 to 11), which operates Monday through Saturday year-round.

Where to Stay

You can stay in historic digs in Colorado Springs in every price range. Famous historic hotels such as the Broadmoor and The Cliff House are pricey. Less expensive, but hardly spartan, are a dozen or so area bed-and-breakfasts, including some in Victorian homes. Least expensive are the many historic motor lodges and motels around Manitou Springs, many of which date to the 1920s and 1930s, when tourists began traveling here by car. Some of these lodges and motels are fine; others need work. Ask to see a room before settling in. If you want a chain hotel, you can find one along I-25 in Colorado Springs.

The Broadmoor
$$$$ **Colorado Springs**

The ultra-luxurious Broadmoor is almost a city for the rich and famous. On its 2,400 acres are 11 restaurants and lounges, 45 golf holes, 12 tennis courts, a 300-seat movie theater, 16 massage rooms, and 700 guest rooms. During high season, 1,700 employees cater to needs you didn't even know you had. That level of service has been maintained for over 80 years, so it's not really news. The best new thing here is the outdoor swimming pool. Like a seashore, the bottom of the pool slopes gradually into a deep end that seems to disappear into the hotel's man-made body of water, Cheyenne Lake. A barely visible wall separates pool from lake. The effect is cool and perfect. Of course, there's a price for all this luxury. Even if you can't or won't pay it, you should still walk through the original 1918 hotel. A recent renovation spruced up the fountains, chandeliers, frescos, marble floors, ceiling murals, and ornate plasterwork, making the entire building a work of art.

Colorado Springs

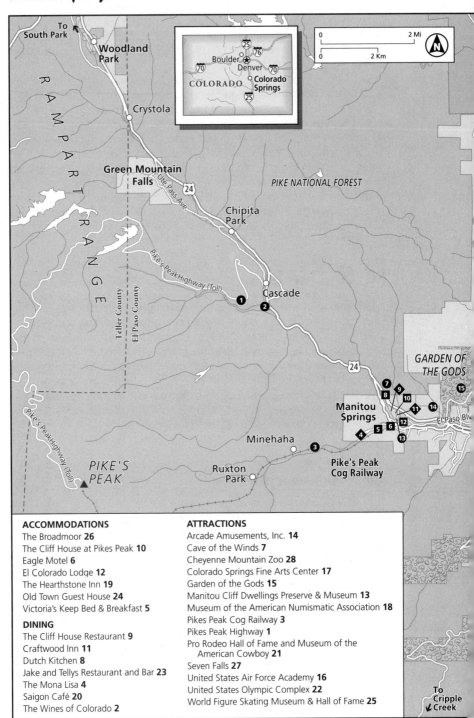

ACCOMMODATIONS
The Broadmoor **26**
The Cliff House at Pikes Peak **10**
Eagle Motel **6**
El Colorado Lodge **12**
The Hearthstone Inn **19**
Old Town Guest House **24**
Victoria's Keep Bed & Breakfast **5**

DINING
The Cliff House Restaurant **9**
Craftwood Inn **11**
Dutch Kitchen **8**
Jake and Tellys Restaurant and Bar **23**
The Mona Lisa **4**
Saigon Café **20**
The Wines of Colorado **2**

ATTRACTIONS
Arcade Amusements, Inc. **14**
Cave of the Winds **7**
Cheyenne Mountain Zoo **28**
Colorado Springs Fine Arts Center **17**
Garden of the Gods **15**
Manitou Cliff Dwellings Preserve & Museum **13**
Museum of the American Numismatic Association **18**
Pikes Peak Cog Railway **3**
Pikes Peak Highway **1**
Pro Rodeo Hall of Fame and Museum of the
    American Cowboy **21**
Seven Falls **27**
United States Air Force Academy **16**
United States Olympic Complex **22**
World Figure Skating Museum & Hall of Fame **25**

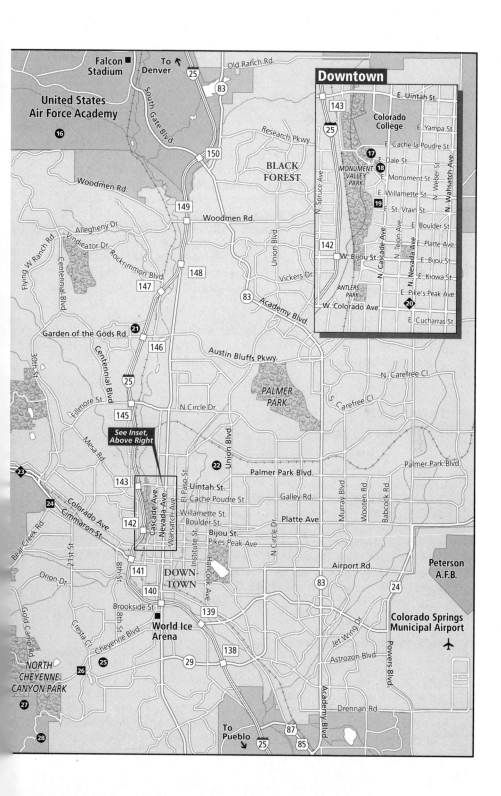

Lake Circle, at Lake Avenue, Colorado Springs. ☎ **800-634-7711.** *Fax: 719-577-5700. Internet:* www.broadmoor.com. *Rack rates: Summer $325–$495 double, $540–$720 suites; winter $230–$350 double, $400–$535 suites. AE, DC, DISC, MC, V.*

The Cliff House at Pikes Peak
$$$–$$$$ **Manitou City**

The Cliff House is the Rocky of Rocky Mountain hotels. In the 1880s, it was a 200-room luxury hotel; in the 1960s, it became a disco and apartment complex; and in the 1980s, it suffered severe damage when it caught fire. After sitting vacant for 16 years, the National Ladmark was restored and it reopened as a luxury hotel in 1999. Now you can once again stay where the likes of Buffalo Bill, P. T. Barnum, and Theodore Roosevelt have slept. Smoke cigars on the veranda, waltz in the ballroom, or listen to music in the music room. The guest rooms still look new and offer a host of amenities, including silk robes, refrigerators, even heated toilet seats. My favorite is the Buffalo Bill suite, where the ceiling, which is the underside of an 18-foot-high cupola, has been painted to resemble the inside of a tepee.

306 Canon Ave., Manitou Springs. ☎ **888-212-7000** *or 719-685-3000. Fax: 719-685-3913. Internet:* www.thecliffhouse.com. *Rack rates: Nov 1–April 30, $129 studios, $179–$249 suites; May 1–Oct 31 $179@@249 studios, $269–$449 suites. AE, DC, MC, V.*

Eagle Motel
$ **Manitou Springs**

Come here when you're ready to rediscover those special motel joys: parking outside your door, free local calls, cable television, and soda pop cooled by hollow ice cubes — not to mention a complimentary continental breakfast. The staff vigorously cleans this 1950s motel every day, so you can live the joy without being reminded of the last guests.

423 Manitou Ave., Manitou Springs. ☎ **800-872-2285** *or 719-685-5467. Fax 719-685-0542. Rack rates: Sept 30–May 22, $54 double; Aug 18–29 and Sept 2–29 $69 double; June 14–Aug 18 and Labor Day weekend $92 double; May 23–June 13 $72 double. Rates include continental breakfast. AE, DISC, MC, V.*

El Colorado Lodge
$–$$ **Manitou Springs**

Built in 1927, this motel consists of real adobe cabins scattered along four acres next to Manitou Avenue in Manitou Springs. The thick adobe walls help muffle the noise of nearby traffic. Not surprisingly, the cabins are decorated in a Southwestern motif, with Native American rugs and art; some even have working fireplaces. The larger accommodations — which sleep up to six people — have refrigerators and microwaves. The

El Colorado claims to have been the first lodge in the area to have used sheets. Fortunately for us, other places caught up, but this one still remains a good value.

23 Manitou Ave., Manitou Springs. ☎ *719-685-5485. Fax: 719-685-4699. Internet:* www.pikes-peak.com/ElColorado. *Rack rates $69–$111 cabins. AE, DISC, MC, V.*

The Hearthstone Inn
$$–$$$ Colorado City

This inn, which occupies an 1885 mansion and a neighboring 1900 tuberculosis sanitarium, feels more formal and reserved than other area B&Bs. Some of its antiques are museum quality, and reproductions of impressionist paintings hang on the walls. The rooms and suites lack the frilly decor found at other B&Bs — you'll find only comfortable antique furniture and well preserved woodwork, floors, and trim. If you can't stand being off-line, you'll be pleased to know that accommodations are wired for high-speed DSL.

506 N. Cascade Ave., Colorado Springs. ☎ *800-521-1885 or 719-473-4413. Fax: 719-473-1322. Internet:* www.hearthstoneinn.com. *Rack rates: $69–$199 double. Rates include full breakfast. AE, DISC, MC, V.*

Old Town Guest House
$$$ Old Colorado City

This inn doesn't have a long history, but it has everything else you could want from a bed-and-breakfast. The uniquely decorated rooms offer luxuries such as steam showers, CD players, VCRs (and complimentary videos), and private decks. The waterbed mattresses are so comfy, you'll wish you were bed-ridden. And tea, soda, and snacks are available around the clock in the common areas. Thick walls and doors make the rooms feel private, especially for a B&B. When you're ready for a gourmet breakfast or driving directions, innkeepers Kaye and David Caster are right there to help.

115 S. 26th St., Colorado Springs. ☎ *888-375-4210 or 719-632-9194. Fax: 719-632-9026. Internet:* www.bbonline.com/co/oldtown. *Rack rates: $99–$185 double. Rates include full breakfast. AE, DC, DISC, MC, V.*

Victoria's Keep Bed & Breakfast
$$–$$$ Manitou Springs

This antique-filled Victorian bed-and-breakfast is convenient to downtown Manitou Springs and the Pikes Peak Cog Railway. There are more than a few B&Bs near Victoria's Keep; what sets this one apart are owners Gerry and Donna Anderson, who hail from the deep South and bring heaping platters of hospitality to your visit. No matter how road-weary you are, you'll feel better when you step inside, meet the innkeepers, and start dipping into the always-full cookie jar. As for the rooms, my favorite is the Turret Room, which has a cozy hiding place inside the house's turret adjoining the main room, as well as a large Jacuzzi tub.

202 Ruxton Ave., Manitou Springs. ☎ *800-905-5337 or 719-685-5354. Fax: 719-685-5913. Internet:* www.victoriaskeep.com. *Rack rates: $90–$175 double. Rates include gourmet breakfast. AE, DISC, MC, V.*

Where to Dine

This is one of two Colorado cities where you can dine in semiformal attire without feeling goofy about it. Dust off that blazer, knot that tie if you know how, and then head for the Cliff House or one of many restaurants at the Broadmoor in search of that perfect meal. Of course, the experience doesn't have to be stodgy. Even the fancy hotels have places where you can dine casually. There are also plenty of mid-priced restaurants in the area. Here are my best dining choices.

The Cliff House Restaurant

$$$ **Manitou Springs** NOUVEAU CONTINENTAL

The Cliff House Restaurant is my favorite Colorado Springs eatery and darn near my favorite in the state. Never mind the Broadmoor Hotel and its huge reputation. Never mind the price — until your credit-card bill arrives. Just enjoy the Victorian surroundings and the French-influenced fare. Seek advice from one of the six licensed sommeliers on staff, then choose one of the 5,000 bottles of wine. The salmon here is so fresh, it can be eaten nearly raw; like most of the other entrees it's cooked — but not overcooked — and topped with a buttery sauce. Don't pass up the cheese appetizer plate, it may have been the best thing I ate on my trip. For dessert, wash down the soufflé with a sip of port. Above all, enjoy.

Suit coats are suggested, but if you don't feel like dressing up, you can dine casually in the cocktail area on the porch.

306 Canon Ave., Manitou Springs. ☎ *888-212-7000 or 719-685-3000. Reservations recommended. Main courses: $25–$32. Open: Breakfast, lunch, and dinner daily. AE, DC, MC, V.*

Craftwood Inn

$$ **Manitou Springs** GAME

Located in a 1912 Arts and Crafts–style mansion on a hillside above Manitou Springs, the Craftwood Inn is the best place to go if you're hungry for game. The choice of meats reads like a who's who of the local zoo. Menu items include elk, trout, roast duck, noisettes of caribou, and grilled loin of wild boar. There's an extensive wine list, and the window and deck seating afford views of Pikes Peak.

404 El Paso Blvd., Manitou Springs. ☎ *719-685-9000. Reservations suggested. Main courses: $12–$24. Open: Dinner daily. AE, DC, DISC, MC, V.*

Dutch Kitchen
$ **Manitou Springs   AMERICAN**

The same family has run this tiny hole-in-the-wall on Manitou Avenue for over 40 years. They make most of their food from scratch, ring up orders on a 1930s cash register, and close on Thursdays and Fridays, which makes sense only to them. You can have one of their famous corned beef sandwiches, a burger, or a straightforward dinner entree such as "golden fried shrimp" or "Italian spaghetti." You can dine here for under $10 even if you sample the award-winning pie.

1025 Manitou Ave., Manitou Springs. ☎ *719-685-9962. Reservations for large parties only. Main courses: $6–$11.50. Open: Sun–Wed lunch and dinner. Closed Dec–Feb. Cash or checks only.*

Jake and Tellys Restaurant and Bar
$$ **Old Colorado City   GREEK**

Two Greek brothers serve the old-world recipes of their grandmother at this quirky restaurant in Old Colorado City. If you'd like to try a collection of her traditional Greek dishes, order the sampler plate. It has *dolmadaki* (grape leaves with meat stuffing), spanakopita, and other delicacies whose names are too long for a guidebook this size. If the food doesn't transport you back to the Old World, maybe the murals of Greece and mounted ocean fish will.

2616 W. Colorado Ave., Colorado Springs. ☎ *719-633-0406. Reservations accepted. Main courses: $14.95–24.95. Open: Lunch and dinner daily. AE, DC, DISC, MC, V.*

The Mona Lisa
$$ **Manitou Springs   SWISS**

If you bring a date to this romantic, candle-lit restaurant, you may end up wearing a satisfied half-smile like the restaurant's namesake. You can dunk breads, bagels, and cheeses into fondues, each with different cheeses and ingredients. If you order meat, the chefs will grill it at your table and serve it with its own dipping sauces. For dessert, the dipping items are cakes, brownies, cookies, and fruit, and the fondues are chocolate. Each of the restaurant's many rooms has windows opening onto a hallway, where there's even a street lamp.

733 Manitou Ave., Manitou Springs. ☎ *719-685-0277. Reservations accepted. Main courses: $14–$23; fondue for two, $33 per person. Open: Tues–Sun dinner only. AE, DISC, MC, V.*

Saigon Café
$ **Colorado Springs** **VIETNAMESE**

Most of Saigon Café's dishes have plenty of fresh vegetables and only a modest amount of meat, served over rice or rice noodles. The best may be the noodle specialties — the meat of your choice served with rice noodles, bean sprouts, cucumber, mint, lettuce, peanuts, and sauce. The restaurant uses linen tablecloths, but if you insist on eating carryout, Saigon Café can rustle up a box for your food.

20 E. Colorado Ave., Colorado Springs. ☎ *719-633-2888. Reservations accepted. Main courses: $7.95–$13.95. Open: Mon–Sat lunch and dinner. AE, DISC, MC, V.*

The Wines of Colorado
$ **Cascade** **AMERICAN**

This restaurant is the only place in the state where you can sample and purchase wines from all of Colorado's 35 wineries. If this sounds like a painful task, taste the wines! You can sample a half-dozen or so for free, then purchase any of 200 bottled varieties or simply order a glass with dinner. As for the food, you can get salads, sandwiches, wine-marinated hamburgers, and entrees such as grilled ahi and chicken pot pie. The deck overlooking the confluence of two creeks is a pretty place to dine.

If you do sit down to dine, don't expect your server to hand over a wine list — you're supposed to have chosen during the tasting process. (Duh.)

8045 W. Hwy. 24 (at turn-off to Pikes Peak Highway), Cascade. ☎ *719-684-0900. Reservations for parties of six or more only. Main courses: $4.95–$10.95. Open: Summer lunch and dinner daily; closed Mondays the rest of the year. MC, V.*

Exploring Colorado Springs

Some of the tourist attractions in Colorado Springs have been operating for so long, they've become historical sites, too. If they weren't worth seeing, most of them wouldn't have lasted so long.

The best things to see and do

Cave of the Winds

Many years ago, on a hillside above present-day Manitou Springs, slightly acidic rainwater flowed through cracks in limestone and gradually dissolved some of the rock, eventually forming a mazelike network of caves — and, as fate would have it, a major tourist attraction. At Cave of the Winds, you can choose between three tours. The mellow, 45-minute Discovery Tour (cost: $15 adults; $8 children ages 6 to 15) is the tour for duffers. It follows paved routes down lighted corridors where tour groups have been going for over 100 years. This tour may not, um, rock your world, but it's still lots of fun, especially if you get a guide who can make light of a script that mixes the right amounts of science, hokum, and humor. Other tours are more demanding. On the Lantern Tour (cost: $18 adults, $9 children ages 6 to 15, children under 6 not allowed), you'll carry your own lantern into an otherwise dark cave, walk uneven dirt floors, and follow a guide into chambers smaller and more pristine than the ones on the Discovery Tour. The extreme, four-hour Explorer Tour (cost: $80 per person) involves real spelunking and is only open to physically fit people over 13. For the Lantern and Explorer tours, call ahead for reservations. The cave's natural temperature is always 54 degrees, so remember to dress warmly.

Six miles west of I-25 on U.S. 24, Manitou Springs. ☎ *719-685-5444. Internet:* www.caveofthewinds.com. *Open: May–Aug, daily 9 a.m.–9 p.m.; Sept–April, daily 10 a.m.–5 p.m.*

Cheyenne Mountain Zoo

The people who named Cheyenne Mountain Zoo weren't kidding about the "mountain" part. It sits on a mountainside at 6,800 feet, with steep forest floors above it. The zoo animals that are suited to this environment wander large, forested plots of land on the hillside. They often seem more comfortable than the zoo-goers, many of whom can't handle the steep climbs. If the climbing wears you out, you can ride on the zoo shuttle (cost: $1 for a full day) alongside other weary Homo sapiens. The zoo has 146 species from around the world, including rarely seen Southwestern animals such as gray wolves and mountain lions. If you bring your kids, make sure to visit the 1920s-era carousel, which costs $2 a ride.

4250 Cheyenne Mountain Zoo Rd. (above the Broadmoor). ☎ *719-633-9925. Internet:* www.cmzoo.org. *Admission: $10 adults 12–64, $8 seniors 65 and over, $5 children 3–11. Open: Summer, daily 9 a.m.–6 p.m. (8 p.m. on Tues); rest of year, daily 9 a.m.–5 p.m.*

Garden of the Gods

When colliding tectonic plates uplifted the most recent incarnation of the Rocky Mountains, a few massive sandstone slabs were pushed out of the earth at the base of the mountains. In 1,300-acre Garden of the Gods Park, erosion has carved this sandstone into fantastic shapes. Admission is free, but with 1.7 million visitors annually, it can be hard to find a parking space, let alone a quiet place. If the park is busy, look for a spot at the Garden of the Gods Visitor Center. Many spectacular rocks line the 1½-mile Perkins Central Garden Trail, which is accessible from this area. If you're curious about the rocks, watch the 12-minute, laser-enhanced video (cost: $2 for adults, $1 for kids 12 and under) at the visitor center, which explains how they were formed.

A stunt becomes a tradition

The second oldest auto race in America, **the Pikes Peak Auto Hill Climb** (☎ 719-685-4400; Internet: www.ppihc.com) started as a publicity stunt. In 1916, Spencer Penrose, owner of the Broadmoor Hotel, organized the race as a way of letting the world know about a new toll road that he had just bankrolled. Today, racers in motorcycles and sports cars still careen up the last 12.4 miles (the gravel portion) of the Pikes Peak Highway every year. The road probably would have been paved long ago if local officials hadn't feared ruining the race.

You can find out more about the history of the race and see old cars and motorcycles from past races at the **Pikes Peak Auto Hill Climb Educational Museum,** 135 Manitou Ave., Manitou Springs. The museum is open daily from 9 a.m. to 7 p.m. during summer (call for off-season hours). Admission is $5 adults, $4 seniors, and $2 for children ages 6 to 12.

Ridge Road (off I-25 Exit 146). ☎ *719-634-6666. Internet:* www.gardenofgods. com. *Admission: Free. Open: May–Oct daily 5 a.m.–11 p.m.; Nov–April daily 5 a.m.–9 p.m. Visitor Center hours: June–Aug 8 a.m.–8 p.m.; Sept–May 9 a.m.–5 p.m.*

Pikes Peak Cog Railway

Unlike many other historic railroads in Colorado, this 1891 railway has always catered to tourists, and today it carries more than a quarter-million people annually from Manitou Springs (elevation: 6,571 feet) to the summit of Pikes Peak (elevation: 14,110 feet). It's a straight, steep, 9-mile climb, with grades of 25 degrees in places. Ordinary trains can't get enough friction to climb this steeply; that's why this one has a cog that grabs onto a toothy center track. The train passes waterfalls, wildlife, and lakes before finally opening onto views that span all the way to Kansas. It takes 1 hour and 15 minutes to reach the windswept summit, where you linger for 40 minutes in or near the gift shop before making the 40-minute trip back down.

515 Ruxton Ave., Manitou Springs. ☎ *719-685-5401. Internet:* www.cograilway. com. *Tickets: $24.50 adults; $12.50 children under 12. Open: Late April–Dec 29. Train departs every 80 minutes during mid-summer, less often during slower periods. Reservations are requested.*

Pikes Peak Highway

This isn't the only road to the top of a 14,000-foot peak in Colorado. The road up Mount Evans, nearer to Denver, goes higher, costs less, and is just as pretty. But this is the more famous road, the one where race cars race every summer. If you plan on driving the 20 miles to the top, remember that a 14,000-foot peak is a serious undertaking, even in an automobile. Make sure you have at least half a tank of gas, because your round-trip will take two hours or more, as well as grippy brakes for the trip down. As for the road, it's wide enough for two city buses to pass each other, but it lacks guardrails and becomes gravel after 7 miles, which makes it plenty scary for flatlanders. And the weather on top is changeable, to say the least. One advantage to the road (over the train) is that it lets you set your own pace and pause at overlooks. In winter, the road stays open but is usually only plowed to around the 13-mile mark.

Turn off U.S. 24 at Cascade (10 miles west of Manitou Springs). ☎ *800-318-9505 or 719-385-PEAK. Internet:* www.pikespeakcolorado.com. *Admission: $10 per adult (16 and over) or $35 per carload. Open: May 19–Sept 5, daily 7 a.m.–7 p.m.; Sept. 6–30, daily 7 a.m.–5 p.m.; rest of year, daily 9 a.m.–3 p.m.*

United States Air Force Academy

The U.S. Air Force Academy is huge. It encompasses 18,000 acres along the foothills of the Rockies, and the drive from the north to the south gates of the academy covers 14 miles. To get your bearings after arriving, follow the signs to the visitor center, which has Air Force videos, displays, gifts, and an information desk. It also has maps for a self-guided driving tour. From there, you can walk a ⅓-mile paved trail to the popular Cadet Chapel. Afterwards, allow at least two hours for the driving tour. During daytime, you can break up the drive by enjoying some of the open space. It's not exactly Woodstock in there, but you can still mountain-bike or hike on the Santa Fe Trail, road bike, play golf, or picnic. Just make sure you have a photo ID.

12 miles north of Colorado Springs, off I-25 Exit 156B (follow signs to the visitor center). ☎ *719-333-8723. Internet:* www.usafa.af.mil. *Admission: Free. Visitor Center hours: Summer daily 9 a.m.–6 p.m.; winter daily 9 a.m.–5 p.m.*

United States Olympic Complex

Unfortunately for the likes of you and me, this 36-acre complex is set up to train world-class athletes and not to entertain bored, frumpy tourists. Still, if you love the Olympics, you'll probably enjoy going on a one-hour tour. After watching a short, unsubtle video highlighting American Olympic achievements, you'll walk through facilities where athletes train for sports such as volleyball, judo, shooting, swimming, and boxing. If you go during mid-morning or late afternoon, you'll probably see at least a few athletes enduring the repetitive, boring, torturous work that you always hear about, after the fact, during the Olympics. If you don't take the tour, you're still allowed to wander the grounds, visit the gift shop, and stop at the U.S. Olympic Hall of Fame (which has changing displays). You may not, however, enter the buildings.

1 Olympic Plaza, corner of Boulder Street (entrance) and Union Boulevard. ☎ *719-578-4618 (visitor center) or 719-578-4644 (hotline). Admission: Free. Open: Mon–Sat 9 a.m.–5 p.m. Last tour leaves at 4 p.m.*

Other things to see and do

In addition to the big draws, Colorado Springs may have more small, quirky attractions than any other Colorado town. While in Colorado Springs, you can

- **Get thrown.** The **Pro Rodeo Hall of Fame and Museum of the American Cowboy,** 101 Pro Rodeo Dr. (☎ 719-528-4764), overflows with trophies, hats, boots, spurs, and chaps belonging to famous rodeo cowboys. So many cowboys have been inducted into the hall, you can't help but wonder who's left. It's open daily from 9 a.m. to 5 p.m. (except holidays). Admission costs $6 adults; $5 seniors 55 and over; $3 children 6 to 12, and is free for kids under 6.

- **See super-high fly balls.** During late spring and summer, the **Colorado Sky Sox** (☎ 719-591-SOXX, Internet: www.skysox.com) of the AAA-level Pacific Coast League play baseball at Sky Sox Stadium, 4385 Tutt Blvd. Tickets are reasonable ($4 general admission, $6 to $7 reserved), and the caliber of play is only one step down from the Majors.

- **Russell up some art.** The **Colorado Springs Fine Arts Center,** 30 W. Dale St. (☎ 719-634-5581), has a large collection of fine regional art, including pieces by Georgia O'Keefe, Charles Russell, and Albert Bierstadt. My favorite gallery showcases pre- and post-Colombian Native American and Hispanic work. There's also a tactile gallery. It's open Monday through Saturday from 9 a.m. to 5 p.m., Sunday from 1 to 5 p.m. Admission is $4 for adults, $2 for seniors, students, and kids 6 to 16. Admission is free on Saturday.

- **Obey the flute.** At **Manitou Cliff Dwellings Preserve and Museum** (☎ 800-354-9971 or 719-685-5242; Internet: www.cliffdwellings museum.com), Native American flute music blares over speakers near the dwellings, mere yards from the parking area. When you hear Native American flute music in Colorado, there's usually a gift shop nearby, and sure enough, there's one here. Worse still, the cliff dwellings aren't even from here; they were moved to this spot in the early 1900s. However, they're very accessible. If this is your only chance to see an Ancestral Puebloan dwelling, take advantage of it. The museum is on U.S. 24 in Manitou Springs, 5 miles west of I-25 (Exit 141). It's open June through August daily from 9 a.m. to 8 p.m.; September through May daily from 9 a.m. to 5 p.m. (weather permitting). Admission is $8 for adults, $7 for seniors, $6 for children ages 7 to 11, and free for kids under 7.

- **Overcome "Numismatism."** People who think *Numismatic* describes a disease will be relieved to discover that the word actually refers to coins. The eight galleries of coins and bills at the **Museum of the American Numismatic Association,** 818 N. Cascade Ave. (☎ 719-632-2646; Internet: www.money.org), constitute the largest such collection outside the Smithsonian in Washington, D.C. The museum also houses a library and has an authentication department, which may just save you an embarrassing moment on *Antiques Roadshow.* Best of all, it's free. The collection is open Monday through Friday from 9 a.m. to 4 p.m., and Saturday from 10 a.m. to 4 p.m.

✔ **Study sequins.** The World Figure Skating Museum and Hall of Fame, 20 First St. (☎ **719-635-5200;** Internet www.worldfigure skatingmuseum.org), isn't so much about skating as about the trappings of the sport — the sequined outfits, polished skates, buttons, trophies, and medals. Seeing these showy historical items up close may pique your curiosity about the people behind the glitter. The museum is open June through August, Monday through Saturday from 10 a.m. to 4 p.m.; September through May, Monday through Friday and the first Saturday of each month from 10 a.m. to 4 p.m. Admission costs $3 adults, $2 for children ages 6 through 17 and seniors over 60.

✔ **Get sprung.** At the **Manitou Springs Chamber of Commerce,** 354 Manitou Ave. (☎ **800-642-2567** or 719-685-5089), you can pick up a map identifying ten mineral water springs in the downtown area. In the late 19th century the town promoted the mineral water as a cure-all. It's a fun way to tour the downtown. Bring a cup so that you can fill up and drink if you get thirsty.

✔ **Fall for something.** The promotional literature for **Seven Falls** (☎ **719-632-0752**) calls this area the "Grandest Mile of Scenery" in Colorado. The claim would probably be true if there weren't so many tourists milling around next to the water, and so many man-made structures to accommodate them. To visit the falls, you pay admission and then drive 1 mile up South Cheyenne Canyon to a long parking lot. From there, you can take an elevator or stairway to the Eagle's Nest Platform, the best vantage point from which to see the entire 181-foot-high falls. What appears to be one waterfall actually tumbles off of seven different ledges. If the viewing platform doesn't seem close enough, you can also climb a staircase right next to the water. And if you think the falls may look better under colored floodlights, you can come back in early evening, when the lights come on. It's pretty. Seven Falls is at the end of South Cheyenne Canyon Road, off Cheyenne Boulevard. It's open daily in summer from 8:30 a.m. to 10:00 p.m.; the rest of the year, it's open daily from 9:00 a.m. to 4:15 p.m. (9:30 p.m. on weekends in May and September). Admission before 5 p.m. is $7 for adults, $4.50 for kids ages 6 to 15; after 5 p.m. it's $8.50 adults, $5.50 kids.

If you prefer a more natural setting, go to the nearby **Helen Hunt Falls** (in North Cheyenne Canyon), which costs nothing to visit.

Guided tours

Pikes Peak Tours/Gray Line, 3704 W. Colorado (☎ **800-345-8197** or 719-633-1181), will pick you up at your hotel and take you on a bus tour of Pikes Peak. The four-hour round-trip tour costs $35 for adults over 12, $20 for children 11 and under.

The **Manitou Trolley** (☎ **719-385-RIDE**) drives one-hour loops past the major sights in and around town, including the Garden of the Gods Trading Post. Because you can get on and off, it also doubles as mass transit. The trolley buses, which are free, depart every 30 minutes from sites around town, including the Manitou Springs Chamber of Commerce at 354 Manitou Ave. They run from 7:00 a.m. to 7:45 p.m. daily from May 25 through September 15 and again between Thanksgiving and New Year's Day.

Staying active

With so many full-blown tourist attractions in and around Colorado Springs, you may not spend as much time on the trails as you would in other parts of the state. If you do want to exercise in the backcountry, consider the following activities:

- ✔ **Biking and hiking:** Trails lace the foothills above Colorado Springs. One especially popular and scenic area is North Cheyenne Canyon. Starting high up in the canyon, an 8-mile stretch of the **Gold Camp Road** is closed to motor vehicles. Once a railroad grade, the wide, gradual trail is ideal for family rides and walks. If you want a more challenging ride, you can branch off the Gold Camp Road onto single-track trail. To reach the trailhead, take Cheyenne Boulevard past Seven Falls and Helen Hunt Falls. The trailhead is at the High Drive parking lot, where the road turns from pavement to dirt. **Criterium Bicycles**, 6150 Corporate Dr. (☎ **719-599-0149**), rents full-suspension mountain bikes for $35 per half-day, $50 per whole-day. **Challenge Unlimited,** 204 S. 24th St. (☎ **800-798-5954** or 719-633-6399), will set you up with bikes and help you coast down all 20 miles of the Pikes Peak Highway. Cost for that excursion is $93 per person in the morning, $80 in afternoon (when storms are more likely).

- ✔ **Golfing:** The preferred public course in Colorado Springs is the 27-hole **Patty Jewett Golf Course,** 900 E. Espanola St. (☎ **719-385-6950**). Non-resident greens fees are $27 for 18 holes, $13.50 for 9 holes.

- ✔ **Rafting:** See "Heading Out to Canon City and Royal Gorge," later in this chapter.

Shopping

Colorado Springs has a big mall in addition to the downtown shops in Colorado Springs, Old Colorado City, and Manitou Springs, where shops generally stay open from 9 a.m. to 6 p.m. Anchored by Mervyns,

J.C. Penney, Foleys, and Dillards, **The Citadel,** 750 Citadel Dr. E.
(☎ 719-591-2900; Internet: www.shopthecitadel.com), has 170 shops
on three levels. It's open Monday through Saturday 10 a.m. to 9 p.m.
and Sunday 11 a.m. to 6 p.m. In the following sections, I fill you in on
some other places worth investigating.

Antiques

At **Nevada Village Antiques,** 405 S. Nevada Ave. (☎ 719-473-3351),
eight dealers share a 7,000-square-foot mall. Upwards of 50,000 articles
are for sale.

Books

The Chinook Bookshop, 210 N. Tejon St. (☎ 800-999-1195 or 719-635-
1195; Internet: www.chinookbook.com), has been selling books in
downtown Colorado Springs since 1959. The shop serves free coffee,
defends privacy, opposes censorship, encourages dogs to visit, invites
browsers, and even tolerates shirtlessness. There's also a children's
area and a map room.

Pottery

Van Briggle Art Pottery, at the corner of 21st Street and U.S. 24
(☎ 719-633-7729; Internet: www.vanbriggle.com), has been a working
gallery since 1899. The artisans here make a style of pottery that was
first created by Artus Van Briggle, who's famous in pottery circles. Some
pieces are cast, others are hand-thrown. The studio sells bowls, vases,
and lamps, at prices ranging from $20 to $1,500. Free tours are available.
It's open Monday through Saturday from 8:30 a.m. to 5:00 p.m.

Especially for Kids

Arcade Amusements, Inc., 930 Manitou Ave. (☎ 719-685-9815), in
Manitou Springs, has old-fashioned, analog amusement games such
as pinball and Skee-Ball for grown ups. It also has kiddie rides for,
um, kiddies. And its state-of-the-art video games are sure to please
teenagers. Some of the attractions are in the open air, so you won't
feel claustrophobic. It's open daily from 10 a.m. to midnight during
summer; 11 a.m. to 7 p.m. (and sometimes later) in other months.

Nightlife

Colorado Springs isn't known for its nightlife, but in recent years the
night scene has expanded along with the city.

Hitting the bars and clubs

Most of the hottest nightspots are within walking distance of one another in the heart of Colorado Springs, but there are also a few fun roadhouses and pubs outside of downtown. Your options include the following:

- ✔ Arguably the most popular gathering place in Colorado Springs, **Phantom Canyon Brewing Company,** 2 E. Pikes Peak Ave. (☎ 719-635-2800), has billiards, handcrafted beers, and a menu that's heavy on comfort food.

- ✔ A bartender at **The Ritz Grill,** 15 S. Tejon (☎ 719-635-8484), described his bar as a "martini bar and meat market." The place does, in fact, serve martinis and food. And, on weekends, R&B, blues, and Ska bands lure big crowds onto the small dance floor.

- ✔ **Rum Bay,** 120 N. Tejon St. (☎ 719-635-3522), is the city's hot dance club, and it fuels the fire with 200 different rums.

- ✔ Strangely enough, the best jazz bar in Colorado Springs is in a Chinese restaurant: **Genghis Khan,** 30 E. Pikes Peak Ave. (☎ 719-328-1852), has local jazz and blues acts on Wednesday, Friday, and Saturday nights.

- ✔ Five nights a week, **Acoustic Coffee Lounge,** 5152 Centennial Blvd. (☎ 719-268-9951), books an eclectic lineup of musical acts — everything from folk to jazz. You can get coffee or a smoothie there, or dip into a full bar.

- ✔ **The Underground,** 130 E. Kiowa St. (☎ 719-634-3522), offers alternative and modern music, sometimes live and sometimes not.

- ✔ **Tres Hombres** (☎ 719-687-0625), 12 miles east of Colorado Springs in Woodland Park, brings in smooth pickers.

- ✔ **Colorado Music Hall,** 2475 E. Pikes Peak Ave. (☎ 719-447-9797), an all-ages venue, attracts well-known national touring acts as well as lesser-known regional rock bands.

Classical music

The **Colorado Springs Symphony Orchestra** (☎ 719-633-6698, or 719-520-7469 for ticket information; Internet: wwwcssymphony.org) performs at the acoustically suburb, 2,000-seat **Pikes Peak Center,** 190 S. Cascade Ave. Tickets to performances run between $8 and $42.

Heading Out to Canon City and Royal Gorge

A quick 43-mile drive from Colorado Springs puts you in Canon City and near the mouth of Royal Gorge, a 1,200-foot-deep canyon cut by the Arkansas River. Royal Gorge is the area's big tourist attraction, but the highest concentration of visitors is usually found at the nearby Colorado State Penitentiary, which is not even so much as a "runner-up hotel" in this book.

Getting there

To reach Canon City from Colorado Springs, take Colorado 115 south for 33 miles, and then follow U.S. 50 west for 10 miles to Canon City. Canon City is 39 miles west of I-15 at Pueblo.

Exploring Royal Gorge

Royal Gorge formed when the Arkansas River cut downward through very hard Precambrian rock. It's one the deepest and most scenic canyons in the state. You'd do well to bypass most of the tourist traps near the gorge, but three attractions are worth checking out:

✔ To see the gorge from the top, go to **Royal Gorge Bridge and Park** (☎ **888-333-5597** or 719-275-7507; Internet: www.royal gorgebridge.com), where you can walk (or catch a ride) across the gorge on the world's highest suspension bridge. Built in 1929, the bridge is 880 feet long and more than 1,100 feet above the Arkansas River. Standing on it and staring straight down at the river, feeling the whole structure sway in the wind, is exciting. The admission price also covers rides across the gorge on an aerial tramway, trips up and down a canyon wall on the "world's steepest incline railway," a rim-side mini-railroad, a petting zoo, and live entertainment. A well-marked turnoff for the park departs from U.S. 50 8 miles west of Canon City. It's another 4 miles to the park. The park is open daily from 8:30 or 9:00 a.m. to dusk. Admission costs $17 adults, $15 seniors 60 and up,and $14 children ages 4 to 11.

✔ To see the gorge from the bottom, take the **Royal Gorge Route** (☎ **303-569-2403**) out of Canon City. Don't be fooled into riding either of the two miniature trains on the rim of the gorge. If you want to take the real train along the bottom of Royal Gorge, you have to drive into Canon City and follow the signs to the Santa Fe Depot (on Third Street south of U.S. 50). You'll be rewarded with close-up views of the Arkansas River and the steep canyon walls. The ride goes out and back from Canon City, lasts two hours, and covers 24 miles round-trip. From May 18 to October 1, the train departs at 9 a.m., noon, and 3 p.m. daily. The rest of the year, it leaves at noon on Saturday and Sunday only. Admission is $26.95 adults, $16.50 children ages 3 to 12.

✔ The third and most exciting way to experience the gorge is on a raft floating down the Arkansas River. Because the gorge has some angry (Class 4) whitewater, this trip isn't for everyone, and kids under 15 aren't even allowed. But if you're strong enough to paddle in real rapids and prepared for an adventure, call **Arkansas River Trips (ART)** at ☎ **800-321-4352.** From mid-May through mid-September, ART offers half-day Royal Gorge paddle trips for $52 and full-day trips for $85. If you've never helped paddle a boat in whitewater before, you'll need to take the full-day trip so that you have time to practice before entering the gorge. ART also offers a handful of oar trips. On oar trips, a guide rows the boat solo, using oars mounted in a metal frame (as opposed to the passengers and guide paddling together).

Where to stay and dine

In 1885, two years after the **St. Cloud Hotel,** 631 Main St. (☎ **800-405-9666** or 719-276-2000; Internet: www.stcloudhotel.com), was completed, the owners dismantled it brick by brick and moved it from Silvercliff to Canon City. Since then, it's been the state headquarters for the Colorado Ku Klux Klan, a bus stop, a long-abandoned eyesore, and an asset seized by the state for back taxes. The new ownership has worked hard to restore it to its short-lived glory. Some rooms look Victorian; others look like sets from *The Big Sleep.* On the upside, it's as solid as a pyramid, it has a convenient downtown location, and the prices — $75 to $85 double — are reasonable.

If you want a place without a history, consider the **Comfort Inn Canon City,** 311 Royal Gorge Blvd. (☎ **800-228-5150** or 719-276-6900; Internet: www.choicehotels.com). Rates (including breakfast) run from $65 to $170, depending on the type of room you get and the season.

A neon sign outside **Merlino's Belvedere,** 1330 Elm Ave. in Canon City (☎ **800-625-2526**), nearly always alerts customers that there is "immediate seating" available — no surprise, since the place maxes out at around 500. Inside, most of the rooms feel Denny's-casual, with pastel colors and booths along the walls. This third-generation family-run business appears about as intimate as the Coors family business, but the food tastes homemade. The kitchen staff cooks spaghetti sauce three times a week in batches of over 60 gallons, bakes bread, and whips up gelato with fresh seasonal fruit. If you don't feel like pasta, you can choose between steaks, seafood, chicken, and burgers. A dinner entree will set you back anywhere from $9 to $26. Open for lunch and dinner daily.

Fast Facts: Colorado Springs

AAA

The American Automobile Association has an office at 3525 N. Carefree Circle (☎ 800-283-5222 or 719-591-2222).

Hospitals

Memorial Hospital, 1400 E. Boulder St. (☎ 719-365-5000), has a 24-hour emergency room and offers all critical-care services.

Information

Colorado Springs Convention and Visitors Bureau (☎ 800-DO-VISIT or 719-635-7506; Internet: www.coloradosprings-travel.com) operates a Visitor Information Center at the corner of Cascade and Colorado avenues. For an update on weekly events, call ☎ 719-635-1723. In Manitou Springs, the Chamber of Commerce (☎ 800-642-2567 or 719-685-5089; Internet: www.manitousprings.org) is at 354 Manitou Ave.

Newspapers

Colorado Springs has its own daily paper, the *Gazette Telegraph.* It also tolerates the two Denver dailies, the *Denver Post* and the *Rocky Mountain News.* For a quirkier approach to the news (and for strong arts and entertainment coverage), pick up the *Springs* magazine or the *Independent,* both of which are free tabloids. Many newsstands also sell national newspapers such as the *Wall Street Journal* and *The New York Times.*

Pharmacies

Walgreens Drug Store, 920 N. Circle Dr. (☎ 719-473-9090), fills prescriptions.

Taxes

State tax is 3%, local sales tax is 7%, and lodging tax is 9% for Colorado Springs and slightly higher in Manitou Springs.

Taxis

Call Express Airport Taxi (☎ 719-634-3111), American Cab (☎ 719-637-1111), or Yellow Cab (☎ 719-634-5000).

Transit Information

Contact Colorado Springs Transit (☎ 719-385-7433).

Weather Updates

Call ☎ 719-475-7599.

Part IV
Northern Colorado

"The scenery here is just magnificent. The trees, the plants, and I've never seen so many soaring eagles in one place."

In this part . . .

By now, you may have visited the big cities, and you may have acclimated yourself to Colorado's thin air. So it's time to go higher, up into the northern regions of Colorado and the mountainous country the state is most famous for. In this part, I introduce you to two great mid-size cities (Fort Collins and Boulder) at the foot of the mountains, then take you up into the alpine beauty of Rocky Mountain National Park and to some of the best ski towns that the U.S., never mind Colorado, has to offer. Take a deep breath, throw on an extra layer, drink a glass of water, and keep reading.

Chapter 15

Rocky Mountain National Park

● ●

In This Chapter

▶ Picking a time to go

▶ Hiking, climbing, and finding other cool things to do

▶ Staying at a classic lodge in the gateway towns

● ●

*T*here are mountains all over the western half of Colorado, but the 416 square miles of Rocky Mountain National Park merit special attention for several reasons. A road through the park — Trail Ridge Road — crosses the continental divide at over 12,000 feet. It's the highest continually paved highway in America and probably the easiest way to experience high-alpine tundra, vibrant with life and color for a few short months every summer. With 147 mountain lakes, the park holds more water naturally than most other Colorado mountains. Countless waterfalls and creeks drain high alpine snowfields and glaciers and feed these languid pools. The peaks themselves aren't the highest in Colorado — Longs Peak, at 14,255 feet, is the park's only fourteener — but inside the park, immense walls of granite impose upon the lowlands like barroom bullies. You can't help but notice their brawn. In all, the park has 114 peaks over 10,000 feet. And it's easy to get to. You can be at the eastern entrances only two hours after arriving in Denver.

Choosing a Season to Visit

The park's combination of stunning scenery and easy access has contributed to overcrowding and parking shortages during peak periods. Rocky Mountain's visitation in 2001–2002 was 3.3 million, roughly the same as Yellowstone National Park — in an area one-eighth the size.

 Don't drive through the park on a July or August weekend and expect to get back to nature. To enjoy these mountains in solitude, you need to come in the off-season or else don a backpack and take a long walk.

Unfortunately, the busiest times are also the most opportune periods for covering ground here. If you want to cross the park by car, you'll need to visit between Memorial Day and mid-October, when Trail Ridge

Road is open. The prime months for hiking are July and August, when the snow melts off the highest elevations and uncovers wildflowers in bloom. Summer doesn't last long at 11,000 feet. In May and June, you may still have to hike snowy trails. In late September and October, the trails should be mostly dry, but an early-season snowstorm may dampen your experience. In winter, most park roads stay open, some of the trails are marked for skiing and snowshoeing, and the area suddenly becomes very quiet.

Getting There

Denver International Airport (DIA), 80 miles to the southwest, is the closest major airport to Rocky Mountain National Park. DIA is served by most major domestic carriers and rental-car companies. For information on contacting individual airlines and car-rental agencies, see the Appendix. After you arrive in the state, your options for getting to the park will definitely involve wheels.

Driving

From the city of Denver, it's only 71 miles to Estes Park. Take U.S. 36 to Boulder and then continue on to Estes Park. In Estes Park, U.S. 36 meets U.S. 34, which goes west through the park to Grand Lake and Granby. Coming from the west, make your way to I-40, which passes through Granby en route from I-80 (near Park City, Utah) to I-70 (at Empire, Colorado). In Granby, you'll need to head east on U.S. 34. If you're coming from the south, you can take either I-40 to Granby or Colorado 7, the Peak-to-Peak Scenic Byway, to the east edge of the park.

Busing in

From May 16 through October 1, the **Estes Park Shuttle and Mountain Tours** (☎ 970-586-5151) makes four round-trips daily to Denver International Airport. The shuttle picks up and drops off passengers at most Estes Park locations. One-way fare is $39 per person; a round-trip coasts $75. Charter service is also available.

Planning Ahead

Call or write **Rocky Mountain National Park,** Estes Park, CO 80517-8397 (☎970-586-1206) for information. You can also get information off the Web at www.nps.gov/room or via e-mail at romoinformation@nps.gov.

Backcountry permits are required year-round for overnight stays in the park's backcountry. There's a $15 charge for backcountry permits issued for hikes May through October; the rest of the year, they're free.

Permits for spring, summer, and fall go on sale March 1. If you're set on a particular hike, buy your permit well in advance. On summer weekends in July and August, the most popular areas fill up. Backcountry offices are located at the **Kawuneeche Visitor Center,** outside the park's Grand Lake entrance; and on U.S. 36 near the **Beaver Meadows Visitor Center.** For more information call ☎ **970-586-1242** or write to Backcountry Office, Rocky Mountain National Park, Estes Park, CO 80517.

Three of the park's five campgrounds are always first-come, first-served. Reservations are accepted for the other two for dates during peak season (late May through mid-September). To make a reservation for the **Moraine Park** or **Glacier Basin** campgrounds, call ☎ **800-365-2267** or surf the Internet to http://reservations.nps.gov.

To find out more about the towns bordering the park, contact

✔ The **Estes Park Area Chamber of Commerce,** P.O. Box 3050, Estes Park, CO 80517 (☎ **800-443-7837** or 970-586-4431)

✔ The **Grand Lake Area Chamber of Commerce,** P.O. Box 57, Grand Lake, CO 80447 (☎ **800-531-1019** or 970-627-3372)

✔ The **Greater Granby Chamber of Commerce,** P.O. Box 35, Granby, CO 80446 (☎ **970-887-2311**)

Learning the Lay of the Land

The continental divide goes right through the heart of Rocky Mountain National Park. The main route through the park and across the divide is **Trail Ridge Road,** which meanders 49 miles from a spot near Estes Park on the east side of the park to Grand Lake on the west. On the way, it snakes for 12 miles across alpine tundra, cresting at 12,183 feet near Fall River Pass. Completed in 1932, Trail Ridge Road is the highest continually paved highway in America.

Trail Ridge Road isn't the only way to climb from the area close to Estes Park to the loftier reaches of the park. Beginning in mid-summer (and sometimes earlier), you can also take **Fall River Road.** The first 2 miles of the road are paved and two-way, but near the Endovalley Picnic Area it becomes a one-way dirt road ascending 9 miles to Fall River Pass. This was the first major road in the park when it was completed in 1920, and it doesn't seem to have changed much since then. It's narrow, exposed to steep drop-offs, and has switchbacks that are too sharp for vehicles longer than 25 feet. It ends at Trail Ridge Road, next to the Alpine Visitor Center. Together with Trail Ridge Road, it makes for a fun loop drive when it's open.

Rocky Mountain National Park

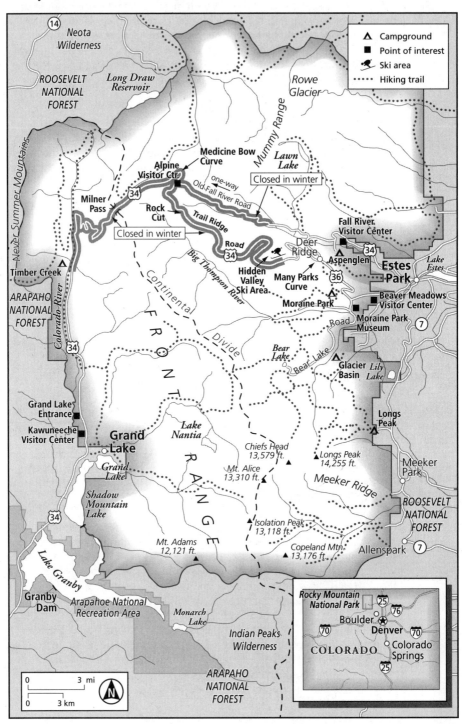

Legend:
- △ Campground
- ■ Point of interest
- 🎿 Ski area
- ⋯ Hiking trail

Neota Wilderness

14

ROOSEVELT NATIONAL FOREST

Long Draw Reservoir

Rowe Glacier

Mummy Range

Medicine Bow Curve

Lawn Lake

Alpine Visitor Ctr.

Milner Pass

34

one-way
Old Fall River Road

Closed in winter

Rock Cut

Trail Ridge

Fall River Visitor Center

Never Summer Mountains

Road

34

Deer Ridge

34

Closed in winter

Aspenglen

Estes Park

Lake Estes

36

Timber Creek

Hidden Valley Ski Area

Many Parks Curve

Beaver Meadows Visitor Center

ARAPAHO NATIONAL FOREST

Colorado River

34

Big Thompson River

Moraine Park

Moraine Park Museum

7

CONTINENTAL DIVIDE

Road

Bear Lake

Bear Lake

Glacier Basin

Lily Lake

FRONT

Grand Lake Entrance

Kawuneeche Visitor Center

Grand Lake

Lake Nantia

Longs Peak

Chiefs Head 13,579 ft.

Longs Peak 14,255 ft.

Meeker Park

Grand Lake

Mt. Alice 13,310 ft.

Meeker Ridge

RANGE

Shadow Mountain Lake

ROOSEVELT NATIONAL FOREST

34

Mt. Adams 12,121 ft.

Isolation Peak 13,118 ft.

Copeland Mtn. 13,176 ft.

Allenspark

7

Lake Granby

Granby Dam

Arapahoe National Recreation Area

Monarch Lake

Indian Peaks Wilderness

ARAPAHO NATIONAL FOREST

Rocky Mountain National Park

25

76

Boulder

70

Denver

70

COLORADO

Colorado Springs

25

0   3 mi
0   3 km

N

Rocky Mountain National Park has three main entrances. From the west, U.S. 34 enters the park near Grand Lake and becomes Trail Ridge Road. On the east, U.S. 34 and U.S. 36 enter the park a few miles apart near Estes Park and then meet at Deer Ridge Junction. You can use either U.S. 34 or U.S. 36 to reach Trail Ridge Road. However, U.S. 34 also provides access to Fall River Road, and U.S. 36 takes you closer to the hiking trails in Moraine Park and Glacier Basin.

Other park roads are spurs leading to trailheads in alpine basins. On the east side of the park, **Bear Lake Road** branches south off of U.S. 36 and provides access to two large campgrounds and some of the park's most popular hiking trails. Because the parking areas near popular trailheads often fill up, the park operates two shuttle-bus routes in this area. You can catch either shuttle at the Visitor Transportation System parking area across from the **Glacier Basin Campground.** (For more on the shuttles, see "Getting around," later in this chapter.)

In the southeast corner of the park, a road goes 2 miles east from Colorado 7 to the **Wild Basin Trailhead.** Just north of there, a spur road off of Colorado 7 goes east to a campground, ranger station, and the parking area for the **Longs Peak Trailhead.** The highest mountain in the park, 14,255-foot **Longs Peak,** is located nearby.

Arriving in the Park

There's a visitor center at each primary park entrance, as well as one right in the middle of the park. All have information desks, interpretive displays, and park literature.

- ✔ The **Beaver Meadows Visitor Center** (☎ 970-586-1206) is on U.S. 36 just outside the Beaver Meadows entrance. It's open daily from 8 a.m. to 9 p.m. from Memorial Day through Labor Day, 8 a.m. to 5 p.m. the rest of the year.

- ✔ The **Fall River Visitor Center,** just outside the Fall River entrance on U.S. 34, opened in 2000. Open daily from 9:00 a.m. to 5:30 p.m. from late March through late October, it has displays on wildlife.

- ✔ The **Alpine Visitor Center** is situated where Fall River Road and Trail Ridge Road converge. Located on the tundra, this visitor center has displays on high-alpine plant and animal life. It's open from 10:30 a.m. to 4:30 p.m. daily, Memorial Day through mid-October.

- ✔ The **Kawuneeche Visitor Center** (☎ 970-586-1206), on U.S. 34 just outside the Grand Lake Entrance, is open daily from 8 a.m. to 6 p.m. from Memorial Day through Labor Day, with shorter hours the rest of the year. It has a backcountry office and an auditorium that shows a 20-minute video on the park.

Paying fees

Park admission, good for seven days, costs $15 per week per vehicle, $5 for individuals on foot, bicycle, or motorcycle. A $50 **National Parks Pass** covers admission to all National Parks for one year from the date of purchase. An **Annual Pass** to Rocky Mountain National Park costs $30. For $10, people over 62 can buy a **Golden Age Pass,** which entitles the holder to free admission for life at all federal fee areas.

Getting around

Driving through Rocky Mountain National Park isn't difficult; the hard part, during high season at least, is finding parking near your favorite trailhead. During mid-summer, the park often has more cars than it can accommodate. The busiest time is in July and August between 10 a.m. and 3 p.m. One of the busiest areas is 10-mile **Bear Lake Road,** where many popular hiking trails are located.

During 2003 and 2004, the last few miles of Bear Lake Road will close to private vehicles, adding to an already challenging situation. If you're on Bear Lake Road but can't park at (or reach) the trailhead you desire, park at the **Visitor Transportation System** parking area (across from Glacier Basin Campground) and use one of two shuttle systems serving the lot.

The **Moraine Park** route makes seven stops between the parking area and the **Fern Lake Trailhead.** Buses on that route run every 20 minutes between 7:30 a.m. and 7:30 p.m. The **Bear Lake Route** makes three stops between the parking area and Bear Lake. Buses on the Bear Lake Route run every 30 minutes between 5 a.m. and 10 p.m. The shuttle service operates daily from May through October. During absolute peak periods, there may be times when even the Visitor Transportation System parking area fills up. When this happens, try the Moraine Park Museum lot. If that's full too, it may be time to find an activity outside the park. In winter of 2003 and 2004, the road will be open to Bear Lake.

Considering safety

Although Rocky Mountain National Park isn't an especially dangerous place, it does sport a few hazards that could sour your visit. Take the proper precautions and you should be fine. Check out the following hazards and tips for dealing with or preventing them:

> ✔ **Animal encounters:** Most bear encounters happen because people aren't careful with food. When car-camping inside Rocky Mountain National Park, stow your food in airtight containers inside your vehicle, out of sight, and never, ever in your tent. Mountain lion encounters are rare, but a lion did attack a child inside the park in 1997. When they do attack, cougars usually go

after children or small adults, often when the victims are running. If you encounter a very large cat in the forest, do your best to act like something other than a deer (seriously). Stand up tall, talk, walk backwards slowly, and toss a few rocks in the general direction of the cat. Whatever you do, don't bound away through the underbrush. As for the elk and moose, a general rule is to keep your distance, especially during the fall mating season or if calves are present. Elk and moose often bluff charges, but real attacks do happen.

✔ **Falls:** Surprisingly, falls are the leading cause of death in the park, and not because there are so many technical climbers here. Most falling deaths are caused by unspectacular tumbles onto rocks. So watch your step.

✔ **Hypothermia:** A summer rain sounds innocent enough, but above 10,000 feet, the water is usually icy enough to make you hypothermic. Even on warm, seemingly clear days, carry insulating layers of synthetic fabrics such as polypropylene and polar fleece — cotton sweatshirts won't do — as well as a water-resistant shell. And eat and drink regularly. Hydration is a key factor in preventing hypothermia.

✔ **Altitude sickness:** Headaches, nausea, and fatigue are common when people move rapidly from sea level to high elevations. The best way to avoid altitude sickness is to acclimate and take it easy for a few days at lower elevations before climbing any mountains. Drink plenty of water, and avoid alcohol and caffeine. If you have a headache or nausea, the symptoms should subside if you descend 2,000 to 3,000 feet. Seek immediate medical attention if you experience vomiting, coughing, or a loss of coordination.

✔ **Avalanches:** In general, staying off of steep snowfields in the backcountry is a wise move if you don't know about snow safety. During late spring and summer, watch for rapidly warming snow. If you're sinking in deeper than your boot tops in soggy snow and your route crosses steep slopes, it's time to switch to another activity.

✔ **Lightning:** Afternoon thunderstorms are common in summer. If a storm approaches while you're in the park, the best thing to do is vacate exposed peaks and ridgelines until it passes. While heading into heavily forested areas is a good idea, *do not stand under an isolated tree during a lightning storm!*

Enjoying the Park

Most people explore Rocky Mountain National Park by driving some or all of Trail Ridge Road, which tops out at 12,183-foot Fall River Pass. Before starting your drive, stop at a visitor center and pick up a *Trail Ridge Road Guide* (cost: 25¢). This self-guided driving tour provides descriptions of 12 numbered sites along Trail Ridge Road. Even if you don't want to make all the stops, don't miss the following:

- ✔ **Never Summer Ranch:** Located on the west side of the park, this well-preserved homestead is one of the best places in the West to see how the ranch families of a century ago lived. The ranch house and outbuildings are full of the belongings, tools, and furniture of the original inhabitants. And the ranch is nestled in a forest near the Colorado River, a half-mile away from the parking lot. (It's a 1-mile round-trip hike.) During summer, volunteers guide free tours of the ranch and outbuildings, open daily from 10 a.m. to 4 p.m.

- ✔ **Alpine Visitor Center:** One of the subtle delights of Rocky Mountain National Park is its tundra. Many well-insulated plants and animals survive above 11,000 feet, enduring a frost-free season of only eight to ten weeks. To find out more about them, stop at the Alpine Visitor Center, and then drive a few miles east to **Rock Cut** and hike a mile round-trip on the **Tundra Communities Trail.** (For more on this trail, skip ahead to "Taking a hike.")

- ✔ **Moraine Park Museum:** Located on the **Bear Lake Road,** this may be the best place in Colorado to learn about mountains. Its exhibits on mountain-building clarify the effects of tectonic activity, glaciation, volcanism, weathering, and other influences. Don't miss it. It's open daily from 9:00 a.m. to 4:30 p.m. from mid-April through mid-October.

Taking a hike

If you start your hike early in the morning, you'll have an easier time parking, and you'll also avoid afternoon thunderstorms, which are common during the summer months. Below are areas with great hiking, and descriptions of prime trails.

The best way to explore Rocky Mountain National Park is by getting out of the car and hiking some of its 350 miles of trails.

East side (Bear Lake area)

With high-alpine lakes, immense snowfields, views of Longs Peak, and thundering waterfalls, Bear Lake is one of the most scenic areas anywhere. As you may expect, the Bear Lake area lures people by the shuttle-load. Even after hiking a mile or so down a trail here, you can still expect company.

Bear Lake Trail

This wide, gravel trail circles Bear Lake and has benches along the way. The trail is considered handicap-accessible, but there are a few steep climbs. (A sign at the trailhead provides detailed information on gradients and widths.) Always busy, the trail opens onto views of Longs Peak and Hallet Peak.

Distance: 0.5 miles round-trip. Level: Easy. Access: At Bear Lake. Follow Bear Lake Road 9.7 miles off of U.S. 36.

Slab avalanches

Colorado leads the nation in avalanche fatalities. Most of these deaths result from *slab avalanches,* in which a slab of snow shears off of the snow underneath it. Imagine tilting a layer cake until the top part slides off, and you'll have a good picture of what a slab avalanche is like. At a critical angle, it may take a little prodding to make the top layer slide. In an unstable snowfield, the weight of one person can sometimes trigger a large avalanche that's been close to happening. If you're unfamiliar with the rules of snow safety, hire a guide before traveling the backcountry in winter and spring.

Bear Lake to Lake Haiyaha

As you climb 745 vertical feet over 2.1 miles (one-way) from Bear Lake to Lake Haiyaha, you'll pass a string of mountain lakes, each with its own unique splendor. First there's Nymph Lake (0.5 miles), a tiny mirror flecked with green lilies and golden flowers. Then comes Dream Lake, flush against mountainsides on which immense, hanging snowfields dribble waterfalls. You'll lose a few people if you continue to Lake Haiyaha. There, you'll have to clamber across boulders to reach the edge of a lake so clear, you can see fish 30 feet away.

Distance: 4.2 miles round-trip. Level: Moderate. Access: At Bear Lake. Follow Bear Lake Road 9.7 miles off of U.S. 36.

East side (Longs Peak area)

Among the dozens of immense peaks in the park, the park's lone fourteener, Longs Peak, attracts the most attention. Thousands of people climb to the top every year, and for some it's the experience of a lifetime.

However, bear in mind that if you're willing to walk far enough to climb Longs Peak, you could also climb a smaller, equally scenic peak in near solitude. That said, here's one trail that heads up Longs Peak.

Keyhole Route up Longs Peak

Unless you're a technical climber, you'll need to take the Keyhole Route to reach the summit. The first 6 miles are on a rocky but clearly defined hiking trail. Where the trail ends in a boulder field, the 2-mile route to the summit begins. You'll alternately clamber across boulder fields and traverse ledges to reach the top. Bull's-eyes on the rocks help make sure you stay on course. You'll need good hiking boots in order to grip on steep, slippery rocks. And you'll need to prepare carefully by bringing lots of food and water, insulating layers, a wind- and water-resistant shell, and a headlamp. The window for summiting via the Keyhole Route is usually mid-July to early September.

Because the round trip usually takes 12 to 15 hours, many hikers break up the climb by spending the night at a mid-mountain campsite. Call the **Backcountry Office** (☎ **970-586-1242**) several months in advance in order to procure a Backcountry Permit for a campsite on Longs Peak.

Distance: 16 miles round-trip, 4,855 vertical feet to from trailhead to summit. Level: Strenuous. Access: Longs Peak Ranger Station, 1 mile off Colorado 7, 7 miles south of Estes Park.

Southeast corner (Wild Basin area)

Trails in Wild Basin are less crowded than ones around Bear Lake — yet still busy during high season. The area is lower and warmer than Bear Lake.

Wild Basin Trail to Ouzel Falls

This trail follows North St. Vrain Creek and then crosses two of its tributaries, climbing gradually for about 900 feet en route to Ouzel Falls. The prettiest sight along the way may be Calypso Cascades, where water dances over boulders as smooth as marble, passing under logs jammed helter-skelter like pick-up sticks. The trail crosses an area where wildflowers have spruced up a scar left by a 1978 forest fire. Then comes Ouzel Falls, where the creek arcs off a ledge and into a pool below.

Distance: 5.4 miles round-trip. Level: Moderate. Access: Across from Wild Basin Ranger Station. To reach the station, follow Colorado 7 for 13.5 miles south of Estes Park; turn off at the Wild Basin Ranger Station sign and follow the signs.

West side

There's a lot of hiking on the west side of the park, including some trails near Grand Lake. Two prime trailheads are right across from each other on Trail Ridge Road, between Farview Curve and Timber Creek Campground. The less strenuous option, **Colorado River Trail,** is on the west side of the road, and **Timber Lake Trail** is on the east side. For a short hike, try **Alpine Communities Trail,** which is east of the continental divide but on the west side of the park.

Alpine Communities Trail

This paved, half-mile trail gradually climbs across alpine tundra to some craggy rocks. I like it because it makes you feel the raw, unfettered elements in the high mountains. The plants here are so low and tiny, they seem to vibrate in the breezes instead of swaying. You can see where the saturated and oft-frozen earth has squeezed broken rocks onto its surface. And on a clear day, there are smatterings of color everywhere: yellow and purple flowers, greenish lichens, and a cornflower blue sky.

Distance: 1 mile round-trip. Level: easy. Access: At Rock Cut parking area on Trail Ridge Road.

Glaciation

The Rocky Mountains get their elevation from tectonic activity. Where the Pacific plate slips under the Continental plates, the land gets pushed up. That elevated land has been shaped by glaciation. In the Ice Ages of the past 2 million years, immense glaciers formed and gradually crept downhill, applying great pressure to the earth. As they did, they scooped out steep bowls known as *cirques* high in the mountains. Further downhill, they widened the mountain valleys and left basins where lakes form today. Like plows, they also pushed rocks off to the sides. These rocks form spines known as *moraines*. A few small glaciers remain inside Rocky Mountain National Park, but they're melting fast.

Colorado River Trail to Lulu City

The National Park Service calls this a moderately difficult trail, but the trail is difficult only because it's 3.7 miles (one-way) to Lulu City. As it follows the Colorado River upstream through forests and meadows, this wide, dusty boulevard climbs only about 350 feet. After 2 miles you'll pass an old mine and two cabins in Shipler Park. Another 1.7 miles takes you to the old mining town of Lulu City — which is hardly a lulu of a city. (Seems that after the miners left, the ranchers who followed carted away most of the wood from the buildings.) The trail continues on to the headwaters of the Colorado River, 8 miles from the trailhead.

Distance: 7.4 miles round-trip. Level: Moderate. Access: Well-marked parking area for trailhead, on west side of Trail Ridge Road between Farview Curve and Timber Creek Campground.

Timber Lake Trail

You have to work hard to reach the high-alpine lakes on the west side of the park, but the extra effort makes the lakes seem more stunning when you get there. (On the east side, you can drive right up to many of them.) This trail steadily climbs 2,060 feet over the course of 4.7 miles to Timber Lake, cupped between Jackstraw Mountain and Mount Ida. The trail is long, but smooth and not particularly steep — most of the grades are user-friendly. Even so, you should set aside most of a day to go up and back. Most of the way, pine forest shelters you. As you near the lake, the trail becomes more rugged and the forest thins, eventually giving way to alpine meadows alongside Timber Creek.

Distance: 9.6 miles round-trip. Level: Strenuous. Access: Well-marked parking area for trailhead, on east side of Trail Ridge Road between Farview Curve and Timber Creek Campground.

Roving with rangers

Ranger programs are scheduled throughout the year, with a full schedule offered from June through September. They include short walks, talks, and guided hikes of up to four hours. For a full schedule, consult the park's free newspaper, *Rocky Mountain National Park High Country Headlines*.

Watching wildlife

It's hard *not* to see wildlife in and around the park. About 3,000 **elk** range from the tundra near the continental divide all the way down to the meadows around Estes Park. They're especially numerous on the eastern side of the park. Look for **Bighorn sheep** on the tundra and near Sheep Lake in Horseshoe Park, on the eastern side of the park. The park no longer has grizzly bears, but it does have a healthy population of **black bears.** Black bears often turn up near campgrounds, residences, and businesses where people have not been careful with their food or trash. Watch for them in the forest. **Coyotes** prefer open areas but can be found anywhere in and around the park. They look like lanky reddish-brown dogs, only, unlike dogs, they carry their tails low between their legs. **Moose** gravitate to damp, boggy lakes, river bottoms, and forest. Most moose sightings occur on the west side of the park.

Staying Active

With mountains, rivers, lakes, trails, and sheer rock walls, Rocky Mountain National Park attracts a range of athletes and outdoor enthusiasts. Outside the park, you'll find still more places to recreate, including less pristine settings such as golf courses and reservoirs.

Inside the park

Hiking isn't the only activity you can do inside the park. Here are some other options:

 ✔ **Biking:** Mountain biking is prohibited inside Rocky Mountain National Park. However, road cyclists often cross the park on Trail Ridge Road. The road is narrow, steep, and high. Traffic can be heavy, and the sightlines for drivers are poor. Experienced cyclists will probably enjoy the ride on weekdays; on weekends, however, you're better off avoiding the crush of traffic.

✔ **Fishing:** The park's lakes and streams have four species of trout, but most of the fish are small. Only artificial lures and flies are allowed inside the park, and fishing is prohibited in certain lakes and streams. Before entering the park, pick up a Colorado fishing license (cost: $5.25 for one day) at **Estes Park Mountain Shop** (☎ 970-586-6548), 358 E. Elkhorn Ave., in Estes Park; or at **Budget Tackle** (☎ 970-887-9344), 255 E. Agate Ave., in Granby. And check at a visitor center about park-specific regulations.

✔ **Horseback riding:** Riding is allowed on 260 miles of trails (also used for hiking) inside the park. **Hi Country Stables** keeps horses near **Glacier Creek** (☎ 970-586-3244) and **Moraine Park** (☎ 970-586-2327) inside the park boundaries. A walking ride, through forest and across streams costs $40 for two hours.

✔ **Mountaineering:** Skilled mountaineers often attempt challenging routes inside Rocky Mountain National Park. The park presents tests ranging from glacier travel to ice climbing to multiday ascents of rock walls. If you'd like to try your hand at technical mountaineering, contact the **Colorado Mountain School (CMS),** P.O. Box 1846, Estes Park, CO 80517 (☎ **888-CMS-7783** or 970-586-5758; Internet: www.cmschool.com). The lone guide service in Rocky Mountain National Park, CMS guides half-day excursions ($170 for one or two people) and full-day excursions ($230 for one person, $320 for two people), in addition to offering a variety of classes.

In the gateway communities

The mountain scenery doesn't end at the park boundaries. There's a lot to do on both sides of the park, including the following:

✔ **Boating:** Just west of the park is **Grand Lake,** the largest natural lake in Colorado. A few steps from the boardwalk in downtown Grand Lake (the town), **Solvista Marina,** 1030 Lake Ave. (☎ **970-627-8158**), offers lake tours (cost: $10 adults, $5 children 12 and under) and rents fishing boats ($45 per hour), pontoon boats ($50 per hour), speed boats ($50 per hour), pedal boats ($10 per hour), canoes ($20 per hour), and one- and two-person kayaks ($15 per hour and $20 per hour, respectively). Kids will enjoy driving the bumper boats ($5 for 10 minutes) — motorized inner tubes in a watery corral that encourages collisions. There's also a sandy public beach and swimming area. Below Grand Lake, the Colorado River has been dammed twice, creating two reservoirs, **Shadow Mountain Lake** and **Lake Granby.** When full, they're considerably larger than Grand Lake, although, unlike Grand Lake, they're not surrounded by forest or particularly scenic. You can also boat on the east side of the park. Just east of downtown Estes Park is a small reservoir, **Lake Estes,** with a sandy beach and wading area. **The Lake Estes Marina** (☎ **970-586-2011**), half a mile east of town on Highway 34, rents fishing boats ($20 per hour), two-person sport boats ($22 per hour), pontoon boats ($34 per hour), large pontoon boats ($42 per hour), paddle boats ($18 per hour), and canoes ($12 per hour).

✔ **Cross-country skiing:** You can skate-ski on 95 kilometers of track at **Snow Mountain Ranch** (☎ **970-726-4628**), on U.S. 40 9 miles south of Granby. Snow Mountain has 5 kilometers of dog-friendly trails and illuminates another 1.5 kilometers of track for night skiing. Passes cost $12 for adults, $5 for ages 6 to 12.

✔ **Golfing:** West of the park, near Granby, championship golf courses are popping up faster than you can say "bogey." The course nearest the park is the 18-hole, par-72 **Grand Lake Golf Course** (☎ **800-551-8580** or 970-887-2709; Internet: www.grandlakegolf.com). Greens fees are $60 for 18 holes, $35 for 9 holes. Estes Park has two courses. Located on the banks of Lake Estes, the **Lake Estes Executive 9-Hole Golf Course,** 690 Big Thompson Ave. (U.S. 34; ☎ **970-586-8176**), costs $13 for nine holes, $9 in the afternoon. The 18-hole **Estes Park Golf Course,** 1080 S. St. Vrain Street (☎ **970-586-8146**), often hosts herds of deer and elk, so you may have company. Greens fees are $36, $22 after 3 p.m.

On the slopes

Solvista Golf and Ski Ranch, near Granby, spans two hills amid gently undulating rangeland where, come spring, sagebrush pokes through melting snow. The 33 mostly gentle trails funnel down to a single base area, so rounding up the kids here is easy.

In the mid-1990s, Solvista's ownership theorized that this environment could be as pleasant for humans as it had been for cows in years past. After trading for 1,000 acres of Bureau of Land Management land near the old Silver Creek Ski Area, they laid plans for a year-round resort with recreation options ranging from cross-country skiing on a groomed, 40-kilometer trail system, to golf on a 7,200-yard, championship golf course. The development is in its fledgling stage — during the next 20 years, Solvista hopes to build as many as 5,000 single-family homes and condominiums. If the resort can complete this build-out without disrupting what today is a remarkably serene place — no easy task — Solvista will remain a nice place for family ski vacations.

For the lowdown on the trails, terrain, and other vital information on Solvista Golf and Ski Ranch, see Table 15-1.

Table 15-1: Ski Report: Solvista Golf and Ski Ranch
Location: 1.5 miles south of Granby on U.S. 40
Trails: 33
30 percent beginner
50 percent intermediate
20 percent advanced/expert
Vertical drop: 1,000 feet
Base elevation: 8,202 feet
Summit elevation: 9,202 feet
Skiable terrain: 287 acres
Average annual snowfall: 220 inches
Lifts: 5
Snow phone: ☎ 800-754-7458
Central reservations: ☎ 888-283-7458
Internet: www.solvista.com
2002–2003 high-season adult lift ticket: $41

Where to Stay

There's no lodging inside Rocky Mountain National Park. However, the park does have 5 campgrounds totaling 587 sites. The **Timber Creek, Aspen Glen,** and **Longs Peak** campgrounds are always first-come, first-served. Reservations are accepted for the **Moraine Park** or **Glacier Basin** campgrounds for dates during peak season (late May through mid-September). To reserve a spot, call ☎ **800-365-2267** or surf the Internet to http://reservations.nps.gov. The cost per site is $18. Although you can't stay in the park, accommodations are available in the gateway communities of Estes Park, Grand Lake, and Granby.

The top hotels east of the park

Most of the lodging east of Rocky Mountain National Park is in the tourism-happy town of Estes Park. Estes Park seems to have more candy stores, T-shirt shops, and ice cream parlors per capita than anywhere else in the state — with the possible exception of Grand Lake, on the park's west side. Yet it's also pretty. All around town, elk and deer wander grassy hillsides amid greenish, lichen-stained rocks and ponderosa pines. When it comes to lodging, you'll find everything from tiny riverfront cabins to immense historic hotels.

Aspen Lodge at Estes Park

$$ **Estes Park**

Aspen Lodge sits on a forested hillside overlooking Longs Peak, and the Longs Peak Trailhead, inside Rocky Mountain National Park, is just a few miles away. The Lodge's American Plan covers three meals a day plus activities such as nature walks, guided hikes, campfire stories, and sing-alongs. The price also includes rackets and balls for the lodge's two tennis courts, horseshoes for the horseshoe pit, and boats and fishing poles for the small pond. If you prefer exploring on your own, ask for the standard rate, which includes only breakfast. Some of the rooms are in a 30,000-square-foot conference center and lodge — the largest log structure in Colorado. Others are in 1940s and 1950s cabins. The rooms are unspectacular, but the views of Longs Peak are hard to top.

8120 Highway 7, Estes Park. ☎ *800-332-6867 or 970-586-8133. Fax: 970-586-8133. Internet:* www.aspenlodge.com. *Rack rates: May 23–Aug 25 lodge rooms and one-bedroom cabins $199–$219, two-bedroom cabins $219–$239; Aug 26–May22 lodge rooms and one-bedroom cabins $109–$139; two-bedroom cabins $139–$159. Six-day American Plan (available June 15–Aug. 22) $1,299 single adult, $999 adult in family, $699 children 3–12. Three-day American Plan $699 single adult, $549 adult in family, $359 children 3–12. AE, DC, DISC, MC, V.*

Chalet at Marys Lake Lodge

$$–$$$ **Estes Park**

Built between 1919 and 1925, this immense log building sat abandoned for more than two decades after half the structure burned down in 1978. The original windows remain, but the floor plan of the lodge has been reconfigured. Instead of having 300 rooms, the place now has 13 suites and 3 studios, all of which have replicas of Country Victorian antiques. The studios are compact and have limited views, but the suites have sitting rooms and plenty of floor space, and they overlook Marys Lake and the Mummy Range. Perhaps because the inn didn't reopen until 2001, the prices are down-to-earth. Like the nearby Stanley Hotel, it's rumored to be haunted.

2625 Marys Lake Rd., Estes Park. ☎ *877-442-6279 or 970-586-8958. Fax: 970-586-5308. Internet:* www.maryslakelodge.com. *Rack rates: Studios $79–$99, suites $109–$189. AE, DISC, MC, V.*

Olympus Motor Lodge
$$ **Estes Park**

Saying that Estes Park has a lot of motels would be an understatement. Still, this motel is a little different. Each room has a unique quilt, and the walls are painted to match the colors in the quilt. (Whatever you do, don't spill.) The owners deliver fresh-baked muffins to the rooms every morning, and they serve tea and espresso in the 1922 lodge building. Perched on a hillside with distant views of Longs Peak, every room has a patio complete with old-style metal lawn furniture.

2365 Big Thompson Ave. (P.O. Box 547), Estes Park. ☎ *800-248-8141 or 970-586-8141. Fax: 970-586-8142. Internet:* www.estespark.us/olympuslodge. *Rack rates: Jun 16–Sept 14 $78–$92; Sep 15–Jun 15 $55–$75. AE, DC, DISC, MC, V.*

Stanley Hotel
$$$–$$$$ **Estes Park**

The Stanley Hotel may have inspired Stephen King's horror story *The Shining,* but the place is more picturesque than ominous. It's a wide, symmetrical building, four stories high, with a white exterior and a red roof. Fanlights in the windows, Corinthian columns, and a bell tower together give it a classical appearance, and its position on a hillside lends it extra prominence. The hotel's rooms have been recently renovated and all are bright and full of either genuine antiques or reproductions. The superior rooms, which look south to the peaks along the continental divide, cost $20 more than the standard rooms, which look north toward the hotel's courtyard gardens and smaller hills.

333 Wonderview Ave. (P.O. Box 1767), Estes Park. ☎ *800-976-1377. Fax: 970-586-3673. Rack rates: Standard $129–$159; superior, $149–$189; deluxe $169–$209. AE, DC, DISC, MC, V.*

A shining inspiration

In 1973, a stay at the Stanley Hotel helped inspire Stephen King to write *The Shining.* King was experiencing what must have been a rare case of writer's block when he heard about Trail Ridge Road — the road that runs through Rocky Mountain National Park — closing for the winter. An idea took root. In King's book, the haunted hotel called the Overlook is a dead ringer for the Stanley. Parts of the original film version show Timberline Lodge in Oregon, but the made-for-TV remake was set at the Stanley Hotel, and King himself oversaw the production.

YMCA of the Rockies Estes Park Center
$$ Estes Park

Families and groups come here to experience a wholesome, summer-camp-style atmosphere. Situated on 860 acres, the YMCA of the Rockies has huge playing fields, hotel rooms for 450, and vacation homes and cabins for 210 (the small, rustic cabins are especially good values). You can swim in an indoor pool; play horseshoes, basketball, or volleyball; ride horses; or shoot archery. There's a restaurant on the premises, plus three other dining rooms for groups. It's a family-oriented place, but anyone can come here. For $5 per day, you can buy a temporary YMCA membership that allows you to rent a room.

2515 Tunnel Rd., Estes Park. ☎ ***970-586-3341***, *ext. 1010. Fax: 970-586-6078. Internet:* www.ymcarockies.org. *Rack rates: Rustic cabin, $71; four-bedroom vacation home, $266. MC, V.*

The top hotels west of the park

Located just outside the west entrance to the park, **Grand Lake** mirrors the touristy surroundings of Estes Park (on the park's east side), with a few differences. Grand Lake is more remote and, with a year-round population of around 400, much smaller. It's built on the shores of the largest natural lake in Colorado. It also has a downtown boardwalk. For lodging, Grand Lake has a historic lodge, lakeside cabins, and motels. For less expensive lodging, drive another 12 miles southwest on U.S. 34 to the ranching town of **Granby.**

Grand Lake Lodge
$–$$ Grand Lake

Built in 1920, this lodge sits on a hilltop high above Grand Lake. Because Rocky Mountain National Park surrounds the lodge on three sides, guests can hike out of their cabins and keep going into the park. On the lodge's forested acreage, you can choose among activities such as basketball, volleyball, or horseshoes, or best of all, recline next to a pool that seems to hover over the lake. Most cabins sleep two to six people, and the larger units have fully equipped kitchenettes; the smallest cabins look like standard motel rooms and only sleep two. The setting of the lodge is stunning, and some of the rooms offer great views of the lake.

15500 U.S. 34, just outside the west entrance to Rocky Mountain National Park (P.O. Box 569), Grand Lake. ☎ ***970-627-3967***. *Fax: 970-627-9495. Internet:* www.grand lakelodge.com. *Rack rates: Cabins $75–$170. AE, DC, DISC, MC, V. Open May 31–Sept. 15.*

Kicking Horse Condominiums

$$–$$$$$ **Granby**

In 2001, Solvista Golf and Ski Ranch, formerly Silver Creek Ski Area, constructed 115 new luxury "ski-in, golf-out" condominiums as part of an expansion that's slated to continue for years to come. Sandwiched on a hillside between the ski area (above) and the golf course (below), the condos have huge windows that open onto the golf course fairways, rangeland, and the far-off foothills of Rocky Mountain National Park. They sleep four to eight people, and all have private decks, full kitchens, washer/dryers, gas fireplaces, and TV/VCRs. Solvista offers ski and golf packages that include lodging in a variety of accommodations, including these units.

1000 Village Road, (P.O. Box 1110), Granby. ☎ *888-283-7458. Internet* www.solvista.com. *Rates: One-bedroom $101–$333; two-bedroom $126–$405; two-bedroom with loft $143–$425. AE, DC, DISC, MC, V.*

Trail Riders Motel

$ **Granby**

This is the little 1930s motel that could — and can. After 70 years or so, it's still tidy, well maintained, and thick walled. In addition to old-time features such as knotty wood paneling, nooks with wooden benches and tables, and steam heat, the rooms also have modern amenities such as microwaves, refrigerators, and coffeemakers. Ask for a spot away from Grand Avenue — the rooms nearest the road look noisy, though one employee begs to differ. This motel charges up to $20 less for one person than for two people, making it an attractive option for those traveling alone. (Prices listed here are for two sharing a room.)

On U.S. 40 (P.O. Box 1005), Granby. ☎ *970-887-3738. Rack rates: $55–$65 double. DISC, MC, V.*

Lemmon Lodge

$$–$$$$ **Grand Lake**

Lemmon Lodge rents out 19 cabins and houses that are on or near the shore of Grand Lake (the water) and a short walk from Grand Lake (the town). Privately owned, they range from luxury homes with lake views to a rustic cabin. All of them have full kitchens or kitchenettes. The lodge employees do their best to honestly describe the different offerings. No matter what you choose, you'll be in a nice spot.

1224 Lake Ave. (P.O. Box 514), Grand Lake. ☎ *970-627-3314 (summer) or 970-725-3511 (winter). Internet:* www.lemmonlodge.com. *Rack rates: May 17–Jun 20 $75–$225; Jun 21–Sep 2 $100–$330. MC, V.*

Silver Creek Lodging
$–$$$$ Granby

This large condominium hotel stands alone in high desert along I-40, a mile south of Granby. It's convenient to Winter Park, Rocky Mountain National Park, and Grand Lake. The closest attraction is Solvista Golf and Ski Ranch, just a mile up the road. Fortunately, the hotel is self-sufficient. It has an indoor/outdoor pool, four hot tubs, a restaurant and bar, an exercise room, a small store, a game room, and tennis courts. The rooms are privately owned. The studio I stayed in seemed to belong in the early '80s: A staircase spiraled up to an upstairs loft; the walls were lined by thin, vertical mirrored stripes; there was a gas fireplace; and in the full kitchen, the microwave had a dial for a timer.

P.O. Box 4222, Silver Creek. ☎ *800-926-4386 or 970-887-2131. Fax: 970-887-4090. Internet:* www.silvercreeklodging.com. *Rack rates: Standard $69–$139; studios $89–$189. AE, DC, DISC, MC, V.*

Where to Dine

Rocky Mountain National Park doesn't have any full-service restaurants. However, the gateway communities of Estes Park, Grand Lake, and Granby have dozens of restaurants.

Be careful: There are some bad restaurants in these parts. But if you stick to my recommendations, you should be safe.

The top restaurants east of the park

Hunan Restaurant
$ Estes Park   MANDARIN/SZECHUAN

Everything about this eatery sounds familiar: Hunan Restaurant serves Mandarin cuisine, has daily lunch specials, accepts no substitutions, fries egg rolls, steams rice, and gives out fortune cookies for dessert. You've already eaten at similar restaurants a hundred times, even if you've never been to Estes Park. But three factors make this particular Hunan Restaurant worthwhile: Despite being in a tourist town, its prices are barely higher than at the other Hunan Restaurants of the world; it serves tasty fare; and, most importantly, a lot of nearby eateries are horrible. Another bonus is that you can usually get a table here, even when the town is packed.

460 W. Riverside Drive (in Picadilly Square). ☎ *970-586-8287. Reservations accepted. Main courses: $6.25–$13.95. Open: Mon–Sat lunch and dinner; Sunday dinner only. DISC, MC, V.*

Notchtop Bakery & Café

$–$$ Estes Park   NATURAL FOODS

Notchtop Bakery serves the type of fresh, light, creative food that's popular in Boulder and all too rare in Estes Park. To supplement its gourmet baked goods, the Notchtop cooks omelettes and home fries every morning, and serves sandwiches, salads, and burgers at lunch and dinner. Among the delicacies: deep-fried mahimahi on a bun; fire-roasted green chilies stuffed with herbed mashed potatoes; and a tuna melt on focaccia bread. On Friday nights, folk singers croon to small but enthusiastic crowds.

459 E. Wonderview (in upper Stanley Village). ☎ *970-586-0272. Reservations accepted after 4:30 p.m. Main courses: $6.25–$11. Open: Summer daily for breakfast, lunch, and dinner; rest of year Fri–Mon breakfast, lunch, and dinner; Tue–Thurs breakfast and lunch. DISC, MC, V.*

Poppy's Café

$–$$ Estes Park   PIZZA

Like other restaurants in the heart of downtown Estes Park, Poppy's gets slammed in summer. Waves of tourists wash over the place and then ebb away, leaving pizza crusts, dropped silverware, and napkins behind. Yet Poppy's does a good job of turning tables, and it serves fare that's consistently palatable. The restaurant has pizza, but you can also get sandwiches, burgers, and salads. During warm weather, it's worth waiting the extra 15 to 30 minutes for creekside seating.

342 E. Elkhorn Ave. (on the Riverwalk in Barlow Plaza). ☎ *970-586-8282. Reservations not accepted, but you can call ahead to put your name on the waiting list. Sandwiches and burgers: $5–$7; large pizza $12 plus $1.85 per topping. Open: Daily lunch and dinner. DISC, MC, V.*

Sweet Basilico

$–$$ Estes Park   SOUTHERN ITALIAN

During summer, you'll need to plan ahead to get a table at Sweet Basilico. Because the restaurant charges little, seats only 32, and serves flavorful Italian food, it often sells out two weeks in advance (though a few tables are set aside for walk-ins). Sweet Basilico's marinara sauce tastes gourmet on pasta. You can also order chicken, veal, seafood dishes, and pizza. Try the chicken Marsala sautéed with mushrooms, wine, garlic, and sweet basil.

If you forget to book ahead, you can order to go and then take your food to a table on the roof of the restaurant.

401 E. Elkhorn Ave. ☎ *970-586-3899. Reservations highly recommended. Main courses: $8.95–$15.25. Open: Summer daily lunch and dinner; rest of year Tues–Sun lunch and dinner. AE, DISC, MC, V.*

The top restaurants west of the park

Grand Lake Lodge
$–$$ Grand Lake   AMERICAN

The grandiose reputation accorded Grand Lake Lodge doesn't seem to prevent the place from putting out a tasty spread at a fair price. The lunch menu has burgers, soups, salads, and sandwiches. At dinner, the prime rib is the main attraction, but you can also get steak, fish, chicken, and pork dishes. Vegetarians will enjoy the linguini with sun-dried tomatoes, capers, artichoke hearts, and kalamata olives. Families traveling with small children will appreciate that children under 5 eat free at the breakfast buffet. You'll pay a few dollars more than you would in Grand Lake, but the lake views make it worthwhile. The best vantage point, by far, is on the porch.

Starting at the beginning of the season, you can make dinner reservations for the end of the season. Make your reservations far in advance and ask for a porch seat when you do.

15500 U.S. 34, just outside the west entrance to Rocky Mountain National Park. ☎ *970-627-3967. Reservations accepted for dinner and Sunday brunch. Main courses: $15.50–$26.95. Open: May 31–Sept 15 Mon–Sat breakfast, lunch, and dinner; Sun brunch and dinner. AE, DC, DISC, MC, V.*

Pancho and Lefty's Restaurant
$ Grand Lake   MEXICAN/AMERICAN

Pancho and Lefty's looks like a fish place, sort of. In the bar, a stuffed blue marlin is mounted on the wall, across from a tropical plant and a rowboat that dangles, upside down, below the ceiling. Huge windows overlooking Grand Lake give you an eyeful of water. Given the atmosphere, the place should serve bluefish, but instead it cooks up Tex-Mex items such as rellenos, enchiladas, and burritos, many of them smothered in chili. Other options include steaks; burgers; and baskets of deep fried fish, chicken, and onion rings.

If the restaurant is full, look for a seat in the bar. You can order off the full menu there and enjoy the best lake views. If you're lucky, you may catch some live entertainment, too.

1120 Grand Ave. ☎ *970-627-8773. Reservations not accepted. Main courses: $6.25–$13.50. Open: Daily lunch and dinner. AE, DISC, MC, V.*

Silver Spur Steakhouse & Saloon
$–$$ Granby   AMERICAN

Once a bar with a rugged reputation, the Silver Spur has reinvented itself as the most popular family restaurant in Granby — though there's still a saloon in the back. With no apologies to the Beef Council, it now claims to serve "real food for real people." Tex-Mex, burgers, steaks, and sandwiches all seem to meet the restaurant's definition of real food. As for "real people" — don't worry, the place isn't discriminating. To prove your mettle, try the Mile High Brownie Sundae for dessert.

15 E. Agate. ☎ *970-887-1411. Reservations accepted. Main courses: $7–$17. Open: Daily lunch and dinner. AE, DC, DISC, MC, V.*

The Longbranch Restaurant
$–$$ Granby   GERMAN/MEXICAN

In a building on Granby's main drag, the somber, old-looking Longbranch Restaurant serves up an international array of German, American, and Mexican dishes. You're better off ordering the Longbranch's Teutonic fare, which includes Hungarian goulash, *sauerbraten* (marinated beef served with red cabbage and potato pancakes), and *jaeger schnitzel* (pork tenderloin smothered with creamy mushroom sauce, served with authentic German spaetzle).

175 E. Agate (in downtown Granby). ☎ *970-887-2209. Reservations for large groups only. Open: Jun–Aug daily lunch and dinner; rest of year Mon–Fri lunch and dinner, Sat–Sun dinner only. DISC, MC, V.*

Fast Facts: Rocky Mountain National Park

Emergency

Dial ☎ **911.**

Hospital

East of the park, the Estes Park Medical Center, 555 Prospect Ave. (☎ 970-586-2317), provides 24-hour emergency care. West of the park, you can get 24-hour emergency care at Granby Medical Center, 480 E. Agate Ave. (☎ 970-887-2117), in Granby. For a full-service hospital, go to Kremmling Memorial Hospital District, 214 S. Fourth Street (☎ 970-724-3442), in Kremmling.

Road Conditions

Dial ☎ 877-315-7623 or 303-639-1111.

Chapter 16

Boulder and Fort Collins

· ·

In This Chapter

▶ Breaking down your Boulder options

▶ Finding fun in Fort Collins

▶ Hitting the brewery circuit

· ·

*B*oulder and Fort Collins have several things in common. For starters, they're college towns, home to the University of Colorado and Colorado State University, respectively, each of which has about 25,000 students. Situated roughly 40 miles apart on the eastern slope of the Rockies, Boulder and Fort Collins are both fun, fast-growing communities of around 100,000 residents. Each has a river running through it, and alongside that river, a busy pedestrian path. Both cities brim with artsy shops, lively bars, and excellent restaurants in a variety of price ranges. And both should appeal to you even if you're far past 21, especially if you enjoy an active lifestyle.

Yet despite their similarities, their personalities diverge. In Fort Collins, the occasionally rowdy nightlife centers around beer, including a number of brands brewed right in town. Boulder likes its beer, too, but it also appreciates juices, derivatives, and extracts, all of which combine to give the town a healthy glow. In Fort Collins, farm kids still cruise their pick-up trucks up and down College Avenue on Saturday nights. In Boulder, at least a few people understand that *everything is right here now;* they hardly move. Fort Collins raises cows; Boulder reveres them. And while Fort Collins likes all kinds of loud music, Boulder gravitates to acoustic jams and polyrhythmic international sounds. In sum, Fort Collins absorbs a little wildness from its neighbors to the north in Wyoming and a little earthiness from the farms to its east; Boulder, for its part, takes inspiration from the Far East and the coasts, and never, ever from Wyoming.

What's Where: Boulder and Fort Collins and Their Major Attractions

To enjoy these towns, you don't have to go on campus — in fact, I don't recommend it unless there's a football game. You're better off staying in town and going where the students go to spend their parents' money. Think about it — if all the action were on campus, there wouldn't be so many kids in town.

Boulder

Home of the University of Colorado Buffaloes, Boulder is as much a journey as a destination — especially if you get caught in traffic. After you find a parking space, you'll have a ball. While you're there, make sure to visit the following:

- ✔ **Pearl Street Mall,** where the pedestrian is king and street performers and vendors are footservants who dazzle and entertain you.
- ✔ **The Boulder Creek Path,** a 16-mile riverside path thronged with cyclists, hikers, and inline-skaters, as well as softly treading people in search of deep relaxation.
- ✔ **The Chautauqua Institute,** which for a century has brought lofty ideas and challenging music to regular folks.

Fort Collins

Home to the Colorado State University Rams, Fort Collins can be a wild ride on a Saturday night. Here are a few places to start your visit:

- ✔ **Poudre Canyon,** which is home to the free-flowing Cache La Poudre River and, in the surrounding foothills, some premium hiking trails.
- ✔ **Brewery tours** at local suds houses range in size from enormous (Anheuser-Busch) to miniscule (Odells).
- ✔ **Swetsville Zoo,** proof positive that a dairy farmer with a blowtorch and a can-do attitude can work an Ark's worth of miracles.

Boulder

If you're a liberal who has cash to burn, Boulder may be the most desirable community this side of San Francisco. You can eat great vegetarian food, hike on 200 miles of trails in 30,000 acres of open space on the eastern slope of the Rockies, do yoga, meditate, and contemplate the universe. Even as Boulder's real-estate prices have soared, the city has kept the idealism that put it on the map many years ago. Like other places, Boulder faces challenges, not least of which are a homeless population, occasionally cantankerous college students, and a rapidly growing population of 95,000. Yet the town still tends to side with the underprivileged, the young and rebellious, and the defenders of open space and nature.

As a visitor, you don't need to get embroiled in politics, but you can still enjoy Boulder's frame of mind. The best way is to blend a little movement, a little culture, and a lot of relaxation. During the day, you can walk the Boulder Creek Path or hike into the foothills in one of Boulder's mountain parks. You can buy books at one of many independent booksellers. And you can enjoy the zany street entertainers in the Pearl Street Mall. Come nighttime, you can almost always hear funky music or take in a performance of some kind. Though Boulder doesn't have a lot of great museums, it values spontaneity, creativity, and sound. You won't have to work hard to find a good show.

Getting there

Denver International Airport (DIA), 40 miles southeast of Boulder, is the closest airport with commercial service. Most major domestic carriers and a few international ones fly into DIA, and major rental-car companies have desks at the airport. For information on contacting individual airlines and car-rental agencies, see the Appendix at the back of this book.

Between 3 a.m. and 9 p.m. daily, Denver's **Regional Transportation District (☎ 303-299-6000)** provides hourly bus rides to Denver International Airport (and other Denver locations) from the Boulder main terminal at 14th and Walnut streets. Service from DIA to Boulder runs from 6 a.m. to 11 p.m. (Call for the exact schedule.) Known as skyRide, the service costs $10, and exact change is required in either bills or coins. To catch the skyRide buses leaving DIA, go to Level 6 of the main terminal.

SuperShuttle Boulder (☎ 800-BLUE-VAN or 303-444-0808) offers van service between Boulder and Denver International Airport. The drivers make regular stops at major hotels, and they detour to residences upon request. To go from Boulder to the airport, make your reservation at least 24 hours in advance. Coming from Denver to Boulder, just go to the SuperShuttle desk on Level 5 of the main terminal. Cost for the trip to a regular SuperShuttle stop is $19, $10 ages 8 to 16. There's no charge for children under 8. The fare to an unscheduled stop is $25 for the first person, $10 for each additional person. (Children under 8 are still free.)

A more expedient — and expensive — way to go from DIA to Boulder is in a cab. Just go to the taxi stand and ask for a ride. To go from Boulder to DIA, call **Boulder Yellow Cab (☎ 303-777-7777),** which charges a $70 flat rate for up to five passengers.

To drive from Denver to Boulder, take I-25 north and then head northeast on the Boulder Turnpike (U.S. 36). From Fort Collins and points north, take I-25 south and then head southeast on Colorado 119. Boulder is 55 miles from Fort Collins.

Boulder

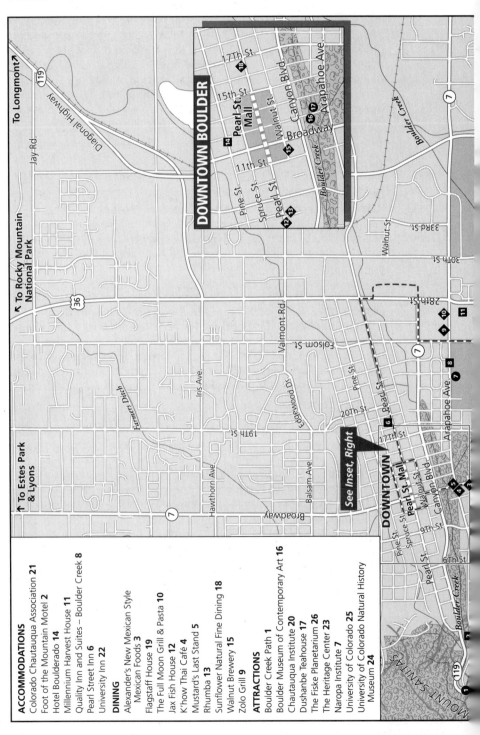

ACCOMMODATIONS
Colorado Chautauqua Association 21
Foot of the Mountain Motel 2
Hotel Boulderado 14
Millennium Harvest House 11
Quality Inn and Suites – Boulder Creek 8
Pearl Street Inn 6
University Inn 22

DINING
Alexander's New Mexican Style
    Mexican Foods 3
Flagstaff House 19
The Full Moon Grill & Pasta 10
Jax Fish House 12
K'how Thai Café 4
Mustard's Last Stand 5
Rhumba 13
Sunflower Natural Fine Dining 18
Walnut Brewery 15
Zolo Grill 9

ATTRACTIONS
Boulder Creek Path 1
Boulder Museum of Contemporary Art 16
Chautauqua Institute 20
Dushanbe Teahouse 17
The Fiske Planetarium 26
The Heritage Center 23
Naropa Institute 7
University of Colorado 25
University of Colorado Natural History
    Museum 24

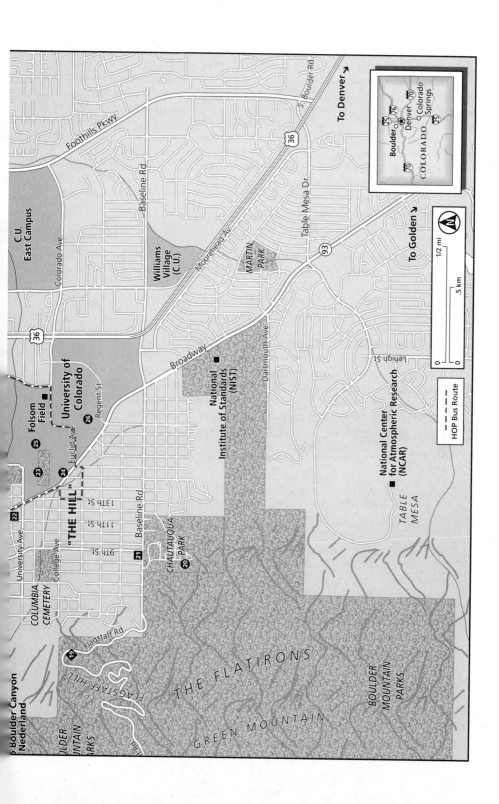

Getting around

Boulder's north-south streets are numbered, with Third Street flush against the foothills and the numbers increasing as you head from west to east. Foothills Parkway (Colorado 157) is the main north-south artery on the east side of town. However, U.S. 36 brings you closer to the downtown area. Heading northeast from Denver, it veers north in Boulder and becomes 28th Street. From U.S. 36 you can reach the heart of the downtown by turning west on Canyon Boulevard (Colorado 119 and 7) and then north on Broadway (Colorado 7). Two blocks north of Canyon Boulevard on Broadway, you'll cross Pearl Street, the hub of downtown Boulder. If you continue west on Canyon Boulevard, you'll head up into the mountains via Boulder Canyon.

Driving in Boulder is fairly easy, though not always expedient. Certain roads get congested, and parking spaces can be hard to find. In the downtown area during daytime, you usually have to pay for a spot. The curbside meters take nickels, dimes, and quarters. Every 5¢ buys just 4 minutes of liberty, so empty out your piggybank before going to town.

Boulder also has a highly efficient bus system that serves destinations throughout the city and travels as far away as Denver. Many routes run at ten-minute intervals during peak periods, making the bus a great way to get around. The City of Boulder operates the **HOP** line, which makes 40 stops on a loop through the downtown area. Call ☎ **303-447-8282** for information on HOP service. Another useful line, **SKIP**, goes north and south on Broadway. Denver's **Regional Transportation District** oversees SKIP and other Boulder County routes. For information on those lines, call ☎ **800-366-7433** or 303-299-6000, or surf the Internet to www.rtd-denver.com. You can also pick up an RTD Boulder County Bus Map at locations throughout town. HOP and SKIP fares are 75¢, 25¢ for seniors 60 and over. Most other local RTD routes cost $1.10 for adults, 55¢ for seniors over 60. Exact change is required.

If the bus doesn't show up, you can always call **Boulder Yellow Cab** ☎ **303-777-7777** or **Metro Taxi** ☎ **303-666-6666.** The taxi companies don't have a strong presence on the streets, so you'll usually need to pick up a phone and dial.

You can easily ride a bike through much of downtown Boulder. Many roads have bike lanes, and you can also use the pedestrian-only Boulder Creek Path, which extends 16 miles on a general east-west course through town. **University Bikes,** Ninth and Pearl (☎ **303-444-4196**), rents town bikes ($20 for one day, $30 for two) and mountain bikes ($25 for one day, $45 for two). Locks and helmets are included in the price.

Where to stay

Lodging in Boulder costs a lot. You can save a few dollars by staying in a chain hotel on the east side of town, but the best way to find an affordable room is to time your visit carefully. Besides its busy summer season, Boulder's hotels fill up during college events such as parents' weekends, graduation, and home football games. If you want to visit Boulder on a budget, schedule your trip around these events — and, if possible, around July and August.

The top hotels

Foot of the Mountain Motel
$–$$ Boulder

Located near the mouth of Boulder Canyon, this motel is nine blocks from downtown, so the walk to the shopping district is a little farther than from other area lodges. The trade-off is the motel's wooded location across from the Eben G. Fine Park, where you can cool off in Boulder Creek. Built in the early 1930s, the one-story motel buildings look like lodging for Santa's elves. They — the buildings, that is — have rough-hewn pine exteriors, red trim, and green roofs. Inside the 19 rooms, you'll find knotty pine walls and desks, as well as old-style bathrooms with medicine cabinets and (usually) showers instead of tubs. There's no air-conditioning, but two windows in each room help create a draft, especially when you turn the fan on.

200 Arapahoe, Boulder CO 80302. ☎ *303-442-5688. Fax: 303-442-5719. Internet:* www.footofthemountainmotel.com. *Rack rates $70–$85. AE, DISC, MC, V.*

Colorado Chautauqua Association
$–$$$ Boulder

Anyone who has a cultural bent should spend a few days in one of the 60 cottages rented out by the Colorado Chautauqua Association. Situated on 26 acres at the base of the Flatiron Mountains, these clean, rustic, Arts and Crafts–style dwellings date back to the early 1900s. They have hardwood floors, screened-in porches, and gas stoves, but no TVs. Rather than watch Regis, you're supposed to become part of a community that's engaged in intellectual and cultural endeavors. This isn't as daunting as it may sound. In between naps, you just go to any concerts, forums, classes, and films that interest you. During summer at least, there are many to choose from. (For more on cultural offerings at Chautauqua, see the hotel's Web site.) As for food, you can cook in your room or eat in the Chautauqua Dining Hall, which is fancier than the name implies. Chautauqua borders a large mountain park, so you can start hiking right outside your door.

900 Baseline Rd., Boulder. ☎ ***303-442-3282.*** *Fax: 303-449-0790. Internet:* www.chautauqua.com. *Rack rates: Efficiency $70–$81, one-bedroom cottage $81–$98, two-bedroom cottage $95–$190. MC, V.*

Hotel Boulderado
$$$$ **Boulder**

You can easily recognize this Boulder landmark by the bright green canopies on the building, by its imposing five stories of red brick, and by its location mere steps from the Pearl Street Pedestrian Mall. Built in 1909, its sumptuous lobby has Victorian furniture, a cherry-wood staircase, and colorful rugs, all under a ceiling of Italian stained glass. You can stay in the historic hotel, where the rooms are old and full of antiques, or in a more recent addition, where the rooms are full of reproductions. For the most memorable experience, ask for a corner room in the older building — these rooms provide a little more light, air, and history.

2115 13th Street, Boulder. ☎ ***800-433-4344*** *or 303-442-4344. Fax: 303-442-4378. Internet:* www.boulderado.com. *Rack rates: Weekday $185 –$325; weekends May 24–Oct 31 $169–$299, Nov 1–May 23 $135–$235. AE, DC, DISC, MC, V.*

Millennium Harvest House
$$$ **Boulder**

I loved my fifth-floor king room at this hotel, the largest in Boulder. The furnishings seemed perfect for a town that's perched between the plains and the mountains: The leather easy chair belonged in a den in Chicago; the quilted bedspread could have come from Kansas, and the coppery lamps hinted at points farther west. A spacious desk faced the mountains out the wall-to-wall windows. And the staff provided small luxuries, including nightly turndowns and three complimentary morning newspapers. If you want to exercise, you can use the pool, the tennis courts, or the fitness room, or you can jog on the Boulder Creek Path, which skirts the edge of the property. The hotel also has a good restaurant and room service.

1345 28th Street, Boulder. ☎ ***303-443-3850.*** *Fax: 303-443-1480. Internet:* www.millennium-hotels.com. *Rack rates: mid-Oct–mid-March $79–$129; rest of year $119–$180; University of Colorado graduation and parent's weekend $215. AE, DC, DISC, MC, V.*

Quality Inn and Suites — Boulder Creek
$$ **Boulder**

This inn is tucked into a mostly residential neighborhood at the southeast edge of downtown. Most of the rooms are distanced from Arapahoe Avenue, so they're quiet even though the Boulder Creek Path passes nearby, and the heart of Boulder's downtown is only about five blocks away. Rooms have furniture made from pine branches, watched over by framed photographs of the owner's dog, and all of them have refrigerators and microwaves. There's also a workout room, hot tub, pool, and guest laundry. A hot breakfast is included in the rates.

2020 Arapahoe Ave., Boulder. ☎ *888-449-7550 (outside Colorado only) or 303-449-7550. Fax: 303-449-1082. Internet:* www.qualityinnboulder.com. *Rack rates: Standard $89–$130, suites $119–$150. AE, DC, DISC, MC, V.*

The runner-up hotels

Pearl Street Inn

$$$ Boulder   This bed-and-breakfast has a prime location near the action on Pearl Street but is surprisingly quiet. The rooms have such amenities as quilts and antiques, and all but one has a wood-burning fireplace. The prices could be lower, but this really is a prime spot. *1820 Pearl St., Boulder.* ☎ *888-810-1302 or 303-444-5584. Fax: 303-444-6494. Internet:* www.pearlstreetinn.com.

University Inn

$$ Boulder   This two-story 1960s-era motor lodge, just two blocks from Pearl Street, has rooms that look older than those at the Quality Inn, and it's near a busy intersection. But dozens of shops and restaurants are within walking distance, the rooms are clean, and the prices are fair. *1632 Broadway, Boulder.* ☎ *800-258-7917 or 303-442-3830. Fax: 303-442-1205. Internet:* www.texasguides.com/university.html.

Where to dine

Boulder restaurants don't allow smoking, tend to be health-conscious, and have great chefs, many of whom have come here for the lifestyle. As you'd expect in a college town, there are a lot of cheap ethnic places and pizza joints, plus a few brewpubs. Near the Pearl Street Mall, you'll also find brightly decorated, trendy, expensive restaurants, much like the ones in Denver's LoDo area (see Chapter 13 for more on Denver). Many of these restaurants have popular bars that border the regular seating. If you give them a try, you may end up eating gourmet food in an environment that's surprisingly festive.

The top restaurants

Alexander's New Mexican–Style Mexican Foods
$ Boulder   NEW MEXICAN

There's something scary about buying inexpensive Mexican food at a former gas station, but Alexander's serves premium fare. The menu features the usual enchiladas, tacos, burritos, and tostadas. What's unique are the fillings — lard-free beans and lean meats; vegetables such as white cabbage, asparagus, zucchini, and spinach; grains such as quinoa, bulgar wheat, and barley; and a soft white substance known as tofu. You can eat out back on a patch of grass or try to find a spot in the tiny indoor dining area, which usually has more plants than people.

1650 Broadway. ☎ *303-444-6699. No reservations. Main courses: $5–$11. Open: Daily lunch and dinner. Cash only.*

The Full Moon Grill & Pasta
$$–$$$ Boulder   NORTHERN ITALIAN

If you love fresh seafood served with handmade pasta, head for the Full Moon Grill before the opportunity wanes. Succulent dishes such as the *Free Form Ravioli* (house made pasta, scallops, fennel, fresh fish, tomatoes, saffron-chardonnay broth) and the *Linguini Alla Sardegna* (swordfish, tomato, garlic, saffron mint, and white wine) may be gone tomorrow. Dip your bread in olive oil and balsamic vinegar, and wax eloquent over a bottle from the immense wine list. Unlike many other Boulder eateries, here, you won't have to howl to be heard. Once a hamburger joint, the sun-splashed, octagonal dining room takes on ambience when the sun's last glow gives way to candlelight — and moonlight, too.

2525 Arapahoe Ave. (inside the Village Shopping Center). ☎ *303-938-8800. Reservations accepted. Main courses: $13–$25. Open: Mon–Fri lunch and dinner; Sat–Sun dinner only. AE, DISC, MC, V.*

Jax Fish House
$$–$$$ Boulder   SEAFOOD

Along with the best martinis in town, Jax has some of the freshest fish. It flies in fresh oysters, clams, and mussels daily, and its nearly living "Filet Mignon of Tuna" has a devoted following. (The filet is a 2-inch-thick slab of tuna, barely seared and served with scallion hash browns, sweet soy, and pickled ginger.) Because Jax serves seafood, it covers its tables with paper. And because it covers its tables with paper, it gives crayons to customers. The restaurant learned too late that customers who have crayons and martinis in hand can be trouble; that's why the brick walls in here look like a coloring book. If you're looking for a quiet, romantic evening, forget Jax. This place rocks on the weekends, especially when the bar at the front of the room fills up.

928 Pearl St. ☎ *303-444-1811. Reservations not accepted. Sandwiches $8–$17, entrees $16–$25. Open: Nightly for dinner. AE, DC, MC, V.*

Rhumba
$$ Boulder   CARIBBEAN

On certain summer nights, this place becomes a huge party. Servers in tropical shirts push through crowds of singles to make sure the people on the patio get their rum drinks in time. The enthusiasm swells when those potent drinks take hold, and the crowds from the bar spill over into the seating area. During my meal here, I couldn't help feeling as if my gourmet dinner and I had together parachuted into a Club Med. With so much activity, it's easy to overlook the delicious food, which has sweet

Caribbean ingredients such as mango, coconut, and pineapple. Among the many options, you can get half jerk chicken over black beans with coconut rise, or simplify things (sort of) by ordering a cheeseburger with boniato french fries and banana guava ketchup.

950 Pearl St. ☎ 303-442-7771. Reservations accepted sometimes. Main courses: $9–$22. Open: Fri–Sun lunch and dinner; Mon–Thurs dinner only. AE, DC, MC, V.

Sunflower Natural Fine Dining
$$ Boulder   GOURMET NATURAL FOODS

The Sunflower's menu announces that the restaurant shuns preservatives, additives, and artificial ingredients; that it seeks organically grown ingredients free of synthetic chemical fertilizers, herbicides, and pesticides; and that it uses only aluminum-free cookware, non-irradiated herbs and spices, and Celtic sea salt. That part of the menu has about as much charm as your average corporate mission statement, but the food itself is surprisingly flavorful. Naturally enough, the restaurant serves many vegetarian dishes, but you can also order meaty items such as buffalo steak, seafood cioppino, and fresh Alaskan halibut.

1701 Pearl St. ☎ 303-440-0220. Reservations accepted. Dinner entrees: $13.95–$24.50. Credit cards: Open Mon– Fri lunch and dinner, Sat–Sun brunch and dinner. AE, MC, V.

Zolo Grill
$$ Boulder   CONTEMPORARY SOUTHWESTERN

This trendy restaurant presents a spicy, smoky, gourmet version of southwestern food. Key ingredients include jabanero and chopotle peppers, strong cheeses, and succulent meats such as duck, ahi tuna, and pulled pork. The tough part is deciding which way you'd like to be overpowered. Choices include the likes of barbeque duck tacos, blackberry jabanero pork chops (served with goat cheese), and wild mushroom enchiladas. The room, which is mostly red and yellow, feels just as warm and rich as the food.

2525 Arapahoe (in the Village Shopping Center). ☎ 303-449-0444. Reservations not accepted. Main courses: $11–$20; brunch $6.50–$11.50. Open: Mon–Sat lunch and dinner; Sun brunch and dinner. AE, DC, MC, V.

The runner-up restaurants
Flagstaff House

$$$$ Boulder   NEW AMERICAN   Half the locals I interviewed loved this pricey Boulder landmark; the other half expressed disappointment. Yet everyone could appreciate the sweeping views of the plains through the mostly glass walls, and all agreed that the service stood out. *1138 Flagstaff Rd. ☎ 303-442-4640.*

K'how Thai Café
$ Boulder   THAI

The salads, curries, noodle dishes, and fried rice all leave the kitchen with spice to spare, and the heat hits your sinuses long before your belly. Most of the meals start out vegetarian, but you can add chicken, pork, shrimp, beef, or seafood. 1600 Broadway. ☎ *303-447-0273.*

Mustard's Last Stand
$ Boulder   HOT DOGS

Inside Mustard's Last Stand, fallen vegans and defiant meat-eaters wait in line to order Chicago-style hot dogs, polish sausage, burgers, hoagies, and specialty sandwiches. If you're unimpressed by the phrases "all beef" and "natural casing," you can still get a tempeh burger, veggie dog, or tofu Rueben. After all, this is Boulder. Corner of Arapahoe and Broadway. ☎ *303-444-5841.* Cash only.

Walnut Brewery
$–$$ PUB FARE

The busiest brewpub in Boulder, Walnut Brewery occupies an old firehouse that's been converted into a roomy, high-ceilinged dining area and bar. These days, the only sirens are the ones drinking at the bar, and the only three-alarm fires are caused by buffalo wings. The food is above average, and the beer is first rate, especially the Indian Peaks Pale Ale. 1123 Walnut St. ☎ *303-447-1345.*

Exploring Boulder

In Boulder, you don't have to do much to have a good time. You just have to be there and see what happens. Sometimes it's best not to even judge what's good and bad.

The best things to see and do

Okay, some of us get paid to judge things. If fate smiles upon you, you will

> ✔ **Sip tea in paradise. Dushanbe Teahouse,** 1770 13th St. (☎ 303-442-4993), looks like something the deep subconscious might unveil in an enlightened state. A gift from the city of Dushanbe, Tajikstan, it took 40 artisans three years to hand-carve and hand-paint the teahouse. When they finished, they shipped it in crates to the U.S., where it sat for several years before being reassembled next to Central Park in downtown Boulder. Under a large skylight, at the center of the room sits "The Fountain of the Seven Beauties," whose name pretty much describes the scene. The teahouse serves hundreds of teas and a variety of international dishes,

including some Tajik fare. If you don't feel like eating, come between 3 and 5 p.m. for tea. Or simply look around — this was meant to be a gathering place, and you're encouraged to visit even if you buy nothing. Admission is free. It's open Sunday through Thursday from 8 a.m. to 9 p.m., and Friday and Saturday from 8 a.m. to 10 p.m.

✔ **Watch human tricks.** Shopping is anything but dull at **Pearl Street Mall,** on Pearl between 11th and 15th streets (☎ **303-449-3774**). During summer, you'll pass street vendors, sidewalk cafes, and, best of all, street performers, including balloon-artists, escape masters, contortionists, opera singers, and tightrope-walkers. The performers yell in order to be heard over the crowds, single out audience members for special attention, and aggressively pass the hat when they're done. Together they make the place more medieval than mall-like. The shops are fun, too — at least five independent bookstores dot the area, as well as stores selling everything from kites to CDs.

✔ **Hide out near the Boulder Creek Path.** Like Boulder itself, this paved pedestrian path connects the mountains and the plains. It parallels Boulder Creek downstream for 16 miles, beginning 4 miles up Boulder Canyon and ending on the east side of town, within mooing distance of the plains. The path crosses no streets and has many small, leafy parks alongside it. Starting from the west end, you'll pass Elephant Rocks, a rock-climbing and bouldering hotspot. Just below the mouth of the canyon, you'll go through shady Eben G. Fine Park, perfect for picnicking, soaking, and cooling off. Another mile or so to the east, behind the Millennium Hotel, you can look at trout through small, murky windows into the creek. Speed-walkers, inline-skaters, runners, and cyclists all blaze down the path, yet many others use the area as a giant natural sedative. On summer afternoons, if you peek through the foliage at the water-smoothed boulders and the creekside park benches, you'll see dozens of people relaxing. It doesn't matter how you use the path, just make sure to spend some time there.

Other things to see and do

Boulder also has a host of smaller museums, libraries, and galleries, including ones on two local campuses:

✔ When a Tibetan meditation master, Chogyam Trungpa Rinpoche, founded Boulder's **Naropa Institute** in 1974, he envisioned a place "where East meets west and sparks . . . fly" — and fly they did, especially when free-thinkers such as Allen Ginsberg and Ann Waldman were teaching there. Today **Naropa University** (☎ **800-603-3117** or 303-245-4819) still merges Western scholarship and Eastern contemplation. The college is home to Ginsberg's personal library and one of the country's most important spoken-word archives. The institute opens certain workshops, classes, and performances to the public. And its library is a must-see for people interested in Eastern religion and alternative therapies. To find out more about what's happening, go to www.naropa.edu. For information on performances, call ☎ **303-245-4715.**

✔ The **Boulder Museum of Contemporary Art,** 1750 13th St. (☎ **303-443-2122**), displays cutting-edge work by nationally known artists. The exhibits change every three months and include paintings, collages, mixed media, ceramics, and installations. There's also an area for readings, performances, and discussions. Admission is $4 for adults, $3 for students and seniors 55 and up. The museum is open Tuesday through Saturday from 10 a.m. to 6 p.m.

✔ Think twice before blindly wandering where the Buffalo roam. **The University of Colorado at Boulder** is big enough to accommodate 25,000 students, and its many pinkish, Italian Renaissance–style buildings look strikingly similar to the untrained eye. My walk on campus reminded me of a recurring nightmare where it's my freshman year again and I can't find my classes. You can avoid a similar plight by going straight to the circulation desk at the University Memorial Center, 1669 Euclid (at Broadway), and picking up a campus map. Then you'll be able to locate attractions such as **The University of Colorado Natural History Museum, The Heritage Center** (dedicated to the history of the university), and **The Fiske Planetarium,** all of which are open to the public.

Campus tours for prospective students are offered weekdays at 9:30 a.m. and 1:30 p.m. and Saturdays at 10:30 a.m., but first you'll need to make a reservation by calling ☎ **303-492-6301,** option 2. The university discourages regular visitors from taking them, but if you're curious, go ahead. Tours leave from the University Club, on the southeast corner of Broadway and Euclid.

Staying active

The national media regularly lauds Boulder as one of the most fit, healthy, and recreation-friendly towns in the country. Some of the praise goes to the town's abundant water, rock, and forest, including over 30,000 acres of open space. The rest goes to the townspeople themselves, who make a point of getting out and enjoying their resources. When in Boulder, set aside a few hours for:

✔ **Climbing:** Boulder has challenging climbing within a few miles of the city limits. One hot spot is **Elephant Rocks,** just west of town in Boulder Canyon. At **Eldorado Canyon State Park** (☎ **303-494-3943**), 8 miles southwest of town in Eldorado Springs, climbers creep up 800-foot canyon walls. There are also great climbs in the Flatirons near Chautauqua Park. For climbing gear and information, visit **Mountain Sports,** 2835 Pearl St. (☎ **303-442-8355**).

✔ **Cycling and mountain biking:** Bicycling isn't just a sport here; it's a form of viable transportation. On 100 miles of bike lanes and multiuse paths, you can pedal most places in Boulder without risking your neck. Alas, the mountain biking in Boulder could be better. To avoid conflicts between cyclists and hikers, the city closed many of the hiking trails nearest town to bicycling. Most of the best off-road cycling is a few miles farther out — or uphill — from the city limits. One prime place to pedal is in **Eldorado Canyon State Park** (see the preceding bullet).

✔ **Hiking:** The hiking in Boulder starts right at the west edge of town, where you can hike into city-owned open space in the foot-hills of the Flatiron Range. You'll find great trail-running and hiking in **Chautauqua Park,** just south of Baseline Road. Take Baseline Road west from town and park near Chautauqua. From the Ranger Cottage, climb the obvious fire road up the long grassy hillside. The road takes you to the trailhead for the **Mesa Trail,** which undulates through ponderosa pine forest and meadows for 6 miles along the base of the Flatirons. If you want to do a loop hike through this area, go to the ranger station and pick up the free *Circle Hikes Guide,* published by the **City of Boulder Open Space and Mountain Parks** (☎ 303-441-3440). It describes two loop hikes in Chautauqua Park and four others a short drive away.

✔ **Running:** Boulder has a huge population of joggers and runners who take advantage of the elevation, clean air, and hilly terrain to get in top shape. You can run trails all around town, but if you want to test yourself against some maniacally fast Boulderites, go to the busy **Boulder Creek Path.**

Hitting the slopes

Given its location near Boulder, **Eldora Mountain Resort** gets skied hard throughout the winter. Its 12 lifts can deposit plenty of skiers in a relatively small, 680-acre area, nearly half of which has snowmaking capability in case Mother Nature's supply falls short. Skier traffic and manmade snow often combine to create ice and moguls. As you descend the Eldora's 1,400 vertical feet, don't be surprised if you encounter either of the two (and tortuous combinations thereof), especially if it hasn't snowed in a while. On the upside, you won't have to battle traf-fic on I-70 to get there, and the place is low-key and has a few challeng-ing spots.

See Table 16-1 for a rundown of the resort's statistical and contact information.

Table 16-1	Ski Report: Eldora Mountain Resort
Location: 21 miles west of Boulder, near Nederland	
Trails: 53	
20% beginner	
50% intermediate	
30% advanced/expert	
Vertical drop: 1,400 feet	
Base elevation: 9,200 feet	
Summit elevation: 10,600 feet	
Skiable terrain: 680 acres	
Average snowfall: 311 inches	
Lifts: 12	
Phone: ☎ 303-440-8700	
Internet: www.Eldora.com	
2002–2003 all-day adult lift ticket: $47	

Shopping

Even unenthusiastic shoppers should browse the stores on Pearl Street. Not only will you be constantly entertained as you walk, you'll see products ranging from Tibetan imports to kites. Starting from the top of Pearl Street and working your way down, here are a few interesting stops:

✔ **Belle Star,** 385 Pearl St. #7 (☎ **303-249-6958**), will analyze your auric field photograph for $20. The digitally enhanced photograph reveals blotches of color and light around your head. The color and light may not mean much to you — to the ungifted, it just looks like you're at a disco. That's where Belle Star comes in. She can read these photographs to reveal things about you. For example, you may find out that you're a healer, mystic, or teacher. The entire process takes just a few minutes.

✔ **West End Wine Shop,** 777 Pearl St. (☎ **303-245-7077**), carries 350 wines, all of which have been tasted and approved by one of the shop's owners, Manuel Sanchez. Sanchez appears no worse for the wear, and he'll gladly share his opinion of each bottle. The store also carries a small selection of handcrafted beers and liquor.

✔ With 100,000 books on three floors, **Boulder Book Store,** 1107 Pearl St. (☎ **800-244-4651** or 303-447-2074), is the largest of the local independents. Open since 1973, it resembles a downsized version of Denver's popular Tattered Cover Bookstores. Chairs and tables are tucked into corners on the different floors, making it easy to hunker down and browse.

✔ If it can fly, float, soar, or spin in the wind (without carrying humans along with it), you can probably find it at **Into the Wind,** 1408 Pearl St. (☎ **800-541-0314;** Internet: www.intothewind.com). The store sells human-controlled floaters such as boomerangs, kites, and flying discs, as well as yard decorations like windmills, mobiles, and twisters. The store even sells hats with propellers.

✔ If you need direction, try finding your way to **Boulder Map Gallery,** 1708 13th St. (☎ **303-444-1406**). This store has all manner of trail maps, road maps, globes, and compasses. If you need a USGS topographical map for anywhere in the country, order it in the morning and you can pick it up that afternoon.

✔ Since 1971, the **Boulder Arts and Crafts Cooperative,** 1421 Pearl St. (☎ **303-443-3683**), has represented local artists. Right now the co-op has 50 members, including painters, sculptors, and jewelry-makers. Most of the artists charge reasonable prices for their work, making this a great place to shop for gifts.

✔ **Grassroots Hemp,** 1537 Pearl St. (☎ **303-786-8105**), sells shirts, bags, blankets, and socks made of hemp, one of the most durable fibers on the planet. In addition to selling hemp products, Grassroots Hemp is an information center advocating changes in hemp-related laws.

✔ **Beat Book Shop** (☎ **303-444-7111**) is my favorite store in town. Its proprietor, Tom Peters, has amassed a sizeable collection of used books by Beat writers and poets, as well as other vintage paperbacks, LPs, CDs, and magazines. This time capsule of the '50s and '60s occupies a tiny space at 1713 Pearl St.

Nightlife

Even when the students are out of town, Boulder has a vigorous nightlife. The hottest restaurants — Jax, Rhumba, and The Med, to name a few — also have bars that are popular with young professionals. In addition to these trendy mingling spots, the town has basement dives, brewpubs, and places specializing in live music. The music distinguishes this town. Boulder attracts some great pickers who turn up solo for jam sessions as well as in formal gigs alongside their own groups.

Hitting the clubs and bars

Generally speaking, bars and clubs usually heat up around 11 p.m. and close around 2 a.m. Pick up the latest copy of *Boulder Weekly* to see who's playing where. If nothing captures your fancy, poke your head into some of these bars, cafes, and clubs:

- ✔ **Mountain Sun Brew Pub,** 1535 Pearl St. (☎ 303-546-0886), seems to have the strongest brewpub beer in Boulder. A pint of Hogback Dopplebock hit me so hard, I had to have a Java Porter to sober up. Mountain Sun has no bar, so friends congregate around tables as if at a coffee shop. The decor consists of tapestries and Grateful Dead concert posters, watched over by a mural of a setting (or rising) sun.

- ✔ The **Rio Grande Mexican Restaurant,** 1101 Walnut St. (☎ 303-417-1322), offers further proof that great food and great margaritas are mutually exclusive. In this case, the margaritas rule.

- ✔ Popular national touring acts gravitate to the **Boulder Theater,** 2032 14th St. (☎ 303-786-7030). Offerings include everything from jam bands to comedies and community forums. Most shows at this 1906 Art Deco–style venue are open to all ages.

- ✔ Big-name acts that don't go to the Boulder Theater often turn up at the **Fox Theatre and Café,** 1135 13th St. (☎ 303-447-0095). Being close to the University of Colorado, the Fox Theatre attracts more students than the shows downtown, and the place can get a little rowdy.

- ✔ If you're hungry for blues, check out **The Catacombs,** 2115 13th St. (☎ 303-443-0486), which consists of a maze of underground chambers, including poolrooms, smoking rooms, lounging areas, and a music room. Blues bands often play the music room. It's hard to pinpoint who hangs out here, because every room is different.

- ✔ **Tulagi,** 1129 13th St. (☎ 303-443-3399), books some noisy, rowdy acts plus the usual Colorado jam band fare. It also has cheap drink specials.

- ✔ For jazz and R&B, try **Trios Wine and Martini Bar,** 1155 Canyon Blvd. (☎ 303-442-8400). The bar has live music Wednesday through Sunday, usually for no cover.

- ✔ **Penny Lane,** at the corner or 18th and Pearl streets (☎ 303-443-9516), isn't a bar but it does have some quirky entertainment. A coffee shop, Penny Lane has an open mike two nights a week, as well as readings, drop in jams, and folk singers. There's something every night, usually starting at around 8:00 or 8:30 p.m.

Looking for culture

The auditorium at the **Chautauqua Institute** is one of the neatest music venues going. Erected in 1898, it's like a huge, rickety barn, only with comfortable seating and a large stage. Daylight peeks through cracks in the walls; the air smells as fresh as if you were outside. During silences in performances, you may hear the rain and wind. Because of the superb acoustics and unusual setting, musicians love playing here. Every summer, two major music festivals are based here.

Several nights a week from late June to mid-August, the **Colorado Music Festival** takes over the auditorium for classical music performances. The festival has its own orchestra, which often plays alongside visiting musicians. It also has a chamber series. Every performance is different, and the offerings include everything from Bernstein to Dvorak. The least expensive tickets always cost $10; prime seats go for $33 to $37. Tickets for the upcoming season go on sale May 1. To find out more about the Festival, visit the **Colorado Music Festival Box Office,** 1525 Spruce St., Suite 101 (☎ **303-449-2413;** Internet: www.colorado musicfest.org).

When it's not hosting the Colorado Music Festival, Chautauqua has its own summer festival, which brings dance troupes, folk singers, intellectuals, comedians, and other entertainers. Recent performers include John Hiatt, Joan Baez, the Cleo Parker Robinson Dance Ensemble, and the essayist Andrei Codrescu. Prices for the **Chautauqua Summer Festival** range in cost from free (for the season-ending show) to $35 or more for the most popular acts. Surf the Internet to www.chautauqua. org for more information.

Tickets for both the Colorado Music Festival and Chautauqua Summer Festival are available through the **Chautauqua Box Office** (☎ **303-440-7666**), open Monday through Friday from 10 a.m. to 4 p.m., Saturday from noon to 4 p.m., and 90 minutes before show time. It's on the Chautauqua grounds between the auditorium and the dining hall. **TicketsWest** carries tickets to these shows at area King Soopers Stores. You can order online at www.ticketswest.com or call ☎ **866-464-2626.** Tickets to the Chautauqua Summer Festival only are available at the **Boulder Theater Box Office,** 2032 14th St. (☎ **303-786-7030**).

Chautauqua also hosts many lower-profile events, including forums, concerts, classes, and film screenings. For information on these events, surf the Internet to www.chautauqua.com or call ☎ **303-442-3282,** ext. 24.

The **Colorado Shakespeare Festival** takes place at the Mary Rippon Outdoor Theater on the University of Colorado campus from late June through mid-August every summer. This talented company does three Shakespearean plays every year, including at least one tragedy. A few students and graduate students take part, but most of the performers are seasoned pros. Best of all, you can picnic (without glassware) beforehand, and then take in the evening sky during the performance. Tickets cost $10 to $46. No children under 5 are admitted. Order tickets by phone (☎ **303-492-0554**) or by visiting the box office in the basement of the Dance and Theater Building on the University of Colorado Campus, near the intersection of Broadway and Euclid. For more on the festival, surf the Internet to www.coloradoshakes.org.

Fast Facts: Boulder

Hospital

Boulder Community Hospital, 1100 Balasam Ave., at North Broadway (☎ 303-442-4521) has 24-hour emergency care.

Information

Boulder Convention and Visitors Bureau, 2440 Pearl St. (☎ 800-444-0447 or 303-442-2911; Internet: www.bouldercolorado usa.com), is open 8:30 a.m. to 5:00 p.m. Mon–Thurs and 8:30 a.m. to 4:00 p.m. on Fridays.

Internet Access

The Boulder Public Library, 11th and Arapahoe (☎ 303-441-3099), provides free Internet access.

Pharmacies

King Soopers Supermarket, 1650 30th Street (☎ 303-333-0164), fills prescriptions.

Post Office

There is a local branch at 15th and Walnut streets. Call ☎ 800-275-8777 for hours and other Boulder post office locations.

Road Conditions

Call ☎ 303-639-1111.

Weather

Call ☎ 303-494-4221.

Fort Collins

Maybe because of the farms at the edge of town, Fort Collins feels closer to the plains than the mountains — even though the mountains are just a few miles away. The air feels a little heavier and the earth looks more fertile than in the hills. And the homes in the downtown section are, for the most part, basic and solid. Except for a few spots along College Avenue, Fort Collins appears less busy than Denver and Boulder. It has uncrowded biking trails, exciting boating on the Cache La Poudre River, and scenic hikes in Poudre Canyon. Because Fort Collins is home to Colorado State University, you can also enjoy the benefits of a college town, including inexpensive food, a lively night scene, and the occasional stage production.

Getting there

You can't fly to Fort Collins unless you charter a plane, but Denver International Airport (DIA) is only 70 miles away. Most major domestic carriers and a few international ones serve DIA, and major car-rental companies have desks at the airport. For information on contacting individual airlines and car-rental agencies, see the Appendix.

If you don't feel like driving, you can catch a shuttle with **Shamrock Airport Express** (☎ 970-482-0505), which makes hourly trips from DIA to the Fort Collins Area. Shamrock stops at the University Park Holiday Inn (at the corner of Prospect and Center) and the Marriott Courtyard

Fort Collins

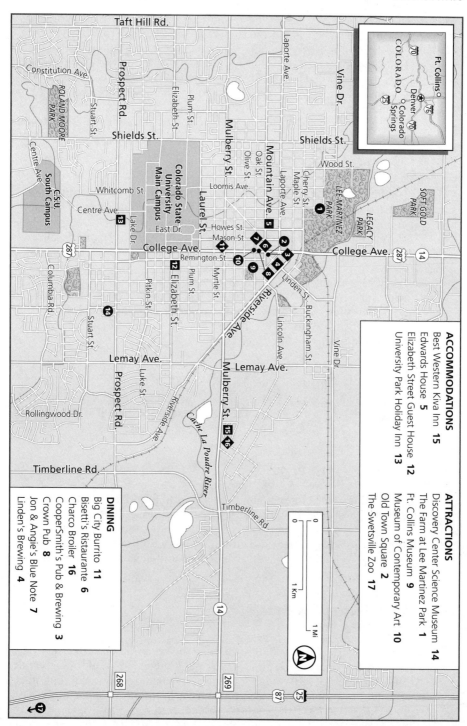

ACCOMMODATIONS
Best Western Kiva Inn **15**
Edwards House **5**
Elizabeth Street Guest House **12**
University Park Holiday Inn **13**

ATTRACTIONS
Discovery Center Science Museum **14**
The Farm at Lee Martinez Park **1**
Ft. Collins Museum **9**
Museum of Contemporary Art **10**
Old Town Square **2**
The Swetsville Zoo **17**

DINING
Big City Burrito **11**
Bisetti's Ristaurante **6**
Charco Broiler **16**
CooperSmith's Pub & Brewing **3**
Crown Pub **8**
Jon & Angie's Blue Note **7**
Linden's Brewing **4**

0   1 Km
0   1 Mi

(at Lemay and Harmony). The shuttles operate between 4 a.m. and 9 p.m. A ride costs $21 each way.

To drive to Fort Collins from Denver, take **I-25** north to Mulberry Street/Colorado 14 (Exit 269). Go 4 miles west on Mulberry Street to Colorado Avenue. Take Colorado Avenue north into the downtown area. **Interstate 80** passes 30 miles north of Fort Collins. If you're coming from the northwest on I-80, exit in Laramie and take **U.S. 287** 40 miles southwest to Fort Collins. If you're coming from the east on I-80, head south on I-25 for 40 miles to the eastern edge of Fort Collins.

Getting around

Driving around Fort Collins is easy, though College Avenue, the main north-south road in the downtown, can get slow during busy times. You'll find lots of free parking downtown, and you can usually locate a spot within a few blocks of your destination if you turn off of College Avenue.

Fort Collins's bus service, **Transfort (☎ 970-221-6620)**, provides city-wide service every day but Sunday. The buses run every half-hour and sometimes less frequently. A one-way fare, including transfers, is $1 for adults, 50¢ for seniors over 59, and free for youths 17 and under. Exact fare is required.

As in Boulder, the best way to negotiate Fort Collins may be by bicycle. Many roads, with the noteworthy exception of College Avenue, either pass through residential areas or have bike lanes. You can hang your bike on a bus if your legs fail you. **Lee's Cyclery,** 202 W. Laurel St. (☎ **800-748-BIKE** or 970-482-6006), rents bikes for $25 per day.

Where to stay

Fort Collins has a lot of chain hotels near I-25, and a few more on the streets bordering the university. The hotels closer to the university cost a little more. Because it's only a five-mile drive from I-25 into the downtown, staying near the Interstate is a viable option. If you come during a college event, such as a home football game, graduation, or parents weekend, you're going to pay a lot, no matter where you stay.

Best Western Kiva Inn
$$ Fort Collins

If the University Park Holiday Inn (see the review later in this section) is full, try the Kiva Inn, on Mulberry Street between I-25 and the University. Like a Pueblo Indian *kiva* (a subterranean ceremonial chamber), the lobby is nearly circular and has a fireplace in the middle. Fully refurbished in 1997, the rooms are decorated with Southwestern art and have microwaves and refrigerators. There's also an outdoor pool and an indoor exercise area. You can step back into the 1950s by dining next door at Charco Broiler (skip ahead to "Where to dine" to read my review of this restaurant).

1638 E. Mulberry St. ☎ ***888-299-5482*** *or 970-484-2444. Fax: 970-221-0967. Internet:* www.bestwestern.com/kivainn. *Rack rates: May 1–Sept 1 $99–$135; rest of year, $81–$125. Rates include continental breakfast. AE, DC, DISC, MC, V.*

Edwards House
$$–$$$$ Fort Collins

This bed-and-breakfast in a 1904 Denver Four Square home feels so elegant, luxurious, and proper, you can't help thinking that a wedding may break out at any moment. The Denver Four Square style came about after the price of silver crashed and Colorado's wealthiest people either decided, or were forced, to stop building ornate Victorian exteriors. On the inside, these homes were often very luxurious, and you won't suffer in this one. All eight guest rooms have gas fireplaces, armchairs, four-poster beds, and televisions with VCRs. You can borrow a book or a video from the library, or, if you feel like breaking a sweat, use the exercise room and sauna. Complimentary afternoon refreshments are offered, plus a full breakfast.

402 W. Mountain Ave. ☎ ***800-281-9190*** *or 970-493-9191. Fax: 970-484-0706. Internet:* www.edwardshouse.com. *Rack rates: $89–$159. Rates include full breakfast. AE, DISC, MC, V.*

Elizabeth Street Guest House
$–$$ Fort Collins

This 1905 home is pure, old-style country. Downstairs, you'll walk on hardwood floors of oak and pine, next to a solid oak staircase. Upstairs, sponged paint gives the walls an old-world appearance. Folk art lines the shelves and hangs from the walls. You'll find needlepoint, miniatures, rag dolls, and other knickknacks. Because there are only three guest rooms, you're sure to get extra attention from the innkeepers, Sheryl and John Clark, and the house mutt, Louie. Two rooms share baths but have private wash basins. This B&B is a great value for solo travelers, who can stay here in a room with shared bath for $48 (breakfast included).

202 E. Elizabeth St. ☎ ***970-493-2337***. *Fax: 970-416-0826. Internet:* www.bbonline.com/co/Elizabeth/index.html. *Rack rates: Double room with shared bath $73, double room with private bath $95. Rates include full breakfast. AE, MC, V.*

University Park Holiday Inn
$$–$$$ Fort Collins

Located right across the street from Colorado State University, the rooms in this hotel surround a nine-story atrium, where the restaurant, lounge, and lobby are located. The atrium once housed living plants, but the greenery attracted insects and caused allergies, so management removed the plants, waxed them leaf-by-leaf, and then returned them to the lobby. With the atrium on one side and huge windows with panoramic views on the other, you'll feel like part of the sky above the plains when you stay here. The suites are spacious and comfortable. Each has a king bed and a separate area with a sofa-sleeper, recliner, and desk. The standard guest rooms are smaller, with one queen bed or two doubles. The hotel also has a pool, exercise room, hot tub, and dry sauna.

425 W. Prospect Ave. ☎ *970-482-2626. Fax: 970-493-6265. Internet:* www. holiday-inn.com/ftcollinsco. *Rack rates: Standard rooms $79–$129, suites $129–$159. Rates may rise slightly higher during key college events. AE, DC, DISC, MC, V.*

Where to dine

Because Fort Collins brews beer by the truckload, it comes as no surprise that many locals head for pubs when suppertime rolls around. Some of the town's best dining is in its brewpubs and in one English-style tavern. Most of these pubs have nonsmoking areas and patios, so you can usually find a good place to sit with children. The town also has gourmet restaurants, and cheaper places that cater to students.

Big City Burrito
$ **Fort Collins   MEXICAN**

Because so many variables come into play, you could dine at this hole-in-the-wall every meal and never have two burritos taste alike. Choose between two burrito sizes, six varieties of tortillas, eight fillings (including potato and chicken mole), and four salsas, not to mention rice and cheese. For a little extra, add sour cream and/or guacamole. Throw in the human factor — this is significant, because the workers can be distracted — and the burritos become entertainingly random. If you ever did get a burrito like your last one, you could use any of several dozen bottles of hot sauce to permanently alter it (and maybe you). It seems the customers bring in their favorite sauces and leave them by the counter, just in case.

510 S. College. ☎ *970-482-3303. No reservations, but phone orders accepted. Main courses: $1.79–$8.99. Open: Daily lunch and dinner. AE, DISC, MC, V.*

Bisetti's Ristorante
$$ **Fort Collins   ITALIAN**

When Bisetti's opened in 1979, the owners lacked the money they needed to decorate their basement dining room. Customers signed a Chianti bottle, and the owners hung the bottle from the ceiling. Twenty-some years later, the restaurant no longer lacks decor. Its hearty fare has made friends through time, as illustrated by the thousands of empty Chianti bottles hanging from the ceiling. Almost all dishes come with homemade pasta, so you really can't go wrong. But if you're at a loss for what to order, look for the little Chianti bottles on the menu, which indicate customer favorites. Afterwards, have some cheesecake; it's the best dessert in town.

120 S. College Ave. ☎ *970-493-0086. Reservations accepted. Main courses: $8.95–$17.95. Open: Mon–Fri lunch and dinner; Sat–Sun dinner only. AE, DC, DISC, MC, V.*

Charco Broiler
$–$$ Fort Collins   STEAKS

It's hard to say exactly what's inside this 1957 steakhouse, because the place is so dark, but there seems to be a lounge, three dining rooms, barn-wood walls, wagon wheels, and booths of red Naugahyde. You can get eggs and pancakes in the morning; sandwiches, salads, and burgers in the afternoon; and the best steaks in town at night. The clientele includes cops, truckers, and, during college-football weekends, alumni and TV camera crews.

1716 E. Mulberry. ☎ *970-482-1472. Reservations not accepted. Main courses: $3.25–$36. Open: Mon–Sat breakfast, lunch, and dinner; Sun dinner only, starting at 11 a.m. AE, DC, DISC, MC, V.*

CooperSmith's Pub & Brewing
$–$$ Fort Collins   AMERICAN

The oldest brew pub in northern Colorado, CooperSmith's attracts a diverse crowd of tourists, locals, and students, who drink a wide range of brews — everything from ginger ale to chili beer (spiced by real Anaheim chilis) — while dining on good if unremarkable pub fare and wood-fired pizzas. No matter what you order, you're sure to enjoy one of Fort Collins's most active spots. It has a spacious, high-ceiling bar, a nonsmoking dining room, and two patios, one of which opens onto the pedestrian-only Old Town Square. The brewpub also runs a pool hall next door.

5 Old Town Square. ☎ *970-498-0483. Reservations for large parties only, but not on weekends. Main courses: $4.95–$18.95. Open: Daily lunch and dinner. AE, MC, V.*

Crown Pub
$–$$ Fort Collins   PUB FARE

This English-style pub serves fish and chips, half-pound burgers, a London broil with "starch du jour," and sautéed chicken in curry sauce. You can drink a dark English beer next to dark wooden walls, gilded mirrors, and paintings of sailing ships. Because it has so much character, this may be my favorite place in town.

134 S. College Ave. ☎ *970-484-5929. Reservations not accepted. Main courses: $6.95–$15.95. Open: Lunch and dinner daily. AE, MC, V.*

Screamin' ice cream

A trip to Fort Collins isn't complete without a cone of handmade ice cream. At **Walrus Ice Cream Company,** 125 W. Mountain Ave. (☎ 970-482-5919), the teenagers behind the counter jam candy into bowls of homemade ice cream and don't stop until the whole thing comes close to avalanching. Offerings include sundaes, splits, homemade ice-cream cakes, and *tusks* (vanilla ice cream dipped in chocolate, on a stick). If Walrus Ice Cream is too crowded, try **Kilwins Chocolates & Ice Cream,** 114 S. College Ave. (☎ 970-221-9444). Kilwins may have the town's best ice cream, but it loses points for its Plain Jane presentation. Try a scoop of the chocolate caramel cashew. The big guys — **Ben & Jerry,** that is — have a shop at 1 Old Town Square (☎ 970-407-0899).

Jon and Angie's Blue Note
$ Fort Collins   COFFEE

Jon and Angie's Blue Note may be the most conspicuously Bohemian coffee shop in Colorado. Once-revolutionary books line the shelves, a back room holds bongo drums and guitars that you're free to play, and you can even plug in one of the electric guitars if you really want to. If your playing isn't so hot, pick out an album and spin it on a turntable. The coffee shop also has a pool table and a chessboard. The emphasis here is on the strong coffee, but the joint also sells tasty breakfast burritos, veggie lasagna, and muffins for cheap. On certain nights, stick around and hear poetry, spoken-word, and open-mike jams.

147 W. Oak St. ☎ *970-490-2695. No reservations. All items under $4. Open: Daily breakfast and lunch. Credit cards not accepted.*

Linden's Brewing
$$ Fort Collins   AMERICAN/CAJUN

Linden's Brewing deserves a special award for christening one of its past beers "Red Ass Ale," presumably in honor of a charismatic mule. Linden's has more than just a great beer name. It serves tasty Cajun fare — including gumbo, crawfish étouffée, and shrimp Creole — and offers live entertainment on Wednesday through Saturday nights. Performers like Widespread Panic and Big Head Todd and the Monsters have passed through on their way up; other, even bigger names, have passed through on their way down. Black lights throw purple and blue hues against the brick walls. The stage is in the back, surrounded by tables and some space for milling and dancing. It's a cool room, and a nice fit for the many jazz acts who play here. It's open until around 2 a.m. on most nights, so it's a good late-night spot.

214 Linden St. ☎ *970-482-9291. Reservations accepted. Main courses: $8.95–$21.95. Open: Lunch and dinner daily. AE, DISC, MC, V.*

Exploring Fort Collins

Fort Collins has such an understated attitude, it's easy to overlook the many great (and mostly free) activities in town. All the attractions I describe in this section (except for the Discovery Center) cost nothing and are fun.

The best things to see and do

Discovery Center Science Museum

Don't be put off by this museum's inauspicious location in an elementary-school building. The 120 exhibits in six rooms could just as easily be in a glitzy big-city museum. They explore energy, motion, force, flight, machines; structural designs, electricity, health, waves, vibration, and other phenomena. Kids. in particular, will get a charge out of the hands-on exhibits.

703 E. Prospect Rd. ☎ *970-472-3990. Internet:* www.dcsm.org. *Open Tues–Sat 10 a.m.–5 p.m., Sun noon to 5 p.m. Admission: Adults 13–59, $6.50; children 3–12, $4.50; seniors 60 and over, $5.*

The Farm at Lee Martinez Park

This 1920 farm adjacent to a Fort Collins City Park lets you stroll into America's farming past. For 25¢, you can get a scoop of feed and hand-nourish the many barnyard animals, including goats, chickens, sheep, turkeys, ducks, cows, and geese. Pigs are also present, but they're ornery, dirty, lazy and uncooperative — in other words, they're pigs. Don't feed them. For $3, kids under 12 can ride the ponies on weekends. There's also a small museum devoted to farming, replete with attention-grabbing exhibits such as "Dairy Cows: Past and Present" and "Harvesting through Time."

600 N. Sherwood St. ☎ *970-221-6665. Summer hours: Tues–Sat 10:00 a.m.–5:30 p.m., Sun noon to 5:30 p.m. Free admission.*

Fort Collins Museum

The Fort Collins Museum explores the city's history using exhibits focusing on a variety of topics. When I visited, this museum was changing exhibits, moving offices, and refurbishing some of the historic cabins on its property. But a downstairs room had an exhibit on Colorado League Baseball, with vignettes from players and photos of old teams. The league, which flourished in the 1930s, '40s, and '50s, consisted mostly of Latino players who competed on Sundays — their one day off from work in the nearby sugar-beet fields. The exhibit is an example of the museum's creative side and shows why it merits a stop.

200 Matthews St. ☎ *970-221-6738. Internet:* www.ci.fort-collins.co.us/museum. *Open Tues–Sat 10 a.m.–5 p.m.; Sun noon–5 p.m. Admission free.*

Museum of Contemporary Art

Some contemporary artists make a living by going postal with paint, so it makes sense that this museum is in Fort Collins' old Post Office. The ground floor houses rotating national and international exhibits. Upstairs is a second gallery for local artists as well as co-ops where artists create and sell their work. The Museum of Contemporary Art likes to display art that incorporates innovative materials and techniques, but it also makes room for pieces by contemporary artists working in traditional forms (read: landscape paintings). Because it's free, convenient, and full of intriguing art, it's an all-around winner.

201 S. College Ave. ☎ 970-482-2787. Open Tues–Fri, 10 a.m.–6 p.m.; Sat noon to 5 p.m. Donations accepted.

The Swetsville Zoo

The Swetsville Zoo began life in 1985 when an alfalfa farmer named Bill Swets began welding together farm equipment, car parts, and scrap metal and turning it into dinosaurs, dragons, bugs, vehicles, and any combination thereof. Drivers started pulling off nearby I-25 to see what Swets had come up with, and the national media soon followed. Nowadays, an estimated 20,000 visitors stop by the farm every year to see the 143 fanciful sculptures on display. Swets, in his early 60s, hangs around and is approachable, but he won't sell any of his creations — he says they're "meant to be fun." This is a can't-miss roadside attraction. If you happen to be passing near Fort Collins on I-25, be sure to see it.

4801 E. Harmony Rd. (at the southeast corner of the I-25/Harmony Road junction). ☎ 970-484-9509. Open: During daylight hours. Donations accepted.

Staying active

Fort Collins may not look like much when it comes to mountain sports. But that's to your advantage because it helps keep the people away. Ignore the silos and head for the foothills west of town. There's plenty to do, including the following:

- ✔ **Fishing:** You can fish the Cache La Poudre River right in Fort Collins, but the trout get bigger and hungrier the closer you get to the headwaters. You can drive partway there by taking Colorado 14 up Poudre Canyon. For a guide, rod, advice, and the mandatory fishing license, go to **St. Peter's Fly Shop,** 202 Remington St. (☎ 970-498-8968).

- ✔ **Golfing:** Like Denver, Fort Collins offers low-key, inexpensive golf. The city operates three courses. Greens fees top out at $24 for 18 holes during peak periods. Courses include the 9-hole **City Park Nine,** 411 S. Bryan (☎ 970-221-6650); the 18-hole **Collindale Golf Course,** 1441 E. Horsetooth Rd. (☎ 970-221-6651); and the **South**

A crash course in malted beverages

Fort Collins has three breweries to go with its three brewpubs. If you're 21 or older and appreciate an occasional malted beverage, find a designated driver and visit the breweries, all of which offer free tours and tastings. The tours repeat similar information about the brewing process. Unless you're more interested in brewing than beer, I recommend taking just one tour and spending the rest of your time in the tasting rooms. Here's what you need to know about each brewery:

One of five major **Anheuser-Busch** breweries in North America, the one at 2351 Busch Drive (at I-25, exit 271) produces roughly 6 million barrels of 22 different alcoholic beverages a year. The brewery is immense, so the tours last up to an hour and involve a mile of walking. Skip the tour and go look at the Budweiser Clydesdales, which live in a luxurious stable next to the tasting room. They're one of five traveling hitches owned by the company. Each horse has hooves the circumference of pizzas, weighs about a ton, and stands 18 hands (6 feet) high at the withers (shoulder). After that, go to the tasting room. *What you'll taste:* Two 12-ounce glasses of the Anheuser-Busch beverages of your choice. Usually there are ten taps running and other selections are available in the bottle. Products range from a nonalcoholic energy drink to King Cobra malt liquor. *The best souvenirs:* You name it — everything from golf balls to piggy banks. *Watch out for:* Budweiser-themed music playing constantly in the tasting room. Call ☎ 970-490-4691 for more information. The brewery is open June through August daily from 9:30 a.m. to 5:00 p.m.; in September daily from 10 a.m. to 4 p.m.; and December through May Thursday through Monday from 10 a.m. to 4 p.m.

New Belgium Brewery, 500 Linden St. (☎ **888-NBB-4044**), produces 250,000 gallons of some of the nation's best beer every year in its wind-powered brewery. New Belgium's Belgian-style beers include the hot-selling Fat Tire Ale, which is huge in Colorado. Brewery employees guide tours once a day on weekdays, and the tours do get crowded. Skip the tour and stay behind in the tasting room after everyone leaves. *What you'll taste:* Usually, eight 5-ounce glasses — six of the brewery's regular beers, and two of its specialty beers. *The best souvenirs:* Bicycle jerseys and flying disks. *Watch out for:* Crowds around 2 p.m. on weekdays. Tours are given Monday through Friday at 2 p.m.; hourly on Saturdays from 11 a.m. to 4 p.m. The tasting room is open Monday through Saturday from 10 a.m. to 6 p.m.

Like New Belgium, **Odell Brewing Company,** 800 E. Lincoln (☎ **970-498-9070**), makes rich, flavorful beer, but its brewery produces only about 25,000 gallons annually. Because the brewery is small, the average tour lasts about 20 minutes and involves only about 100 yards worth of walking. You can even sip one of Odell's English-style beers along the way. If you haven't already guessed, this is the brewery tour I recommend. Afterward, you may have to fight with your traveling partners for a spot at the counter in the tiny tasting room. *What you'll taste:* A 3-ounce sample of each of the 8 to 12 beers on tap. *The best souvenirs:* Fly-fishing shirts and free bumper stickers. *Watch out for:* Your spot at the counter. The brewery is open from Monday through Friday from 10 a.m. to 3 p.m., with a Saturday tour at 2 p.m.

Ridge Golf Club, 5750 S. Lemay Ave. (☎ **970-226-2828**). You can reserve tee times up to three days in advance.

✔ **Hiking:** For quick, scenic walks, visit the same parks described in the following bullet. For a longer excursion, drive into Poudre Canyon and climb **Greyrock.** The 2.8-mile (one-way) Summit Trail and the 3.8-mile (one-way) Meadows Trail both leave from the same trailhead and meet near the mountaintop, making a loop hike possible. Whichever way you go, it's a little over 2,000 vertical feet to the summit. Perhaps 300 vertical feet from the top, where the Summit Trail reconnects with the Meadows Trail, you'll spy the top of Greyrock — a foreboding buttress of rock, shaped like the top of a Stetson Hat. A challenging route departs from the junction and climbs to the top. If you take this route, pay close attention to where you are and don't try anything daring. If you're on the right track, you won't have to do anything scary. From the summit, you'll have a 360-degree view of the area, including distant views of the Great Plains and Wyoming. To reach the Greyrock trailhead, drive 8 miles up Poudre Canyon on Colorado 14.

✔ **Mountain biking:** Intermediate and advanced mountain bikers will enjoy the single track at 2,500-acre **Horsetooth Mountain Park,** 4 miles west of Fort Collins on County Road 38 East (☎ **970-679-4570**). The park has 27 miles of technically challenging trails in the grassy foothills west of Horsetooth Reservoir. The cost is $5 per carload or $2 per individual cyclist. Don't sneak in — you'll be fined if you're caught. For more benign terrain, go to **Lory State Park,** 708 Lodgepole Dr. (☎ **970-493-1623**), or pedal the paved 8.35-mile **Poudre River Trail,** which parallels the river from North Taft Hill Road to East Drake Road. For $25 per day, you can rent a front-suspension mountain bike from **Lee's Cyclery,** 931 Harmony, at Lemay (☎ **970-226-6006**).

✔ **Rafting:** The name Cache La Poudre doesn't have the cachet associated with, say, the Arkansas, but experienced boaters know it well. Like the Arkansas, it poses a variety of challenges, has a long season, and boasts a lengthy stretch of federally designated wild and scenic waters. (Loosely translated, that means it has parts that are undammed, unpolluted, and mostly undeveloped.) From mid-May through mid-August, **Rocky Mountain Adventures** (☎ **800-858-6808** or 970-493-4005; Internet: www.shoprma.com) offers half- and full-day trips on the Cache La Poudre. The full-day trips include some challenging Class 4 waters, so be ready for action. Prices range from $42 to $60 for the half-day trips; the full-day trip costs $88.

Shopping

For fun shopping and people watching, wander through Fort Collins's Old Town area, on College Avenue between Mulberry Street and Jefferson. If Old Town is the heart of Fort Collins, the aorta is in **Old Town Square,** a pedestrian walkway bordered by College Avenue, Mountain, and Walnut streets. Old Town Café has sidewalk cafes, shops, lots of flowers, and some great places for sitting.

If, however, you prefer a mall, then **Foothills Fashion Mall,** 215 E. Foothills Parkway (☎ 970-226-2441), is for you. It has 120 stores, including a Foley's, JC Penney, Mervyn's, and Sears, not to mention ample (yawn) parking. It's open Monday through Saturday from 10 a.m. to 9 p.m., Sunday from 11 a.m. to 6 p.m.

Nightlife

Fort Collins's downtown has more watering holes than a sprinkler. You may enjoy tipping a few at the following spots:

- ✔ **Jay's Bistro,** 151 S. College Ave. (☎ 970-482-1876), has tapas, martinis and piano jazz.

- ✔ At the opposite end of the sound spectrum, but only a short walk away, twinkles **The Starlight** (☎ 970-484-4974), whose motto is "Drink hard, rock harder." Located at 167 N. College Ave., the Starlight books an occasional national blues or rock act but seems to reserve most nights for bands with names such as "Wretch Like Me" and "Chok."

- ✔ Most of the big-name bands go to the **Aggie Theater,** 204 S. College Ave. (☎ 970-407-1322).

- ✔ For techno, trance, and hip-hop, check out **The Matrixx,** 450 Linden Center Dr. (☎ 970-407-0738).

- ✔ If you want to two-step, you'll have to saddle up and ride across town to **Sundance Steakhouse and Country Club,** 2716 E. Mulberry, (☎ 970-484-1600). The Sundance offers Western entertainment nightly.

Fast Facts: Fort Collins

Hospital

Poudre Valley Hospital, 1024 S. Lemay Ave. (☎ 970-495-7000), has a trauma center and emergency room.

Information

The Colorado Welcome Center, 3745 E. Prospect Rd., near I-25 (☎ 970-491-3388), has information on Fort Collins and on other Colorado destinations.

Internet Access

Fort Collins Library, 201 Peterson St. (☎ 970-221-6740), has free Internet access, but use is limited to 20 minutes when others are waiting.

Pharmacies

City Drug, 101 S. College (☎ 970-482-1234), can fill your prescription in the downtown area.

Post Office

The Fort Collins Post Office Main Office is at 301 E. Boardwalk Dr. Call ☎ 800-275-8777 for information about hours and other area locations.

Road Conditions

Call ☎ 877-315-7623 or 303-639-1111.

Chapter 17

Northern Colorado High Country (West)

- -

In This Chapter

▶ Festival-going in Aspen

▶ Soaking up Glenwood Springs

▶ Seeing Redstone, a Utopia for the road-weary

▶ Riding and roping in Steamboat Springs

- -

*V*isitors to the mountain towns west of Vail (Chapter 18) and north of Crested Butte will find plenty of variety, if not always solitude. Forty miles south of I-70 is Aspen, a historic mining town, cultural hub, and celebrity hotspot. Aspen can be hard to afford for one person, let alone a family, but you can stay in Carbondale and save on lodging while exploring the five nearby ski areas. Glenwood Springs, a small city located right on the interstate, is popular with families and known for its enormous Hot Springs Pool.

If you detour onto less-traveled mountain roads, you can choose between two fine destinations. Redstone offers a quiet retreat into nature — and the past. The town has some stunning historic buildings — including an enormous Tudor mansion built in the early 1900s — but the real allure is the quiet setting in the West Elk Mountains. For a truly Western experience, your best bet is Steamboat Springs, a bustling town that happily blends recreation and ranching.

What's Where?: The Region and Its Major Attractions

You can have a lot of fun in this region if you set up a base camp in Glenwood or Carbondale and make short excursions to area attractions. Steamboat Springs, however, is a destination unto itself, and its Western flavor makes the trip worthwhile.

Northern Colorado High Country (West)

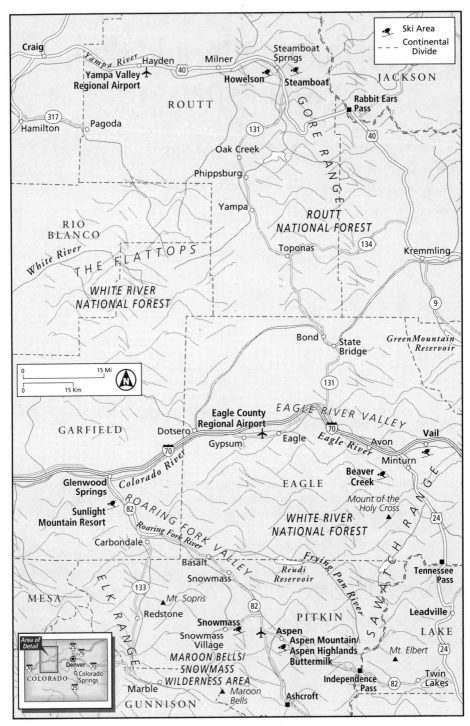

Ski Area
Continental Divide

Craig
Yampa River
Hayden
Milner
Steamboat Sprngs
JACKSON

Yampa Valley
Regional Airport
Howelson
Steamboat

ROUTT
Rabbit Ears
Pass

317
Hamilton
Pagoda
131
40

Oak Creek

Phippsburg

RIO
BLANCO
White River
THE FLATTOPS
Yampa
ROUTT
NATIONAL FOREST

WHITE RIVER
NATIONAL FOREST
Toponas
134
Kremmling

9

Bond
State
Bridge
GreenMountain
Reservoir

15 Mi
15 Km

EAGLE RIVER VALLEY

GARFIELD
Dotsero
Eagle County
Regional Airport
Gypsum
Eagle
Eagle River
Avon
Vail

Minturn

Glenwood
Springs
Colorado River
Beaver
Creek

EAGLE

Sunlight
Mountain Resort
82
Mount of the
Holy Cross
24

Carbondale
ROARING FORK VALLEY
Roaring Fork River
WHITE RIVER
NATIONAL FOREST

Basalt
Reudi
Reservoir
Frying Pan River
Tennessee
Pass

133
Snowmass
82
Leadville

MESA
Mt. Sopris
PITKIN
LAKE

Redstone
Snowmass
Mt. Elbert
24

Snowmass
Village
Aspen
Aspen Mountain
Aspen Highlands
Buttermilk

MAROON BELLS
SNOWMASS
WILDERNESS AREA
Independence
Pass
82
Twin
Lakes

Marble
Maroon
Bells
Ashcroft

GUNNISON

Area of
Detail
25
76
70
Denver
70
COLORADO
Colorado
Springs
25

Aspen

Aspen can be snooty, and its prices inspire awe, but at least you get something in return. It has buildings that date to a mining boom in the 1880s and 1890s; it has culture to rival any town of its size in the West; and it has wilderness to spare. Among its finest attractions are

- ✔ **Four ski areas,** including prime choices for beginners **(Buttermilk),** intermediates **(Snowmass),** experts **(Aspen Highlands),** and celebrities **(Aspen Mountain).**

- ✔ The **Aspen Music Festival,** a nine-week celebration and school with up to six classical performances daily.

- ✔ Hiking and backpacking in the stunning **Maroon Bells/Snowmass Wilderness Area.**

Glenwood Springs, Carbondale, and Redstone

A popular resort since 1888, Glenwood Springs has some of the most appealing family attractions in the state. Carbondale offers fine restaurants and inexpensive lodging near Aspen. And farther off the beaten path, in the heart of the West Elk Mountains, hides Redstone, an unincorporated town that was once a Utopian community for coal miners. When you're in this area, don't miss

- ✔ **Hot Springs Pool,** the largest public hot springs in the world

- ✔ **Glenwood Caverns,** where two newly opened rooms showcase pristine, ornate limestone formations

- ✔ **Redstone Castle,** a 42-room, lavishly decorated mansion built 100 years ago by one of the world's richest men

Steamboat Springs

Ranching remains a major industry in the Yampa Valley, and you can sample Western culture just by walking down Lincoln Avenue in Steamboat Springs. While you're in the neighborhood, you should also visit

- ✔ **Steamboat Ski Area,** home to Colorado's best glade skiing

- ✔ **Strawberry Park Hot Springs,** where a frosty river and 147-degree geothermal springs together stir up a natural paradise

- ✔ **Ranches near town,** where you can ride, rope, and relax

Aspen

Aspen has a lot going for it. It's a historic mining community near stunning wilderness. It has traditionally been home to some of the nation's finest skiers and mountaineers, including members of the 10th Mountain Division, who helped develop the ski area on Aspen Mountain after World War II. And since the 1940s, the town's leaders have worked hard to promote recreation, music, culture, and ideas — all of which exist in spades in today's Aspen.

Aspen remains fun, stimulating, and scenic, but don't kid yourself: It isn't for everyone. Prices are high, traffic in and out of town can be heavy, and the locals don't always embrace the common folk.

If you're a Hollywood producer or the permanently elected president of a small Caribbean republic, you should plan a long vacation here. For you, Aspen has designer shops, prestigious galleries, and some of the finest restaurants in the nation. You can tip your mug in historic barrooms where the locals really do get out and party. With four ski areas, Aspen offers plenty of variety on the slopes, and the town's luxury hotels will treat you like royalty (probably because you *are*). If, however, you don't have the do-re-mi or are just plain regular, you may need to consider basing yourself in a satellite town, such as Glenwood Springs or Carbondale. Both have bus service to Aspen and offer lodging at a fraction of the cost. Plus, they're pretty attractive places themselves.

Getting there

Aspen is 172 miles west of Denver and 130 miles east of Grand Junction. During winter and early spring, the only way to reach Aspen is by taking Colorado 82 southeast for 42 miles from Glenwood Springs (on I-70). In summer and early fall, you can sometimes shorten the trip from Denver by taking Colorado 91 south to Leadville, continuing south for 17 miles on U.S. 24, and then taking Colorado 82 east over Independence Pass 44 miles. This route stays closed until road crews clear the snow off 12,094-foot Independence Pass in spring.

Don't drive over the pass during stormy weather of if you're tired. Though paved, this stretch of Colorado 82 has only one lane (total) in places and some sobering drop-offs alongside it.

Aspen is far enough from Denver International Airport to make flying closer a good idea. There are two airports within easy striking distance of town. The closest is **Aspen-Pitkin County Airport** (☎ 970-920-5380), 3 miles northwest of Aspen on Colorado 82. **United Express** offers daily nonstop service from Denver to Aspen; **America West Express** offers a similar service from Phoenix. During winter, you can also fly to Aspen nonstop from Minneapolis/St. Paul on **Northwest Jet Airlink.** Another option is to fly into **Eagle County Airport,** 70 miles from Aspen on I-70.

Many hotels offer complimentary ground transfers into town from **Aspen-Pitkin County Airport.** If a transfer is unavailable, call **High Mountain Taxi** (☎ 970-925-TAXI). **Avis, Budget, Dollar, Thrifty, and Hertz** all have desks at Pitkin County Airport. For information on contacting individual airlines and car-rental agencies, see the Appendix.

To catch a shuttle to Aspen from Eagle County Airport or Denver International Airport, call **Colorado Mountain Express** (☎ 800-525-6363). The one-way trip from Eagle County costs $62 per person; from Denver, it's $102.

Amtrak (☎ 800-872-7245) trains stop at Glenwood Springs Station (☎ 970-945-9563). In Glenwood, you can rent a car through **Enterprise,** 124 W. Sixth St. (☎ 970-945-8360), or **Glenwood Springs Ford-Lincoln-Mercury,** 2222 Devereux Rd. (☎ 877-330-0030 or 970-384-2460). You can also catch a bus to Aspen; for more information on schedules and fares, contact the **Rubey Park Transit Center** (☎ 970-925-8484; Internet: www.rfta.com).

Getting around

In Aspen, ditch your car and take the bus. Free, regular shuttle buses serve most popular destinations around Aspen. This includes Aspen Mountain, Aspen Highlands, and Buttermilk ski areas. (Most of the time, rides to Snowmass cost $3 for adults, $2 for kids ages 6 to 16, but during winter you can take a free skier shuttle during the day.) The local shuttles usually run from around 6 a.m. to 2 a.m. You can also catch rides to far-flung locales such as Carbondale ($5 one-way), Glenwood Springs ($6), and Rifle ($9). This is how a lot of workers reach this parking-deprived community. For the latest schedules and fares, stop by the **Rubey Park Transit Center** (☎ 970-925-8484; Internet: www.rfta.com), on Durant Avenue between Mill and Galena streets.

By taking the bus, you can avoid some of the parking challenges around town. Though you can usually find a spot, you'll have to pay $1 an hour for many downtown spots on Monday through Saturday; in other areas, you'll have to move the vehicle every two hours (or right when you start having fun).

If you need a ride, call **High Mountain Taxi** (☎ 970-925-8294).

Where to stay

Over the last 20 years, Aspen has gradually lost most of its affordable lodging. As they opened, the town's big, expensive hotels began sharply discounting their rooms during slow periods, all but wiping out business for the small, cheap motels. As a result, the so-called little guys have closed shop, sold their land, and been replaced by newer and ever more expensive hotels.

If you're on a budget and don't care when you see Aspen, come during late spring and late fall, when you can stay in palatial digs for around $100 a night.

Hotel Jerome
$$$$$ Aspen

When he built the Hotel Jerome in 1889, the silver and retail magnate Jerome Wheeler hoped it would rival the famous Ritz Hotel of Paris for luxury. Wheeler seems to have started a trend in Aspen. Nowadays his hotel isn't the only opulent place in town, but it is *the* place if you want your luxury in a historic setting. The hotel's common areas feel more authentic than the rooms do. As you wander these areas, you'll pass arched hallways, an oak fireplace mantle, tiles colored with gold and cobalt, and the hotel's old paging system and front desk. The 92 guest rooms sport the same feeling of newness as modern luxury units, only with Victorian furniture and eccentric floor plans.

330 E. Main St., Aspen. ☎ *800-331-7213 or 970-920-1000. Fax: 970-920-2050. Internet: www.hoteljerome.com. Rack rates: Oct–Nov 21 $225–$335; Nov 22–April 20 $425–$710; April 21–May21 $230–$335; May22– September $425–$555. AE, DC, DISC, MC, V.*

Limelite Lodge
$$–$$$$ Aspen

If you can afford the rates here, then you can vacation in downtown Aspen. The inn, which has some of the cheapest prices in town, encompasses three motel-style buildings. Don't worry; none is a dump. Rooms are clean and come with refrigerators; a few come with full kitchens. The inn serves a free continental breakfast in a sunny lounge area. The lodge is within walking distance of the gondola at Aspen Mountain.

228 E. Cooper, Aspen. ☎ *800-433-0832 or 970-925-3025. Fax: 970-925-5120. Internet: www.limelightlodge.com. Rack rates: April–Dec 14, $57–$177; Christmas week $127–$277; Jan–March $147–$257. Rates include continental breakfast. AE, DC, DISC, MC, V.*

The Little Nell
$$$$ Aspen

The Little Nell competes directly with The St. Regis for Aspen's ultra-wealthy clientele, but the two hotels have little in common other than luxury. The Little Nell is considerably smaller and more intimate. Owned by the Aspen Skiing Company, it's right at the base of the gondola (which is a short walk away for guests of the St. Regis). It welcomes dogs and even has biscuits at the bell stand. And its rooms, each with a gas fireplace and most with balconies, are generally larger than the ones at the St. Regis. The hotel does not, however, have as many places that invite public lounging, mingling, and star-gazing.

675 E. Durant, Aspen. ☎ *888-843-6355 or 970-920-4600. Fax: 970-920-4670. Internet:* www.thelittlenell.com. *Early June–Sept $395–$520; Oct–mid-Nov and mid-May–early June $250–$325; mid-Nov–mid-Dec and mid-April $425–$575; Dec 20–New Year's $850; Jan–early April, $595–$795. Closed April 20–May 15. AE, DC, DISC, MC, V.*

The St. Regis
$$$$$ **Aspen**

The St. Regis recently spent $12 million on new decor that one employee described as "Colorado Ralph Lauren." Loosely translated, Colorado Ralph Lauren seems to mean rocks, leather, wood, rawhide, earth tones, and a higher price tag than "Colorado Wal-Mart." This sprawling luxury hotel, which opens onto splendid views of Aspen Mountain, has everything you'd expect for a small fortune: a swimming pool, spa, health club, enormous bronze sculptures, bellhops, views, a concierge, ultra-trendy restaurants, and the occasional celebrity sighting. You can even acquire your own ski butler — someone who will tune your skis, warm your boots, and guide you around the hill.

315 E. Dean St., Aspen. ☎ *888-454-9005 or 970-920-3300. Fax: 970-925-8998. Internet:* www.stregisaspen.com. *Rack rates: $225 to $1,140 double. AE, DC, DISC, MC, V.*

Skier's Chalet Motel
$$–$$$$ **Aspen**

This budget motel lets you experience the trappings of the old Aspen. Built in 1962 and decorated like a Swiss Chalet, the lodge is right next to the remaining towers on the old Lift 1, which was Aspen's first chairlift and was once the longest lift in America. In the morning, you can easily walk to a modern, functioning chairlift; when you're done skiing, you can glide back to the door. The motel has more character than the Limelite Lodge, but its rooms are darker and older-feeling, and they get noisy when people in ski boots clomp past on the wooden walkways. Ask for a room facing the ski area. It won't cost extra, and the views of the skiers and ski hill are spectacular.

233 Gilbert St., Aspen. ☎ *970-920-2037. Fax 970-920-6504. Internet:* www.stayaspen.com. *Rack rates: Jan 3–Feb 8, $145; Feb 9–March 31, $160; Dec 21–Jan 2, $190; rest of year, $110. MC, V.*

Where to dine

Within a few square blocks in downtown Aspen are a half-dozen of Colorado's best restaurants — and some of the finest in America. Prices are high, but many gourmet eateries have reasonably priced bar menus, and other places offer early-evening and off-season specials. Choose your spots carefully and you can dine well here without breaking the bank. (It's lodging that presents the biggest challenge in Aspen.) Here are a few places to get you started.

Cache Cache

$$–$$$ **Aspen** **FRENCH**

Cache Cache opened with just eight tables 17 years ago and has moved the walls back twice since then. Many locals have been coming here for years when they want a scrumptious meal. Inside the open, relaxed dining area, you can take in the activity around you, study the black and white photos of French street life, or simply enjoy the warm colors and candlelight. The offerings include terrines, seafood, meats, and rotisserie-cooked chicken and duck. (Try the rabbit stew.) If you're on a budget, order off the bar menu, which consists entirely of meals costing $12.

205 S. Mill St., Aspen. ☎ 970-925-3775. Reservations recommended. Main courses: $12–$34. Open: Dinner daily. Closed late spring and late fall. AE, MC, V.

Campo de Fiori Ristorante

$$ **Aspen** **NORTHERN ITALIAN**

Campo de Fiori has one of those rustic rooms that make wine and bread seem like an imperative. Fallen leaves have been painted on the floors, empty jugs and old books clutter shelves above the tables, and the brightly painted wooden furniture seems to have come from an Italian yard sale. Among other options, you can choose between veal, a thick seafood soup, stuffed chicken breast, rack of lamb, steaks, and fish-and-pasta dishes. Don't be surprised if you taste garlic, vinegar, or gourmet cheese in your food.

205 S. Mill St., Aspen. ☎ 970-920-7717. Reservations accepted. Main courses: $12–$29. Open: Dinner daily. AE, MC, V.

Hotel Jerome Garden Terrace/Century Room

$$$–$$$$ **Aspen** **AMERICAN**

For a blow-out meal, head for the Hotel Jerome and dine on the Garden Terrace in summer and in the Century Room in winter. Aspen has better-known restaurants than this one and rooms more inviting than the Hotel Jerome's stodgy Century Room, but no local chef is doing better work than Todd Slossberg. In the last two years, Slossberg has twice been nominated by the James Beard Foundation for the honor of "Best Chef in the Southwest." His dishes are symphonies of fresh regional produce and native game such as elk, lamb, and trout. The hotel describes proper attire as being "Aspen casual," meaning anything from jeans to furs — and sometimes both.

330 E. Main St., Aspen. ☎ 800-331-7213 or 970-920-1000. Reservations recommended. Main courses: $21–$34. Open: Dinner daily. AE, DC, MC, V.

Little Annie's Eating House
$$ Aspen   AMERICAN

Little Annie's opened its doors in 1972 and has been crammed with cus-
tomers much of the time since then. During winter, people line up for a
chance to eat the restaurant's reasonably priced steaks, salmon, trout,
chicken, and burgers. The decor is as all-American as the food: checker-
board tablecloths, wagon wheel lanterns, a yoke, and hundreds of pin
flags from golf courses.

*517 E. Hyman Ave., Aspen. ☎ 970-925-1098. Reservations not accepted. Main
courses: $7–$18. Open: Lunch and dinner daily. AE, DISC, MC, V.*

Mogador
$$–$$$ Aspen   MEDITERRANEAN

One of the most atmospheric rooms in town, Mogador has jeweled light
fixtures, Moroccan lanterns, stone walls, colorfully painted cement floors,
and candelabras that, come nighttime, provide most of the light in the
room. In case you start thinking you're in Aspen, the owners send a belly
dancer through the place on weekends. The chef, C. Barclay Dodge, usu-
ally prepares hot and cold appetizers, plus fish, shrimp, poultry, and
meat dishes. Desserts are serious business here, and many of the 50
Spanish wines go swimmingly with sweets.

*430 E. Hyman, Aspen. ☎ 970-429-1072. Reservations recommended. Main courses:
$18–$35; bar menu $5–$15. Open: Dinner daily. Closed Oct–Dec 15, April–Jun 6. AE,
MC, V.*

The Red Onion
$–$$ Aspen   MEXICAN

Even if you're not hungry, come here for a beer and a look at the original
Brunswick bar, which dates to 1892. Atop the bar, two painted gypsy figures have been perching for even longer than the bar's most devoted
patrons. If you dine here, you'll probably sit in a back room that was once
a hidden gambling area, surrounded by photos of famous musicians who
performed here when the place was a nightclub. The fare consists mostly
of Mexican combination plates, and the bar serves un-historic beverages
such as Jell-O shots and Colorado microbrews.

*420 E. Cooper Ave., Aspen. ☎ 970-925-9043. Main courses: $9–$15. Open: Lunch
and dinner daily. Closed in late April and early May. AE, MC, V.*

Exploring Aspen

In Aspen, you can walk through Victorian neighborhoods left over from
the early 1890s, when Aspen was briefly the nation's biggest silver producer. You can attend more high-profile cultural events than in any

other mountain town; and you can also escape into some of the tallest and most majestic peaks in the state. To get a well-balanced view of Aspen, do your best to sample each of the town's gifts.

The best things to see and do

If you don't feel like spending your day on Aspen's trails, you may enjoy

- ✔ **Getting the royal treatment.** The 77,000-square-foot **Aspen Club and Spa,** 1450 Crystal Lake Rd. (☎ **866-4VITALITY** or 970-925-8900), has everything you need to exhaust your muscles, including a swimming pool, tennis courts, a large weight room, personal trainers, and group-fitness workouts. Afterwards, recover with a massage, a healthy meal, or a treatment at the full-service spa. Three-day club memberships cost $180. No membership is required for the spa.

- ✔ **Mining for fun.** If you reserve ahead, you can tour two Aspen-area silver mines. One tour goes into the **Smuggler Mine,** 2 miles east of town off Colorado 82, which produced the world's largest silver nugget (1,840 pounds) in 1894 — right after silver lost most of its value. On this 90-minute tour (cost: $20 for adults, $15 for children under 12), you'll walk 1,200 feet into the mine, usually with a former miner. Tours are conducted by appointment only. Offered on Saturdays during summer, the **Compromise Mine Tour** generates more excitement. You'll be picked up at your hotel, driven high up Aspen Mountain to the mine entrance, and then get towed more than 2,000 feet underground behind an electric mine locomotive. The tour takes two hours and costs $30 for adults, $20 for children under 12. Children under 5 are not allowed on either tour. Call ☎ **970-925**-2049 for reservations.

- ✔ **Visiting the low-rent district.** From Memorial Day through Labor Day, you can go on a guided tour of the mostly abandoned 1890s mining town of **Ashcroft,** 14 miles southeast of Aspen on Castle Creek Road. At 11 a.m. and 2 p.m. daily, one of the ghost town's caretakers will walk you through the eight remaining buildings, including a saloon that's been converted into a museum. The tour costs $3 for ages 10 and over and lasts 20 to 30 minutes. You can also visit the town on your own, free of charge. For more information, call or visit **HeritageAspen: Aspen's Historical Society,** 620 W. Bleeker St. (☎ **970-925-3721**; Internet: www.aspenhistory. org). If you like Ashcroft, you'll also enjoy the ghost town of **Independence,** 17 miles east of Aspen on Colorado 82.

- ✔ **Remembering John Denver.** For the next few years, the **Wheeler/ Stallard House,** 620 W. Bleeker St. (☎ **970-925-3721**) will devote a room to Aspen's own John Denver, replete with the singer's platinum records, tour jackets, and guitar case. The Denver shrine notwithstanding, this 1889 Queen Anne Revival–style house is hardly the Hard Rock Café — it's the town's historical museum and has a large, permanent exhibit on Aspen's past. It's open Tuesday through Saturday from 10 a.m. to 4 p.m. Admission is $6 for people over 10, $5 seniors 65 and older, and free for kids 10 and under.

✔ **Admiring art.** Because Aspen brims with people who have an inordinate amount of wall and floor space — and the means to fill it with fine art — the town has more than 25 galleries, many of which sell museum-quality pieces and even masterpieces. Published by *Aspen Magazine,* the town's *Art Gallery Guide* describes the current galleries and has a map of where to find them. Don't miss the **Aspen Art Museum,** 590 N. Mill St. (☎ **970-925-8050**), which brings world-class art exhibitions to Aspen. The museum is open Tuesday through Saturday from 10 a.m. to 6 p.m.; Sunday from noon to 6 p.m. Admission costs $3 for adults, $2 for students and seniors, and is free for kids under 12.

Tours

Okay, maybe you feel embarrassed about wanting to gawk at the homes of the rich and famous. Get over it. If the stars and CEOs hadn't built such ostentatious homes, you wouldn't be driving around looking at them. For a tour of Aspen that blends scenery, history, and — yes — celebrity homes, call **Ambassador Tours** (☎ **800-734-6506**). The company's guide, a local party disc jockey whose stage name is "Disco Dan," has spun records at many celebrity gatherings and has a few innocuous stories to tell. A two-hour tour for two people costs $160; for a family, the same tour runs $290. People obsessed with Hollywood will probably enjoy themselves, but those less star-struck may find better places to spend their vacation budget.

Staying active

There are so many ways to pass a day in the mountains near Aspen, it's hard to home in on just a few. The ones listed here are particularly enjoyable:

✔ **Cycling:** Hardcore road cyclists should get up early, beat the traffic, and attempt the 4,000-vertical foot, 20-mile grind to 12,000-foot **Independence Pass.** Other times, consider a more gradual 12-mile climb up the length of the **Maroon Creek Road,** a valley-bottom drive that's closed to most motor vehicles from 8:30 a.m. to 5:00 p.m. daily. If you'd rather avoid cars altogether, you can pedal on paved bike trails throughout the Roaring Fork Valley. The mountain biking is just as much fun — and even more extensive. To rent a bike and obtain area maps, go to **Aspen Velo Bike Shop,** 465 N. Mill St. (☎ **970-925-1495**).

✔ **Golfing:** At **Aspen Golf Course,** 1 mile west of Aspen on Colorado 82 (☎ **970-925-2145**), greens fees are $80 for 18 holes, $45 for 9 holes, with sharply reduced rates late in the day.

✔ **Hiking and backpacking:** You can hike straight out of the downtown area, but the most stunning scenery is deep inside the **White River National Forest,** which encompasses the 161,000-acre **Maroon Bells/Snowmass Wilderness Area.** For a fun day in the mountains, visit the ghost town of Ashcroft and then hike the **Cathedral Lake Trail,** located 15 miles southeast of Aspen off the **Castle Creek Road.** The 2.7-mile (one-way) trail climbs 2,000 feet to a small lake. If you want to hike near the two red-brown, pyramid-shaped peaks known as **Maroon Bells,** take a bus ($5.50 adults, $3.50 ages 6 to 16) from the **Rubey Park Transit Center (☎ 970-925-8484;** Internet: www.rfta.com) to the end of Maroon Creek Drive and walk 1.8 miles to **Crater Lake.** Backpackers and aggressive hikers sometimes forge onward through the Snowmass/Maroon Bells Wilderness all the way to Crested Butte. Most private vehicles are barred from Maroon Creek Drive between 8:30 a.m. and 5:00 p.m. You can, however, take the drive for a $10 fee between 7:00 and 8:30 a.m. and between 5 and 7 p.m. Backpackers and people with disabilities can always drive the road after paying the $10. For maps and information visit the **White River National Forest Aspen Ranger District Office,** 806 W. Hallam St. (☎ **970-925-3445**).

✔ **Horseback riding:** From May 1 through November 15, **Aspen Wilderness Outfitters (☎ 970-963-0211)** keeps horses in stables at **Snowmass Village** and offers rides ranging from one-hour strolls to multiday trips. Prices start at $40 for one hour. Children under 7 are not allowed.

Hitting the slopes

Lift tickets sold by **Aspen/Snowmass** are good at any of four mountains, linked by a free shuttle system from downtown Aspen. In 2002–2003, a high-season, adult, all-day lift ticket cost $68. See Table 17-1 for the technical lowdown on each resort.

Table 17-1   Ski Report: Aspen Highlands, Aspen Mountain, Buttermilk, and Snowmass

Aspen Highlands	Aspen Mountain	Buttermilk	Snowmass
Location Off Colorado 82 just west of Aspen	Downtown Aspen	Off Colorado 82 west of Aspen	Off Colorado 82 west of Aspen
Named trails 115 (20% easiest, 33% more difficult, 17% most difficult, 30% expert)	76 (0% easiest, 48% more difficult, 26% most difficult, 26% expert)	42 (35% easiest, 39% more difficult, 26% most difficult)	83 (7% easiest, 55% more difficult, 18% most difficult, 20% expert)
Vertical drop 3,635 feet	3,267 feet	2,030 feet	4,406 feet

Aspen Highlands	Aspen Mountain	Buttermilk	Snowmass
Base elevation 8,040 feet	7,945 feet	7,870 feet	8,104 feet
Summit elevation 11,675 feet	11,212 feet	9,300 feet	12,510 feet
Skiable terrain 720 acres	673 acres	420 acres	3,010 acres
Average annual snowfall 300 inches	300 inches	200 inches	300 inches
Aspen Highlands	**Aspen Mountain**	**Buttermilk**	**Snowmass**
Lifts 4	8	7	20
Snow phone ☎ 888-277-3676	☎ 888-277-3676	☎ 888-277-3676	☎ 888-277-3676
Aspen Central Reservations ☎ 800-262-7336 or 970-925-9000	☎ 800-262-7336 or 970-925-9000	☎ 800-262-7336 or 970-925-9000	☎ 800-262-7336 or 970-925-9000
Internet www.aspen snowmass.com	www.aspen snowmass.com	www.aspen snowmass.com	www.aspen snowmass.com
Cost of 2002–2003 high-season, adult, all-day lift ticket $68	$68	$68	$68

The low-key mountain for locals is **Aspen Highlands,** an area that boasts some formidable expert terrain and one of the largest vertical drops in the nation. Accessible only by hiking (sometimes with assistance from a Sno-Cat that takes skiers partway to the top) and inbounds at Aspen Highlands, Highland Bowl serves up long, precarious, leg-burning descents, and it also affords stunning views of 14,156-foot Maroon Bells and other immense peaks. If you like skiing steep, classic lines, you need to get to Highland Bowl.

The main advantage to **Aspen Mountain** is its convenience to Aspen's chic downtown area. The Silver Queen Gondola climbs 3,267 vertical feet from the base area in town directly to the 11,212-foot summit. Below the summit, the terrain consists mostly of advanced and intermediate runs — including some steep mogul runs — all of which seem to funnel into gullies brimming with skiers who have a certain je ne sais quoi. If possible, ski this mountain with a local who knows the hidden powder stashes and can steer you away from those gullies. Also, keep in mind that Aspen Mountain has just 673 acres — hardly a lot by Western standards.

Buttermilk is a small area catering mostly to beginners. One of its instructors described it as an assembly line churning out new skiers. Former home to the X-Games, Buttermilk also has the largest terrain park at the four resorts. It's more than 2 miles long, with a superpipe for snowboarders and 30 rails.

With 3,010 acres of skiable terrain and the nation's largest vertical drop (4,406 feet), **Snowmass** is the second-largest ski area in the state behind Vail. More than half of its runs are classified as "more difficult" terrain, making Snowmass arguably the single most attractive resort in the state for intermediate skiers.

Shopping

Aspen's downtown area is ornamented by designer boutiques with one-word names and cryptic window displays. Every so often the names change, guaranteeing that shoppers can find the very latest of whatever it is that these stores sell.

Meanwhile, at least two Aspen standbys keep doing a brisk business. Since the mid-'70s, **Curious George Collectibles,** 426 E. Hyman Ave. (☎ 970-925-3315), has traded well-preserved relics from the area's recent past — including antique belt buckles, chaps, guns, and native American jewelry. And for 25 years, **Explore Booksellers,** 211 E. Main St. (☎ 970-925-5336), has carried a thought-provoking selection of contemporary fiction and regional titles. Located in a small Victorian home on Main Street, it has a vegetarian bistro upstairs.

Nightlife

Six nights a week at **The Grottos,** 320 S. Mill St. (☎ 970-925-3775), the owners move the tables out of the way and make room for dancers and a live band. The bar keeps its kitchen open until 10 p.m., so you can load up on wings, pizza, or the popular she-crab soup during the first set.

The most popular club acts often play at **The Double Diamond,** 450 S. Galena St. (☎ **970-920-6905**).

A quiet, dark, celebrity-studded hotspot is **Whiskey Rocks,** 315 E. Dean St. (inside the St. Regis Hotel; ☎ **970-920-3300**). Managed by supermodel Cindy Crawford's husband, Rande Gerber, this is the place to come for gourmet appetizers, Manhattans, and shooters.

The **J-Bar,** 330 E. Main St. (inside the Hotel Jerome; ☎ **970-920-1000**), is equal parts sports bar, historic barroom, and neighborhood pub. Even when there's a big game on the tube, it's hard to ignore the ornate, hand-carved bar that has been here since the hotel opened in 1889.

And if you want to visit Hunter S. Thompson's haunts, go to **Woody Creek Tavern,** 0002 Woody Creek Plaza (☎ **970-923-4585**), in Woody Creek.

Culture

Aspen has been an oasis of culture ever since the 1940s, when an eminent Chicago couple not only bankrolled the first chairlift on Aspen Mountain but also established the Aspen Music Festival and the Aspen Center for Humanistic Studies. Today, the town is particularly rich in classical music, especially from mid-June to mid-August, when the **Aspen Music Festival and School** (☎ **970-925-9042;** Internet: www.aspenmusic festival.com) schedules as many as six concerts a day at venues throughout town. The offerings range from free student performances to recitals by virtuosos, for which tickets may cost as much as $55.

Another notable festival is **Jazz Aspen Snowmass** (☎ **970-920-4996**), which brings top jazz performers to Snowmass Village during June. Herbie Hancock, Roy Hargrove, and Dr. John have performed in recent years. Tickets cost $43 to $48.

From mid-June to late August, you can sit in a partly open tent and take in plays by **Aspen Theater in the Park** (☎ **970-925-9313;** Internet: www.aspentip.org). This professional theater company usually does four selections every summer, with tickets costing $25 and $30.

The culture doesn't stop coming in winter. To catch up on happenings in town, stop by the box office inside the **Wheeler Opera House,** 320 E. Hyman Ave. (☎ **970-920-5770;** Internet: www.wheeleroperahouse.com). While there, see what film screenings are on tap in the Opera House. **The Wheeler Film Society** (☎ **970-925-5973**) regularly screens foreign, independent and vintage films there. Tickets cost $7.50.

Fast Facts: Aspen

Hospital

Aspen Valley Hospital, 0401 Castle Creek Rd. (☎ 970-925-1120), has a 24-hour emergency room and a Level III trauma center.

Information

You can pick up information in two places in downtown Aspen. The main office for the Aspen Chamber Resort Association is at 425 Rio Grande Place (☎ 970-925-1940; Internet: www. aspenchamber.org). The Chamber Resort Association also operates a visitor center inside the Wheeler

Opera House, at Hyman Avenue and Mill Street.

Pharmacy

Carl's Pharmacy, 306 E. Main St. (☎ 970-925-3273), has ample parking and will happily fill your prescription.

Post Office

The main Aspen Post Office is at 235 Puppy Smith Street.

Weather and Road Conditions

Call ☎ 970-920-5454 for the latest road conditions.

Glenwood Springs, Carbondale, and Redstone

In the past few years, some of Aspen's millionaires have relocated to the less showy towns of Glenwood Springs and Carbondale, where they're now rubbing elbows with the people who used to wait on them. Each of these towns has a lot going for it. Back when Aspen residents were still mining silver and not born with it in their mouths, **Glenwood Springs** had already established itself as a world-famous resort. It still has historic hotels, a thriving shopping district, and the largest hot springs pool in the world. In the past hundred years or so, **Carbondale** profited from coal mining, potato farming, railroads, ranching, and construction; each industry left a mark on this curiously zoned community. The upshot is that it really *is* a community. The townspeople, including many artists and mountain athletes, gather on the town's historic Main Street, which seems relaxed even when most of the Roaring Fork Valley crawls with people. The unincorporated community of **Redstone** is the smallest, most remote, and prettiest of the three. Situated on the banks of the Crystal River inside the White River National Forest, it was built around 1900 as a Utopian town for coal miners. Across from a row of historic brick coke ovens is the Craftsman-style Redstone Inn, once a lodge for the unmarried miners. Redstone Castle, a Tudor mansion where the mine's owner once lived, sits atop a grassy hill a mile up the road from the inn.

Getting there

Interstate 70, the Colorado River, and busy railroad tracks all rush down the same corridor through the heart of **Glenwood Springs.** It's 169 miles west of Denver and 84 miles east of Grand Junction. **Carbondale** is 12 miles southeast of Glenwood Springs via Colorado 82. **Redstone** is another 17 miles south of Carbondale on Colorado 133. To reach Aspen from Carbondale, continue east for another 30 miles on Colorado 82.

Amtrak (☎ 800/872-7245) trains stop twice daily in Glenwood Springs Station (☎ 970-945-9563).

In Glenwood, you can rent a car through **Enterprise,** 124 W. Sixth St. (☎ 970-945-8360), or **Glenwood Springs Ford,** 2222 Devereux Rd. (☎ 877-330-0030 or 970-384-2460).

If you want to fly closer than Denver International Airport, your best bet is **Vail/Eagle County Airport** (☎ 970-524-9490), 31 miles east of Glenwood Springs on I-70. See the Vail section in Chapter 18 for information on flights and rental cars at that airport. You can arrange a shuttle from Eagle County into Glenwood Springs (cost: $46.50) through **Colorado Mountain Express** (☎ 800-525-6363).

Getting around

Many locals in Carbondale, Glenwood Springs, and Aspen use buses to travel between towns. The **Roaring Fork Transit Authority** (☎ 970-925-8484) serves all three communities, but not Redstone. To get to Aspen from Glenwood Springs, it'll cost you $6 one way. Service runs from about 6 a.m. to midnight.

Inside Glenwood proper, **Ride Glenwood Springs** offers bus service between Wal-Mart, in the south part of town, and Roaring Fork Marketplace at the town's west end, for $2 per day. There's ample parking at the ends of town, so this service comes in handy when the downtown lots fill up. The bus usually runs daily from 7 a.m. to 10 p.m. Call ☎ 970-945-2575 to find out more about stops and schedules.

Where to stay

If you stay in Glenwood or Carbondale when skiing Aspen, you can choose between clean family-run motels, chain hotels, and historic digs, usually for about $100 to $200 less per night than you'd pay for a comparable spot in you-know-where. And you save on meals, too. As for Redstone, it's in its own universe, one that I'm dying to revisit soon. You only have a few options there, but they're good ones.

Cedar Lodge Motel
$ Glenwood Springs

This nifty budget motel has two swimming pools, a hot tub, a sauna, a breakfast room, and a small exercise room. Most of the comfy rooms come with a small refrigerator and microwave. The motel is close to the turnoff for Sunlight Ski Area.

2102 Grand Ave., Glenwood Springs. ☎ **800-854-3761** *or 970-945-6579. Fax 970-945-4420. Internet:* www.cedarlodgemotel.net. *Rack rates: $50–$69.50. Rates include continental breakfast. AE, DC, DISC, MC, V.*

Hotel Colorado
$$$ Glenwood Springs

Once one of America's preeminent resorts, this 1889 hotel lost some of its luster when it was converted to a Naval Hospital during World War II. (Its size and proximity to a train station made it an ideal location.) Yet it still has character, partly because of its perch on a hillside above Glenwood's Hot Springs Pool, originally part of the hotel grounds. Styled after an Italian palace, it also has courtyard gardens, two original fireplaces, grand staircases, and a sunny sitting area. The rooms, which are clean and comfortable, have some of the quirks you'd expect at a historic hotel: There's no air conditioning, and the hot water can be as unpredictable as Amtrak. But I still savored being here.

526 Pine St., Glenwood Springs. ☎ **800-544-3998** *or 970-945-6511. Fax: 970-945-7030. Internet:* www.hotelcolorado.com. *Rack rates: $139–$452. AE, DC, DISC, MC, V.*

Redstone Castle
$$$–$$$$ Redstone

John Osgood was the fifth richest man in America when he built what was then known as Cleveholm Manor in a remote river canyon in the early 1900s. He spent $2.5 million on the 24,000-square-foot mansion in an effort to outdo his friends, who included the likes of John D. Rockefeller, J.P. Morgan, and Jay Gould. Situated on a hilltop surrounded by 500 fenced, landscaped acres, the 42-room English Tudor castle was his prize possession. If you stay here, you'll have the run of the place. You can shoot pool on the original billiards table, read in the leather-walled library, and snack in a dining room that has a gold-leaf ceiling and walls of Honduran Mahogany. It's like being in a Richie Rich comic.

Even if you don't stay here, call ahead and reserve a space on a 90-minute tour so that you can see the place and hear Osgood's bizarre story.

58 Redstone Blvd., Redstone. ☎ **970-704-1430**. *Fax: 970-704-1394. Internet:* www.theredstonecastle.com. *Rack rates: $150–$400. Tours (by appointment only): $12 adults, $10 seniors 65 and up, $5 children 5 to 12. AE, DISC, MC, V.*

Redstone Inn
$–$$$ **Redstone**

I love old Arts and Crafts–style lodges in remote locations, and the Redstone Inn may be my favorite anywhere. It was built by a steel and coal baron named John Osgood, who envisioned — or at least advertised — a Utopian community for his coal miners. In 1904, the inn and the surrounding buildings offered miners a theater, dining room, changing area, reading room, electricity, and hot and cold running water. The inn still has a four-sided clock tower just like the ones in European mountain villages. Today, the miners have been replaced by tourists who oversleep, swim, lift weights, play tennis, hike, and fish — all of this on or near the grounds of the inn. The property also has two restaurants and a bar. During summer, the dining room and guest rooms fill up far in advance, so make sure to reserve ahead.

0082 Redstone Blvd. (18 miles south of Carbondale on Colorado 133), Redstone. ☎ _**800-748-2524** or 970-963-2526. Internet:_ www.redstoneinn.com. _Rack rates: $46–$150 double; $110–$211 suite. AE, DISC, MC, V._

Thunder River Lodge
$ **Carbondale**

This lodge offers basic motel rooms for a reasonable price. Not counting telephones and televisions, the most noteworthy amenity is an unlimited supply of free ice cubes — enough, even, to fill coolers. You'll love the prices, especially if you use copious amounts of ice cubes and also take advantage of ski packages that let you stay here and ski Aspen for just a few dollars more than the price of lift tickets. (Call the inn or visit the inn's Web site for information on ski packages.) All the rooms are pleasant, but I prefer the upstairs ones, which were added in 1999 and still feel brand-new.

179 Highway 133, Carbondale. ☎ _**970-963-2543**. Internet:_ www.thunderriver lodge.com. _Rack rates: $40–$70. AE, DISC, MC, V._

Where to dine

Of the three communities, my favorite place to eat is Carbondale. It has one exceptional restaurant and several good ones, and you can usually find a table right away. Most Glenwood Springs restaurants don't take reservations, and they fill up fast on summer nights.

If you're in Glenwood Springs during July, avoid eating during the 7 p.m. crunch. If you're staying in Redstone, make sure to reserve a table at the Redstone Inn ahead of time, because you don't have many dining options in this community.

Glenwood Canyon Brewing Company

$–$$ Glenwood Springs   PUB FARE

Like most Colorado brewpubs, this one has hardwood floors, high ceilings, ceiling fans, and glass partitions exposing brewing vats (presumably to remind you that the beer wasn't, in fact, brewed by Schlitz). And, as at the other breweries, this one offers salads, sandwiches, pasta, steaks, and some tasty brews. The unique selections here are the soups in bread bowls. My favorite is the Wisconsin cheddar cheese beer soup, which tastes just right after a day on the slopes, especially when washed down with a Shoshone stout.

402 Seventh St., Glenwood Springs. ☎ *970-945-1276. Reservations for large groups only. Main courses: $5.95–$16.95. Open: Lunch and dinner daily. AE, MC, V.*

Juicy Lucy's

$$ Glenwood Springs   STEAKS AND SEAFOOD

Juicy Lucy's is a rarity among Colorado's upscale restaurants — a place where you can picture in advance what your food is going to look like. Entrees include grilled fresh Atlantic salmon, three lamb chops with mint jelly, and chopped sirloin steak with mushroom gravy, as well as steaks of different heft. Top it off with any of 22 wines available by the glass. You'll eat in a pleasant, historic dining room with split bamboo floors, copper light fixtures, and a ceiling of molded plaster.

308 Seventh St., Glenwood Springs. ☎ *970-945-4619. Reservations not accepted. Main courses: $12–$29. Open: Lunch and dinner daily. Closed Nov. MC, V.*

Sapphire Grill

$$ Glenwood Springs   ITALIAN GRILL

Because Sapphire Grill is in an inconspicuous upstairs spot, you can often walk in and get a table when other Glenwood restaurants are jammed. Another plus is that the chef loves garlic. After eating the bulb of roasted garlic that comes with your home-baked bread, order the escargot in garlic butter as an appetizer. Follow it with linguine with spicy garlic shrimp sauce. The Sapphire also serves grilled steaks, salmon, and pork chops, as well as a popular rack of ribs. The dessert list, entirely garlic free, includes homemade tiramisu and crème brûlée.

710 Grand Ave., Glenwood Springs. ☎ *970-945-4771. Reservations accepted. Entrees: $10–$20. Open: Dinner daily. AE, MC, V.*

689 Main Kitchen and Wine Bar

$$$ Carbondale   WORLD CUISINE

In 2002, the chef here cooked a meal at the James Beard House in New York, putting this Carbondale eatery in the ranks of America's finest. Yet the place still feels easygoing. Servers in loose-fitting, patterned shirts deliver delicacies such as herb-crusted chicken and apricot-mustard bar-beque pork tenderloin without fanfare. The restaurant's sommelier, who loves to fly-fish, offers tips on wines as casually as he may discuss lures during off-hours. On clear summer nights, the patio opens and seating doubles, so you can sometimes walk right in and get a table.

689 Main St., Carbondale. ☎ *970-963-6890. Reservations accepted. Main courses: $16–$25. Open: Tues–Sun dinner. AE, MC, V.*

Village Smithy
$ **Carbondale   ECLECTIC**

Since 1975, the Village Smithy has been Carbondale's spot to enjoy an extended breakfast. Its omelets, pancakes, smoothies, and sunny patio seating have probably cut into the town's productivity, but no one around here seems to mind. At lunch, the restaurant serves big salads, soups, sandwiches, and South-of-the-Border fare. You can eat in an old black-smith's shop or on the patio, which stays open, thanks to the miracles known as space heaters, even during winter.

26 S. Third St., Carbondale. ☎ *970-963-9990. Reservations not accepted. Main courses: $3–$10. Open: Breakfast and lunch daily. MC, V.*

White House Restaurant and Bar
$ **Carbondale   PIZZA, PASTA, AND BARBEQUE**

Despite having an Italian version of Uncle Sam on its menu, the White House seems to belong in New England more than it does in Washington, D.C., Italy, or, for that matter, Colorado. Its low ceilings, intimate barroom, and friendly servers call to mind those East Coast village taverns where everyone thinks they know your name. A locals' favorite in Carbondale, the White House serves above-average pizzas and calzones. Its wine list consists entirely of $10, $12, and $16 bottles.

801 Main St., Carbondale. ☎ *970-704-9400. Reservations accepted Mon–Thurs only. Main courses: $7.75–$11. Pizzas: $10–$20. Open: Dinner daily; lunch Fri–Sun. DISC, MC, V.*

Zocalito Latin Bistro
$$ **Carbondale   SPANISH/SOUTH AMERICAN**

Zocalito's chef and owner, Michael Beary, used to cook French food in Aspen. Then his cooking went south — to Guatemala, southern Mexico, and Spain. Now he uses hard-to-find South American ingredients to flavor seafood, beef, pork, and chicken. In the dining room, masks and festival costumes hang on pumpkin-colored walls, and panels of stamped glass sit atop the dividers between the booths.

568 Colorado 133., Carbondale. ☎ *970-963-6804. Reservations accepted. Main courses: $18–$20. AE, MC, V. Open: Dinner daily.*

Exploring Glenwood Springs, Carbondale, and Redstone

Glenwood Springs has endless activities for families. Redstone is an attraction unto itself, especially for historians looking for well-preserved relics from the early 1900s. And Carbondale is the place to get away from tourist attractions, relax, and enjoy being in the mountains.

The best things to see and do

In the Hot Springs Pool, Glenwood Springs has one of the best kid-friendly attractions in Colorado. If you're hurtling down I-70 past Glenwood, make sure to get off the freeway and soak.

Glenwood Caverns

On this tour, you'll ride a bus up a winding road onto a hillside high above Glenwood Springs and then go deep inside mountain caves. Some of these caverns opened as a tourist attraction known as Fairy Caves in the late 1800s and early 1900s. The operation closed in 1917, and then reopened in 1998. The new two-hour family tours visit the original Fairy Caves, where many formations have been damaged, and then continue on into two newly opened rooms with nearly pristine formations. These rooms, known as The Barn (for its size, the second largest in Colorado) and Kings Row (for its perfectly preserved stalactites and stalagmites) make this tour a winner. The family tour requires participants to climb 100 stairs, but the three- to four-hour "Wild Tour" is even harder. It requires you to wear a headlamp and crawl on your hands, knees, and belly in order to squeeze into caves far off the beaten path. It's an unforgettable adventure for families with teenagers.

508 Pine St., Glenwood Springs. ☎ *800-530-1635 or 970-945-4CAV. Internet:* www. glenwoodcaverns.com. *Family-tour admission: adults $12, children 3–12 $7, under 3 free. Wild Tours: $50 per person; you must be 13 or older to go. Open: Daily 9 a.m.–4 p.m. in May; daily 9 a.m.–5 p.m. June–Oct.*

Hot Springs Pool

At Glenwood's famous Hot Springs Pool, the pools are so huge and hold so many people, it can take a while to get used to the sheer mass — and believe me, I mean *mass* — of humanity. But you'll still have fun. You can swim in a 400-by-100-foot, 90-degree pool, which has lap lanes and diving boards, or soak in a 100-by-100-foot therapy tub, kept at around 104 degrees. Two 300-foot-long waterslides will spin you and then send you skittering across a watery run-out. My favorite time to soak is on winter nights, when you can watch the steam rise in something like solitude. As for the pool's history, the Ute Indians once soaked here, but the first official pool was built in 1888.

401 N. River Road, Glenwood Springs. ☎ *970-945-6571. Admission: $10.25 adults, $6.75 children 3–12. Open: 7:30 a.m.–10:00 p.m. in summer, 9 a.m.–10 p.m. rest of year. Closed second Wed of month in Sept, Nov, Jan, March, and May.*

Yampah Spa and Vapor Caves

Like the nearby Hot Springs Pool, the vapor caves are fed by 125-degree geothermal springs. Instead of soaking, however, you'll descend into rock-walled rooms sculpted out of actual caves, sit on marble benches, and inhale the steamy air, which is hottest in the rooms farthest underground. The caves' detractors find the rooms, the air, and the company all a bit too close. But if you enjoy steam baths, you'll love this place. For over a century, a variety of cures and treatments have been offered in the building above the caves, and today a modern spa sells massages, facials, and wraps.

709 E. Sixth St., Glenwood Springs. ☎ *970-945-0667. Vapor-cave admission: $8.75 (includes one towel); 2-day pass $15. Open: Daily 9 a.m.–9 p.m.*

Staying active

Three rivers that flow from towering peaks all meet in this area, providing great boating and fishing. If the water doesn't keep you entertained, you can always climb high into the mountains.

✔ **Fishing:** The Crystal River passes through Redstone and then empties into the Roaring Fork River near Carbondale. The Roaring Fork, in turn, drains into the Colorado River near Glenwood. All have their share of trout, but you have to make sure not to trespass when you go after them. To find out the rules, contact the **Colorado Division of Wildlife,** 50633 U.S. 6 and 24, Glenwood Springs (☎ 970-947-2920). **Roaring Fork Anglers,** 2114 Grand Ave., Glenwood Springs (☎ 970-945-0180), can help you find the best holes.

✔ **Biking and hiking:** The **Glenwood Springs Chamber Resort Association,** 1102 Grand Ave., publishes a free **Trails Guide** to the Glenwood Springs area. Your options include long Forest Service roads, narrow mountain paths, and the 16-mile, paved **Glenwood Canyon Path,** which has stretches right alongside I-70 but also branches off and follows the Colorado River. You can ride up the Glenwood Canyon Path starting at the east end of Sixth Avenue, right next to Yampah Vapor Caves in Glenwood. Because of the proximity to the freeway, it's a better choice for cyclists than for hikers. If you want to take a quick hike or ride in **Carbondale,** park your car in the lot north of the intersection of Colorado 133 and Colorado 82. The trailhead for the **Red Hill System** is about a quarter-mile up the obvious dirt road, on your left. It's less than a half-mile from the trailhead to **Mushroom Rock,** which has views of the surrounding valley. You can go farther by completing one of several possible loops through the area, on trails that are equally popular among hikers, advanced mountain bikers, and dogs.

The **White River National Forest Supervisor's Office,** 900 Grand Ave., Glenwood Springs (☎ **970-945-2521**), oversees seven wilderness areas, including the nearby **Maroon Bells–Snowmass** wilderness. The office can provide maps and information on the area hikes as well as on the forest trails near **Redstone.**

✔ **Golfing: The Ranch at Roaring Fork,** at 14913 Highway 82, Carbondale (☎ **970-963-3500**), has the cheapest greens fees in the Roaring Fork Valley: $15 for 9 holes. **Glenwood Springs Golf Club,** 0193 Sunny Acres Rd., West Glenwood (☎ **970-945-7086**), charges $19 for 9 holes, $29 for 18. Many other courses in the valley are private, with greens fees running up to $250.

✔ **Rafting:** Local raft companies offer half- and full-day trips on the Roaring Fork and Colorado rivers. In this area, neither river makes for a scary trip, but each has enough whitewater to entertain an average American family. **Whitewater Rafting,** 2000 Devereux Rd., Glenwood Springs (☎ **800-963-7238** or 970-945-8477; Internet: www.whitewaterrafting.com), can set up a trip for you.

Hitting the slopes

It's hard *not to* like small ski areas such as **Sunlight Mountain Resort** and **Monarch** (see Chapter 21), places with dirt parking lots, roaming dogs, and base areas that seem to belong on *That '70s Show.* Here are a few of the advantages to Sunlight: A $34 lift ticket, the cheapest in Colorado; equally cheap digs in nearby Glenwood Springs; and free rides (check for the schedule) to and from town in Sunlight's colorfully painted school bus. The ski instructors and the lift attendants greet each other by name, and they'll probably greet you, too. Sunlight's 460 acres include some serious steeps, challenging glades, and an abundance of intermediate runs. Best of all, Sunlight bundles its vacation packages with the world-famous Hot Springs Pool in Glenwood Springs, so that après-ski soaking is included in the cost. If this mountain doesn't relax you, the springs will. If you want to look at the technical data for the resort, see Table 17-2.

Table 17-2	Ski Report: Sunlight Mountain Resort
Location: 10901 County Road 11, Glenwood Springs	
Trails: 67	
20% beginner	
55% intermediate	
20% advanced	
5% expert	
Vertical drop: 2,010 feet	
Base elevation: 7,885 feet	

Summit elevation: 9,895 feet	

Summit elevation: 9,895 feet

Skiable terrain: 470 acres

Average annual snowfall: 250 inches

Lifts: 4

Phone: ☎ 800-445-7931

Internet: www.sunlightmtn.com

2002–2003 high-season adult all-day ticket: $34

Shopping

Carbondale's Main Street has some fun boutiques and galleries. Make sure you stop at **Kahhak Fine Arts and School,** 411 Main St. (☎ 970-704-0622). The school's proprietor, Majid Kahhak, uses the same studio to teach, create, and sell spontaneous art that he calls *essence painting.*

Glenwood Springs has a thriving shopping district along Grand Avenue, just south of the bridge over the Colorado River. One worthwhile stop: **Summit Canyon Mountaineering,** 732 Grand Ave. (☎ 800-360-6994), which sells gear, clothing, coffee, books and maps.

Redstone has a number of small galleries and boutiques, some of which are in historic cottages once reserved for miners.

Nightlife

A quarter-century ago the **Black Nugget,** 403 Main St., Carbondale (☎ 970-963-4498), was a notoriously rough bar that catered mostly to coal miners. Today, it's a friendly locals hangout, with live music Wednesday through Saturday nights year-round. Smoking is allowed only in a back room. In Glenwood Springs, head for the **Glenwood Canyon Brewing Company,** 402 Seventh St. (☎ 970-945-1276).

Fast Facts: Glenwood Springs, Carbondale, and Redstone

Hospital

Valley View Hospital, 1906 Blake Ave., Glenwood Springs (☎ 970-945-6535), has 24-hour emergency care. It's off 19th Street, one block east of Colorado 82.

Information

The Glenwood Springs Chamber Resort Association (☎ 970-945-6589; Internet: www.glenwoodsprings.net) has a visitor center at 1102 Grand Ave. For information on Carbondale and

Redstone, visit the Carbondale Chamber of Commerce, 569 Main St. (☎ 970-963-1890; Internet: www.carbondale.com).

Pharmacy

In Carbondale, you can fill your prescriptions at City Market,1051 Hwy. 33 (☎ 970-963-5727). In Glenwood Springs, go Downtown Drug, 825 Grand Ave. (☎ 970-945-7987).

Post Office

The Glenwood Springs Post Office is at 113 Ninth St. The Carbondale Post Office is at 655 Main St. Call ☎ 800-275-8777 for hours and other information.

Weather and Road Conditions

Call ☎ 970-920-5454 for the latest road conditions.

Steamboat Springs

Tourism has long-since overtaken ranching as the top industry in and around Steamboat Springs, and new developments keep cropping up on subdivided ranchland. Yet the town still values its cows and cowboys. The town, which markets itself as "Ski Town, USA," has always been as proud of its Western hospitality as it is of the many skiers it has sent to the Winter Olympics. And it still is today.

Of course, it's not a perfect marriage. The area has two different neighborhoods, each with its own personality. The base area of Steamboat Ski Area feels like a modern-day, mega-ski area, with immense hotels, fine restaurants, expensive boutiques, and homes the size of airport terminals. A few miles northwest of the ski area, along U.S. 40, sprawls the redbrick Western town of Steamboat Springs. Here, bike shops and the microbreweries share the main drag with Western stores such as F.M. Light and Soda Creek Outfitters. Next to a skate park, across from a network of mountain-bike trails, there's a historic rodeo ground. This older part of town is my favorite — it's a place where a visitor can enjoy the best of both the old and the new West.

Getting there

Steamboat Springs is 158 miles northwest of Denver, 194 miles east of Grand Junction, and 335 miles east of Salt Lake City. If you're driving from Denver, you'll need to take I-70 68 miles west to Silverthorne, then take Colorado 9 38 miles north to Kremmling. In Kremmling, turn west on U.S. 40 and go 52 miles to Steamboat Springs. If you're coming from the west on I-70, exit at Rifle and go 88 miles north on Colorado 13 to Craig. In Craig, head east on U.S. 40 for 42 miles to Steamboat Springs. Coming from the Northwest, you can take I-40 all the way from Park City, Utah, to Steamboat, a distance of about 300 miles.

During winter, **Yampa Valley Regional Airport** (☎ **970-276-3669;** Internet: www.yampa.com), 25 miles west of Steamboat Springs off of U.S. 40 (near Hayden), has daily nonstop service to Denver (on United

Express), Dallas–Fort Worth (American), Minneapolis–St. Paul (Northwest), Chicago (American) and Newark (Continental).

Upon landing, you can rent a car through **Avis** or **Hertz.** For information on contacting individual airlines and car-rental agencies, see the Appendix. **Alpine Taxi** (☎ 800-343-7433 or 970-879-8294) offers round-trip ($43 per adult) and one-way ($27 per adult) shuttle service between the airport and town. Call ahead for a reservation.

Getting around

Steamboat Springs Transit (☎ 970-879-3717) provides free bus service between Steamboat Springs and Steamboat Ski Area. The buses run every 20 minutes during peak hours. From mid-April to mid-December, the buses run from 7:00 a.m. to 10:45 a.m. The hours are even longer during the ski season.

If you miss the last bus, call **Alpine Taxi** (☎ 800-343-7433 or 970-879-2800) for a lift.

Steamboat Springs is easy to figure out. Most of the activity is along **Lincoln Avenue,** a stretch of U.S. 40. Lincoln Avenue runs northwest and southeast through town, paralleling the Yampa River, which borders the town on the southwest side. A series of numbered streets (3rd through 13th) cross U.S. 40, with the highest numbers being farthest north and west. Across the Yampa River from the downtown area, you'll find the town's rodeo grounds, skate park, and softball fields, as well as the historic Howelsen Hill Ski Area.

About 2 miles southeast of the downtown are developments around the base of the ski area. There are hotels, condos, luxury homes, and shopping plazas. Most of the buildings are larger and newer than the ones downtown. To reach the ski area base, go about 2 miles southeast of downtown on U.S. 40, then turn east on Mount Werner Road and follow the signs.

Where to stay

You can save by staying in Steamboat Springs's downtown area and taking the free shuttle to the mountain. On the outskirts of town along U.S. 40 are newer, chain hotels. The downtown has older but well-maintained motels. I like the downtown area's Western feel and reasonable prices. Bear in mind, however, that a motel along U.S. 40 in downtown Steamboat is hardly a retreat to nature. The highway was built extra-wide to accommodate cattle drives, and it holds a lot of traffic at times. The largest, most luxurious hotels are clustered around the base of the mountain.

Best Western Ptarmigan Inn
$–$$$$ Mountain Village

This ski-in, ski-out hotel at the base of Steamboat Mountain predates the days when luxury hotels dominated the base areas of ski resorts. Built in 1969 (with an addition in 1979), it could as easily be alongside Interstate 80 in Illinois as at Steamboat Ski Area. The smallish basic rooms have gray and tan furnishings. An elevator connects the four levels, but most people just use the stairs. You won't have to dodge any bellhops. (Sometimes, when you ring the front-desk bell, no one hops, period.) But you can ski straight into and out of the hotel, get free newspapers and Internet access, and eat reasonably priced fare at the hotel restaurant. It's cool.

2304 Apres Ski Way, Steamboat Springs. ☎ *800-538-7519 or 970-879-1730. Internet:* www.steamboat-lodging.com. *Rack rates: May 24–Dec 19, $69–$112; Dec 20–Jan 1, $239; Jan 2–March 29, $159–$199; March 30–April 13, $109. Closed mid-April–May 24. AE, DC, DISC, MC, V.*

Nordic Lodge Motel
$–$$$ Downtown Steamboat Springs

When I asked the front-desk person about this motel's age, she shrugged, said she didn't care and instead offered me a beer. It was the kind of pretzel logic that makes guidebook-writing fun — and dangerous. As it turned out, this lodge, in downtown Steamboat Springs, was built in 1960 but fully refurbished in 2001. Most of the lodge is one story in height, so you can usually lug your belongings straight into your room. The room itself will be clean and comfy, with a small refrigerator and microwave. It will also be convenient to downtown restaurants and shops.

1036 Lincoln Ave., Steamboat Springs. ☎ *800-364-0331 or 970-879-0531. Rack rates: Spring, summer, and fall, $49–$74; winter, $74–$125. AE, DISC, MC, V.*

Steamboat Grand Resort Hotel and Conference Center
$$–$$$$ Mountain Village

Developed by the New England–based American Skiing Company, this hotel at the base of Steamboat Ski Area has a stylish Western veneer. The lobby area has waterfalls, cozy leather armchairs, and a flagstone chimney that towers nearly three stories above a gas fireplace. With 328 guest rooms and suites, the Grand is as big as its name and offers more than its share of luxuries, including two restaurants, a fitness center, a spa, a swimming pool, concierge services, and an ardent crew of bellhops. Accommodations start with Deluxe Parlor rooms, each with a full kitchen, dining area, and queen-size sofa sleeper. One caveat: The walls are thin and the noise level pretty high for a hotel in this price range.

2300 Mount Werner Circle, Steamboat Springs. ☎ *877-269-2628 or 970-871-5500. Internet:* www.steamboatgrand.com. *Rack rates: April 2–Dec 25 $99–$125;*

Ranch life

To fully experience Steamboat culture, consider spending some time at a ranch. You can choose among several different experiences, which appeal to different types of vacationers. Choose the one that best fits your style.

Independent types, who'd prefer to use a ranch as a home base, should head for **Dutch Creek Guest Ranch at Steamboat Lake,** 25 miles northwest of Steamboat Springs on Colorado 62 (☎ **800-778-8519** or 970-879-8519; Internet: www. dutchcreek.net). This guest ranch offers accommodations in log cabins or A-frames — both have kitchens — and you're free to enjoy your days as you please. You can try your hand at horseback riding (for an additional fee), Ping-Pong, and horseshoes, or curl up by a fire with some hot cocoa and a copy of _Colorado & The Rockies For Dummies._ Rates, which include breakfast, for the more desirable log cabins run $140 to $165; the A-frames cost $95 to $125.

If you'd prefer an **all-inclusive experience,** try the **Home Ranch,** 54880 County Rd. 129 (☎ **970-879-1780;** Internet: www.homeranch.com). In summer and fall, you'll have to decide between guided hiking, fly-fishing, or horseback riding. Later on, you can soothe your aching muscles in the pool, sauna, or hot tub. The lodge schedules lots of kids' activities, so you can leave the young ones behind — or not. And after the family-style dinner, join a campfire sing-along or adjourn to your luxuriously appointed room. Accommodations are in cabins and lodge rooms, and prices vary according to how large and luxurious your digs are, but no matter what you choose, you're going to pay big bucks. Prices drop in winter, when you shell out only for your room and your breakfast. Summer and fall double-occupancy rates for seven nights run $4,249 to $5,404; add $1,554 for each additional person. Winter nightly double-occupancy rates (two-night minimum stay required) run from $250 to $375, plus $50 per night for each additional person.

For a true **working vacation,** head for **Saddleback Ranch,** 37350 County Rd. 179 (☎ **970-879-3711**). You can't stay overnight at this 7,000-acre working cattle ranch, but you're welcome to help out with chores. From June through mid-September, you can help round up, move, and tend the ranch's 800 mother cows. Mostly, however, you just ride alongside the cowboys and watch them work. Each ride lasts about four hours, and kids have to be at least 8 years old to go along. Come evening, you can also go for a 1½-hour dinner ride, capped off with a meal of chicken, steak, or fish. The cattle drive costs $65 per adult, $60 per child; a dinner ride is $49 adults, $39 per child.

Christmas week, President's Week, $299; Jan 6–Feb 12, Feb 18–April 1, $209. AE, DC, DISC, MC, V.

Where to dine

Steamboat has more than a few first-rate restaurants and many others providing tasty food at reasonable prices. There are more choices downtown, but my two favorites are at the base of the ski area.

Café Diva

$$$ Torian Plum Plaza   NEW AMERICAN

Every night, Café Diva's small staff creates a special experience for diners near the base of Steamboat Ski Area. Both owners are sommeliers, and the chef came here from one of Manhattan's hottest restaurants. Together, they've created the best all-around dining experience in Steamboat Springs. The menu changes seasonally, but you can always order a few standbys. Start with crab and tomato bisque, then, for an appetizer, get the Cajun crab cakes in Creole remoulade. Finish with the elk tenderloin and roasted-garlic mashed potatoes in veal brown sauce.

The experience is especially nice in summer, when you can dine on a patio with mountain views.

1875 Ski Time Square Dr. (in Torian Plum Plaza across from Terry Sports), Steamboat Springs. ☎ *970-871-0508. Reservations recommended. Main courses: $16–$35. Open: Dinner daily. AE, DISC, MC, V.*

Creekside Café and Grill

$–$$ Downtown   AMERICAN/ECLECTIC

Creekside Cafe serves three meals most days, but I'd come here in the morning for the "Legendary Creekside Benny's," usually known as eggs Benedict. Creekside serves eight variations on the dish, ranging from *traditional* (poached eggs, English muffin, hollandaise sauce, and black forest ham) to *Yampa* (with smoked trout and tomatoes instead of ham). The staff can be distracted, the coffee is strong, and the creek-side patio gets just the right amount of sunlight. In other words, this is the perfect ski-town breakfast joint. At lunch, the Creekside switches to a diverse menu that includes falafels, gyros, sandwiches, wraps, burgers, and salads. The dinner menu consists mostly of pasta dishes.

131 11th St., Steamboat Springs. ☎ *970-879-4925. Reservations for dinner only. Main courses: $7–$20. Open: Wed–Sat breakfast, lunch, and dinner; Tues and Sun breakfast and lunch only. MC, V.*

The French Bistro at Mattie's

$$–$$$ Mountain Village   FRENCH BISTRO

This restaurant, which opened in late 2001, occupies a space big enough for a sporting goods store. That's too bad, because its tasty food deserves an intimate setting. A husband-and-wife team runs Mattie's, with the husband, Marc Pauvert, serving as the master butcher, and the wife, Rebecca, as head chef. The first courses include such delicacies as pâtés, terrines, baked artichokes, and mussels; the entrees are mostly hand-cut meats with delicate sauces. You can choose from 17 domestic and French wines available by the glass, as well as bottles ranging in price from $19 to $150.

1890 Mount Werner Rd. (on the mountain in Ski Time Square), Steamboat Springs. ☎ *970-879-2441. Reservations recommended. Main courses: $9.50–$24. Open: Tues–Sun lunch and dinner. Closed Oct–Nov, April 15–June 15. AE, DISC, MC, V.*

La Montana

$$–$$$ Steamboat Base Area   SOUTHWESTERN/MEXICAN

It's easy to see why this is one of the most acclaimed Southwestern restaurants in Colorado. An old-style tortilla roaster works overtime, throwing heat across the bar patrons and wafting the scent of warm dough throughout the restaurant. One dining room has immense prints of nature photographs taken by the owner; the other room displays masks and traditional Mexican art. It's worth a trip here just to dip a fresh tortilla chip in the tomatillo-and-avocado salsa. The menu has Tex-Mex dishes and fajitas, but there are also creative, gourmet entrees such as coriander tofu with toasted quinoa in black-bean reduction sauce, and grilled elk loin with a cilantro pesto crust.

2500 Village Dr. (off of Apres Ski Way), Steamboat Springs. ☎ *970-879-5800. Reservations recommended. Main courses: $12–$28. Open: Dinner daily Dec 1– April 15 and June 1–Sept. 1. Closed Sun–Mon during spring and fall. AE, DISC, MC, V.*

Slopeside Grill

$–$$ Torian Plum Plaza   GRILLED ITEMS, PIZZA, AND PASTA

This is one of those places where the walls seem to be vying with the menu for the title of "Most Eclectic Items on Display." The walls flaunt old signs, ice skates, skis, snowshoes, photos, bridles, and saddles, among other items. Not to be outdone, the menu features everything from peanut butter and jelly sandwiches to *salciccia Ricardo* (red and green bell peppers roasted in olive oil and garlic with Italian sausage and served over fresh fettuccini). You can also buy several flavors of dog food, but only if you and your four-legged friend are on the patio. Best of all, Slopeside offers 11 kinds of handmade pizza for under $10 each, and it keeps serving those pizzas at reduced prices after 10 p.m. in winter, 9 p.m. in summer.

1855 Ski Time Square Dr. (at Steamboat Ski Area base), Steamboat Springs. ☎ *970- 879-2916. Reservations suggested. Main courses: $6.45–$16.95. Open: Lunch and dinner daily. AE, DISC, MC, V.*

Steamboat Brewery and Tavern

$–$$ Downtown   PUB FARE/NEW AMERICAN

Fashioned after an old Chicago tavern, Steamboat Brewery has a colorful tile floor; cherry woodwork; and high-backed booths. It also has at least two mouth-watering beers: the Alpenglow Strong Ale and the Pinnacle Pale Ale. The food consists of standard brewpub offerings, including soups, salads, pizzas, sandwiches, burgers, and more expensive entrees.

If you crave onion rings but know you should have a salad instead, split the difference and get the goat cheese and fried onion salad with fresh tomatoes and balsamic vinaigrette.

Fifth Street and Lincoln Avenue, Steamboat Springs. ☎ *970-879-2233. Reservations accepted. Main courses: $11–$15. Open: Lunch and dinner daily. AE, DISC, MC, V.*

Exploring Steamboat Springs

The Yampa Valley has over 150 hot springs, produced by geothermal activity. In Steamboat, you should soak in the springs first and then figure out the rest of your itinerary — if there *is* a rest of your itinerary. Later on, time permitting, you can shop, absorb history, ride a horse, or pursue almost any kind of recreation known to man.

The best things to see and do

First get the soaking out of the way. You can

✔ **Soak and exercise.** Kids love the **Steamboat Springs Health and Recreation Center** (☎ **970-879-1828**), where the waters are perfect for kinetic young people and adults pursuing active lifestyles. Located at the east end of town on Lincoln Avenue, this community hub has hot mineral pools (98 to 102 degrees), an 82-degree lap pool, a wading pool, and a waterslide, not to mention a weight room, tennis courts, snack bar, and playground. The springs stay open year-round even though they're outdoors. They're open Monday through Friday from 5:30 a.m. to 10:00 p.m., Saturday and Sunday from 8 a.m.to 9 p.m. Admission costs $7.50 adults; $5 students 13 to 17; $3.50 kids 3 to 12 and seniors over 61. The waterslide costs $5 for ten rides, $3 for five rides.

✔ **Soak and — what's exercise?** The **Strawberry Park Hot Springs** (☎ **970-879-0342;** Internet: www.strawberryhotsprings.com) have little in common with the Health and Recreation Center. Privately owned, they're in a remote, forested canyon and cater mostly to adults who like sitting still in beautiful places. The park has four terraced rock pools, each fed by a mixture of 147-degree mineral water and icy creek water. After sunset, kids are no longer allowed, and the adults may remove their suits. The place is informal: You buy your tickets outside and change in a tipi. There are no lights, so a small flashlight comes in handy after dark. You can camp here or rent a rustic cabin. The road to the springs is rough and often unsuitable for two-wheel-drive vehicles. Call the springs before attempting the drive in winter, no matter what you're driving, but don't pass up a chance to soak here. It's located 7 miles north of town at the end of County Road 36. (Turn east on Seventh Street and follow the signs.) Weekdays before 5 p.m it costs $5 for adults, $3 for children under 18. Weekdays after 5 p.m., weekends, and holidays it costs $10 for adults, $5 for kids under 18. It's open daily from 10:00 a.m. to 10:30 p.m.

Other things to see and do

When you're done soaking, you can further stimulate your senses by:

- ✔ **Hitting the rodeo.** You can immerse yourself in cowboy culture at the pro rodeos held every Friday and Saturday night from mid-June through August at Romick Arena. The arena is at the base of Howelsen Hill, on the opposite side of the Yampa River from downtown Steamboat Springs. (Use Fifth Street to cross the river.) Live country music kicks off the festivities at 6 p.m., followed by the rodeo, including bull riding, at 7:30 p.m. The cost is $11 for adults, $6 for ages 7 to15, with kids 6 and under free. Call ☎ **970-879-0880** to find out more.

- ✔ **Treading through the past. The Tread of Pioneers Museum,** 800 Oak St. (☎ **970-879-2214**), has the usual artifacts from Victorian life, some of which are displayed in a 1908 Queen Anne–style home. It also has some stunning historic photographs of Native Americans, an exhibit on skiing in Steamboat, and a videotape of a historic hotel burning down. Cost is $5 for adults, $4 for seniors over 62, and $1 for children under 12. It's open Tuesday through Saturday from 11 a.m. to 5 p.m.

Especially for kids

A few places in Steamboat are especially fun for kids:

- ✔ During summer at **Howelsen Hill,** 845 Howelsen Parkway (☎ **970-871-1104**), you can ride a chairlift and then descend 400 vertical feet on the **Alpine Slide.** Howelsen Hill is located across the Yampa River from downtown Steamboat Springs, via Fifth Street. One ride costs $8 for ages 13 and over, $7 for children 7 to12, and $1 for children 3 to 6. It is open June through September on weekdays from 11 a.m. to 6 p.m., and weekends from 10 a.m. to 6 p.m.

- ✔ A short walk from the alpine slide, check out the town's **skate park** next to Howelsen Hill and the rodeo grounds. It's free and open to the public.

- ✔ At the base of **Steamboat Ski Area** (☎ **970-871-5252**), you (or your kids) can dangle from bungee cords while bouncing on the trampoline. The setup allows people to safely flip, and flip, and flip. The cost is $6 for two minutes. There's also a climbing wall (two climbs for $6).

Staying active

Steamboat may not have the "best" ski area, the "best" mountain biking, the "best" fishing, or the "best" whitewater, but if you want a well-rounded recreation scene, it may be, well, the best. No matter what you want to do, Steamboat has something for you. While you're here, think about:

✔ **Boating:** During years when a lot of snow has fallen, the Yampa River and its tributaries offer some of the most turbulent whitewater in North America. Even if your "boat" is a half-inflated car inner tube, you're still in luck — certain stretches of the Yampa are so mellow and civilized, you could call AAA to fix a flat. One prime tubing zone starts right in downtown Steamboat Springs. To float the Yampa through town, go to **Backdoor Sports,** at the corner of Ninth and Yampa (☎ **970-879-6249**). Rent a tube for $12; and start your 2-mile float trip down the river right there. For people who are more serious about the water, **Backdoor Sports** also gives six-hour kayak lessons for $90, after which you'll be ready to float some of the milder whitewater.

✔ **Hiking:** On Steamboat Ski Area, your basic easy-to-find hiking trail is the **Thunderhead Trail,** which starts near the base of the Silver Bullet Gondola and climbs 2,180 feet over 3 miles to its terminus at the upper gondola station. The uppermost portions, which skirt rock outcroppings and drift through aspen groves flecked with wildflowers, are the most scenic. To save energy, you can ride the gondola up (cost: $15 adults, $10 kids 13 to 17, and $6 kids 5 to 12) and then hike down. The most stunning trails near town are at **Fish Creek Falls** (☎ **970-879-1870**). For a short hike and picnic, walk ⅛ mile to the falls overlook, where you can sit at picnic tables and watch the falls thunder 165 feet downhill through a mossy gorge. To get closer to the water, take the lower trail (as opposed to the one to the overlook) ¼ mile to the base of the falls. You can continue hiking on this trail and make a 2½-mile (one-way), 1,600-vertical-foot ascent to **Upper Fish Creek Falls.** The trailheads start 4 miles east of town on County Road 32, inside the Routt National Forest. Cost is $3 per vehicle. Serious hikers and backpackers should drive north of Steamboat Springs and to the edge of the **Mount Zerkel Wilderness Area,** which encompasses parts of the Sawtooth, Park, and Sierra Madre mountain ranges. For more information and maps of this area, go to the **Medicine Bow–Routt National Forest Office,** 925 Weiss Dr., Steamboat Springs (☎ **970-879-1870**).

✔ **Golfing:** Picture a golf course with bottomless bunkers, rolling fairways, thick roughs, and lots of water. If the course you imagine is in Scotland and not in Hell, then you should go play a round at **Haymaker,** 32500 U.S. 40 (☎ **970-870-1846**). Modeled after top Scottish courses, the 18 holes are surrounded by undeveloped land, making the experience even more pure. Greens fees are $79 from June 8 through September 22, $54 after 4:30 p.m. The rest of the season, 18 holes costs $54 at all times. There's also a driving range on the premises.

✔ **Horseback riding:** A number of area ranches offer horseback riding. If you want to ride in a pretty spot at the edge of Steamboat Springs, head for **Sombrero Ranches.** Located next to the rodeo grounds at the base of Howelsen Hill, Sombrero Ranches offers one-hour ($25) and two-hour ($40) rides on Emerald Mountain, as well as breakfast ($40) and dinner ($45) excursions by reservation only. Call ☎ **970-879-2306** for more information, or go right to the stables by crossing the river at Fifth Street.

✔ **Mountain biking:** You can access **Steamboat Ski Area's** 50-mile trail system near the base of the Silver Bullet Gondola, or you can start 2,180 feet higher up by riding the gondola (cost: $23 adults, $18 kids 13 to 17, and $14 kids 5 to 12). You can pick up a map of the trails at the base of the resort. There's also prime riding on **Emerald Mountain,** across the Yampa River from the downtown area. Cross the river at 13th Street, then look for the single track trail. The single track meets a Jeep road that climbs steadily for 1,550 vertical feet over 3 miles to the top of 8,250-foot Quarry Mountain. This area is warmer than Steamboat Ski Area, so consider hitting it in early morning or late afternoon. The staff at **Sore Saddle Cyclery,** 1136 Yampa St. (☎ **970-879-1675**), rents mountain bikes ($35 per day) and town bikes ($15 per day) and can tell you more about area trails. Sore Saddle also sells state-of-the-art titanium bike frames made locally by **Moots Cycles** (☎ **970-879-1676**).

Hitting the slopes

Like the town of Steamboat Springs, **Steamboat Ski Area** prides itself on being friendly. Former Olympic medallist Billy Kidd, now the resort's Director of Skiing, often guides complimentary mountain tours, and Nelson Carmichael, the bronze medallist in mogul skiing in the 1992 Winter Games, schedules free bump-skiing clinics for the public. As for the terrain, Steamboat's 2,939 acres make it the third largest area in the state, behind Vail and Snowmass. The 20 lifts efficiently move skiers, and the 142 trails tend to follow fall-line paths down the four linked mountains. More than half the runs are designated as intermediate, so mid-level skiers will relish being here. Advanced skiers will love threading their way through the mountain's seemingly endless aspen glades, which become especially enticing after the resort receives some of its famous dry powder. Beginners have fewer options, since only 13% of terrain is for novices. Still, this is easily one of the top ski areas in the state. See Table 17-3 for the lowdown on the resort's snowfall and other technical details.

Table 17-3	Ski Report: Steamboat Ski Area
Location: 2 miles southeast of downtown Steamboat Springs	
Trails: 142	
13% beginner	
56% intermediate	
31% advanced	

(continued)

Table 17-3 *(continued)*

Vertical drop: 3,668 feet

Base elevation: 6,900 feet

Summit elevation: 10,568 feet

Skiable terrain: 2,939 acres

Average annual snowfall: 330 inches

Lifts: 20

Snow phone: ☎ 970-879-7300

Steamboat Central Reservations: ☎ 800-922-2722

Internet: www.steamboat.com

2002–2003 high-season adult all-day ticket: $64

More than 50 Olympians have trained at **Howelsen Hill Ski Area,** a winter sports center in Steamboat Springs. At 90 years and counting, this is the oldest continuously operating ski area in Colorado, good for a listing on the National Register of Historic Places. Most visitors come here for the night skiing, but Howelsen Hill also has ski jumps, Nordic trails, and a half-pipe course for snowboarders. The hill hosts about 75 competitions every winter. On most days, it's also open to the public. By Western standards, it's puny — come here for the night skiing, the Nordic trails, or the history. If none of these attracts you, you're better off at Steamboat Ski Area. For more on the resort, check out Table 17-4.

Table 17-4   Ski Report: Howelsen Hill Ski Area

Location: Downtown Steamboat Springs

Trails: 19

25% beginner

50% intermediate

25% advanced/expert

Vertical drop: 440 feet

Base elevation: 6,696 feet

Summit elevation: 7,136 feet

Skiable terrain: 30 acres
Average snowfall: 150 inches
Lifts: 3
Snow phone: ☎ 970-879-8499
Internet: www.ci.steamboat.co.us/recreation/howlesen.htm
2002–2003 high-season adult all-day ticket: $15

Shopping

F.M. Light & Sons, 830 Lincoln Ave. (☎ **970-879-1822**), has sold Western clothing in Steamboat since 1905. The store has a huge selection of Lee and Wrangler jeans, Stetson hats, and cowboy boots, plus knives, oiled coats, and even stick horses. **Soda Creek Outfitters,** 335 Lincoln Ave. (☎ **970-879-3146**), has Western goods that, if anything, are more traditional than the selections at F.M. Light. If, for whatever reason, you ever wanted chaps and spurs, this is the store for you.

Nightlife and culture

Slopeside Grill (☎ **970-879-2916**), across from the Sheraton in **Ski Time Square,** serves gourmet pizzas at discounted rates after 10 p.m. Slopeside also offers live entertainment every afternoon during ski season and on Sunday afternoons in the summer.

Not far away is the town's hottest club, **Level'z,** 1860 Ski Time Square Drive (☎ **970-870-9090**), which has a sprawling dance floor and live entertainment nightly, usually in the form of DJs but sometimes featuring nationally known bands. Bands also groove at **The Tugboat Grill and Pub** (☎ **970-879-7070**), also located at Ski Time Square. The town's best sports bar is **The Tap House,** 729 Lincoln Ave. (☎ **970-879-2431**).

Every summer for the past 15 years, Steamboat's **Strings in the Mountains** music festival has attracted dozens of famous folk, as well as bluegrass, country, world, and classical musicians to a tent near the base of the ski area. Recent performers have included Leonard Slatkin, Garrison Keillor, the Colorado Symphony, and Asleep at the Wheel. For more information on Strings in the Mountains, call ☎ **970-879-5056** or surf the Internet to www.stringsinthemountains.org.

Fast Facts: Steamboat Springs

Hospital

Yampa Valley Medical Center, 1024 Central Park Dr. (☎ 970-879-1322), has 24-hour emergency service and plenty of experience treating injured knees.

Information

Steamboat Springs Chamber Resort Association runs a visitor center at 1255 S. Lincoln Ave. (☎ 970-879-0880; Internet: www.steamboatchamber.com).

Pharmacy

Lyon's Corner Drug & Soda Fountain, 840 Lincoln Ave. (☎ 970-879-1114),

can fill your prescription and sell you homeopathic remedies to boot.

Post Office

The Steamboat Springs Post Office is located at 200 Lincoln Ave. Call ☎ 800-275-8777 for hours and other information.

Road Conditions

Call ☎ 970-315-7623 for the latest road conditions.

Chapter 18

Northern Colorado High Country (East)

- -

In This Chapter

▶ Locating the cool spots (temperature-wise): Winter Park and Fraser

▶ Knowing the hotspots (people-wise): Vail and Breckenridge

▶ Finding ski areas galore along I-70

- -

*W*hen people plan a fast-paced Colorado vacation, they often think of destinations in the high country near the continental divide and I-70. This area has some of the state's famous mountain towns, including Vail, Breckenridge, and Winter Park, and boasts four of its five most popular ski areas. It's easy to get to — most towns here are within two hours of Denver. It has stunning mountain scenery, including thundering rivers and 10,000-foot passes where the rocks meet the heavens.

All this beauty hasn't gone unnoticed, or untouched. Near the best-known ski areas are large hotels, parking decks, and pockets of high-density development. The upshot is that these resort communities can really entertain vacationers: They offer varied and challenging recreation, a broad range of lodging, year-round family activities, delicious food, free (or inexpensive) transportation, rowdy nightlife, and summertime culture. I'd go to these towns not for a sleepy mountain getaway but for some aggressive exercise combined with an active nightlife. If, however, you want a drowsy retreat from humanity, look for a B&B, guest ranch, or mom-and-pop motel a few miles outside the town limits.

What's Where?: The Region and Its Major Attractions

Summit County and Vail are right on I-70 and easy to reach from Denver if the weather is fair and traffic is light. To get to Winter Park, you need to detour off the interstate and climb over 10,000-foot Berthoud Pass. That may explain why Winter Park feels a little more secluded than the other ski towns near Denver.

Winter Park and Fraser

These two side-by-side towns have long provided a convenient mountain retreat for Denver residents. Located in a mountain valley just west of the continental divide, they're surrounded by thick spruce and fir forest and alongside the Fraser River. They're also surprisingly peaceful and down-to-earth, like a Colorado version of *Northern Exposure*. Among the attractions are

- ✔ **The Ski Train,** a historic train that brings skiers up for the day from Denver, then takes them home at night
- ✔ **Winter Park Resort,** a Denver-owned park that also qualifies as a mogul-skier's paradise
- ✔ **Mountain biking trails** on the forest floors of the Fraser Valley

Vail

Vail has been a Tyrolean-style resort ever since the first chairlifts went up in 1962. The whole idea worked — and works — because the ski area is as vast as a mountain in the Alps and because many Europeans actually moved here. Though it attracts nearly enough visitors to rival Disney, the town still has surprising character. When in Vail, make sure to check out the following:

- ✔ **Vail Mountain,** easily the largest ski area in the United States
- ✔ **Vail Village,** a pedestrian-friendly hub of upscale stores, restaurants, and bars, including the famous **Red Lion Inn**
- ✔ **Whitewater rafting** on the Eagle River

Summit County

This bustling county is a no-brainer for skiers and vacationers who want a lot of variety but are on a tight timetable. Located a short drive from Denver, it has four major ski areas, historic towns, and a user-friendly infrastructure, including miles of paved pedestrian trails. Some of the best spots include

- ✔ **Copper Mountain Resort,** which the Forest Service once described as "the most nearly perfect ski mountain in the United States"
- ✔ The towns of **Breckenridge** and **Frisco,** each with historic downtown areas and a variety of lodges and restaurants
- ✔ **Peak 8 Fun Park,** a kid-friendly summer fun center at the base of Breckenridge Mountain Resort

Northern Colorado High Country (East)

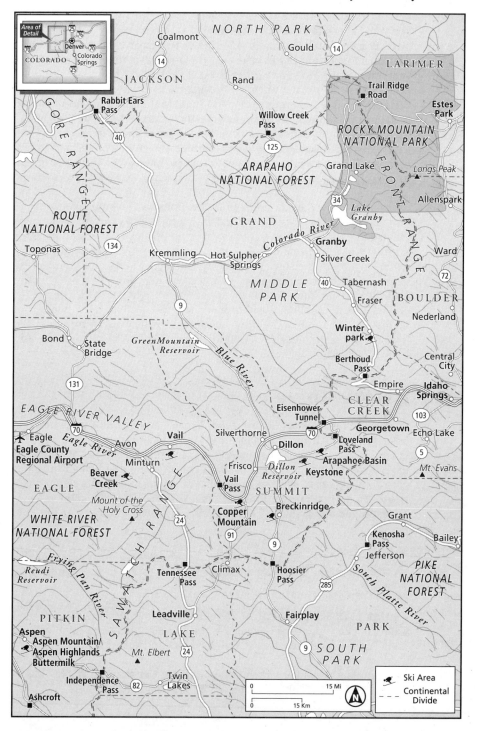

Winter Park and Fraser

For years these two side-by-side towns were best known for their coldness. Fraser, which is usually a degree or two frostier than Winter Park, registers the lowest temperature in the lower 48 states more days per year, on average, than any other town. The daylight hours aren't bad. But on clear nights, the warm air dissipates and cold air plummets from the surrounding mountains onto the 9,000-foot-high valley floor. Partly because of the nighttime cold, and partly because these are railroad towns, the communities have traditionally been slaves to function. Until the 1990s, many local buildings resembled the clunky offspring of a Quonset hut and a mine shack, with colors that ranged from pea green to tan.

Lately the towns have become more fashionable. The management of Winter Park Resort has contracted with a big-money developer to revitalize and expand its base; several large new lodges decorated in the popular Colorado Rustic look have sprung up. Yet there's something endearing about the town's remaining old-style functionality. Area businesses don't look so perfect as to make you nervous. Folks are friendly. And the surrounding mountains appear downright Alaskan. The evergreens here seem thicker and greener, the rivers clearer, the peaks higher than in some of the other mountain towns. Nearby forests could pass for the setting of a Jack London novel, despite being just over an hour's drive from Denver.

Getting there

Winter Park is 67 miles northwest of Denver and 85 miles from **Denver International Airport** (☎ 800-AIR-2-DEN). Most large domestic carriers serve Denver International Airport, and major rental-car companies have desks there. For information on contacting individual airlines and car-rental agencies, see the Appendix. To arrange a shuttle ride to Winter Park from Denver International Airport, call **Home James Transportation** (☎ 800-359-7536 or 970-726-5060). Cost is $41 per person.

To drive to Winter Park from Denver, go 44 miles west from Denver on **I-70,** then take **Highway 40** north over Berthoud Pass and into Winter Park.

Amtrak's (☎ 800-USA-RAIL or 303-825-2583; Internet: www.amtrak.com) California Zephyr stops in **Fraser** when traveling between the Bay Area and Chicago (and vice versa). Call for fares and schedules.

Car rentals are available through **Avalanche Car Rental** (☎ 888-437-4101 and 970-887-3908) and **Hertz** (☎ 970-726-8933).

If you're staying in Denver and want to travel to Winter Park for a day of skiing, consider using **The Ski Train** (☎ 303-296-4754; Internet www.skitrain.com), a Denver tradition since 1940. Every Saturday and Sunday from December 21 through April 6 (and on Fridays during February and March), the 17-car, quarter-mile-long train departs Denver's Union Station at 7:15 a.m., climbs into South Boulder Canyon and the Flatiron Range, and then crosses the continental divide through the 6-mile-long Moffat Tunnel. It emerges from the tunnel at the base of the ski area, 4,000 vertical feet above its starting point, and deposits as many as 750 passengers at 9:30 a.m. The return trip leaves at 4:15 p.m. An estimated 40% of passengers are nonskiers who take the train as a sightseeing excursion (a trend that one Winter Park resident affectionately calls "Throw Mama *on* the train"). Round-trip coach fare is $45 for adults, $25 for kids.

The train's lone drawback: In order to avoid over-packing the train on Saturday morning and Sunday afternoon, your return ticket is valid only on the same day that you travel to Winter Park, so you won't be able to use that ticket if you plan an overnight stay. The train also operates on Saturdays from mid-June through August.

Getting around

These aren't my favorite towns for walking, because the businesses are pretty spread out. They are, however, perfect for bicycling. You can take a paved bike path all the way from Winter Park Resort to Fraser.

The Lift (☎ 970-726-4163) provides regular, free shuttle service linking Winter Park Resort, Winter Park, and Fraser. During ski season, the shuttles run every half-hour from 7:30 a.m. to midnight. From the Fourth of July to Labor Day, there's hourly service between 9:30 a.m. and 4 p.m. The shuttles don't operate during spring and fall.

Home James Transportation (☎ 800-359-7536 or 970-726-5060) offers taxi service at a cost of $4 for the first mile, plus $2 for each additional mile.

Where to stay

Fraser Valley, home to Winter Park and Fraser, has a hodgepodge of lodging. New condos, old condos, luxury hotels, family lodges, B&Bs, guest ranches, and chain motels all vie for your business. Here are some very different possibilities.

Arapahoe Ski Lodge
$–$$$ **Winter Park**

Run by the same family since the mid-'70s, this rustic lodge has a Bavarian exterior and a mostly wooden interior with an intimate, British-style pub.

Knickknacks such as steins, baskets, and ski memorabilia clutter shelves that seem to have been nailed up on an as-needed basis. Near the lobby you can hang your skis on hooks, or tune them on a table. The 11 guest rooms are spare but comfortable. They don't have televisions, so guests spend more time in the tiny indoor hot tub and swimming pool, the shared television room, and the pub. They get to know each other even better over breakfast and dinner, which are included in the wintertime rates. During slow periods, the place calls itself a B&B and serves breakfast only. It's as old-school as they come.

78594 U.S. 40, Winter Park. ☎ *and Fax **970-726-8222**. Internet:* www.arapahoe skilodge.com. *Winter rates (includes breakfast and dinner for two): Dec 20–31 and Feb 1–March 31 $190; Jan $170. Winter B&B rates (includes full breakfast only): Nov 15–Dec 19 and March 30–April 12 $95. Summer B&B rates (includes full breakfast): June–Sept $69. Closed rest of year. AE, DISC, MC, V.*

Devil's Thumb Ranch
$–$$ Tabernash

Devil's Thumb Ranch overlooks meadows at the base of the Indian Peaks Wilderness Area and is 3 miles from the nearest highway (U.S. 40). If, for some reason, you want to leave, it's only a 20-minutes drive from Winter Park. During summer, guests ride horses and fish in the area. Come winter, 100 kilometers of groomed cross-country ski trails meander through the frozen meadows. You'll bunk down in a historic lodge, fully refurbished in 2001. The rooms are small but charming, with lodgepole-pine beds, down comforters, and robes — but no phones or TVs.

Nordic skiers on a budget will love the Ski Bum rooms, which are just as enticing as the other lodge rooms, only with shared baths. They cost $50 less and, unlike the standard rooms, come with complimentary track passes. There's also a cozy and popular restaurant on the premises.

3530 County Rd. 83, Tabernash. ☎ ***970-726-5632***. *Fax: 970-726-9038. Internet:* www. devilsthumbranch.com. *Rack rates: Standard rooms $119 ($143 over holidays); Ski Bum rooms $69 ($83 holidays). MC, V.*

Iron Horse Resort
$$–$$$ Winter Park

Come to this large condominium hotel at the base of Winter Park Resort if you want to get serious about skiing. The resort's privately owned condos range in size from sport studios with Murphy beds to two-bedroom, three-bath units. No matter what size you choose, you'll have a full kitchen, a gas-log fireplace, and a private balcony. You'll also have access to the hot tubs, heated outdoor pool, steam rooms, and exercise room. If you cook a few meals yourself, you can offset the extra dollars you'll spend for this ski-in, ski-out location.

101 Iron Horse Way, Winter Park. ☎ ***800-621-8190*** *or 970-726-8851. Fax: 970-726-2321. Internet:* www.ironhorse-resort.com. *Rack rates: Dec 1–April 14, $99–$239 studio; rest of year $69–$189 studio. AE, DC, DISC, MC, V.*

The Pinnacle Lodge at Winter Park
$–$$$ Fraser

This new two-story motel has perfect paint, sharp edges, large windows, and lots of space. Not much about the place will surprise you. All the rooms have 28-inch TVs, coffeemakers, refrigerators, microwaves, dataports, and ironing boards. Continental breakfast appears every morning inside a bright, sunny breakfast area. There's also a small indoor swimming pool and spa. The only surprise — and it's a modest one — is that the place is in Fraser and not Winter Park, as the lodge's name would seem to indicate.

108 Zerex St., Fraser. ☎ ***970-722-7631***. *Fax: 970-722-7632. Internet:* www.orchard hospitality.com. *Rack rates: June–Sept; $69–$79; ski season $129–$199; late April 14–May and Oct–Nov, $49–$59. AE, DC, DISC, MC, V.*

Where to dine

In Winter Park, dining usually costs a little less than in other ski towns. And most of the town's restaurants are fine for children.

Fontenot's Cajun Café
$–$$ Winter Park   CAJUN

This restaurant's owner and chef, Chris Moore, likes to go on food-tasting trips to the backwoods restaurants and food stands in rural Louisiana. He brings the best recipes home to chilly Winter Park, where the spicy food tastes especially heartwarming. I loved the gumbo — a soup of crawfish, chicken, peppers, okra, tomatoes, and Cajun spices, served over rice. Being a transplanted New Englander who fusses over fish, the owner is partial to the Tilapia Lafayette — blackened tilapia with crawfish tail meat sautéed in garlic, capers, tomatoes, and basil.

78711 U.S. Hwy. 40 (in downtown Winter Park). ☎ ***970-726-4021***. *Reservations for large groups only. Main courses: $6.95–$19.95. Open: Lunch and dinner daily. AE, DC, MC, V.*

Hernando's Pizza Pub
$ Winter Park   PIZZA/PASTA

Using magic markers that the restaurant keeps on hand for the express purpose of defacing currency, customers of Hernando's Pizza have colored and then donated a total of 13,000 one-dollar bills to the restaurant. Rather than open a Swiss Bank account, restaurant employees tape the bills to the walls, posts, beams, and ceiling of the establishment, making the place look like a combination rathskeller, gallery, and U.S. mint. No one around here seems to know the value of a buck, but they do know their pizza — Hernando's bakes one of the best pies in the Rockies. For your sauce, you can choose between white, white with extra garlic, and traditional red. Top it with anything from almonds to jalapenos.

78199 U.S. 40 (at the north end of Winter Park). ☎ *970-726-5409. Reservations not accepted. Pizzas: $7.50–$17.50. Pasta dishes and sandwiches: $6.25–$7. Open: Dinner daily. Closed mid-April–early June. AE, DISC, MC.*

Randi's Irish Saloon

$–$$$ Winter Park   IRISH/AMERICAN

The many high chairs inside the front door of this restaurant indicate how popular the place is — or could be — among families. Every generation should appreciate the menu. Offerings include Irish pub fare such as shepherd's pie and fish and chips; salads; burgers; and entrees such as filet mignon and salmon with blue cheese. Portions are large, and the desserts seem even larger.

78521 U.S. 40 (in downtown Winter Park). ☎ *970-726-1172. Reservations for large parties only. Main courses: $12–$24. Open: Mon–Fri dinner only, Sat–Sun lunch and dinner. AE, DISC, MC, V.*

The Shed

$$ Winter Park   SOUTHWESTERN

This Winter Park landmark changes its entire menu every six months. The owner says that some of his regulars try all the items on every new menu, then wait around for the next one. When I was here, they would have had to eat their way through the likes of corn and chipotle chowder, Cajun chimichangas, portobello mushroom stacks, and lobster and mango fajitas. The bar's enormous margaritas attract locals by the score, especially during the late-afternoon happy hour.

78762 U.S. 40, Winter Park. ☎ *970-726-9912. Reservations not accepted. Main courses: $9–$20. Open: Dinner daily. Closed mid-April–Memorial Day. AE, DC, DISC, MC, V.*

Exploring Winter Park and Fraser

These are small towns surrounded by big mountains. Most of the activity is in the mountains, but you can also find a few things to do around town.

The best things to see and do

If you visit here, plan on spending time exploring the mountains. But if you need some rest, you can try the following:

✔ **Hit the old community center.** Built in 1876, **Cozens Ranch House,** 77849 U.S. 40, between Winter Park and Fraser (☎ **970-726-5488**), was the first homestead in the Fraser Valley and later served as a post office, stagecoach stop, and chapel. The house has displays on area history, including one on World War II–era POWs who worked in the local timber industry. It's open in the summer Tuesday through Saturday from 10 a.m. to 5 p.m., and Sunday from 1 to 5 p.m. Other months, it's open Wednesday through Saturday from 10 a.m. to 4 p.m., and Sunday from 1 to 4 p.m. Admission is $5 for adults, $4 for seniors 62 and up, and $2 for students.

✔ **Be a-mazed.** Kids in particular will enjoy the summer activities at the base of **Winter Park Resort** (☎ **970-726-5514**). Options include an alpine slide, mini golf, a human maze, indoor and out-door climbing walls, and gravity-defying bungee and zip-line activities. You can pay for activities individually, at prices ranging from $4 to $10, or get a half- or full-day park pass (cost: $34 and $40, respectively). Winter Park Resort is open daily from 10:00 a.m. to 5:30 p.m., from early June to early September.

If you do pay for activities individually, you can run up a big tab in a hurry.

Staying active

If you come to the Fraser Valley on a weekday, you can often enjoy the backcountry in near solitude; on the weekends, expect company from Denver. Some of the best recreation choices include the following:

✔ **Cross-country skiing:** The cold temperatures, abundant snowfall, and rolling valley floor make this a mecca for cross-country skiing. The largest Nordic center, **Devil's Thumb Ranch** (☎ **800-933-4339**), grooms 100 kilometers for skate and classic skiing and also has marked trails for snowshoers. Trail fees are $13 for a full day, $9 after 12:30 p.m. Sleigh rides and ice skating are also on the bill, and the bar and restaurant provide a cozy après-ski environment. The ranch is at 3530 County Rd. 83, off U.S. 40 south of Tabernash.

✔ **Golfing:** The **Pole Creek Golf Club** (☎ **800-511-5076** or 970-726-8847; Internet: www.polecreekgolf.com) boasts 27 holes at 8,600 feet above sea level. It consistently ranks among the top public courses in America, and in 1985 it won *Golf Digest*'s award as the best new public course in America. Greens fees are $80 during high season, $55 during low season. To get there, take U.S. 40 11 miles west from Winter Park to County Road 5.

✔ **Hiking:** On foot, you can you use all the same trails (550 miles' worth) that the mountain bikers do, or you can drive a little higher in the mountains and hike in the **Vasquez, Byer's Peak,** and **Indian Peaks** wilderness areas. You can reach two premier trails by taking County Road 73 out of Fraser and then following the signs: The **St. Louis Lake Trail** goes 3.4 miles to St. Louis Lake, and the rugged **Byer's Peak Trail** rises 2,000 vertical feet over 3.7 miles to the 12,804-foot Byer's Peak, affording panoramic views of the Fraser Valley. Allow 30 minutes to drive to these trailheads from Fraser. You'll need a high-clearance vehicle (and no trailer) to get there. The **Arapahoe National Forest Sulphur Ranger District Office,** off U.S. 40 ½-mile south of Granby (☎ 970-887-4100), has maps and information on these areas.

✔ **Mountain biking:** Over 500 miles of trails thread their way through the Fraser Valley, supplementing the 50 miles of lift-served paths at **Winter Park Resort** (☎ 800-979-0330). Because many Fraser Valley trails are on relatively smooth forest floors, this is an ideal place to learn how to mountain bike. You can get free trail descriptions and maps at the **Winter Park Visitor Center** (☎ 800-903-7275). Intermediate and advanced riders will enjoy the **Creekside Trail,** which parallels St. Louis Creek. To find the trailhead, pedal 3 miles west out of Fraser on County Road 73 and then go left at the turnoff for the **St. Louis Creek Campground.** Starting on the Creekside Trail, you can access intermediate and advanced single-track trails known as **Flume, Zoom,** and **Chainsaw,** plus many others. The trails have a few rocky, technical spots but mostly travel through gently undulating forest. Take your map, because you may have to improvise on your return. If you're pedaling with small children or just want to relax, try the **Fraser River Trail,** which parallels the Fraser River between Winter Park and Fraser. **Beaver's Sport Shop,** 79303 U.S. 40 in Winter Park (☎ 970-726-1092), rents full-suspension and front-suspension mountain bikes all day for $30 and $18, respectively.

Hitting the slopes

For a mega-resort that ranks among the nation's busiest mountains, **Winter Park Resort** feels like a throwback. It's still owned by the city of Denver, which established it as a park in 1939. Many skiers arrive here on The Ski Train, via a historic rail line that passes within yards of the base area. And because of cold temperatures and a storm-trapping location just west of the continental divide, the snowpack (the actual amount of snow on the ground) here usually ranks among the deepest in the state, calling to mind the days, etched in every aging skier's memory (or imagination), when it really did snow.

It's the closest full-service mountain resort, mileage-wise, to the Mile High City, so you can get here easily and enjoy the area's mix of terrain. Winter Park serves up a pleasing variety of mogul runs, cruisers, and beginner runs, sometimes in close proximity to one another. If you want to concentrate on expert runs, you can bounce down long, steep mogul runs on Mary Jane, the most challenging of Winter Park's three mountains. For more on the resort, see Table 18-1.

Novices will appreciate the Galloping Goose chairlift, which serves fenced-in, beginner terrain. Tickets for this chairlift cost just $5, making it an ideal place to teach children how to ski.

Table 18-1	Ski Report: Winter Park Resort
Location: On U.S. 40, 65 miles northwest of Denver	
Trails: 134	
Vertical drop: 3,060 feet	
Base elevation: 9,000 feet	
Summit elevation: 12,060 feet	
Skiable terrain: 2,886 acres	
Average snowfall: 369 inches	
Lifts: 22	
Snow report: ☎ 303-572-SNOW	
Winter Park Reservations: ☎ 800-729-5813	
Internet: www.skiwinterpark.com	
2002–2003 high-season adult all-day ticket: $56	

Fast Facts: Winter Park/Fraser

Hospital

Call **911** for emergencies. In most cases, you can obtain treatment at 7-Mile Medical Clinic, at Winter Park Resort (☎ 970-726-8066). Kremmling Memorial Hospital, 214 S. Fourth St. (☎ 970-724-3442), has a 24-hour emergency room.

Information

Winter Park Visitor Center, on U.S. 40 in downtown Winter Park (☎ 800-903-7275 and 970-726-4118; Internet: www.winter-park-info.com), and Fraser Visitor Center, 120 Zerex Ave. (U.S. 40) in Fraser (☎ 970-726-8312), can handle your questions about the area.

Pharmacy

Fraser Drug Store, next to Alco on U.S. 40 in Fraser (☎ 970-726-1000), can fill your prescriptions.

Post Office

The Fraser Post Office (☎ 970-726-5578) is at 520 Zerex Ave. (U.S. 40). The Winter Park Post Office (☎ 970-726-5578) is at 78490 U.S. 40.

Road Conditions

Call ☎ 877-315-7263 or 303-639-1111.

Vail

Vail as we know it didn't exist before 1962, when a former member of the 10th Mountain Division started a small ski area with a lodge and restaurant at the base. He and his friends fashioned the buildings after the mountain villages they had seen in Europe during World War II. They named the area for the highway engineer who had designed the road into the area, and the place took off from there. Like Aspen, Vail is now beyond expensive, but it still welcomes thousands of skiers who drive up from Denver on weekends, not to mention many destination travelers. Some of the people who helped build the town have stuck around, helping preserve Vail's sense of tradition. Forty years after it started, Vail still feels as much like a town for hardy skiers as it does a retreat for the very rich. And it still retains its European flavor.

Don't be put off by your first glimpse of the community. The town extends down a river canyon alongside I-70, but the downtown villages feel less like an off-ramp than you may think. The heart of the town — two adjoining enclaves known as Vail Village and Lionshead — bans most car traffic and seems remote from the freeway. In places, the splashing of Gore Creek is all you'll hear. And lush mountainsides border the south side of the community.

Twelve miles west of Vail is the resort of Beaver Creek, which is a more secluded version of Vail. Like Vail, it has a pedestrian-friendly, European-style village, and it costs a lot to stay there. Unlike Vail, it's a couple of miles uphill from the freeway, and you'll have to pass through a guard-house to drive up there. Most visitors gravitate to Vail.

Getting there

Part of Vail's allure is its accessibility. It's right on I-70, 109 miles west of Denver and 150 miles east of Grand Junction.

During ski season, **Vail/Eagle County Airport,** 35 miles west of town, has daily nonstop service to and from Dallas, Chicago, Minneapolis, Newark, and San Francisco, and weekend service to Detroit, Cincinnati, and Atlanta. **American, Continental, Delta, Northwest,** and **United Airlines** all fly into Eagle County. Call **Colorado Mountain Express** (☎ **800-525-6363** or 970-926-8118) for a shuttle ride (cost: $44 per person) into town. **Hertz, Avis, Enterprise,** and **Budget** all have desks at the airport. For information on contacting individual airlines and car-rental agencies, see the Appendix.

Vail is within a two-hour drive of Denver, so you can also fly into **Denver International Airport (DIA),** served by most major domestic carriers. Numerous companies offer shuttle services between Vail and Denver, including **Colorado Mountain Express** (☎ **800-525-6363** or 970-926-8118), which charges $62 a person for a shared, one-way ride to Vail from DIA.

Getting around

You can get by without a car in Vail. The town has an outstanding transit system, with **free shuttles** serving Vail Village, Lionshead, East Vail, and West Vail from 6 a.m. to 2 a.m. daily during ski season. (Hours of operation are shorter the rest of the year.) During winter, you'll seldom have to wait more than ten minutes for a bus. For local shuttle-bus schedules, call ☎ **970-477-3456. ECO Transit** (☎ **970-328-3520** or 970-477-1606) provides regular bus service (for $2 to $3) to outlying areas such as Avon, Edwards, Beaver Creek, and Leadville.

For a cab, call **Vail Valley Taxi** (☎ **970-476-TAXI**).

Where to stay

Lodging costs a lot in Vail. If you're a skier, you can save by shopping for package deals or by coming before Christmas or in April, periods when the snow can be hit or miss. Some lodges also discount rooms in mid-January, when the snow tends to be light and fluffy and the coverage is more reliable. If you're not a skier, consider visiting during spring, early summer, and late fall, when the town empties and many lodges sharply discount their rooms. If the rates still seem too expensive, look for lodging in the nearby towns of Avon or Edwards.

Even during high season, visitors can sometimes find last-minute lodging deals in Vail by calling the **Vail Visitor Center** (☎ **970-479-1394**) or checking www.vailonsale.com.

The top hotels

Hotel-Gasthof Gramshammer
$$–$$$$ Vail Village

One of the original three buildings in town, this hotel is a bargain by Vail standards. During winter, its 35 rooms cost about $100 less than nearby accommodations, and they're pleasant. Guests stay in the lodge that Pepi Gramshammer, a former Austrian ski racer, and his wife, Sheika, have run since 1964. They live on the premises and do their best to make you feel like family. Accommodations range from a standard hotel room to a deluxe apartment with a full kitchen. You can unwind in the two Jacuzzis, in Pepi's Bar, or on Pepi's Deck, where you can eat goulash and other Austrian dishes.

231 E. Gore Creek Dr., Vail. ☎ *970-476-5626. Fax: 970-476-8816. Internet:* www. pepis.com. *Rack rates: Mid-June–Dec 15, $95–$585; Dec 15–26, Jan 6–25, and April 2–mid-June, $195–$750; Dec 26–Jan 5, Jan 26–April 1, $225–$835. During winter, self-parking costs $10 a night. AE, DC, DISC, MC, V.*

Lift House Condominiums
$$$–$$$$$ **Lionshead**

Built in 1965, the hotel consists entirely of studio condominiums; each with a queen-size bed, rollaway bed, gas fireplace, kitchenette, and dining area. The rooms aren't very roomy, but no space goes to waste. Four very close adults could stay and eat in each room in something like comfort, and the price is almost right. The hotel's literature says it's only "73 seconds" from the Gondola base but doesn't say who's walking. It is pretty close though.

555 East Lionshead Circle, Vail. ☎ *800-654-0635 or 970-476-2340. Fax: 970-476-9303. Internet:* www.lifthousevail.com. *Rack rates: April 14–May 31, Oct–Nov, $81; June–Sept $99–$135; winter high season $249–$310; winter low season $127–$194. DISC, MC, V.*

Park Hyatt Beaver Creek Resort and Spa
$$$$$ **Beaver Creek**

Situated right at the base of Beaver Creek's ski runs, this immense hotel offers luxuries ranging from in-room computers to six roaring whirlpools. The rooms, big enough for a Shriners convention, have been recently redecorated at an inordinate cost in a Western motif. Downstairs, at the feng shui–influenced spa, ultra-content guests drift around in robes, read magazines, or simply relax. If all the deep relaxation and comfort puts you under, you may need to drive into Vail for some nightlife.

At Beaver Creek Resort, Avon. ☎ *970-949-1234 or 800-55-HYATT (reservations only). Fax: 970-845-2830. Internet:* www.beavercreek.hyatt.com. *Rack rates: Dec 20–April 5, $360–$645; rest of year, $100–$325. Add $75 to $150 per night for a room with ski-area views. AE, DC, DISC, MC, V.*

Sonnenalp
$$$$–$$$$$ **Vail Village**

This hotel, my favorite in Vail, has European-mountain touches such as arched entryways and stonework framing heavy wooden doors. At times, there are so many German and Austrians on duty, you can be sure that the guest-to-European ratio is the lowest in town. The rooms come with gas fireplaces, balconies, windows that open, and heated marble bathroom floors. A single switch shuts off all the lights in the room when you leave. After you're done swimming in the creek-side indoor-outdoor pool, you can relax in the full-service spa.

20 Vail Rd., Vail. ☎ ***800-654-8312*** *or 970-476-5656. Fax: 970-479-5449. Internet:* www.sonnenalp.com. *Rack rates: Nov 27–Dec 20 and April 6–13 $235; Dec 20–Jan 5 $560; Jan 5–April 5 $495; April 14–June 16 and Sept 29–Nov 27 $200; June 16–Sept 29 $295. AE, DC, DISC, MC, V.*

The runner-up hotels

Evergreen Hotel

$$–$$$$ Vail Village   Take off your lederhosen and relax in this hotel's large, comfortable, chain-style rooms. Mostly green, they have benches at the foot of the bed, large TVs, mini-refrigerators, and double vanities. They feel crisp and clean, even if they don't make you want to yodel. *250 S. Frontage Rd. W., Vail.* ☎ ***800-284-8245*** *(reservations only) or 970-476-7810. Fax: 970-476-4504. Internet:* www.evergreenvail.com.

The Lodge at Vail

$$$$ Vail Village   The first hotel at Vail, this lodge claimed a prime location mere steps away from the Vista Bahn chairlift. The lodge has two gourmet restaurants, an exercise room, a swimming pool, and four hot tubs. The prime location and attentive service help make up for the smallish rooms. *124 E. Gore Creek Dr., Vail.* ☎ ***800-331-LODG*** *or 970-476-5011. Fax: 970-476-7425. Internet:* www.lodgeatvail.com.

Where to dine

Like the town itself, Vail's dining scene seems to have a spoon in Europe and a fork in the U.S. Many of Vail's best restaurants serve traditional French, German, Swiss, or Italian food, and most of the rest bring European elements to American fare. The town's list of chefs reads like a reunion of James Beard House nominees. Naturally, dinners cost a lot, but a few places do serve affordable fare, and many bars have specials on food and drinks.

The top restaurants

Bully Ranch
$–$$ **Vail   AMERICAN**

This place is a smart choice for a group of friends who can't agree on what type of food to eat. The menu has salads and wraps for light appetites; chops and salmon for big eaters; and pub fare (including baby back ribs, fish and chips, and fisherman's stew) for everyone else. The dining room has a relaxed Western feel, from the antler lamps on the ceiling to the weathered wooden floor underfoot. A lot of locals come here just for the famous *mudslides* (a mixed drink made up of vodka, kahlua, and Irish Cream), which seem to go hand in hand with overgrazing.

20 Vail Rd., Vail. ☎ ***970-476-5656.*** *Reservations not accepted. Main courses: $7.50–$28. Open: Lunch and dinner daily. AE, DC, DISC, MC, V.*

La Tour

$$$–$$$$ Vail FRENCH/AMERICAN

When Vail's chefs go out for a delectable meal, they often order the latest creations of La Tour's owner, Paul Ferzacca. Ferzacca mastered French cooking at some of Chicago's finest restaurants. When he took over La Tour in 1998, he began subtly tinkering with traditional French fare. The result hardly qualifies as "French lite," but the sauces are a little less creamy than in Paris (or so I'm told), and Asian ingredients have turned up in certain dishes. Plan on staying for a while; this is the place to have a leisurely dinner. The menu is broken down into three courses plus dessert; you may as well shoot the moon. For a main course, try the Dover sole in brown butter sauce.

122 E. Meadow Dr. (across from the west end of the Vail Village parking structure), Vail. ☎ 970-476-4403. Reservations preferred. Main courses: $9–$36. Open: Dinner daily. Closed May 10–Memorial Day. AE, DC, DISC, MC, V.

Sapphire Restaurant and Oyster Bar

$$$ Vail INNOVATIVE AMERICAN

This restaurant's press kit says that one owner, Joel Fritz, has been "married for 35 years to the same person and never a cross word." It says the other owner, Susan Fritz, has been "raising great kids and well-mannered dogs." The Fritz's miracles carry over into their restaurant, which has delicious food, attentive servers, and, if the pattern holds, charming prep cooks. Dinner fare consists primarily of steaks and seafood; at lunch, options include fish tacos, salads, burgers, and sandwiches. You can sit on the creek-side deck or go inside to the dining room and oyster bar, where tiny ceiling lights sparkle like stars.

223 Gore Creek Dr., Vail. ☎ 970-476-2828. Reservations recommended. Main courses: $18–$28. Open: Lunch and dinner daily. AE, MC, V.

Sweet Basil

$$$ Vail CREATIVE AMERICAN

Sweet Basil is my first choice for a meal out in the mountains. This isn't exactly a bold choice — this bistro-style restaurant has been earning raves for 25 years. Ask for a table with views of Gore Creek, then choose between the fish, steak, chicken, and veal dishes, all with creative sauces. The saffron linguini with lobster, bay scallops, shrimp, and cream has been on the menu forever, and it's delicious. For dessert, try the hot sticky toffee pudding cake.

193 E. Gore Creek Dr., Vail. ☎ 970-476-0125. Reservations recommended. Main courses: $23–$28. Open: Lunch and dinner daily. AE, DISC, MC, V.

The runner-up restaurants

La Cantina

$ **Vail   MEXICAN/AMERICAN**   A lot of locals fill up on Mexican combination plates and margaritas here before taking the bus home. The margaritas alone are enough to make you miss your ride. The Mexican rugs, painted furniture, sombreros, and strings of lights will brighten your detour into Margaritaville, and the cheap, tasty food will fuel you when you finally decide to move. *241 S. Frontage Rd. W. (inside Vail Transit Center), Vail.* ☎ *719-486-9021.*

Red Lion Inn

$–$$ **Vail   AMERICAN**   One of the first three buildings in Vail, this has been the town's gathering place for après-ski for 40 years. On winter afternoons, steamy riders pack the place in order to sip on local beers, munch appetizers, and simply be in the Red Lion. Dinner offerings include burgers, sandwiches, ribs, and a New York strip steak. The bar stays smoke-free until 9 p.m. *304 Bridge St., Vail.* ☎ *970-476-7676.*

Exploring Vail

Vail doesn't have a lot of must-see attractions, so you can relax and drift from place to place. During summer, you may drift past gardens, mountain trails, people fishing on Gore Creek, a few galleries, and lots of interesting shops. Go slowly and you'll have energy to spare for the cultural events around town, including outdoor concerts at the town's amphitheater.

The best things to see and do

Colorado Ski Museum–Ski Hall of Fame

Being a nerd for old ski stuff, I love this museum. It has timelines showing major developments in skiing and snowboarding, along with gear and memorabilia from the different periods. It displays uniforms and equipment from each winter Olympics. And it devotes an entire room to the 10th Mountain Division. I'm partial to the vintage posters advertising ski areas and ski movies, and the old-time footage of powder skiers shown on the TV.

231 S. Frontage Rd. E. (in Vail Transportation Center, Level 3), Vail. ☎ *970-476-1876. Internet:* www.vailsoft.com/museum. *Open: Tues–Sun 10 a.m.–5 p.m. Closed May and Oct. Admission: $1 adults; free for children under 12.*

Betty Ford Alpine Gardens

The Betty Ford Gardens isn't a rehab center like that other Betty Ford place. Still, your head will feel better when you see the waterfalls, pools, and 2,000 different kinds of high alpine plants, ranging from bristlecone pines to alpine poppies. Almost anything that will legally grow at 8,200 feet is here, including many exotics. It's especially lovely in mid-summer, when the flowers are in full bloom.

In Ford Park, east of Vail Village, Vail. ☎ *970-476-0103. Internet:* www.betty fordalpinegardens.com. *Open: Daily from dawn to dusk when not under snow. Admission: Free.*

Staying active

During winter the activity in Vail centers around the big — make that enormous — ski area. During the rest of the year, Vail just concentrates on big fun. While you're here, think about going:

- ✔ **Fishing:** Even during the peak run-off months, you can usually wade and fish in Gore Creek right in downtown Vail. When the flows drop in mid-summer, you'll fare better if you travel below the confluence of Gore Creek and the Eagle River. **Fly-Fishing Outfitters** (☎ 800-595-8090 or 970-476-FISH) can help you find the best holes. Guide service for wade trips costs $175 for a half-day, $375 for a full day. Guided float trips start at $275 for a half-day.

- ✔ **Hiking: Vail Mountain** publishes a map showing summer hiking and biking trails on the ski area. You can find those maps in the same boxes that hold ski-area trail maps during winter. The resort has separate hiking and biking trails, so you can go for long walks without having to dodge cyclists. For even less crowded trails, go to Beaver Creek. If you want to hike with guides who are knowledgeable in geology, ecology, and history, contact the **Vail Nature Center,** 700 S. Frontage Rd. (☎ 970-479-2291; Internet: www.vail rec.com). The Nature Center schedules guided hikes most weekdays during summer, including mellow half-day strolls near Vail Village and more rigorous all day hikes in the nearby **Holy Cross** and **Eagle's Nest Wilderness Areas.**

- ✔ **Golfing:** On the par-71, 7,008-yard **Vail Golf Course,** 1778 Vail Valley Dr. (☎ 970-479-2260), you can tee off while taking in views of the Gore Range. Don't gawk too much, lest your ball end up in one of many water hazards. You can reserve your tee time 48 hours in advance. On weekdays, greens fees are $105, $80 at twilight; on the weekends, they rise to $115. Designed by Arnold Palmer, **Eagle Ranch Golf Course,** 50 Lime Park Dr., in Eagle (☎ 970-328-2882), is the least expensive course in the area. During summer, greens fees at this par-72, 7,506-yard course are $85 Monday through Thursday and $90 Friday through Sunday.

- ✔ **Ice skating:** Here's proof positive that the people at Beaver Creek are not living in the real world: You can ice-skate there, outside, *year-round.* Weather permitting, the rink operates from 6 to 10 p.m. nightly. Cost for skating, including skate rentals, is $9 for adults, $7 for kids. Call ☎ **970-845-0438** for more information. Meanwhile, Vail has a bonafide indoor hockey rink; call ☎ **970-479-2271** for information on open skates in Vail.

✔ **Mountain biking:** After picking up a free trail map, you can pedal directly onto Vail Mountain at either Vail Village or Lionshead. It's a long grind to gain the ridgeline, where one of the premier rides, the 7-mile **Grand Traverse,** begins. During summer, you can shorten the trip by taking the Eagle Bahn gondola or Vista Bahn chairlift to the top. Lift tickets, valid all day, cost $16 for adults, $10 for children 5 to12 and seniors 65 to 69, and $5 for seniors over 70. You'll also find challenging trails on the north side of I-70. **Diamond Ski Shop,** 520 Lionshead Mall (☎ **970-476-5500**), can provide directions and also rents full-suspension mountain bikes for $30 a day.

✔ **Rafting: Lakota River Guides** (☎ **800-274-0636** or 970-476-RAFT) has trips ranging from mellow half-day family floats on the Colorado River ($69 adults, $59 ages 6 to 12) to all-day white-knucklers on the Arkansas ($119 for ages 16 and up).

Hitting the slopes

It's hard to overstate the immensity of **Vail.** Its 33 lifts serve 193 trails and five bowls strung across a ridgeline more than 7 miles long. Vail's 5,289 skiable acres make it the largest area in the country by 1,700 acres. It took me most of a day just to ski into every *canyon* in the area boundaries. The terrain includes a pine-covered, north-facing lower mountain with groomed trails as wide as I-80; the famous back bowls, most of which are only moderately steep; and the remote, shady glades of Blue Sky Basin. Beginners have an incredible 35 trails to choose from in Blue Sky Basin alone. Advanced intermediates can drift almost everywhere, even into some of the back bowls. Mogul skiers can test their mettle on the Highline run, where the bumps are bunched like bubble wrap. And powder fanatics can float through an average annual snowfall (348 inches) that ranks among the highest in the state. After a storm, the powder skiers race to make fresh tracks in more than 2,600 mostly open acres in the bowls. A few drawbacks do come to mind: Lift lines inevitably slow skiers who don't know their way around the mountain; parking usually costs $12; and because the back bowls face the sun, the powder quickly warms and condenses after late-season storms. But that's quibbling — this is an awesome mountain. For the technical lowdown on the resort, see Table 18-2.

Table 18-2	Ski Report: Vail Mountain
Location: Vail Village	
Total named trails: 193	
Vertical drop: 3,450 feet	
Base elevation: 8,120 feet	
Summit elevation: 11,570 feet	
Skiable terrain: 5,289 acres	
Average annual snowfall: 346 inches	
Lifts: 33	
Snow phone: ☎ 970-476-4888	
Lodging reservations: ☎ 800-525-2257 or 970-845-5745	
Internet: www.vail.com	
2002–2003 high-season adult all-day ticket: $71	

Compared to Vail, **Beaver Creek Resort** is a downright intimate place, where everyone seems eager to assist you. The meet-and-greet process starts right after you park your car in Avon. Attendants lift the skis from your hand and load them onto the shuttle bus for the five-minute ride to Beaver Creek Village, where another set of attendants unloads the skis, bucket-brigade style, and places them in a rack. After finally catching up with your skis, you'll encounter greeters offering trail maps and advice. Then you'll take two short rides, via sheltered escalator, to the base of the slopes. Everything is ultra-luxurious, from the dried flowers in the bathrooms to the heated sidewalks in the base area. When you're on the hill, you'll finally get to know a delightful mountain that evenly balances beginner, intermediate, and advanced terrain. Beaver Creek has roughly one-third the skiable acreage of Vail, making it large enough to be varied yet small enough to comprehend. A lot of this terrain faces north, so the snow tends to stay cold and soft. Grooming is cherished here, but you'll also find some long mogul runs. See Table 18-3 for more information on the resort.

Table 18-3	Ski Report: Beaver Creek
Location: Parking is in Avon, 8 miles west of Vail on I-70	
Named trails: 146	
Vertical drop: 3,340 feet	
Base elevation: 8,100 feet	

Summit elevation: 11,440 feet
Skiable terrain: 1,625 acres
Average annual snowfall: 331 inches
Lifts: 13
Snow report: ☎ 970-476-4888
Grooming report: ☎ 970-845-5950
Central reservations: ☎ 800-578-4979
Internet: www.beavercreek.com
2002–2003 high-season adult all-day ticket: $71

Shopping

The shopping in and around Vail varies by neighborhood. **West Vail** has the big grocery stores, liquor outlets, and strip malls. **Beaver Creek,** near Avon, offers high-end boutiques and stores, but it's a little too secluded to qualify as a thriving shopping district.

Vail Village has the most fun and varied offerings, including some nationally known shops. One landmark store is the **Golden Bear** (☎ 970-476-4082), famous for selling its trademarked golden bear pendants. Located on Bridge Street in Vail Village, the store still crafts and sells a full line of bears, ranging from silver starter-bears (cost: $55) to diamond-studded bears (cost: if you have to ask the price, you can't afford them).

Right across the street, at 273 Gore Creek Dr., is the flagship **Gorsuch** store (☎ 970476-2294). Among other offerings, the store sells ski attire that does more than just keep you dry and warm; it has what the store describes as, ahem, "flawless form . . . and a new sensuality for city, country, and slopes."

American Ski Exchange, 225 Wall St. (☎ 970-476-1477), is the place to go when you need cheap Vail souvenirs for all your gift-greedy cousins and co-workers. Like a Times Square electronics shop, the store always claims to have drastically cut prices. Vail T-shirts have been sharply reduced to two for $15, and Vail fleece vests usually cost around $15, down from $50 or so.

August: Music month in Vail

During July and August, dozens of concerts and performances take place in the Vail Valley, many of them in the Gerald R. Ford Amphitheater, which has a large covered pavilion, an expansive lawn, and a stage from which performers can see the mountains.

From late June to early August, the **Vail Valley Music Festival** (☎ 866-827-5252; Internet: www.vailmusicfestival.org) presents more than 60 chamber, pops, and orchestral concerts featuring three major symphony orchestras and 40 soloists of international renown. Tickets range in price from $12.50 to $40.

The **Vail International Dance Festival** (☎ 970-949-1999; Internet: www.vvf.org/dance) schedules performances of contemporary and classical dance in early August. Tickets range in price from $15 to $85.

In late July and early August, some of the world's hottest jazz musicians come to town for the **Vail Jazz Festival** (☎ 888-VAIL-JAM; Internet: www.vailjazz.org). In addition to dozens of free outdoor concerts, the festival has intimate club gigs (cover charges vary) and a festival-capping party over Labor Day Weekend. Weekend passes cost $195, and tickets for individual shows cost $35 to $40.

The locals' favorite is probably the **Budweiser Hot Summer Nights Concert Series** — free rock, folk, bluegrass, blues, and reggae performances at the Gerald R. Ford Amphitheater on Tuesday nights during June and July.

Nightlife and culture

Vail has a diverse nighttime scene, with offerings ranging from dance clubs to cigar bars, sometimes even in the same location.

The Tap Room, 333 Bridge St. (☎ 970-479-0500), seems like a low-key locals' watering hole, but if you walk upstairs to **The Sanctuary,** you may find a rave-like dance party.

Club Chelsea, 2121 N. Frontage Rd. West. (☎ 970-476-5600), has a cigar bar, a disco-friendly dance club, and a lounge, all under the same roof. **8150,** 143 E. Meadow Dr. (☎ 970-479-0607), pays real live humans to play funk, rock, and reggae.

Go to **Bully Ranch,** 20 Vail Rd. (☎ 970-476-5656), for mudslides; to **Vendettas Italian Restaurant,** 291 Bridge St. (☎ 970-476-5070), for drafts and late-night pizza; and to the **Red Lion Inn,** 304 Bridge St. (☎ 970-476-7676), for après-ski.

If you want to relax with friends and hear acoustic music, **The Club,** 304 Bridge St. (☎ 970-479-0556), is a good choice.

Fast Facts: Vail

Hospital

Vail Valley Medical Center (☎ 970-476-2451) at 181 West Meadow Dr. (between Vail Road and East Lionshead Circle), has an emergency room open 24 hours.

Information

Vail Valley Tourism and Convention Bureau, 100 E. Meadow Dr., Vail (☎ 800-525-3875 or 970-476-1000, Internet: www.visitvail valley.com).

Pharmacy

City Market, 2109 N. Frontage Rd. W. (☎ 970-476-1621), can fill your prescriptions in Vail.

Post Office

Vail's post office is at 1300 N. Frontage Rd. W. (☎ 970-476-5217), across from Donovan Park.

Road Conditions

Call ☎ 970-479-2226.

Summit County

First, the bad news: Summit County is not the most pristine part of the Rockies. In the heart of the county, a large reservoir stalls water before diverting it to Denver via a tunnel through the continental divide. Not far away, I-70 burrows through the divide and emerges in Summit County, where it's soon engulfed by chain restaurants, retail outlets, and some bona fide sprawl. Many historic buildings dot Frisco and Breckenridge, but condominiums and newer communities have sprouted up all around them. Even the river channels have been altered by dredge mining.

Nevertheless, this semi-developed mountain setting has some real advantages, not least of which is its proximity to Denver. In ideal conditions, you can get to Summit County from the Mile High City in an hour and a half. Once you're here, you can use free mass transit to reach all four ski areas and the major towns. You can choose from an array of lodges throughout the county, ranging from slopeside condos to chain hotels near the interstate. And during summer, you can pedal on 55 miles of paved bike paths. If you do need to escape civilization, 315,000 acres of National Forest awaits.

A historic mining town, **Breckenridge** is the largest and best-known community in Summit County. Located alongside I-70, **Frisco** has a relaxed Main Street and a number of quirky lodges and restaurants. Two other towns, **Dillon** and **Silverthorne,** are on the east side of the reservoir, opposite Frisco. This chapter doesn't devote much space to the last two spots, but you should know that Dillon and Silverthorne do have many chain hotels and are viable choices for travelers on a budget.

Getting there

Denver International Airport (☎ **800-AIR-2-DEN**) is your best bet if you want to fly close to Summit County. Most major airlines serve DIA, and the biggest rental-car companies have desks at the airport. For information on contacting individual airlines and car-rental agencies, see the Appendix.

Because Summit County has an excellent mass-transit system, many people bypass the rental-car desks and take shuttles to their accommodations. **Resort Express** (☎ **800-334-7433** or 970-468-0330) will take you from the airport to Summit County for $52 per person.

If you're driving, **Frisco** is 58 miles from Denver on I-70. To reach **Breckenridge,** exit on Colorado 9 at Frisco, and drive 9 miles south into town. To reach **Copper Mountain,** keep going 14 miles west of Frisco on I-70.

Getting around

In Summit County, it's often easier to get around by shuttle than by car. By riding the shuttles, you can spare yourself parking headaches near the ski areas and in downtown Breckenridge. Three different shuttle services operate in Summit County:

✔ In Breckenridge, you can get around town year-round on the **Free Ride** buses (☎ **970-547-3140**). You can avoid paying for parking during peak winter periods by using the free lots at the north end of town and then taking a shuttle downtown. The busiest routes operate from 6:30 a.m. to midnight.

✔ **The Summit Stage** (☎ **970-668-0999**) provides free transportation to major towns and resorts in Summit County, including Copper Mountain, with hourly service between 6:30 a.m. and 10:30 p.m. All the town-to-town routes pass through **Frisco Station,** behind the Safeway store in Frisco, one block west of the junction of Colorado 9 and Interstate 70.

✔ When the ski areas are open, **KAB Shuttle** (☎ **970-496-4200**) offers regular, free service between Breckenridge and Keystone, where connecting service to A-Basin is available. Call for hours of operation.

During summer, the cleanest and most enjoyable way to travel Summit County is by bicycle. Fifty-five miles of paved paths link Frisco, Breckenridge, Copper Mountain, and Vail. Many of these paths travel in forests away from roads. For more on bicycling in Summit County, skip ahead to "Staying active" later in this section.

If the shuttles don't show or your bike breaks its chain, contact **453Taxi** (☎ **970-453-TAXI**).

A condo of your own

Central reservations agencies handle most of the bookings for the many condominiums in Summit County. Agencies can search for accommodations by price range, size, and location. Upon arriving, however, you may not always get the attentive service you expect of a luxury hotel. Still, it's your best (and sometimes only) option if you want to stay next to the chairlifts. Here are some places to start your search:

✔ **Copper Mountain Resort** (☎ 800-458-8386; Internet: www.copper colorado.com) handles the lodging at its base, in three villages linked by a free shuttle service. Accommodations range from studios ($98 to $324) to four-bedroom condos ($310 to $479). All are close to the lifts and, from what I saw, most seemed comfortable. If you're single (or simply rowdy), the main drawback to Copper is the lack of nightlife. Most restaurants and bars close by 10 p.m., even during high season. This could change in the next year as Copper continues a large base-area expansion.

✔ **Keystone Central Reservations** (☎ 800-842-7417 or 970-496-4242; Internet: www.keystoneresort.com) owns or manages 1,600 condominiums near the ski area's base, with a standard slopeside studio that sleeps four costing between $268 and $348. Keystone prides itself on being family-friendly and schedules a lot of activities for kids and parents.

✔ **Breckenridge Central Reservations** (☎ 888-697-7834 or 970-453-7238; Internet: www.gobreck.com) oversees 3,100 rooms and condos in Breckenridge, including some near the base of the mountain. A standard slopeside studio at Breckenridge generally costs between $200 and $365.

Where to stay

You can find almost every type of lodging in Summit County, but condominiums far outnumber hotel rooms.

Most of Summit County's chain hotels are concentrated along I-70 near Frisco, Dillon, and Silverthorne, a few miles from the ski areas. Options include the **Best Western Lake Dillon Lodge,** 1202 N. Summit Blvd., in Frisco (☎ 970-668-5094); **Days Inn,** 580 Silverthorne Lane, in Silverthorne (☎ 970-468-8661); **Holiday Inn-Summit County,** 1129 N. Summit Blvd., in Frisco (☎ 970-668-5000); and **Super 8,** 808 Little Beaver Trail, in Dillon (☎ 970-468-8888).

You may save a few dollars by staying at a chain hotel, but if nightlife is important to you, pay a bit more and get a room or condominium in Breckenridge. For proximity to the slopes, consider the base areas at Breckenridge, Keystone, and Copper Mountain.

Breckenridge Mountain Lodge

$–$$$ Breckenridge

This lodge is downright cheap for downtown Breckenridge. I like the earthy rooms with bed frames of peeled pine logs, quilted bedspreads, and Western paintings. The new manager seems determined to maintain the place meticulously, and that counts for a lot. Next to the bar here, there's a game room with pool tables, foosball, and video games.

600 S. Ridge St., Breckenridge. ☎ *970-453-2333 or 800-800-STAY (reservations only). Fax: 970-453-5426. Internet:* www.snow.com. *Rack rates: April 21–Nov 30 $65–$84; Dec 1–April 21 $90–$140; Christmas Week, Presidents Week, spring break $188. AE, DC, DISC, MC, V.*

Frisco Lodge Bed & Breakfast

$–$$ Frisco

Some of the Frisco Lodge's rooms are in a creaky (but charming) 1885 boarding house; the rest are in a solid, two-story 1965 motel. All are clean, compact, and decorated in flowery patterns. If you want festive surroundings, try the boardinghouse. It has a big TV area where guests gather and watch movies along with the lodge dog, Sugar. The motel rooms feel more private. Unlike some of the lodge rooms, all the motel rooms have their own bathrooms. When you factor into the rate the free breakfast you get here, the price is hard to beat.

321 Main St., Frisco. ☎ *800-279-6000 (reservations), 970-668-0195. Fax: 970-668-0149. Internet:* www.friscolodge.com. *Rack rates: Spring and fall $50–$80; summer $55–$85; winter low-season $55–$90; winter high-season $110–$150. Rates include free breakfast. AE, DC, DISC, MC, V.*

Hunt Placer Inn B&B

$$$ Breckenridge

The keepers of this 9-year-old home baked a chocolate cake that won the "Golden Pig" award at a local chocolate-cooking contest. If you stay here, you can have your cake and afford it, too. This inn has high ceilings, low prices, and immense three-course breakfasts. The rooms are each sumptuously decorated in a different motif. In the next few years, you should be able to ski right to the lodge, because the ski area is planning to build a chairlift and cut new trails through the forest above the inn. For now, however, you'll have to catch a shuttle outside and ride the full two minutes to the mountain.

275 Ski Hill Rd., Breckenridge. ☎ *800-472-1430 or 970-453-7573. Fax: 970-453-2335. Internet:* www.huntplacerinn.com. *Rack rates: $135–$164. A five-night stay is required during high-season. AE, DC, DISC, MC, V.*

Main Street Station

$$–$$$ Breckenridge

Forget about the kitchenettes, fireplaces, and washer/dryers in the guest units of this new condominium hotel. And never mind the fact that the place offers all the amenities you'd expect of a big-city luxury hotel (free newspapers, underground parking, a business center, and a concierge, to name a few). Finally, ignore the location within walking distance of both downtown Breckenridge and the lowest chairlift at Breckenridge Ski Resort. There's only one thing that most of us need to know: In the guest rooms, you'll find complimentary Dove Bars in the freezers.

505 S. Main St., Breckenridge. ☎ *970-453-5995. Fax 970-547-5909. Internet:* www. mainstreetstation.com. *Rack rates: One-bedroom studio, summer $100–$235, fall $100–$200, winter $160–$340, spring $145–$250. AE, DISC, MC, V.*

Where to dine

Summit County pulls a lot of visitors from heartland states such as Texas, Oklahoma, and Kansas, so it should come as no surprise that many restaurants here serve family-friendly American fare like steaks and barbeque. When you pay for dinner, you'll find out you aren't in Kansas anymore. But you're not in Aspen, either.

Blue Spruce Inn

$$ Frisco   AMERICAN

Before Dillon Reservoir submerged the old town site of Dillon, this 1944 inn was trucked in pieces to Frisco. Today the interior feels earthy yet homey, like a log cabin run by a Cub Scout Den Mother. The restaurant serves standbys such as ribs, steaks, trout, and roast pork, as well as some creative pasta dishes. If you want to dine in your flip-flops, you can order the same food in the barroom, where there's a historic Brunswick bar that was trucked here in pieces from a condemned building in Black Hawk.

20 Main St., Frisco. ☎ *970-668-5900. Reservations recommended. Main courses: $15–$28. Open: Dinner daily. AE, DC, DISC, MC, V.*

Boatyard Pizza & Grill

$–$$ Frisco   AMERICAN/PIZZAS

This place was called Uptown Bistro until the owners decided that the name implied something fancy. Truth is, there *could* be fine dining here: The eclectic menu has some delectable pasta and fish dishes, and the dining room looks as if it aspires to be upscale. Yet the owners have gone the other way, preferring to make people aware of the pizzas, big portions, huge selection, and relaxed atmosphere.

The restaurant sometimes closes seasonally in the late fall, so call before you go if you plan on coming here during that time of year.

304 Main St., Frisco. ☎ 970-668-4728. Reservations for large parties only. Sandwiches and burgers: $7.25–$10. Main courses: $11–$19. Open: Mon–Sat lunch and dinner; Sun brunch and dinner. AE, DISC, MC, V.

Breckenridge BBQ
$–$$ Breckenridge   BARBECUE

The jalapenos used by Breckenridge BBQ are devilishly hot, and the main source of fiber in some of the restaurant's dishes. If you bypass the peppers, the rest of the food warms you more gently. Options include chicken fried chicken, half-pound cheeseburgers, Polish pepper sausage, pulled pork, and barbecued ribs. Salads and cole slaw are available for meek people who want something other than jalapenos for their greens. The restaurant's big deck, with views of the ski area, is popular in summer, especially when musicians play.

301 S. Main, Breckenridge. ☎ 970-453-7313. Reservations not accepted. Main courses: $6.50–$16.95. Open: Lunch and dinner daily. AE, DISC, MC, V.

Breckenridge Brewery & Pub
$–$$ Breckenridge   PUB FARE

These days, Breckenridge Brewery produces most of its beer in Denver, but the staff still whips up a few batches on the premises of this restaurant, as it has since 1990. Two huge vats still loom behind the bartender, a sight that beer drinkers may find strangely reassuring. Along with four staple beers and two seasonal brews, the brewery serves appetizers, soups, salads, sandwiches, ribs, and Southwestern fare. It's a popular place among both tourists and locals, so you're sure to fit in.

600 S. Main St., Breckenridge. ☎ 970-453-1550. Reservations not accepted. Main courses: $10–$18. Open: Lunch and dinner daily. Closed early May and late Oct. AE, DC, DISC, MC, V.

Café Alpine
$$–$$$ Breckenridge   UNIQUE AMERICAN

Café Alpine's offerings change daily, but they may include anything from tortilla-crusted tofu with vegetable, bean and green mole chili to grilled ono with wild mushrooms, wilted spinach, brussel sprouts, toasted couscous and cranberry demi. If you think ono and demi belong on the E! Channel and not the Food Channel, take a seat at the tapas bar and ask the chefs behind the counter to explain who's who, or what's what (for the record, *ono* is a Hawaiian fish and *demi* is a food glaze). While you're there, order some wine from one of the most extensive wine lists in town.

106 E. Adams Ave. (½ block east of Main Street), Breckenridge. ☎ *970-453-8218. Reservations recommended. Main courses: $15–$28. Open: Dinner daily; open for lunch daily Jun–Oct. AE, DISC, MC, V.*

Hearthstone Victorian Dining
$$$ **Breckenridge   AMERICAN**

Located in a 19th-century home, the Hearthstone feels more formal than other area restaurants. Most dishes combine comfort food and contemporary elements; but there are also traditional favorites such as crab legs, prime rib, and filet mignon. Locals seem divided about the Hearthstone, saying it's (a) overrated, (b) the best restaurant in Summit County, or (c) unaffordable. One person argued for (d) "all of the above." Still, the Hearthstone has enough local support to have been named Breckenridge's business of the year for 2002.

130 S. Ridge St., Breckenridge. ☎ *970-453-1148. Reservations accepted. Main courses: $17.95–$31.95. Open: Dinner daily. AE, MC, V.*

Exploring Summit County

With ski areas, historic towns, and mountains, you can always find something to do in Summit County. If nothing is happening in the town where you're staying, check on the ski areas, which promote special events most weekends during summer and early fall. To catch up on happenings around the county, pick up a copy of *Summit Daily News* upon arriving, or surf the Internet to www.summitdaily.com.

The best things to see and do
In Breckenridge and Frisco, you can throw a little history into your shopping, and vice versa. Afterwards, look for a cultural event, concert, or show. Here are a few options:

- ✔ **Shop 'til you need oxygen.** Breckenridge's downtown shopping district is home to about 200 shops, many of them tucked into small spaces on the town's Main Street. Frisco's downtown is smaller, but, like Breckenridge, it has fun stores and character.

- ✔ **Breathe your money's worth.** If you get winded from the intense, high-elevation shopping, stop at **The O2 Lounge,** 500 South Main St., in Breckenridge (☎ 970-453-6262), where ten minutes of pure oxygen costs $10. You can breathe as fast as you want. The lounge also has aromatherapy, smoothies, and herbal drinks.

- ✔ **Make a balloon payment.** Colorado Rocky Ballooning (☎ 888-468-9280 or 970-468-9280; Internet: www.coloradoballoonrides.com) offers the highest commercial balloon flights in the U.S. The one-hour, sunrise flights take off near Breckenridge at 9,600 feet and, under ideal conditions, ascend another 2,000 feet from there. The $195 per-person cost includes a photograph and a champagne breakfast.

✔ **Absorb some sounds.** Dillon, Frisco, and Breckenridge all offer free music during summer. Breckenridge hosts a high-caliber classical music festival (☎ 970-453-9142; Internet: www.breckenridge musicfestival.com) during July and August.

✔ **Brake for history.** The **Frisco Historic Park,** 120 Main St., in Frisco (☎ 970-668-3428), comprises 11 historic buildings surrounding a 1911 schoolhouse that now serves as a museum. You can stroll through an 1881 jail, a 1941 log chapel, and an 1890 ranch house, among other options. It's open Tuesday through Sunday from 11 a.m.to 4 p.m. during summer, and Tuesday through Saturday from 11 a.m.to 4 p.m. the rest of the year. Admission is free.

✔ **Seek out Breckenridge History.** The **Summit Historical Society** (☎ 970-453-7798 for recorded information; ☎ 970-453-9022 for tour reservations) can direct you to some of the most intriguing of Breckenridge's 170 historical sites. You can visit some spots alone; to see others, you'll have to sign up for guided tours ($6 adults, $2 children 2 to 12). To get started, stop at the **Free Museum** at 111 Main St., in Breckenridge. Open daily from 10 a.m. to 8 p.m., the museum houses rotating displays on area history. While you're there, you can get information about the other Summit Historical Society sites, including a placer mining gulch, where water was used to blast hillsides to extract gold; an underground gold mine; and the former home of Edwin Carter, whose collection of taxidermy ended up at the Denver Museum of Nature and Science. For more on that museum, see Chapter 12.

Especially for kids

Peak 8 Fun Park at Breckenridge Ski Resort (☎ 800-789-7669 or 970-453-5000) has three different **alpine slides** ($10 per ride, $8 kids ages 7 to 12), **miniature golf** ($6 per round), a **mountain-bike park** ($10 per lift ride, $8 kids), **scenic chairlift rides** ($8 adults, kids $4) a **human maze** ($5 adults, $4 kids), a **climbing wall** ($6 per climb) and **kids' center.**

If you want to keep the kids busy for more than an hour or so, it's worth it to throw down for a half-day ($45) or full-day ($60) pass that lets junior go wild on all of the above. It's open daily from 9 a.m. to 5 p.m. from mid-June to early September.

Staying active

With four ski areas, three Nordic centers, three ice rinks, four golf courses, the state's second-largest body of water, a whitewater park, and 315,000 acres of National Forest, there's a whole lot for an outdoorsy person to do in Summit County. You can scratch the surface by:

✔ **Biking and hiking:** For starters, you can cover 40 miles of paved bike/hiking paths, including one path that climbs 1,500 feet over 14 miles from Frisco to Vail Pass. **Avalanche Sports,** 540 S. Main St., in Breckenridge (☎ **970-453-1461**), rents a variety of bicycles at costs ranging from $18 to $34 per day and has copies of the free *Summit County Bike Trail Guide,* which describes all the paved paths as well as 27 more rugged rides in the area. The **Arapahoe National Forest Dillon Ranger District Office,** 680 Blue River Parkway, in Silverthorne (☎ **970-468-5400**), can help you locate prime areas for high-alpine hiking and mountaineering.

✔ **Cross-country skiing:** With four Nordic centers, Summit County offers just as many options to cross-country skiers as to downhillers. The largest area, the **Frisco Nordic Center** (☎ **970-668-0866**), south of Frisco on Colorado 9, has a groomed 43-kilometer trail system alongside Lake Dillon. **Breckenridge Nordic Center,** 1200 Ski Hill Rd. (☎ **970-453-6855**), sets 32 kilometers of track in meadows and forests at the base of the Breckenridge Mountain Resort. Both areas also have ungroomed trails for snowshoeing. A day pass good at both centers costs $14 for adults, $10 for seniors 55 to 69 and kids 7 to 16. You can also find groomed Nordic trails at Keystone (☎ **970-486-4275**) and Copper Mountain (☎ **970-968-2882**).

✔ **Golfing: Breckenridge Golf Club,** 0200 Clubhouse Dr. (☎ **970-453-9104**), has three distinct, Jack Nicklaus–designed 9-hole courses. You can reserve tee times up to four days in advance. During peak periods, greens fees are $110. On certain days, however, you can pay $65 for unlimited play after 3:30 p.m.

✔ **Kayaking:** After you've had a few whitewater kayaking lessons, you'll be ready to tackle the **whitewater park** on the Blue River in downtown Breckenridge. You can walk there from the **Breckenridge Recreation Center,** 0880 Airport Rd. (☎ **970-547-3125** for recorded information, or 970-547-3125), which is off Colorado 9 at the north end of town.

✔ **Boating and sailing:** At 3,200 acres, **Dillon Reservoir** is the second-largest body of water in the state and plenty big for boating and sailing. However, because it holds drinking water for Denver, you can't swim or use a personal watercraft. You can, however, rent fishing boats, pontoon boats, and sailboats at either of two marinas. **Dillon Marina,** on Lake Dillon Drive in Dillon (☎ **970-468-5100**), would be my first choice for renting a sailboat or taking sailing lessons. It also has a tiki bar and a large public boat ramp. **Frisco Bay Marina,** 900 E. Main St., in Frisco (☎ **888-780-4970**), is the better choice for paddle sports. It rents one-, two-, and three-person canoes, sea kayaks, and paddleboats, and offers kayaking lessons.

Hitting the slopes

Local riders have numerous reasons for adoring the steep little mountain they call A-Basin. Situated inside National Forest, the **Arapahoe Basin Ski Area** has free parking right near the base, so you won't need a travel agent to get from your car to the chairlift. The 13,050-foot summit — the highest inbounds terrain of any North American ski area — leaves flat-landers breathless but lets the area stay open into summer for die-hard riders. And, finally, the terrain is a hoot. A-Basin is less than one-tenth the size of Vail yet has as much really steep terrain as you'll find in Vail's entirety. When not hiking the chutes on the area's East Wall, skilled riders gravitate to the steep gullies and glades below the Pallavinci Lift. Intermediates can cruise the gentle bowls nearer the summit. Beginners are relegated to the lower mountain — or Keystone. Even the trail map seems relaxed and familiar, as befits an area for locals. It advises that the message boards at the bottom of the hill "are especially helpful if your friends are flaking out" and recommends that skiers "use sunscreen by the gallon." For more on the resort, see Table 18-4.

Table 18-4	Ski Report: Arapahoe Basin Ski Area
Location: 28194 U.S. 6 (between Keystone and Loveland Pass)	
Trails: 66	
15% easiest	
40% more difficult	
20% most difficult	
20% expert	
Vertical drop: 2,270 feet	
Base elevation: 10,780 feet	
Summit elevation: 13,050 feet	
Skiable terrain: 490 acres	
Average snowfall: 367 inches	
Lifts: 5	
Information: ☎ 888-ARAPAHOE	
Internet: www.arapahoebasin.com	
2002–2003 high-season adult all-day ticket: $47	

For the past few years, **Breckenridge Ski Resort** has rivaled and some-times bypassed Vail as the most popular ski area in North America. Visitors seem most enthusiastic about the easy access, the fun town, the abundant intermediate terrain, and the multiday lift tickets, which are also good at Vail, Keystone, and Beaver Creek. As for the mountain, it's big: 139 trails slice through pine and aspen forest on the flanks of four side-by-side peaks (numbered 7, 8, 9, and 10). Higher up, Breckenridge has nearly 800 acres of ungroomed bowl skiing, some of which are accessible only by hiking. This terrain is exhilarating on a powder day, but because of the resort's popularity, the powder often gets tracked quickly. Breckenridge also enjoys preferred status among snowboarders. Readers of *Snowboard Life* voted Breckenridge's SuperPipe number-one in the nation and judged its terrain park number-two. Check out the technical information on the resort in Table 18-5.

Table 18-5	Ski Report: Breckenridge Ski Resort
Location: On the west side of Breckenridge, off Ski Hill Road	
Trails: 139	
	14% beginner
	26% intermediate
	60% expert/ advanced
Vertical drop: 3,398 feet	
Base elevation: 9,600 feet	
Summit elevation: 12,998 feet	
Skiable terrain: 2,043 acres	
Average snowfall: 300 inches	
Lifts: 25	
Snow phone: ☎ 970453-6118	
Reservations: 877-593-5260	
Internet: www.breckenridge.com	
2002–2003 high-season adult all-day ticket: $65	

Part of a project that has grown steadily since opening in 1972, **Copper Mountain Resort** now ranks among the busiest resorts in Colorado. Because of its proximity to I-70, you can watch tractor-trailers rumble past while standing in line for the High Point chair. And the base area, though pleasant for families, lacks the character (and *characters*) found in nearby mining towns. But that's all at the bottom. After hopping on a chairlift, you'll discover terrain that a Forest Service researcher once called "the most nearly perfect ski mountain in the U.S." Intermediates have two huge areas of the mountain to themselves. Beginners can ski from near the summit to the base and even have access to a very gradual bowl. Advanced riders make out best of all. They can choose from mogul runs such as "Triple Threat" or look for untracked powder in any of four 12,000-foot bowls. This mountain was the biggest surprise during my tour of Colorado ski areas — fun, varied, and challenging. See Table 18-6 for further details on Copper Mountain.

Table 18-6	Ski Report: Copper Mountain Resort
Location: 72 miles west of Denver on I-70	
Trails: 125	
21% beginner	
32% intermediate	
54% advanced/expert	
Vertical drop: 2,601 feet	
Base elevation: 9,712 feet	
Summit elevation: 12,313 feet	
Skiable terrain: 2,450 acres	
Annual snowfall: 250 inches	
Lifts: 23	
Snow phone: ☎ 800-789-7609	
Central reservations: ☎ 800-458-8386	
Internet: www.coppercolorado.com	
2002–2003 high-season adult all-day ticket: $64	

Most families who go on ski vacations aren't looking to appear in a Warren Miller movie. They just want to be safe, be comfortable, and have fun. For them, there's **Keystone,** the third most popular resort in Colorado (see Table 18-7). Keystone offers specially priced packages for families and throws in "passports" good for activities away from the slopes (anything from Nordic skiing to yoga). As for the skiing, a high intermediate could handle about 80% of the runs on Keystone Mountain and North Peak. A few expert skiers have ventured to Keystone in recent years to attack the glades and chutes in the Outback, the highest and most challenging part of the resort. Because most expert riders thumb their noses at Keystone, the powder tends to last longer here than at other Summit County ski areas. Keystone also illuminates 17 trails for night skiing.

Table 18-7	Ski Report: Keystone
Location: 21996 U.S. 6, 5 miles east of Dillon	
Trails: 116	
12% easiest	
34% more difficult	
54% most difficult	
Vertical drop: 2,900 feet	
Base elevation: 9,300 feet	
Summit elevation: 12,200 feet	
Average snowfall: 230 inches	
Lifts: 23	
Snow phone: ☎ 800-427-8308	
Reservations: ☎ 800-427-8308	
Internet: www.keystoneresort.com	
2002–2003 high-season adult all-day ticket: $63	

Nightlife

Breckenridge jumps on the weekends, when young professionals from Denver check into condos and then check out the scene. A lot of them go to **Cecilia's,** 500 S. Main St., in Breckenridge (☎ **970-453-2243**), which has a large dance floor, a big selection of martinis, and a walk-in humidor where you can pick your own cigar. DJs usually generate the sounds, which vary from night to night.

For live music, go to **Sherpa & Yeti's,** 318 S. Main St. (☎ **970-547-9299**), a basement barroom that books bands ranging from punk to reggae. The best historical bar in the area is the **Gold Pan Restaurant,** 105 N. Main St., in Breckenridge (☎ **970-453-5499**). In Frisco, **Moosejaw Pub,** 208 Main St. (☎ **970-668-3931**), is a friendly neighborhood tavern.

Fast Fact: Summit County

Hospital

Summit Medical Center, Highway 9 at School Road in Frisco (☎ 970-668-3300), offers 24-hour emergency care.

Information Centers

In Frisco, stop at the Summit County Visitor Information Center, 916 N. Summit Blvd. (☎ 970-668-2051). Breckenridge Resort Chamber (☎ 970-453-2913) has an office at 309 N. Main St.

Pharmacy

The Breckenridge Drug Store, 111 Ski Hill Rd., in Breckenridge (☎ 970-453-2362), can fill your prescription. There are numerous other drugstores scattered throughout Summit County.

Post Office

The Breckenridge Post Office is at 300 S. Ridge St. In Frisco, go to 35 W. Main St. Call ☎ 800-275-8777 for hours and other information.

Road Conditions

Call ☎ 970-668-1090 for the latest road conditions.

Part V
Southern Colorado

The 5th Wave   By Rich Tennant

"Yes sir, our backcountry orientation programs are held at the Footblister Visitor Center, the Lostwallet Ranger Station or the Cantreadacompass Information Pavilion."

In this part . . .

The mountains in the north may be more famous, but the southern reaches of Colorado are home to some of the state's highest peaks. South Central and Southwestern Colorado are also graced with smaller surprises such as hot springs, desert canyons, sand dunes, relaxed towns, and ancient Indian dwellings. Hang on to your hats as I take you on a wild ride that passes through history- and mineral-rich Leadville, topographically bizarre Great Sand Dunes National Monument and Preserve, the dark depths of Black Canyon of the Gunnison National Park, and the largest archaeological preserve in the country at Mesa Verde National Park. There's no danger of saddle sores on this ride, so start reading.

Chapter 19

South Central Colorado

. . . .

In This Chapter

▶ Touring history-, mineral-, and mountain-rich Leadville

▶ Exploring Alamosa's amazing dunes

▶ Taking in the theater at Creede

▶ Art-shopping and river-running in Salida

. . . .

*W*arm winds blow north from New Mexico into the river valleys of South Central Colorado. Flanking those valleys are some of America's highest, frostiest mountains — and a mother lode of mining history.

What's Where?: South Central Colorado and Its Major Attractions

South of I-70, tucked between the continental divide (to the west) and the Front Range mountains, Pikes Peak, and Sangre de Cristo range (to the east), South Central Colorado has four easily overlooked towns, each with its own treasures. Alamosa appears to be just another agricultural community — that is, until you come across the 350-foot-high sand dunes and the geothermal springs a few miles away on the valley floor. When you drive into the tiny mountain town of Creede, you'll know immediately from the rows of Victorian homes and mine shacks that the town has a rich past. Given its population of just 300, you wouldn't expect it to have a top-notch repertory theater, too. Entering Leadville, you may first notice mine tailings, broken-down machinery, and dilapidated trailers, but if you drive a few more miles and look again, you'll find what may be the best-preserved historic district in the state. And if you're driving through Salida on U.S. 50, the town looks like the type of place where you'd gas up and keep moving, but a detour downtown will put you at the heart of a thriving arts community.

South Central Colorado

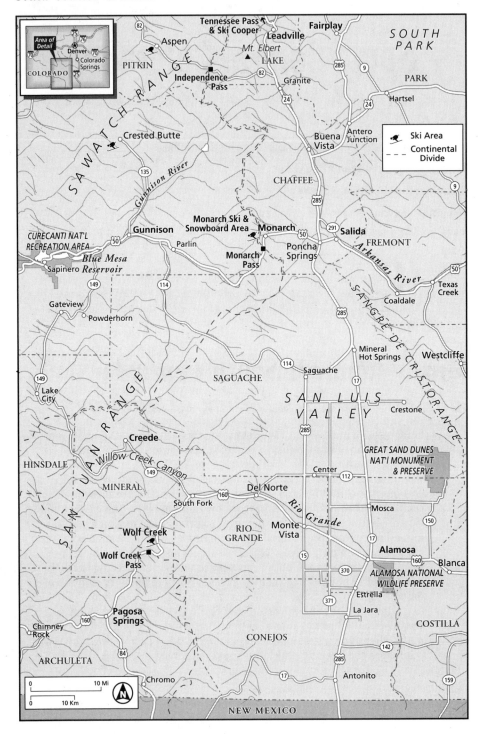

Leadville

The highest incorporated town in the Nation, Leadville also sits within striking distance of the state's highest peak, Mount Elbert. The town's outskirts were mined as hard as anywhere in Colorado, so the place has plenty of history. When you're here, check out

- ✔ **Mining history** at the Matchless Mine, at the National Mining Hall of Fame and Museum, and in the historic mining district.
- ✔ The **Mineral Belt Trail,** a 12½-mile hiking and biking loop that passes pines, mountains, and mines.
- ✔ The buildings in the town's historic district, including the 120-year-old **Silver Dollar Saloon.**

Alamosa/Creede

Creede fills the mouth of a small box canyon high in the mountains; Alamosa sits in an agricultural valley larger than Rhode Island. Yet a river (the Rio Grande) runs past both of them and contributes to the fun, which includes

- ✔ **Great Sand Dunes National Monument and Preserve,** as improbable as a giant pink rabbit and even more fun to look at.
- ✔ Perfectly preserved mines alongside the roads on the **Bachelor Historic Tour** near Creede.
- ✔ The **Creede Repertory Theater,** a risk-taking ensemble that flourishes in the smallest of towns.

Salida

Depressed 20 years ago, this former railroad hub has been revitalized, thanks in part to an influx of river runners and artists. As you may imagine, this is pretty mellow place. While you're here, try to experience

- ✔ The many **studio galleries** in Salida, where artists create and sell their work.
- ✔ A **river trip** on the Arkansas River.
- ✔ The **Monarch Crest Trail,** atop the continental divide.

Leadville

Most people either fall in love with Leadville or can't wait to escape. Your response depends partly on how you handle a chilly mountain climate. Being the highest incorporated town in the United States,

Leadville can get frosty at night, and its summers aren't exactly torrid. But there are other reasons for people's *polar*ized responses. At 10,000 feet and higher, Leadville sits just below the tree line, in a limbo between the warm river valleys below and the 14,000-foot peaks above, including the state's highest — 14,433-foot Mount Elbert. People drawn to the highest peaks find this a perfect base camp; others may feel uncomfortably exposed.

Meanwhile, history buffs gravitate to the historic mines around town. Many of these mines date to the early 1880s, when the prospectors uncovered some of the richest silver reserves in the nation and the town grew to have as many as 30,000 residents. Yet hard-rock mining also left tailings and toxins that taint the experience for some visitors. Personally, I love this town and its clutter of tailings, trailers, shacks, and Victorian homes. It feels and looks like a time capsule of Colorado's past.

Getting there

The closest commercial air service to Leadville is **Vail/Eagle County Airport,** 68 miles to the northwest, but it's cheaper to fly to **Denver International Airport** (☎ **800-AIR-2-DEN**), 113 miles away. Most major airlines fly into DIA, and major rental-car companies have desks at the airport. For information on contacting individual airlines and car-rental agencies, see the Appendix.

To drive to Leadville from Denver, take I-70 west to Exit 195 (Copper Mountain), then go south on Colorado 91 for 24 miles. If you're coming from Aspen during summer and early fall, take Colorado 82 east for 44 miles (crossing Independence Pass), then go north on U.S. 24 for 15 miles. Independence Pass is closed in late fall, winter, and spring. If you're coming from the west on I-70, take Exit 171 (Minturn) and follow U.S. 24 South for 33 miles to Leadville.

Getting around

U.S. 24, the main route through Leadville, enters town from the south as Harrison Avenue. The historic part of town lines Harrison Avenue between Second and Ninth streets. At the north end of the historic district, U.S. 24 jogs east for a block on Ninth Street, then continues north as Poplar Street. A number of museums and historic attractions are near the area where the highway jogs east. Finding parking in Leadville is easy, especially on the side streets. Public transportation isn't an option in Leadville, but after parking your car, you can easily cover the historic part of town on foot.

Where to stay

Leadville has a number of Victorian B&Bs and one 19th-century brick hotel. The historic accommodations are the best places to stay in the town, which also has some unspectacular older motels for travelers on a budget.

Apple Blossom Inn

$$–$$$ Leadville

Where there isn't a window (or a stained-glass window) inside this 1879 Victorian home, there's usually woodwork. The most stunning room, the Library, has maple and mahogany flooring, floor-to-ceiling fir wainscoting, a four-poster queen-size bed, and a fireplace. The inn is remarkably well preserved — even the original brass light fixtures remain. For wood buffs like me, this is one of the prettiest homes anywhere. Groups or large families can take advantage of a two-bedroom suite with a full kitchen.

120 W. Fourth St., Leadville. ☎ *800-982-9279 or 719-486-2141. Fax: 719-486-0994. Internet:* www.theappleblossominn.com. *Rack rates: $69–$169 double, $129–$199 suite. Suite rate is for quadruple occupancy. $20 charge per extra person in room. Rates include breakfast. AE, DC, DISC, MC, V.*

Delaware Hotel

$$ Leadville

Open since 1886, the Delaware Hotel became a flophouse in the 1970s before being fully renovated in 1992. Fortunately, much of the oak woodwork survived the lean years, and today this antique-filled hotel comes close to reproducing its silver-boom opulence. It's not as cozy as the nearby B&Bs, but it has more activities, including regular murder-mystery weekends.

700 Harrison Ave., Leadville. ☎ *800-748-2004 (reservations) or 719-486-1418. Fax: 719-486-2214. Internet:* www.delawarehotel.com. *Rack rates: June–Sept and Dec–March, $79–$139 double; April–May and Oct–Nov $65–$99 double. Rates include continental breakfast. Children under 12 stay free (with some restrictions) in parents' room. AE, DISC, MC, V.*

Leadville Country Inn

$$–$$$ Leadville

This cozy B&B has nine rooms in an 1892 home and its carriage house. The rooms are all individually decorated; some feel more historic than others, but my favorites are in the home itself. Polly's Room has a sunroom with a cushy area where you can curl up, cat-like, and nap in the window. Built into the home's turret, Lillian's room has bay windows, a brass-and-iron queen-size bed, and a claw-foot tub in the bathroom. Stay in either for quiet, comfort, and lots of light when you want it.

127 E. Eighth St., Leadville. ☎ 800-748-2354 or 719-486-2354. Fax: 719-486-0300. Internet: www.leadvillebednbreakfast.com. *Rack rates: $68–$160 double. Rates include breakfast. AE, DISC, MC, V.*

Where to dine

Leadville has some great lodges, but its cuisine doesn't compare to food in the fancy mountain towns. Even so, you'll probably enjoy the places listed here.

Boomtown Brew Pub
$ **Leadville   PUB FARE**

There's less oxygen in the town's atmosphere, so your body absorbs alcohol more quickly. But if you think that Boomtown's brewmeister has cut back on the alcohol to compensate, have another pint. Along with its seasonal brews, Boomtown offers four power-packed regular brews, the most potent being the Poverty Flats Malt Liquor, which weighs in at a whopping 7.1% alcohol. If you remember to eat after visiting Poverty Flats, you can choose between burgers, steaks, and chicken dishes — or go for the owner's favorite: the blackened tuna sandwich with "nuclear" mayonnaise.

115 E. Seventh St., Leadville. ☎ 719-486-8297. Reservations for large groups only. Main courses: $6–$15.95. Open: Lunch and dinner daily. AE, DISC, MC, V.

Callaway's Restaurant
$ **Leadville   AMERICAN**

This restaurant serves straightforward American fare inside the Victorian surroundings of the Hotel Delaware. At lunch, choose between soups, salads, sandwiches, burgers, and entrees such as chicken-fried steak and chili-stuffed baked potato. At dinnertime, the restaurant has entrees from the ocean (grilled salmon), barnyard (stuffed chicken), range (hamburgers and steaks), and garden (pasta primavera).

700 Harrison Ave., Leadville. ☎ 719-486-1418. Reservations accepted. Main courses: $8.95–$15.95. Open: Breakfast, lunch, and dinner daily. AE, DISC, MC, V.

Cloud City Coffee House
$ **Leadville   SANDWICHES/BAKED GOODS**

At this coffeehouse in the sun-splashed lobby of the former Tabor Grande Hotel, you can warm up with coffee or espresso drinks, cool down with a microbrew or iced tea, satisfy your sweet tooth, or get a hearty sandwich made to order. Even during the afternoon, the staff will gladly rustle up breakfast fare such as vegetable quiche, a veggie-and-egg bagel sandwich, or hot or cold granola.

711 Harrison Ave., Leadville. ☎ *719-486-1317. Reservations not accepted. All menu items under $6. Open: Mon–Sat breakfast, lunch and dinner; Sun breakfast and lunch. MC, V.*

Manuelita's Restaurant
$ Leadville TRADITIONAL MEXICAN/SEAFOOD

This isn't the most popular Mexican place in town, but the food here is the most authentic. The menu favors fresh seafood over Tex-Mex. Among the offerings are chicken and steak fajitas, grilled octopus, shrimp with hot sauce, deep-fried fish, and Vera Cruz–style red snapper, as well as Mexican-style sandwiches with marinated pork, shrimp, beef, or chicken. Don't be surprised if your server speaks little English, or if he or she asks for a personal check or cash instead of plastic.

311 Harrison Ave., Leadville. ☎ *719-486-0292. Reservations not accepted. Main courses: $2–$14. Open: Lunch and dinner daily. Credit cards not accepted.*

Quincy's Steak and Spirits
$ Leadville STEAKS

Quincy's serves only filet mignon Sunday through Thursday, and has only prime rib on Friday and Saturday. Each dinner comes with a roll, salad (with house dressing), and baked potato. You just have to choose the size of your portion: filets range from 6 to 15 ounces, and prime rib from 8 to 20 ounces. If you insist on having something less meaty, the restaurant will defrost some lasagna for you.

416 Harrison Ave., Leadville. ☎ *719-486-9765. Reservations accepted for large parties only. Filet mignon dinners $5.95–$12.95; prime rib dinners $7.95–$14.95. Open: Dinner daily. MC, V.*

Exploring Leadville

Leadville is heaven for history buffs. The town had the most lucrative silver mines in the country for a time, and the land around town yielded minerals from silver to molybdenum until the 1980s. Leadville's mining history remains right in plain view, unadorned, and there's a lot to explore. In addition to those looking for historical offerings, Leadville also attracts mountaineers, who can climb to the heavens near town.

The best things to see and do

Instead of visiting all of Leadville's museums in succession, you're better off mixing up your activities in order to absorb the town's history as many ways as possible. The four options in this section can get you started.

National Mining Hall of Fame and Museum

A trip to this museum will help you understand the mine buildings and machinery you see all around Leadville. It has exhibits on all types of mining, ranging from ancient Egyptian gold mines to modern strip mines. There are dioramas of local mining history, re-creations of tunnels (built to scale), and miniatures of historic mines. The Gold Room and the Crystal Room hold samples of gold and crystal, respectively, and the top floor houses a Hall of Fame honoring legendary figures in mining.

120 W. Ninth St., Leadville. ☎ 719-486-1229. Admission: $4 adults, $3.50 seniors 62 and over, $2 children 6–11. Open: May–Oct, daily 9 a.m.–5 p.m.; rest of year, Mon–Fri 10 a.m.–2 p.m.

Matchless Mine (Baby Doe Tabor Museum)

At the Matchless Mine, you'll pay to hear a storyteller recount a heart-breaking tale in the very place where its sad ending played out. It's the story of Baby Doe Tabor and Horace Tabor, a married couple who struck it rich in silver and for years lived lavishly, holding extravagant parties and building sumptuous opera houses, homes, and hotels. Suffice it to say that the story ends poorly for the couple. While you're here, you can look down into the mine shaft that helped enrich Horace and visit the shack where Baby Doe spent her last years, but it's the story, told right, that makes this experience special.

Located 1¼ miles east of town on E. Seventh St. ☎ 719-486-4918 or 719-486-8578. Admission: $4 adults, $1 children 6–12. Open: Summer daily 9 a.m.–5 p.m.; rest of year Tues–Sun 10 a.m.–4 p.m.

Leadville, Colorado, and Southern Railroad

Pulled by diesel engines, this train rumbles away from a historic depot in downtown Leadville and then climbs forested hillsides high above U.S. 91. After 11½ miles, it approaches the Climax Mine, the world's largest molybdenum mine, which operated through 1986. Soon after the mine-scarred mountainside comes into view, the train reverses direction and returns to Leadville on the same track, arriving in town about two and a half hours after departing.

326 E. Seventh St., Leadville. ☎ 719-486-3936. Departures: May 25–June 16 daily 1 p.m.; June 17–Sept 2 daily 10 a.m. and 2 p.m.; Sept 3–29 weekdays 1 p.m. and weekends 10 a.m. and 2 p.m. Cost: $24 adults, $12.50 children 4–12.

Another cool thing to do

Even in a two-wheel-drive car, you can easily cruise through the heart of Leadville's 20-square-mile historic mining district, passing tailings piles, head frames, rusting machinery, and abandoned buildings. Before you go, pick up a free *Route of the Silver Kings* pamphlet at the **Chamber of Commerce Visitors Center,** 809 Harrison Ave. (☎ **888-LEADVILLE** or 719-486-3900). The pamphlet has maps and directions for three self-guided driving tours of area mines. Each drive covers roughly 10 miles and takes one to two hours. The pamphlet explains major landmarks, which are numbered both on the map and in person.

Touring Leadville's historic downtown

Leadville's downtown area is one of the largest National Historic Districts in the U.S. At the **Chamber of Commerce Visitors Center,** 809 Harrison Ave. (☎ **888-LEADVILLE** or 719-486-3900), you can get a printed *Leadville Walking Tour* identifying 73 landmarks in Leadville's National Historic District. Besides some of the other lodges and museums I've recommended, consider these other stops:

- **Heritage Museum and Gallery,** 102 E. Ninth Street (☎ **719-486-1878**). This museum has a Victorian Room; a display on the 10th Mountain Division; and folksy, big-hearted exhibits that pay tribute to Leadville's past. It's open mid-May to mid-October from 10 a.m. to 6 p.m. daily. Admission is $3.50 adults, $3 seniors 62 and over, and $2.50 kids ages 6 to 16.

- **Healy House and Dexter Cabin,** 912 Harrison Ave. (☎ **719-486-0487**). The same ticket admits you to these two historic buildings a few yards from the Leadville Historical Museum and the Museum of Mining History. **Healy House** is an 1878 home that was later converted to a boardinghouse. It now contains Victorian artifacts, including antique toys, dressing screens, and landscape paintings. **Dexter Cabin Museum** is in an 1879 cabin once used by a Leadville businessman. Both buildings are open in summer from 10:00 a.m. to 4:30 p.m. daily, and in September from 10:00 a.m. to 4:30 p.m. on weekends. Admission costs $4 for adults, $3.50 for seniors 65 and over, and $2.50 for children ages 6 to 16.

- **Tabor Opera House,** 308 Harrison Ave. (☎ **719-486-8409**). Built in 1879, the 880-seat opera house was once part of the "Silver Circuit" that brought famous actors and singers west to perform for the newly minted millionaires and miners. For $4 ($2 for kids under 12), you can walk through the opera house while listening to an audiotaped history play over the theater's speakers. It's fun to see the catacombs, dressing rooms, and stage, but for $4, it'd be nice to see a movie, too. It's open daily in summer from 10 a.m. to 5 p.m.

- **Silver Dollar Saloon,** 315 Harrison Ave. (☎ **719-486-9914**). When you're finished walking, cool off at this saloon. The Brunswick back-bar has been here ever since the place opened for business in 1883. The walls are plastered with darn near everything a bar can accumulate in 120 years, including serving trays, musical instruments, historic photos, and masks.

Those hooks really carry

Because of the thin air at Colorado's higher elevations, golf shots carry about 5% farther on Denver's courses and 10 to 15% farther in the mountains than they do elsewhere. But before you rush off to pack your clubs, you should also know that high handicappers seldom score better in the highlands. The thin air allows for added *lateral* movement on shots as well as added distance (though balls do spin more slowly). And people from the flatlands often get confused when they try to read greens against a mountainous backdrop.

Staying active

The two highest peaks in the state are near Leadville in the Sawatch Range. At 14,433-feet, Mount Elbert is the second highest in the lower 48 states, behind 14,494-foot Mount Whitney, in California. Yet it's only 12 feet higher than nearby Mount Massive. You can climb mountains here, but there are a host of other activities to engage in as well. Here are your options:

✔ **Biking/walking:** The **Chamber of Commerce Visitors Center,** 809 Harrison Ave. (☎ **888-LEADVILLE** or 719-486-3900), publishes a free guide called *Mountain Bike and Recreation Trails.* If you're not interested in the area's rugged trails and forest roads, try the **Mineral Belt Trail,** a paved 12½-mile loop around the outskirts of town. Perfect for families, the trail passes old mines, meadows, and thick forest while serving up mountain views. It's closed to motorized vehicles. At the visitor center, you can pick up a free guide that explains the many landmarks along the trail. **Bill's Sport Shop,** Third and Harrison (☎ **719-486-0739**), rents mountain bikes for $25 per day, or $8 for an hour.

✔ **Cross-country skiing:** Located near Tennessee Pass, **Piney Creek Nordic Center** (☎ **719-486-1750**) grooms 25 kilometers of track in gently rolling meadows. Track passes cost $8 for adults, $6 for seniors and kids.

✔ **Golfing:** At 9,800 feet, the 9-hole **Mount Massive Golf Course** (☎ **719-486-2176**) is the highest in North America. The strokes you gain by driving in thin air you may lose when putting with 14,000-foot peaks as a backdrop. Greens fees cost $18 for 9 holes, $28 for 18. It's located 3½ miles west of town at 259 County Rd. 5.

✔ **Hiking/mountain-climbing:** Three non-technical hiking trails go to the summit of 14,433-foot **Mount Elbert.** The easiest one, the **South Main Elbert,** climbs more than 4,000 vertical feet over 5½ miles (one-way) to the summit. To safely reach the top, you'll need to prepare carefully, start early, and use common sense. If you start before dawn, you can summit and then make your way back down before the afternoon thunderstorms spark. For additional information on these trails, contact the **San Isabel National Forest Office,** 2015 Poplar St. (☎ **719-486-0749**). Surprisingly, there's no guide service in Leadville, but the climbs above don't require technical mountaineering skills; most fit people should be able to do them if they take a few days to acclimate, start early, and keep an eye on the weather.

Hitting the slopes

Ski Cooper may have played a historic role in preparing soldiers for World War II, but you don't have to be a warrior to conquer its slopes. (In fact, bunnies do quite well here.) Ski Cooper sits on a long hillside that is gradual enough for all but the most wobbly beginners. Its snow, which is seldom skied and entirely natural, tends to stay soft and fresh. It's a great place to learn, relax, save money, and simplify the skiing experience.

For those who crave more exciting terrain, Ski Cooper offers Snowcat Tours (☎ **719-486-2277**) on nearby **Chicago Ridge.** The daylong tours usher skiers to seldom-skied runs of up to 1,400 vertical feet on 2,500 acres of terrain — more than six times the acreage inside the ski area. Cost is $234 per day (including lunch), and reservations are required. For more on Ski Cooper, see Table 19-1.

Table 19-1	Ski Report: Ski Cooper
Location: 10 miles north of Leadville on U.S. 24	
Trails: 26	
	30% beginner
	40% intermediate
	30% expert
Vertical drop: 1,200 feet	
Base elevation: 10,500 feet	
Summit elevation: 11,700 feet	
Skiable terrain: 400 acres	
Average snowfall: 260 inches	
Lifts: 4 (includes two surface lifts)	
Snow phone: ☎ 719-486-2277	
Other information: ☎ 719-486-3684	
Internet: www.skicooper.com	
2002–2003 high-season adult lift-ticket: $31	

The 10th Mountain Division and Tennessee Pass

In the early 1940s, the U.S. Army erected Camp Hale just north of the current location of **Ski Cooper** in order to house a special division of American servicemen who would study technical mountaineering, alpine skiing, and mountain survival. (Think Outward Bound with artillery.) The men at Camp Hale, also known as the 10th Mountain Division, trained at Ski Cooper and on the larger nearby peaks, and then proceeded to win critical battles in Italy during World War II. You'll find a monument to the 10th Mountain Division at Tennessee Pass, just outside the ski-area entrance. If you continue past the ski area toward Vail, you'll pass roadside markers identifying the old location of the encampment, but there's not much left to see.

Fast Facts: Leadville

Hospital

St. Vincent's General Hospital, 822 W. Fourth St. (☎ 719-486-0230), handles medical emergences 24 hours a day.

Information

Go to the Chamber of Commerce Visitors Center, 809 Harrison Ave. (☎ 888-LEADVILLE or 719-486-3900).

Pharmacy

Sayer-McKee Drug, 615 Harrison Ave. (☎ 719-486-1846), fills prescriptions in downtown Leadville.

Post Office

The post office is one block west of Harrison, at the intersection of West Fifth and Pine streets. Call ☎ 800-275-8777 for additional information about post office locations and hours.

Road Reports

Contact the Lake County Sheriff's Office (☎ 719-486-1249).

Alamosa and Creede

You can take in a month's worth of sights just by spending a few days in Alamosa and Creede, two unsung towns along the Rio Grande River. Alamosa, the larger of the two, is an agricultural and railroad community that could pass for Anywhere USA. Yet it sits in the San Luis Valley, one of the most curious spots in the state. Bordered by the San Juan Mountains to the west and the Sangre de Cristo range to the east, the 50-mile-wide, 100-mile-long valley would be steep-walled and deep if tons of sediment hadn't washed into it from the mountains through the ages. Today the sandy valley floor is nearly flat. Through that floor, artesian springs bubble up, creating wetlands and geothermal pools in an otherwise arid area. You can watch waterfowl in some of the wetlands or soak in certain pools yourself. When the wind blows, it transports sand from the west side of the valley to the east, adding to the wavelike dunes more than 750 feet high inside Great Sand Dunes National Park, one of Colorado's little-known treasures.

If you follow the Rio Grande River upstream into the San Juan Mountains, you'll eventually reach Creede, a former silver-mining town at the mouth of a shadowy box canyon (a canyon that's closed on three sides). Above the town, spectacular old mine buildings seem to cling to the dark walls of Willow Creek Canyon. The Rio Grande River passes just below town. It's popular among fishers and boaters, and the surrounding forests lure outdoorsmen and athletes. With just 300 year-round residents, Creede is the type of place where businesses open their doors whenever an employee happens to be around — and that's not very often during the off-season. In summer, however, visitors cram into the tiny downtown area to experience its unspoiled Victorian architecture and one of the West's finest repertory theater companies.

Getting there

United Express (☎ 800-241-6522) offers daily service between Denver and **Alamosa San Luis Valley Regional Airport** (☎ 719-589-9446), 3 miles south of town on U.S. 285.

Upon landing, you can rent a car through **Budget** (☎ 719-589-0103) or **L & M Auto Rental** (☎ 719-589-4651). For a cab, call **Lil Stinkers Taxi Service** (☎ 719-589-2500).

If you're driving in, Alamosa is at the junction of east-west U.S. 160 and north-south U.S. 285. It's 173 miles north of Santa Fe via U.S. 285. Denver is another 212 miles northeast of Alamosa via Colorado 17 and U.S. 285. U.S. 160 passes through Alamosa en route from Durango (149 miles to the west) to Walsenberg (73 miles to the east). To reach Creede from Alamosa, drive 47 miles west on U.S. 160, then go 22 miles on Colorado 149 west. If you continue past Creede on Colorado 149, it's 48 miles to Lake City.

Getting around

U.S. 160 takes you into the heart of **Alamosa**. The town has wide Western-style streets and ample parking. **Colorado 149** makes a giant U-turn in **Creede's downtown** area. It heads straight into town and toward Willow Creek Canyon, then (wisely) doubles back toward the valley carved by the Rio Grande. There's free parking in the small downtown area. Neither town has mass transit, so you'll have to drive, walk, or ride.

Where to stay

In Alamosa, you can go to a serene bed-and-breakfast, or choose among a number of chain hotels, including the **Best Western Alamosa Inn,** 1919 Main St. (☎ **719-589-2567**); **Comfort Inn of Alamosa,** 6301 County Rd. 107 (☎ **719-587-9000**); **Days Inn,** 224 O'Keefe Parkway (☎ **719-589-9037**); **Holiday Inn,** 333 Santa Fe Ave. (☎ **719-589-5833**); and **Super 8,** 2505 W. Main St. (☎ **719-589-6447**).

You won't find chain properties in Creede, but you can choose between guest ranches, historic hotels, B&Bs, and family-run motels. The prices in this area generally run a little lower than in other parts of the Rockies. Here are a few good choices in this part of the state.

Antlers Rio Grande Lodge
$$ Creede

Most of the accommodations at this guest ranch are flush on the banks of the Rio Grande River. They have no phones or televisions, but the splashing of the river more than substitutes. If you cross the Rio Grande via the suspension bridge near the lodge, you're immediately on National Forest land, and you can climb as far and as high into the mountains as you please. You can also fish for trout without leaving the property. I like the cabins best. Rented in one-week blocks during summer, each has a full kitchen, living area, and porch. The motel rooms share a riverside deck, have kitchenettes, and are smaller than the cabins. The ranch also has a fine restaurant that offers dining both indoors and on a riverside deck.

26222 Colorado 149, Creede. ☎ *719658-2423. Fax 719-658-0804. Internet:* www. antlerslodge.com. *Weekly rack rates: 1-bedroom cabins $700–$725, 2-bedroom cabins, $700–$875. Daily rack rates: $80 double, $25–$29 RV site. MC, V.*

Cottonwood Inn B & B and Gallery
$$ Alamosa

Whether you're sitting on the porch swing, soaking in the hot tub, or lying on a comfy bed, you won't hear much at this B&B. You'd never know that Alamosa's main drag is just two blocks away. Come nighttime, you'll feel yourself cocooned in layers of serenity: valley, town, inn, room, and covers. Before turning off the lights, you can take in the works of local artists, which are on display in the hallways and guest rooms.

123 San Juan, Alamosa. ☎ *800-955-2623 or 719-589-3882. Fax: 719-589-6437. Internet:* www.cottonwoodinn.com. *Rack rates: March–Oct, $70–$99; Nov–Feb $55–$85. Rates include breakfast. AE, DC, DISC, MC, V.*

Creede Hotel

$$ Creede

Located on Main Street, just a few doors down from the **Creede Repertory Theater,** this 19th-century hotel rents out four simple rooms. Each has its original walls and flooring, not to mention spare, tasteful furnishings. The most desirable rooms share a large balcony overlooking Main Street. They don't have phones or televisions, so there's little to distract you from the past. The only real drawbacks are the bathrooms, which look more historic than you may prefer.

120 N. Main St., Creede. ☎ *719-658-2608. Fax: 719-658-0725. Internet:* www.creede hotel.com. *Rack rates: $70–$85 double. Rates include breakfast during peak season only. AE, DISC, V, MC.*

Snowshoe Lodge

$ Creede

Located a few blocks from Creede's downtown and the repertory theater, this lodge offers some great values. Large families can stay in a homey, two-bedroom suite with a cozy downstairs den for only $85 to $100 during high season. The motel rooms are decorated in themes ranging from "John Wayne" (the actor once stayed here) to "Bear/Moose." They're clean, appealing, and ideal for groups that include kids or pets.

On Colorado 149 at the south edge of town, Creede. ☎ *719-658-2315. Internet:* www. creede-co.com/snowshoe. *Rack rates: Motel rooms $35–$70, suite $65–$100. AE, MC, V.*

Where to dine

In Alamosa, the restaurants stay open year-round and the scene is pretty consistent. Many of Creede's restaurants close seasonally, then start fresh the next year. That makes the dining scene less predictable, but it does lend itself to, um, innovation.

Bullfrog Bar and Restaurant (at Cattails Golf Club)

$–$$ Alamosa AMERICAN

You can often find Alamosa locals dining at this restaurant next to the pro shop at the local golf club. Bullfrog serves sandwiches, burgers, and salads all day, and has pasta dishes, steaks, and seafood at dinner. Try the green chili pasta — fettuccini noodles topped with creamy sauce spiced with roasted green chilies. The restaurant closes in mid-afternoon and often shuts down for the night by 8 p.m., so if you roll into town late, call ahead to make sure they're open.

6615 N. River Rd. (head north out of town on State Street then turn left ⅓ mile past the bridge), Alamosa. ☎ 719-587-9999. Reservations accepted. Main courses: $5.95–$17.95. Open: Mon–Sat lunch and dinner, lunch only on Sun. AE, DISC, MC, V.

Café Ole

$ **Creede** **PIZZA**

Café Ole serves hearty, inexpensive breakfasts and lunches and has pizza on Thursday nights. Locals get fired up about the pizza — a relatively scarce commodity around here. Yet only the boldest order the "Slumgullion," with a landslide-sized pile of toppings. Lunch fare includes salads and hot and cold sandwiches.

112 N. Main St., Creede. ☎ 719-658-2880. Reservations accepted. Sandwiches $5–$7, pizzas $6–$18. Open: Mon, Wed, Fri, Sat breakfast and lunch; Thurs evenings for pizza only. AE, DC, DISC, MC, V.

Creede Hotel and Restaurant

$$ **Creede** **AMERICAN**

This restaurant, housed in a 19th-century hotel, packs in theatergoers during the summer months. Once a rowdy bar — the atmosphere still feels like the Old West — it now serves gourmet meals such as merlot-braised lamb shank, New York strip with gorgonzola crust, and free-range pan-roasted chicken. The hotel changed hands in 2002, but its restaurant still enjoys a stellar reputation.

120 N. Main St., Creede. ☎ 719-658-2608. Reservations recommended. Main courses: $13–20. Open: Summer, lunch and dinner daily; rest of year, dinner Fri–Sat, brunch Sun. AE, DISC, V, MC.

Taqueria Cal Villo

$ **Alamosa** **MEXICAN**

Tucked between a liquor store and gas station, this taqueria serves $5 meals with flavors worth $50. The chefs slow-cook, marinate, steam, dice, and shred their meats, then pair them with fresh vegetables and sauces using family recipes. The *La Gringa* (a large flour tortilla filled with your choice of meat, plus guacamole and refried beans) dissolves into rich juices after you bite into it. It costs under $5 and will more than satisfy your hunger.

119 Broadway, Alamosa. ☎ 719-587-5500. Reservations accepted. Menu items $3–$12.75; lunch buffet $7.45. Open: Mon–Sat lunch and dinner; Sun lunch only. Cash only.

Exploring Alamosa and Creede

Even by Colorado standards, there's a lot to do in this area. Besides the usual (glorious) hikes and fishing holes, you can somersault down a sand dune, explore a mineshaft, feed alligators, or see a play.

The best things to see and do

The can't-miss attraction in this area is Great Sand Dunes National Monument and Preserve. Go to the monument first, then choose some other activities in the San Luis Valley. Set aside another day or two to explore the mines and mountains around Creede.

Great Sand Dunes National Monument and Preserve

The sight of 750-foot-high sand dunes on the otherwise flat floor of the San Luis Valley is flat-out bizarre. Blown across the valley by steady west-to-east winds, the sand has piled up across a 39-square-mile area at the base of the Sangre de Cristo Mountains, on the east side of the valley. Now the dunes are part of **Great Sand Dunes National Monument and Preserve.** Wind has sculpted them into striking shapes, with gradual ramps on the windward side and steep slopes on the lee side. For finishing touches, it etches delicate ridges, ripples, and waves in the sand.

To enjoy the dunes, stop first at the visitor center to view displays on the area. Then, drive to the Dunes parking area, hike a quarter-mile across the flats to the dunes, and start climbing, preferably when it's not hot or stormy. Wear closed-top shoes on hot days and carry plenty of water. The summit of High Dune is only about 1¼ miles from the parking lot, but the deep sand will slow you. When you reach the top, have fun! You can run, jump, roll, snowboard, or ride a saucer downhill.

If you want to stay longer, camp at **Pinyon Flats Campground,** which has 88 first-come, first-served sites ($10 per car), drinking water, and sunset views.

Located 35 miles northeast of Alamosa on Colorado 150. ☎ *719-378-2312. Internet:: www.nps.gov/grsa. Admission: $3 per adult (children under 17 free). Open: Visitor Center daily 9 a.m.–6 p.m. in summer; call for hours during the rest of the year.*

Underground Mining Museum

Before driving the **Bachelor Historic Tour** (described in the next listing), go to this museum. That way, you'll know what transpired in all the old mine buildings you see on your drive. Located in an old mine tunnel near the mouth of Willow Creek Canyon, this museum displays mining equipment, memorabilia, and the precious rocks that attracted so much attention in the late 1800s. Alongside each display, interpretive panels explain how miners extracted and moved ore. This may not sound riveting on paper, but the underground setting makes the experience more chilling. Most tours are self-guided, but sometimes former miners take groups through the museum.

In Willow Creek Canyon, at the north edge of Creede. ☎ *719-658-0811. Self-guided tours: $6 adults, $5 seniors over 60, $4 kids ages 6–12. Guided tours: $10 for all ages. Hours vary so call ahead for opening times and tour information.*

Bachelor Historic Tour

This 17-mile driving tour, which begins and ends in Creede, passes dozens of 19th-century mine buildings that look as if they were built yesterday. Propped against and perched atop dark cliffs, these wooden structures seem to exist outside both gravity and time.

Before starting out, stop at the **Creede/Mineral County Chamber of Commerce** (☎ **800-327-2102** or 719-658-2374) on Main Street at the north end of town and pick up the 25-page booklet explaining the numbered stops along the road (cost: $1). Then proceed up Willow Creek Canyon at the north end of town. The most impressive structures are in the first 2 miles of the drive.

Even if you don't want to do the full tour, consider driving as far as the **Commodore Mine** (Stop No. 2). Beyond that point, the mines become less spectacular and the mountain scenery steals the show. Allow at least an hour for the whole loop. When dry, the road is passable (barely) for two-wheel-drive vehicles, but steep grades, bumps, and curves will slow you down. If the road is wet, consider doing the loop backward — this lets you descend the steepest grades instead of climbing them. You can also rent a Jeep for $105 per day from **Continental Divide Services** (☎ **719-658-2682**).

Another cool thing to see and do

In addition to dunes, the San Luis Valley has geothermal pools, and is home to migrating birds and captive alligators.

Flanked on the west by the Rio Grande River, the wetlands at **Alamosa National Wildlife Refuge** (☎ **719-589-9759**) are a sanctuary to mallards, Canada geese, avocets, egrets, herons, and eagles, among other species. The best times to visit are spring and fall, when many migrating birds stop over. You can watch them from an overlook or stroll down a riverside trail. To reach the refuge, go 4 miles east of Alamosa on U.S. 160, then south 3 miles on Rancho Lane. Visitor Center hours are Monday through Friday from 7:30 a.m. to 4:00 p.m. The refuge is open daily from sunrise to sunset. Admission is free.

Especially for kids

Colorado Alligator Farm

The Colorado Alligator Farm is above all a fish farm, raising tilapia in geothermal pools on the property. In 1987, the owners bought a few baby alligators to eat the fish byproducts. People started coming to see the reptiles, and some began dropping off exotic pets that had outgrown tanks in private homes. Now the place crawls with alligators up to 11 feet and other scary critters like monitor lizards, caiman, and snakes. You can fish for carp (cost: $10, including admission) in pools on the property and then feed the fish to the gators. Adults can also sign up for gator wrestling class, taught by a man with badly scarred arms.

9162 County Rd. 9 North (17 miles north of Alamosa on Colorado 17). ☎ *719-378-2612. Open: May 27–Sept 4, 7 a.m.–7 p.m. daily; rest of year, 9 a.m.–5 p.m. daily. Admission: $5 ages 13–79; $2.50 kids 6–12; free for all others.*

Staying active

While in this area, don't limit your physical activity to an ascent of the dunes. Try

- ✔ **Golfing: Cattails Golf Club,** 6615 North River Rd. (☎ 719-589-9515), offers 18 holes along the Rio Grande River outside Alamosa. Greens fees are $28 for 18 holes, $18 for 9 holes, and $10 for unlimited play after 5 p.m.

- ✔ **Hiking:** As you drive from **Alamosa** to Great Sand Dunes National Park on Colorado 150, consider a stop at **Zapata Falls.** From its trailhead 10 miles north of U.S. 160, you can walk a quarter-mile to a waterfall in a shadowy canyon. During spring and early summer, you'll have to battle strong, icy currents to approach the falls, but during late summer you can get right up under them. If you feel like going farther, hike past the falls and climb into the **Sangre de Cristo Wilderness** on the 4-mile Zapata Lake Trail. For more information contact the **Rio Grande National Forest Supervisors Office,** 1803 W. U.S. 160, in Monte Vista (☎ 919-852-5941). There's also great hiking around **Creede. Mineral County** consists of 96% public land and has two wilderness areas. For maps and information on area hikes, stop by the **Creede Ranger Station** (☎ 719-658-2556) on South Main Street or duck into **San Juan Sports,** 102 S. Main St. (☎ 719-658-2359).

Hitting the slopes

With the entire ski area above 10,000 feet and the summit at 11,900 feet, **Wolf Creek** averages 450 inches of snow a year, easily the highest total in the state. The abundant snow usually lets Wolf Creek open in mid-November, long before most other resorts get rolling, and it keeps skiers and riders knee-deep in powder for much of the winter. As for the terrain, it's a mixed bag, with some nice glades, but there aren't many long, consistently steep slopes. Check out Table 19-2 for the resort's technical details.

Table 19-2	Ski Report: Wolf Creek Ski Area
Location: On U.S. 160, 16 miles east of Pagosa Springs and 63 miles west of Alamosa	
Named trails: 50	
	20% beginner
	35% intermediate
	45% advanced/expert
Vertical drop: 1,600 feet	
Base elevation: 10,300 feet	
Summit elevation: 11,900 feet	
Skiable terrain: 1,600 acres	
Average snowfall: 450 inches	
Chairlifts: 6	
Snow phone: ☎ 800-SKI-WOLF	
Information: ☎ 970-264-5639	
Internet: www.wolfcreekski.com	
2002–2003 high-season adult all-day lift ticket: $43 adult	

Culture

In 1966, the **Creede Repertory Theater,** 124 N. Main St. (☎ **719-658-2540;** Internet: www.creederep.com), opened shop as part of an economic development project for what was then a depressed mining town. Today this company of around 15 actors is one of the top performing-arts groups in the state. (As for the town, it's doing a lot better, too.) From June through September every year, the company stages eight or more different plays — and as many as five in a single week — spread over two stages. The summer performances are mostly classics, and they sell out during the peak months of July and August. In early fall, the theater switches to riskier material, including regional and world premieres. The company announces its schedule for the next season in the fall of the previous year, and season tickets go on sale January 1.

If you think you might stay in Creede for a week or more, consider buying a ticket package in order to get the best seats. The least expensive package includes tickets to three Main Stage plays, which you could conceivably use in a week. Individual tickets go on sale May 1. Tickets to Main Stage shows cost $15 to $16. General admission to the more intimate Black Box theater, where the productions are smaller and possibly more experimental, is $5.

Fast Facts: Alamosa/Creede

Information

The Alamosa County Chamber of Commerce (☎ 800-258-7597 or 719-589-4840; Internet: www.Alamosa.org) has a visitor center at the corner of Third Street and Chamber Drive. The Creede/Mineral County Chamber of Commerce (☎ 800-327-2102 or 719-658-2374; Internet: www.creede.com) is located in the County Annex Building, on Main Street at the north end of town.

Hospital

24-hour emergency health care is available at the San Luis Valley Regional Medical Center, 106 Blanca Ave. (☎ 719-589-2511), in Alamosa.

Pharmacy

You can fill prescriptions at Alamosa Pharmacy, 2111 Stuart Ave. (☎ 719-589-1766).

Post Office

The Alamosa Post Office (☎ 719-589-4908) is at 505 Third St. The Creede Post Office (☎ 719-658-2615) is at 10 S. Main St.

Road Conditions

Call ☎ 719-589-9024.

Salida

Salida came of age in the late 1800s as a railroad hub linking Denver and the mines and mine camps of the southern Rockies. Eventually the rails shut down, as did the smoke-belching foundry just east of town. Even the surrounding ranches took some hits. By the 1980s, much of the downtown had been shuttered, but Salida has transformed itself. Inspired by the lovely scenery and cheap rent, artists began opening studios and galleries in the storefronts. Today, splashy handmade signs mark the dozens of art and sculpture galleries in Salida's downtown. During warm-weather months, the artists share the town with boaters and river guides who come here for the whitewater on the Arkansas River, which flows along the northeast side of town. Everyone here seems to enjoy the slow pace, the warm banana-belt weather, and the views of the surrounding 14,000-foot peaks.

Getting there

If you're coming by car, Salida is on U.S. 50 between Gunnison (66 miles to the west) and Pueblo (96 miles to the east). In Pueblo, U.S. 50 meets I-25, Colorado's primary north-south thoroughfare. Five miles west of Salida, U.S. 50 intersects U.S. 285, which goes from Denver (138 miles northeast of Salida) to Alamosa (82 miles south of Salida) and points beyond.

If you want to fly to near Salida, your best bets are **Denver International Airport** (140 miles northeast) and **Colorado Springs Airport** (105 miles to the east). Nearly all the major domestic carriers fly into DIA. Eight commercial airlines serve Colorado Springs Airport (CSA).

In Denver, you can choose from among all the major rental-car companies. At Colorado Springs Airport, your choices are **Avis, Dollar, Hertz,** and **National.** For information on contacting individual airlines and car-rental agencies, see the Appendix.

Getting around

Most people drive, walk, or ride bikes around Salida. **U.S. 50** crosses the town's southern edge. As you reach the east side of town on U.S. 50, take **Colorado 291** (Oak Street) north to reach the downtown area. Seven blocks later, Colorado 291 becomes First Street and turns to the northwest, roughly paralleling the course of the Arkansas River, which borders the north and east sides of town. As First Street, Colorado 291 goes through the heart of Salida. The historic part of town surrounds the intersection of First Street and F Street.

Where to stay

I love the selection of bed-and-breakfasts in Salida. If you have an aversion to enormous stacks of pillows, however, you may want to look into a privately owned motel downtown or a chain hotel along U.S. 50. Choices include the **Comfort Inn,** 315 E. U.S. 50 (☎ 719-539-5000); the **Econo Lodge,** 1310 E. U.S. 50 (☎ 719-539-2895); and the **Holiday Inn Express,** 7400 W. U.S. 50 (☎ 719-539-8500). The prices are reasonable in this area, especially during winter.

Gazebo Country Inn Bed and Breakfast
$$–$$$ **Salida**

The guest rooms in this 1901 home are fluffy even by B&B standards. They come complete with quilts, vintage furniture, robes, extra-plush towels, large bathtubs, and pillows galore. My favorite may be the Rainbow Room, which offers a private door and a spiral staircase to the hot tub. Guests in other rooms have to go around the side of the house. The Rose Room is most romantic, with pink and white striped wallpaper, rose-colored carpeting, and a king-size bed that seems particularly imposing.

507 E. Third St. (at B Street), Salida. ☎ *800-565-7806 or 719-539-7806. Internet:* www.gazebocountryinn.com. *Rack rates: May 20–Sept 30 $80–$150; Oct 1–May 19 $70–130. Rates include breakfast. AE, MC, V.*

River Run Inn
$$ Salida

This inn occupies an 1895 building that once served as the Chaffee County poor farm. If anything can make you wish that you'd been born into a destitute family a century ago, a night here may do it. The seven guest rooms are airy and spacious, with four-poster beds, huge windows, and lace curtains that billow in the afternoon breezes. You can walk a few hundred feet from the inn down to the Arkansas River or simply porch-sit and take in the silence — the inn is on a spacious 5-acre plot, 3 miles outside Salida. If you want to save a few dollars, choose one of the four rooms with shared baths, which cost $15 to $20 less.

8495 County Rd. 160, Salida. ☎ *800-385-6925 or 719-539-3818. Internet:* www.riverruninn.com. *Rack rates: Double $70–$90; group room $32 per person. Rates include full breakfast, afternoon refreshments, and evening sherry. AE, MC, V.*

Woodland Motel
$ Salida

This family-owned motel has snug, immaculate rooms, each with Southwestern decor, 27-inch TVs, air-conditioning, and coffeemakers. The prices are usually among the lowest in town, and the innkeepers will do everything possible to put you at rest — even if it means lugging a mini refrigerator or a microwave to your room. The cheapest rooms come with a single queen-size bed, but others have two queens. Ask for a spot away from the road, and bring your dog if you want, too.

903 W. First St., Salida. ☎ *800-488-0456 or 719-539-4980. Internet:* www.woodlandmotel.com. *Rack rates: $35–$68 double. AE, DC, DISC, MC, V.*

Where to dine

Salida has just enough good restaurants to see you through a long weekend, and none of them will bust your bank account. If you're at a loss for where to dine next, you can always repeat one of your favorites.

Amicas
$ Salida   BREW PUB/PIZZA

Amicas's 14 varieties of thin-crusted, wood-oven pizza perfectly complement its award-winning beers. The restaurant also serves calzones, panini sandwiches, lasagna, and salads. It occupies a streamlined room with hardwood floors, a brick wall, and paintings of peppers and tomatoes. The experience is probably worth twice the cost, which, for an entree, is usually around $7.

136 E. Second St., Salida. ☎ 719-539-5219. No reservations. Main courses: $5.25–$7.95. Open: :Lunch and dinner daily. MC, V.

Bongo Billy's Salida Café
$ **Salida CAFE**

This is one of those espresso-and-pastry shops that gracefully changes to a sandwich-salad-and-microbeer place sometime around midday. The customers, mostly locals, seem to remain pretty much the same all day, with substitutions about as frequent as in a World Cup soccer match. There's a lot to do while you linger. You can browse free reading materials, look at local art, get some sun on the riverside deck, and, on weekends, listen to folk singers.

300 W. Sackett Ave., Salida. ☎ 719-539-4261. Reservations not accepted. Main courses: $5–$7. Open: Breakfast, lunch, and dinner daily. AE, DISC, MC, V.

Dakota's Bistro
$$ **Salida CONTINENTAL**

You can tell that the chef loves food from different regions when you look at his menu. Offerings include such seemingly unrelated entrees as buffalo stroganoff, blackened catfish, and lasagna. On Friday and Saturday nights, he gets even more creative and whips up traditional dishes from a new global region each week.

122 N. F St., Salida. ☎ 719-530-9909. Reservations accepted. Main courses: $10–$18. Open: Lunch and dinner, Tues–Sat. AE, DISC, MC, V.

Laughing Ladies Restaurant
$$ **Salida AMERICAN**

As of 2002, this was the best restaurant in Salida, a funky cafe with rotating art displays, nontraditional American food, and servers who shun uniforms. The place is known for its great salads and appetizers. For starters, try the grilled polenta, portobello mushrooms, and blue cheese. The honey-grilled pork chop with poblano chile is the most popular entree. Over a dozen wines are available by the glass.

128 First St., Salida. ☎ 719-539-6209. Reservations accepted. Main courses: $10.50–$14.95. Open: Lunch and dinner Thurs–Mon; brunch and dinner Sun. DISC, MC, V.

Exploring Salida

There are two things that everyone should do in Salida. First, take a river trip. Then wind down by strolling through the galleries in the downtown area. When you're done, you're only a few miles' drive from Monarch Pass and the continental divide.

The best thing to do

If you want to *look at* art, go somewhere like Aspen, where the galleries have works by the likes of Picasso, Chagall, Warhol, and others whose names ring a cash-register bell. But to *buy* art, go to Salida, where many artists create their pieces right where they sell them. The prices are low, and a lot of the work will move you. Many of my favorite studios are on or near First Street in downtown Salida. Don't miss

- ✔ **The Green Cat,** corner of First and G streets (☎ **719-530-0466;** Internet: www.thegreencatart.com). This gallery displays colorful, clunky, light-hearted paintings by Steph Brady, whose subjects include cats, cows, and the legs of old ladies.

- ✔ **Brodeur Art Gallery,** 151 W. First St. (☎ **719-221-1272;** Internet: www.brodeurart.com). Paulette Brodeur works in a variety of media, but her most recognizable works may be her contemporary paintings of musicians, cafes, and other Bohemian scenes. Her art is sold internationally and this is where it's made.

- ✔ **Broadminded,** 132 W. First St. (☎ **719-539-3122**). The gallery has ceramics, paintings, and sculptures by some really talented women.

- ✔ **Articulation Gallery**, 131 E. First St. (☎ **719-539-0600**). This isn't a storefront studio, but it features challenging works in a variety of media by 20 artists. The prices are far lower than you'd pay for the same art in other towns, including Aspen.

More cool things to see and do

You won't get soaked when you shop for art in Salida, so you should have a few dollars left over to spend on other area attractions, including hot springs. You can

- ✔ **Soak inside.** The Works Progress Administration (WPA) erected a building around the **Salida Hot Springs** (☎ **719-539-6738**) in 1937, thereby creating the largest indoor hot springs pool in the state. Under one roof is a six-lane, 25-yard lap pool where the water is a temperate 90 degrees, a 4-foot-deep, 110-degree pool, a wading pool for toddlers, and four toasty, private, 113-degree tubs that you can rent by the hour for $6 per person. The springs are at 410 W. Rainbow Blvd. (U.S. 50). Admission is $6 adults, $4 ages 6 to17, $2 kids 5 and under. In summer, it's open daily from 1 to 9 p.m.; the rest of the year, it's open Tuesday through Sunday from 4 to 9 p.m., and Friday through Sunday from 1 to 9 p.m.

✔ **Soak outside.** At **Mount Princeton Hot Springs,** 15870 County Rd. 162 (☎ **719-395-2361**), you can soak outside in geothermal water at the base of white cliffs. The springs are open 9 a.m. to 9 p.m. daily. Admission is $6 adults, $3 children 12 and under.

✔ **Soar to the highest Subway.** The ads for **Monarch Scenic Tram** (☎ **719-539-4091**), 22 miles west of Salida on U.S. 50, make it sound as if the tram takes you to the top of the Great Divide, but you're already atop the divide when you reach the parking lot. If, however, you want to take a 670-vertical-foot gondola ride, or if you simply crave a sandwich from "the highest Subway sandwich shop in the world," then the tram is for you. The tram runs mid-May to mid-September daily from 8:30 a.m. to 5:30 p.m. Admission costs $7 adults, $6 seniors over 54, $4 kids 3 to 12.

✔ **Visit a ghost town.** Established in 1880, St. Elmo used to be a rail-road way station, moving ore from Aspen and other mountain towns down the east slope of the continental divide. Then it became a ghost town, with a short main street lined by well-preserved build-ings. A few year-round residents live there now, and sometimes you can shop at the general store. To reach St. Elmo, drive to Nathrop, 17 miles north of Salida, then head west on County Road 162 for 15 miles to St. Elmo.

Staying active

Air currents from the south keep Salida warm even during winter. Yet it's also in Chaffee County, home to 15 of Colorado's fourteeners — the highest concentration of peaks over 14,000 feet in the nation. This unusual environment lets you bicycle in winter and cool your feet on mountain snow (or melted snow) during summer. While you're here, think about:

✔ **Hiking and biking:** Salida's wintertime zephyrs let you bicycle around town even during the coldest months. However, the classic trails are higher up near the continental divide. For a great hike or mountain bike ride, drive to the parking area at Monarch Pass and get on the **Monarch Crest Trail.** To pick it up, follow the dirt road that begins just left of the lower tram station. About a quarter-mile up this road, the trail branches off on the right. It's a surprisingly smooth terrain, given its perch near the divide. You can do a long (12 miles each way) out-and-back or descend off the ridge on other trails. For maps and detailed directions, consult the free *Monarch Bike Guide,* available at **Absolute Bikes,** 330 W. Sackett (☎ **888-539-9295** or 719-539-9295; Internet: www.absolutebikes. com). Absolute Bikes rents full-suspension bikes for $35 a day; front-suspension bikes cost $25. For information on hiking trails, stop by the **San Isabel National Forest Office,** 325 W. Rainbow Blvd. (☎ **719-539-3591**), in Salida.

✔ **Golfing: Salida Golf Club,** at the corner of Crestone and Grant Street (☎ **719-539-1060**), charges $15 for 9 holes. You can play this city-owned 9-hole course twice for $25.

✔ **Rafting:** A half-day trip down the Arkansas River costs about as much as a day at an amusement park, and it's a lot more rewarding. You'll experience both the force of the mountains (via snowmelt) and the peacefulness of a scenic river canyon. You can run rivers throughout Colorado, but the best one for commercial rafting may be the Arkansas, a river known for having a long season (usually May through August) and stretches of water perfect for everyone from novices to experts. More than 60 companies are licensed to run the Arkansas, so it's easy to get on a trip.

Families with children ages 12 and up will love the half- and full-day trips through **Brown's Canyon.** These trips have stretches of calm water where you can scan the craggy canyon walls for bighorn sheep, interrupted by rapids with names such as Pinball, Staircase, and Zoom Flume. Brown's Canyon is genuinely exciting, but not as wild (and potentially abusive) as **The Numbers,** which features continuous Class IV/V waters. Trips down The Numbers are for fit, experienced rafters only.

You can usually choose one of two kinds of boat: Paddle boats, where you help the guide paddle, or oar boats, where the guide does all the rowing using oars mounted on a metal frame. I recommend paddling, because it involves you in the action. One experienced company is **Four Corners Rafting** (☎ **800-332-7238** or 719-395-4137; Internet: www.fourcornersrafting.com), in Nathrop. Four Corners has been in business since the mid-'70s, and offers half- to three-day trips on different sections of the Arkansas. Half-day trips cost $39 for adults and $33 kids under 15, and full-day trips go for $71 for adults and $61 for kids.

Hitting the slopes

I'd love to be at **Monarch Ski and Snowboard Area** during a January storm. Situated against the continental divide on the east side of Monarch Pass, the mountain receives 30 feet of snow annually — one of the state's higher totals. The area's 670 acres include lots of open,

---

The continental divide

The continental divide meanders on a general north-south course through the Rocky Mountains just west of the center of Colorado. If you drive to a point on the divide, get out of the car, and then spill a very large cup of coffee, half of your java will flow into the rivers that empty into the Gulf of Mexico and the Atlantic Ocean. The other half will pour into rivers that head for the Sea of Cortez and the Pacific Ocean.

ungroomed terrain that's perfect for powder skiing. Because it sells inexpensive lift tickets and is farther southeast than most Colorado ski areas, Monarch lures a lot of gung-ho skiers from heartland states such as Kansas, Oklahoma, Texas, and Arkansas. For some reason, these skiers tend to gravitate to the run known as Lower Christmas Tree, leaving the rest of the area unpopulated — and untracked. Even if you're a novice, you can still enjoy the view from the top of the aptly named Panorama chair, which takes in peaks in the Sangre de Cristo, Uncompahgre, Sawatch, and Collegiate ranges. For a rundown of the resort's technical information, see Table 19-3.

Table 19-3	Ski Report: Monarch Ski and Snowboard Area
Location: On Highway 50, 18 miles west of Salida	
Trails: 54	
21% beginner	
37% intermediate	
42% advanced	
Vertical drop: 1,170 feet	
Base elevation: 10,790 feet	
Summit elevation: 11,960 feet	
Skiable terrain: 670 acres	
Annual snowfall: 360 inches	
Lifts: 5	
Snow phone: ☎ 800-228-7943	
Reservations: ☎ 888-996-SNOW	
Internet: www.skimonarch.com	
2002–2003 high-season adult all-day lift ticket: $41	

Taking a side trip to Fairplay

Fairplay probably helped inspire the popular cartoon *South Park*. Once known as South Park City, it's the only incorporated town in Park County, which consists mostly of a 9,000-foot-high, grassy basin known as South Park. One of the cartoon's creators, Trey Parker, hails from Conifer, 53 miles east of Fairplay, and seems to have observed some of the town's quirks. (The townspeople concede that certain characters on the show resemble certain people.) Yet the connection won't be obvious when you roll in: You'll meet few obscenity-spouting third graders, and, if my experience is any indication, your odds of encountering Christ are slim. Instead, you should come here for the sleepy downtown, the historic attraction now known as South Park City (see the following section), and the ghost-riddled Hand Hotel. Fairplay is 58 miles north of Salida on Colorado 9.

Exploring Fairplay

After paying your $5 admission ($2 for children 6 to 12) to **South Park City,** 100 Fourth St. (☎ **719-836-2387**), you can walk through 35 fully stocked historic buildings, including a newspaper office, a doctor's office, and a morgue. What's most amazing is the sheer number of antiques on display. The people of Park County moved the buildings here from elsewhere in the county in the late 1950s and positioned them at the north end of Front Street, so that they'd look like a part of the town, and then they donated 60,000 items, including tools, furniture, appliances and machinery. It's open from May 15 to October 15, daily from 9 a.m. to 5 p.m. (until 7 p.m. from Memorial Day to Labor Day).

Where to stay and dine

Built in 1931, the **Hand Hotel Bed & Breakfast,** 531 Front St. (☎ **719-836-3595;** Internet: www.handhotel.com), has character to burn. As at many other historic lodges, each of the rooms has a theme, only here the innkeepers have gone really wild. For example, the room I stayed in, the Miner's Room, had minerals, a hard hat, frying pans, an old lantern, metal cups, and some bone-chilling photos of miners — all under a burlap ceiling. The hotel is also said to be haunted. In Grandma's Room, the late Grandma Hand will visit if she disapproves of how you unpack. Rates, including breakfast, are $49 for one person, $65 for two.

The **Front Street Café,** 435 Front Street (☎ **719-836-7031**), looks like an espresso-and-smoothie place but instead does lunch, dinner, and a twice-weekly brunch. Plants and fresh-cut flowers soak up the light from the street-side windows, and the servers seem to be dressed for morning coffee — even when they're serving lamb gyros, chicken and dumplings, or homemade lasagna. The prices for a main course at dinner range from $11 to $20. It's open Wednesday through Sunday for lunch (or brunch) and dinner.

Fast Facts: Salida

Hospital

24-hour emergency service is available at Heart of the Rockies Medical Center, 448 E. First St. (☎ 719-539-6661).

Information

Visit the Heart of the Rockies Chamber of Commerce, 406 W. Rainbow Blvd. (☎ 877-772-5432 or 719-539-2068; Internet: www.salidachamber. org).

Pharmacy

To fill a prescription, call Lallier Pharmacy, 147 F St. (☎ 719-539-2591).

Post Office

Salida's post office is at 310 D. St. Call ☎ 800-275-8777 for additional information about post office locations and hours.

Road Conditions

Call ☎ 719-539-6688.

Chapter 20

Black Canyon of the Gunnison and Western Colorado

● ●

In This Chapter

▶ Visiting the darkest, deepest canyon in Colorado

▶ Finding the steepest, scariest ski area

▶ Making your way through down-to-earth Western towns

● ●

*W*estern Colorado may not attract as many visitors as the central part of the state, but it offers a smorgasbord of scenery — everything from vineyards to towering peaks to colorful canyons of sedimentary rock.

What's Where?: Western Colorado and Its Major Attractions

If you follow the Gunnison River through western Colorado, you'll pass a few low-key Western towns and lots of crazy geology. The story began millions of years ago, when the (as yet unnamed) Gunnison River flowed between two intermittently erupting volcanic fields — soon to become mountain ranges. The two fields spewed lava across the land, pushing the river back and forth until it ultimately scraped out the Gunnison Valley. Today, the main hub of the valley is the town of Gunnison, a ranching community nestled between the Elk and San Juan mountain ranges. Crested Butte, a former mining town turned skiing mecca, sits 28 miles north of Gunnison in the West Elk Mountains. Lake City, a tiny, historic mining town, is 55 miles south of Gunnison in the San Juan range. Both towns border rivers that drain into the larger Gunnison, and both open onto seemingly endless alpine forests and wilderness.

West and downstream of Gunnison, the river has been dammed three times inside the Curecanti Recreation Area. One dam creates the state's largest body of water, the 20-mile-long Blue Mesa Reservoir. At the west

Western Colorado

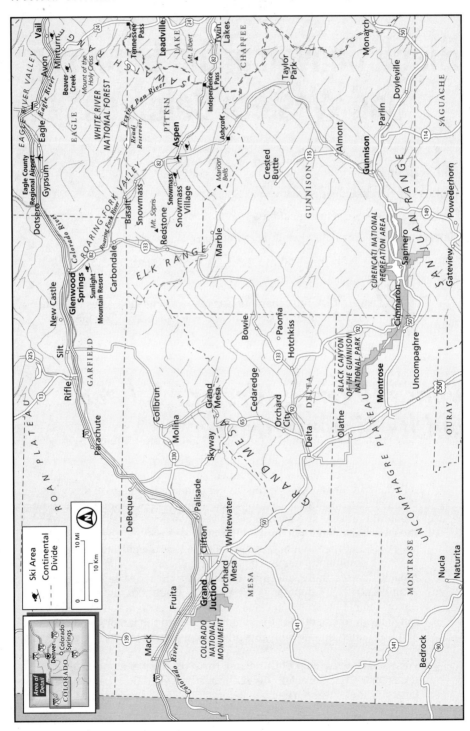

end of the recreation area, the river enters the 2,000-foot-deep Black Canyon of the Gunnison. Fifteen spectacular miles of this gorge are inside Black Canyon of the Gunnison National Park. Further downstream, thanks to modern diversion techniques, the river helps irrigate orchards and farms near the small cities of Delta, Montrose, and Grand Junction. The Gunnison River drains into the Colorado River south of Grand Junction. In this part of the state, the mountains give way to horizontal layers of sedimentary rock, which have partly eroded to form colorful mesas, buttes, and canyons. They're yet another twist in a striking region. To see more of this picturesque terrain, visit Colorado National Monument or Dinosaur National Monument.

Grand Junction

Grand Junction is the largest city in western Colorado and has a relaxed downtown graced with many sculptures. But what's really amazing are its immediate surroundings, including

- ✔ **Grand Mesa,** an 11,000-foot, flat-topped mountain with hundreds of small lakes and reservoirs
- ✔ **Colorado National Monument,** where erosion has sliced four colorful canyons into the edge of the Uncompahgre Plateau
- ✔ **Orchards and vineyards** east of Grand Junction in Palisade

Montrose, Delta, and Black Canyon of the Gunnison National Park

The Gunnison River accomplished the nearly impossible east of Montrose, slicing 2,000 vertical feet downward through some of the oldest, hardest rock on the planet. When you drift into this area, make sure you see

- ✔ **Black Canyon of the Gunnison National Park,** home to a chasm far deeper than it is wide
- ✔ **Montrose's Main Street,** site of the most down-to-earth shopping in Colorado
- ✔ The **Ute Indian Museum,** full of beadwork and other art by members of the Ute tribe

Gunnison, Crested Butte, and Lake City

This area includes three strikingly different towns, one devoted to skiing (Crested Butte), another to ranching and education (Gunnison), and a third to plain-old quiet and relaxation (Lake City). While in this area, be sure to visit

- ✔ **Crested Butte Mountain Resort,** home to some of the nation's steepest skiing and hottest riders

- ✔ **Lake San Cristobal,** near Lake City, the second largest natural body of water in Colorado, created when a mountainside slumped into a river

- ✔ The **wildflowers and wilderness** in the high-alpine basins of the Elk and San Juan Mountains

Grand Junction

From Interstate 70 on a hot summer day, the west side of Grand Junction appears as a bleached sprawl of chain stores and hotels. This isn't a mirage. With a population around 40,000, Grand Junction is the largest town in western Colorado and people come from all around for shopping, medical care, and entertainment. That's one reason why the west side of town sprawls with malls. If, however, you drive south off the interstate into the downtown, you'll find attractive homes from the early 1900s, an artsy Main Street shopping district, and a real-world community that evenly balances business and pleasure. When the light softens in the evening, the colors surface in the town's verdant, irrigated parks and golf courses; in the salmon-colored rocks of Colorado National Monument; and in the blue-brown Colorado River, which absorbs the smaller Gunnison River at the south end of town. Water from the rivers, and from the earth itself, helps grow fruit in the nearby valleys and moistens the vineyards of eight area wineries.

Getting there

Grand Junction is in far western Colorado on I-70, 251 miles west of Denver. U.S. 50 enters Grand Junction from the southeast. Montrose is 61 miles southeast of Grand Junction on U.S. 50.

Walker Field, 2828 Walker Field Dr. (☎ **970-244-9100;** Internet: www. walkerfield.com), has daily service to Phoenix (on America West Express) and Denver (on United Express). Upon landing, you can rent cars from **Avis, Budget, Enterprise, Hertz, National,** and **Thrifty,** or call **Sunshine Taxi** (☎ **970-245-TAXI**) or **American Spirit Shuttle** (☎ **970-523-7662**) for a ride to your hotel. For information on contacting individual airlines and car-rental agencies, see the Appendix.

Amtrak's California Zephyr train (☎ **800-USA-RAIL;** Internet: www. amtrak.com), which runs from Chicago to the Bay Area, stops at the station on 331 S. First St. (☎ **970-241-2733**) in Grand Junction twice daily, once in each direction.

Getting around

Many of Grand Junction's most splendid attractions are in the surrounding countryside, so the best way to get around is by car. Most of the city is between the Colorado River (on the south) and **I-70** (on the north).

When driving in town, keep in mind that the town's numbered streets run north and south, perpendicular to Main Street and the named avenues, which go east and west. The downtown borders Main Street between First Street and Seventh Street.

Where to stay

Chain hotels line Grand Junction's Horizon Drive where it crosses I-70. These hotels cater both to passersby and people vacationing in the city, and their rates fluctuate along with the ebb and flow of freeway traffic. Scattered through the downtown and surrounding valley are older motels and some pleasant bed-and-breakfasts. An hour southeast of Grand Junction, Grand Mesa has cabins and historic lodges alongside lakes in deep pine forests.

Adam's Mark Grand Junction
$$ Grand Junction

The Adam's Mark sits right across I-70 from the Holiday Inn — the other major hotel in town — but the two are as different as east and west. Remodeled in 2002, the Adam's Mark is better for couples and business travelers. It costs more, has an upscale restaurant and popular sports bar, and offers amenities such as room service and extra phones in the bathrooms. Because the Adam's Mark towers eight stories above the vertically challenged town of Grand Junction, it has the most expansive views in the area, including ones of the hotel tennis courts and outdoor swimming pool.

743 Horizon Dr., Grand Junction. ☎ *970-241-8888. Fax: 970-242-7266. Internet:* www. adamsmark.com. *Rack rates: $59–$129. AE, DC, DISC, MC, V.*

Alexander Lake Lodge
$$ Grand Mesa

The seven cabins on this property overlook one of those perfect little alpine lakes that seem to belong in a sepia-toned movie scene. The cabins sleep anywhere from two to seven people. Some are in almost perfect condition; others need work. Some have full kitchens; others just have microwaves. The owners have hired a full-time construction team to add a few cabins and bring the whole place up to snuff. Construction aside, most of the activity is inside the 100-year-old Alexander Lake Lodge, which has an immense fireplace, hanging pelts, and an enclosed porch with lake views. The lodge has a fine, moderately priced restaurant inside. It's open for lunch and dinner Thursday through Sunday, year-round.

2121 AA 50 Rd., Cedaredge. ☎ ***970-856-ALEX.*** *Fax: 970-856-2540. Internet:* www.alexanderlakelodge.com. *Rack rates: June–Sept $90–$140; Jan–May $55–$110. MC, V.*

Holiday Inn Grand Junction
$–$$ Grand Junction

Close your eyes (briefly) and picture a guest room at an especially nice Holiday Inn. Now that you know what the accommodations look like, we can discuss the real advantage to this hotel: a HoliDome entertainment zone that will tie up your kids for hours, if not days. Children love the indoor swimming pool, hot tub, pool tables, table tennis, and video arcade. Parents can either suffer the children or suffer on the cardiovascular machines. There's also an outdoor swimming pool and hot tub in a wind-sheltered, sun-splashed courtyard. As at all Holiday Inns, kids stay free, and the hotel restaurant (a Coco's) caters to youngsters. The location, mere yards from I-70, makes this a viable choice even if you're only passing through.

755 Horizon Dr., Grand Junction. ☎ ***970-243-6790.*** *Fax 970-243-6790. Internet:* www.holiday-inn.com/grandjunction. *Rack rates: $69–$99. AE, DC, DISC, MC, V.*

Two Rivers Winery
$–$$ Grand Junction

If the words *pitching woo* remind you of Japanese baseball, it's time to relearn romance by taking your partner to the Chateau at the Two Rivers Winery. Named for the world's prime grape-growing regions, the eight immaculate guest rooms all have French decor and views of the surrounding vineyards. There won't be any HoliDome here to distract you, so you can lavish all your attention on your partner — perhaps even over a bottle of wine. Come morning, you can breakfast on bright-yellow tablecloths in a sunny dining area or take your food onto an outside deck.

2087 Broadway, Grand Junction. ☎ ***970-241-3155.*** *Fax: 970-241-3199. Internet:* www.tworiverswinery.com. *Rack rates: $79–$145. Rates include breakfast. AE, MC, V.*

Where to dine

Grand Junction is only now getting used to the idea of gourmet dining. It has a handful of fine restaurants and many others that serve good eats. Unlike many other Colorado towns, it also has plenty of suburban-style chains.

Chefs' New World Cuisine

$$ **Grand Junction** NEW WORLD CUISINE

The two chefs here went to cooking school together before opening this restaurant. One is in his 20s, the other in his 50s. One cooks meaty entrees with rich sauces; the other bakes fruity, frothy, chocolaty desserts. Both change their offerings in order to use what's ripe. This is Grand Junction's only true fine-dining establishment and it even boasts an award-winning wine list. But that doesn't mean you'll need a blue blazer. When I asked one of the chefs about the dress code, he shrugged forlornly and said he wasn't big on tank tops.

936 North Ave., Grand Junction. ☎ *970-243-9673. Reservations appreciated. Main courses: $14.75–$27.50. Open: Tues–Sat for dinner only. AE, MC, V.*

Fiesta Guadalajara

$–$$ **Grand Junction** MEXICAN

Fiesta Guadalajara has tapped into the same successful formula used by chain Mexican eateries across America. In a sprawling, Technicolor dining room, the restaurant serves cheese-heavy, south-of-the-border fare in portions large enough to make you feel as if you've entered an eating contest. This formula, which also involves flavored margaritas and fried ice cream, seems to play as well in Grand Junction as it does in metropolitan suburbs — which is to say, very well indeed.

710 North Ave. (at Seventh Street), Grand Junction. ☎ *970-255-6609. Reservations accepted. Main courses: $4.95–$13.95. Open: Lunch and dinner daily. Closed Thanksgiving and Christmas. AE, DISC, MC, V.*

Il Bistro Italiano

$–$$ **Grand Junction** ITALIAN

Brunella Gualerzi, who does the cooking here, hails from northern Italy and prepares entirely Italian fare, ranging from seafood to traditional pizza and lasagna. All the pastas, breads, and desserts are handmade. Except for a few token Colorado wines, the wine list consists of Italian selections. Even the music is by Italians and Italian-Americans (but not Madonna). The dining area, with high ceilings, a brick wall, and tiny lamps strung through an elaborate pulley system, seems stylish enough to be Italian.

400 Main St., Grand Junction. ☎ *970-243-8662. Reservations accepted. Main courses $12–$18. Open: Tues–Sat lunch and dinner. AE, DISC, MC, V.*

Pablo's Pizza

$ **Grand Junction** PIZZA

On its Spudstacular pizza, Pablo's Pizza dumps roasted potatoes, sour cream, chives, green onions, and cheese; on the Bangkok, it drops Thai peanut sauce, large shrimp, green onions, bell peppers, cilantro, and cheese. The kids' menu even has a Mac 'n' Cheese pizza. Named for Pablo Picasso, the restaurant calls its pizza "a slice of art," but it seems more like pizza underneath a meal. In all, Pablo's offers 14 specialty pizzas as well as made-to-order pies and basic slices. And everything does taste good.

319 Main St., Grand Junction. ☎ *970-255-8879. No reservations. Cheese slice: $1.75. Small specialty, 12-inch pizzas: $4.75–$10.50. 18-inch pizzas: $12.75–$18.50. Open: Mon–Sat lunch and dinner. DISC, MC, V.*

Rockslide Restaurant and Brewery
$–$$ Grand Junction   STEAKS AND SEAFOOD

A kayak and hang glider dangle above the smoke-free dining area at this restaurant, making the meals here a potential thrill sport. Rather than worry about things crashing, keep your eyes on the fish, burgers, pizza, pasta, and steaks, as well as on the beer. It's all tasty. The restaurant also has a smoking area and a bar where you can watch televised sports and sip any of the half-dozen or so Rockslide brews available on tap.

401 Main St., Grand Junction. ☎ *970-245-2111. Reservations not accepted. Main courses: $7.50–$17. Open: Mon–Sat lunch and dinner; Sun brunch and dinner. AE, DC, DISC, MC, V.*

Exploring Grand Junction

No matter which direction you go from Grand Junction, you'll find awesome country. Grand Mesa rises to the southeast, towering 4,000 feet higher than the 7,000-foot Uncompahgre Plateau, which is immediately to Grand Junction's southwest. Vineyards and orchards dot the valley floor east of the city, alongside the Colorado River. And if you drive two hours north from Grand Junction, you'll end up at Dinosaur National Monument.

The best things to see and do

A trip to Grand Junction feels most rewarding if you spend time in the surrounding territory. Go to Colorado National Monument for red-rock desert canyons, or make the hour-long drive to Grand Mesa if you prefer alpine lakes. Afterwards, you can enjoy the rewards of the town itself.

Colorado National Monument

Inside 20,000-acre Colorado National Monument, runoff has carved four 800- to 1,000-foot-deep canyons into the northeast edge of the 7,000-foot Uncompahgre Plateau. You can enter the monument from either Fruita or Grand Junction on Colorado 340, but either way, you'll climb 2,600 vertical feet from the valley floor to the top of the plateau. Inside the National Monument, Colorado 340 becomes Rim Rock Drive, which skirts the northeast edge of the plateau for most of its 23 miles. The drive passes 18 overlooks of the four canyons. From the overlooks, you can see balancing rocks, spires, arches, and other unusual landforms. During breaks from your journey on Rim Rock Drive, you can:

✔ **Go to the Visitor Center.** The Rangers here will answer your questions, and you can purchase maps and books. A 12-minute video flaunts stunning pictures of the surrounding landscape and offers almost no information. (The message seems to be "Feel good about nature.") The visitor center is open from 8 a.m. to 6 p.m. daily in summer, 9 a.m. to 5 p.m. the rest of the year.

✔ **Take a short rim hike.** The National Monument has six short, well-marked trails on or near the canyon rim. Start with the **Canyon Rim Trail,** which goes from the Visitor Center along the rim for ½ mile, affording views of Wedding and Monument canyons.

✔ **Hike down into a canyon.** There are also longer, more demanding trails (or routes) that descend into the canyons. Though less panoramic than the rim walks, these trails let you see the rock formations up close, feel the scratchy desert vegetation, and smell the sun-baked soils. Plus, they take you farther away from the crowds. You can walk the **Monument Canyon, Liberty Cap,** and **Ute Canyon** trails all the way to parking areas in Grand Valley or else climb back up to the rim. Be sure to discuss your plans with a ranger before hiking into a canyon, and carry plenty of water.

✔ **Camp.** The first-come, first served **Saddlehorn Campground** has sites with picnic tables and grills, and access to drinking water and restrooms. The cost per site is $10.

Colorado National Monument (☎ 970-858-3617) is on Colorado 340 between Grand Junction and Fruita. Admission, valid for seven days, costs $5 per car, $3 for individuals on foot, bicycle, or motorcycle. It's free from October through March.

Grand Mesa

Other than being flat-topped and near Grand Junction, Grand Mesa and the Uncompahgre Plateau have little in common. With an apex over 11,000 feet, Grand Mesa is higher by more than 4,000 feet. Because of its lofty elevation, it's much wetter. Unlike the mostly arid Uncompahgre Plateau, it has 300-some lakes, ponds, and reservoirs. Grand Mesa's forests of pine and aspen belong to the mountains and not the desert. Even the rock layers are different. Grand Mesa has a cap of erosion-resistant lava atop shale and other soft layers; the Uncompahgre Plateau consists mostly of hard sandstone. You can drive up and over Grand Mesa on Colorado 65 as you go from Cedaredge to Mesa. When you reach the top, stop at the **Grand Mesa Visitor Center** (☎ 970-856-4153). The rangers there can point out places for fishing, picnicking, boating, and hiking. One premier hike is the **Crag Crest National Recreation**

Trail, a 10.3-mile loop that climbs 1,000 vertical feet to an 11,000-foot razor-like ridge — the highest area on the mesa. You don't have to do the whole loop to reach the ridgeline. Just park at the west trailhead, near Island Lake, and follow Trail 711 to the Crest.

Other things to see and do

When you need a break from the hiking, fishing and boating of Grand Mesa, try one of the many other relaxing and enjoyable activities in Grand Valley. You can

✔ **Find a perfect peach.** Grand Valley not only has two rivers, it sits atop artesian wells that provide extra irrigation water for fruit and grape growers. The sunny days, dry air, and cool nights also help fatten the fruit. If you're taking I-70 through Grand Valley during summer, check to see what the farmers are selling in **Palisade** (I-70, Exit 42), 13 miles east of Grand Junction. Look for cherries in June, apricots in July, peaches in August, and apples in September.

✔ **Get in the van and start "wining."** Palisade is also home to seven of the eight Grand Junction wineries. All offer free tastings and sell wine by the bottle. (The eighth winery, Two Rivers, is in Grand Junction proper.) You can pick up a free guide to area wineries at the **Grand Junction Visitor and Convention Center,** 740 Horizon Dr., in Grand Junction (☎ **800-962-2547** or 970-244-1480).

American Spirit Shuttles (☎ **888-226-5031** or 970-244-8425) offers custom tours of area wineries for a minimum of $130 (or $25 per person for groups of six or more). They also offer regularly scheduled group tours on Wednesdays and Saturdays (cost: $25 per person).

✔ **Brave the Jurassic Robots. Dinosaur Journey Museum,** 550 Jurassic Court (off I-70, Exit 19), in Fruita (☎ **970-858-7282**), has some dinosaur skeletons, but the real attractions are its robotic dinosaurs. They look realistic, move convincingly, and, except for an occasional metallic clunking noise, make all the shrill cries and howls that people in the Age of Spielberg have come to expect of dinosaurs. Later, you can shift your attention to a simulated 5.3 magnitude earthquake. It's open May through September, daily from 9 a.m. to 5 p.m.; and October through April from Monday through Saturday 10 a.m. to 4 p.m., Sunday noon to 4 p.m. Admission is $7 adults, $6 seniors 60 and over, and $4 children ages 3 to 12.

✔ **Dig it.** The **Museum of Western Colorado** (☎ **888-488-DINO**) lets visitors participate in one-day (cost: $95) and three-day (cost: $695) digs alongside real paleontologists at a site west of Grand Junction. You can get information about these digs at the Dinosaur Journey Museum.

✔ **Scale an "educational tower."** The **History Museum and Smith Tower,** 462 Ute Ave., in Grand Junction (☎ **970-242-0971**), has a 125-foot high tower with 360-degree views of Grand Junction.

Lower down in the museum, you can duck through a simulated uranium mine, visit a historic schoolroom, and even admire a vintage photo of "Miss Atomic Energy." Gun fanatics will get fired up about the collection of sidearms, including ones that belonged to Kit Carson, Annie Oakley, and Buffalo Bill. All in all, it's a fun museum. Open Monday through Saturday from 9 a.m. to 5 p.m., Sunday noon to 4 p.m. Admission costs $5.50 adults, $4.50 seniors 60 and over, and $3 children ages 3 to 12.

✔ **Savor sidewalk sculpture.** Long before Denver created its 16th Street Mall, Grand Junction converted its Main Street (between Second and Fifth avenues) into a pedestrian-friendly shopping park. Besides having restaurants and shops, the park is home to **Art on the Corner** — 26 permanent and 28 loaned sculptures that brighten the downtown sidewalks. You can purchase the loaned sculptures at prices ranging from $400 to $30,000. The many whimsical pieces make a trip downtown (and off of the interstate) special. Call the **Downtown Development Agency** at ☎ 970-245-9697 for more details.

Staying active

At less than 5,000 feet, Grand Junction is one of the low spots in western Colorado and a prime area for year-round, snow-free sports. If you're fixing to freeze, you can always drive to Grand Mesa, more than 6,000 feet higher than the Grand Valley. Here are a few options to consider:

✔ **Cross-country skiing: The Grand Mesa Nordic Council** (☎ 970-434-9753) grooms up to 35 kilometers (22 miles) of track for free skiing on Grand Mesa. Some trails are regularly maintained, others are groomed sporadically. There's also an extensive network of forest roads that are packed down for snowmobiling. For information on winter sports atop the mesa, contact the **Grand Mesa Visitor Center** at ☎ 970-856-4153.

✔ **Golfing:** *Golf Digest* recently named the **Golf Club at Redlands Mesa,** 2325 West Ridges Boulevard, in Grand Junction (☎ 970-263-9270), one of the nation's best new affordable courses. Greens fees for 18 holes are $59.

✔ **Hiking:** There are great hikes both atop Grand Mesa and inside the Colorado National Monument. If you simply want a convenient, pretty place to walk, ride, or inline skate, head for any of four **Colorado Riverfront Trails,** which range in length from ½ to 4 miles. One easy one to find is the **Watson Island/Old Mill Bridge Trailhead,** at the intersection of Seventh Street and Struthers, where the city's **Botanic Garden** is located.

✔ **Mountain biking:** Abundant public lands, a dry climate, and a mixture of forest and desert have combined to make this one of the nation's newest mountain-bike hotspots. If you want to go really far, perhaps even with vehicle support, you have two good options. The **Tabeguache Trail,** a mix of double track and some steep, technical single track, drifts 144 miles from Grand Junction south to Montrose, climbing as high as 9,500 feet on the Uncompahgre Plateau. One trailhead is on Monument Road south of Broadway. The **Kokopelli Trail** meanders 142 miles from the Loma Boat Launch, 15 miles west of Grand Junction, all the way to Moab, Utah, passing through spectacular and remote desert canyons in eastern Utah. **Ruby Canyon Cycles,** 301 Main Street, in Grand Junction (☎ **970-241-0141**), rents mountain bikes and can tell you more about area trails.

To get your bearings, pick up a free copy of *Biking Guide to the Grand Valley* at visitor centers and bike shops around town.

Hitting the slopes

Powderhorn Resort, on the north face of Grand Mesa, has the closest lift-served skiing to Grand Junction. At just 510 acres, this is one of the smaller ski areas in the state, but it has a respectable 1,650-foot vertical drop, including some direct fall line skiing off the Take Four Chairlift. Powderhorn doesn't always get enough snow at its base. The ski area's 9,850-foot summit is low by Colorado standards, and the resort isn't in a major snow belt. But the terrain is fine, especially if you can catch it during a big snow year. For more details on Powderhorn, see Table 20-1.

Table 20-1	Ski Report: Powderhorn Resort
Location: On Colorado 65, 7 miles south of Mesa	
Trails: 27	
	20% beginner
	50% intermediate
	15% advanced
	15% expert
Vertical drop: 1,650 feet	
Base elevation: 9,200 feet	
Summit elevation: 9,850 feet	
Skiable terrain: 510 acres	
Average snowfall: 250 inches	
Lifts: 4 (includes one surface lift)	
Snow phone: ☎ 970-268-5700	
Reservations: ☎ 970-268-5700	
Internet: www.powderhorn.com	
2002–2003 high-season adult all-day lift ticket: $38	

Shopping

With over 160 stores and restaurants, **Mesa Mall** (☎ **970-242-0008**), at the junction of 24 Road and U.S. 6 and 50, is the largest mall between Denver and Salt Lake City. Anchor stores include Target, Sears, J.C. Penney and Mervyn's. In the downtown area, the pedestrian-friendly **Main Street Shopping District** (Main Street between Second and Fifth avenues) has galleries, restaurants, and shops — and more than 50 sculptures.

A side trip to Dinosaur and Dinosaur National Monument

Surrounded by windswept high desert, the town of Dinosaur is home to 400 people, a handful of motels and restaurants, and not much else. The town has a memorable personality, but the big surprise comes when you visit nearby Dinosaur National Monument: Only a small portion of the monument has anything to do with dinosaurs. The first 80 acres or so were set aside in 1915 to preserve a quarry full of remarkably well-preserved dinosaur fossils; the remaining 210,000 acres encompass scenic desert canyons, including the confluence of the Green and Yampa rivers.

Getting there

Dinosaur National Monument straddles the Utah-Colorado border and has a paved entrance road on each side. The monument's headquarters are on U.S. 40, 2 miles east of the town of Dinosaur. The town of Dinosaur is 3 miles east of the Utah border and 110 miles north of Grand Junction (about a two-hour drive). To reach Dinosaur from Grand Junction, take I-70 12 miles east to Colorado 139 north. Follow Colorado 139 north for 75 miles, then turn left (west) on Colorado 64 and follow it for 20 miles to the town of Dinosaur. The dinosaur quarry is 7 miles north of Jensen, Utah. To reach Jensen, go 20 miles west of Dinosaur on U.S. 40.

Seeing the sights

The main attraction in this area, sure enough, is **Dinosaur National Monument,** but you'll find many different sights within the monument itself. Two main roads go into the monument, one from the Utah side and one from the Colorado side:

✔ To see dinosaur bones, you'll need to enter the monument on the **Utah side** and pay a $10-per-car admission fee. To reach the bones, you'll immediately park at a staging area and wait for a free shuttle, which takes you ½ mile to the quarry. The fossils inside the quarry date to 145 million years ago, when floods swept dinosaur carcasses onto a sandbar, where they were buried by river sediment.

Through time, the sediment turned to rock and the bones fossilized. Today, the quarry consists of an exposed rock wall in which hundreds of bones are imbedded. Archeologists removed many bones in the past, then left others for future generations. They even put up a roof to protect the area. Opposite the wall of bones is a two-story viewing area with displays, reconstructed skeletons, and an area for ranger discussions. After seeing the quarry, drive 11 miles on **Cub Creek Road.** You'll pass 800-year-old rock art, viewpoints above the Green River, hiking trails, a historic cabin, and the most conveniently situated campground in the park. Alongside Cub Creek Road, just inside the entrance gate, you can pick up a brochure that interprets key landmarks along the way.

✔ It costs nothing to enter the National Monument on the **Colorado side.** First, stop at the **Monument Headquarters.** The headquarters has no dinosaur bones, but it does have maps and information as well as a short video about the monument. If you enter from this side, you won't see dinosaur bones, period. Instead, you'll drive **Harpers Corner Road** and climb onto the broad Yampa Plateau, reaching overlooks of the confluence of the Green and Yampa rivers. Twenty-three different geological strata are exposed in the park, and many can be seen in the colorful canyons visible from this road.

I recommend driving all 31 miles to the end of the road and then hiking another mile (one-way) to the end of **Harper's Corner Trail.** This puts you at the tip of a peninsula from which you can see a broad sweep of the canyon carved by the Green River, more than 3,000 feet below, including a massive fin of rock where the Green meets the Yampa. If you have a high-clearance vehicle and the weather is fair, and if you also have a high tolerance for rugged, bumpy roads, you may enjoy a 13-mile detour (one-way) down **Echo Park Road,** which descends to the shady campground near the confluence. En route, it passes more hiking trails, rock art, and a historic cabin. This road becomes impassable when wet, even for four-wheel-drive vehicles, so don't try it if it's been raining.

Where to stay

Lodging choices are few in Dinosaur. I'd stay at the **Terrace Motel,** 312 Brontosaurus Blvd. (U.S. 40; ☎ **970-374-2241**), provided that Charles and Vivian Gabrielson are still running it. They've been operating the motel since 1964 and are hoping to sell the place soon. If they don't, your room should be fine. Mine had a tilting bathroom and a desk with the drawers painted shut, but it was spotless and the mattress felt brand new. The Gabrielsons keep the same rates, no matter how busy they are: $36 for a room with a double bed; $64 for a two-room suite with four beds.

Where to dine

At **Miner's Café,** 420 E. Brontosaurus Blvd. (U.S. 40; ☎ **970-374-2020**), in Dinosaur, you'll hear your food before you taste it. Entrees include the likes of chicken fried steak, hamburger steak, popcorn shrimp, and battered halibut. A hamburger patty on cottage cheese constitutes a "Diet Delight." Nothing costs over $10. The restaurant also sells fossils and tie-dyes, has Christian literature on the tables, and allows smoking. It's open Monday through Saturday for breakfast, lunch, and dinner.

Fast Facts: Grand Junction

Hospital

St. Mary's Hospital (☎ 970-244-2273), at Seventh Street and Patterson Road, offers 24-hour emergency room services.

Information

The Grand Junction Visitor & Convention Bureau (☎ 800-962-2547 or 970-244-1480, Internet: www.visit grandjunction.com) is at 740 Horizon Drive, off I-70, Exit 31.

Post Office

The main Grand Junction Post Office is at 241 N. Fourth St. (☎ 970-244-3400).

Road Conditions

Call ☎ 970-245-8800.

Weather

Call ☎ 970-243-0914.

Montrose, Delta, and Black Canyon of the Gunnison National Park

The main attraction in this area is the Black Canyon of the Gunnison, where the Gunnison River has cleaved downward for 2,000 feet into a tableland known as Black Mesa. Because the canyon is deeper than it is wide, little sunlight reaches the river. This lack of light, along with the dark walls of Precambrian gneiss (a hard rock formed during a geologic age more than 543 million years ago), makes the canyon seem strangely imposing — primordial even. The mood changes when you descend off of Black Mesa and enter the sun-baked agricultural communities of the Uncompahgre Valley. The largest of them, Montrose, has 13,000 residents and a diverse economy that's anchored by agriculture. In Montrose and nearby Delta, farmers grow everything from sweet corn to barley. On the land northeast of Delta and near the canyon's north rim, vineyards produce many of the grapes used by Colorado's burgeoning wine industry. In this area, the villages become smaller and seemingly more eccentric. One especially popular stopping point is Crawford, home to musician Joe Cocker's Mad Dog Café.

Getting there

In winter, **Montrose Regional Airport** (☎ **970-249-3203**) has daily service to and from Dallas/Fort Worth (on **American**) and Houston (on

Continental); frequent service to and from Denver (on **United Express**) and Phoenix (on **America West Express**), and Saturday-only service to and from Newark (on **Continental**). During summer, you'll probably have to fly into Grand Junction. **Budget, Dollar, Thrifty,** and **National** all have rental desks at the airport. For information on contacting individual airlines and car-rental agencies, see the Appendix.

From Grand Junction, Delta is a relatively brisk 40-mile drive southeast on **U.S. 50.** Montrose is another 21 miles south of Delta on U.S. 50. If you're coming from the east, you can take U.S. 50 all the way from Pueblo, 226 miles away, where the highway dead ends at **I-25.** If you're coming from the northeast on I-70, get off in Glenwood Springs and follow **Colorado 82** south for 12 miles toward Aspen, then take **Colorado 133** south to Carbondale. Keep going on Colorado 133 for 90 miles southwest to Delta. This is an exquisite drive. From the south, pick up **U.S. 550** in Durango and take it north for 108 miles to Montrose.

Getting around

To get around in Montrose and Delta, you'll need to trade in your current vehicle for a 20-year-old Ford pick-up. Just kidding. You'll probably want to have a car, though, because there's no local bus service. Though walking in these towns is fun, their business districts span several miles, so walking isn't always your best choice.

For a cab in Montrose, call **Western Express Taxi** (☎ **970-249-8880**). **Delta Transit Co.** (☎ **970-874-1529**) can give you a ride in Delta.

Where to stay

Montrose and Delta have a number of chain hotels, but they also have a few bed-and-breakfasts and some vintage motels. If you want to use Montrose as a home base, start with the places listed here.

Delta has two historic motels that could either become substandard or classic in the next few years, depending on what the owners do with them. If you like old digs or are on a tight budget, stop by the **Westways Court Motel,** 1030 Main St. (☎ **970-874-4415**), or the **El-D-Rado Motel,** 702 Main St. (☎ **970-874-4493**), and see whether the rooms meet your standards. The Westways Court is older (1938), displays a classic neon sign, and has quirky rooms with knotty pine walls and ceilings. The Pueblo-style El-D-Rado has fresher rooms, including ones with refrigerators and microwaves. Its rates, usually $30 to $50, run a few dollars lower than at the Westways Court.

If the preceding relics don't cut it or you prefer the familiarity of a chain, you can choose between newer, chain hotels. In Montrose, there's the **Best Western Red Arrow,** 1702 E. Main St. (☎ **970-249-9641**); the

Comfort Inn, 2100 E. Main St. (☎ **970-240-8000**); the **Holiday Inn Express,** 1391 S. Townsend Ave. (☎ **970-240-1800**); and the **Days Inn,** 1655 E. Main St. (☎ **970-249-3411**). In Delta, try the **Best Western Sundance Motel,** 903 Main Street (☎ **970-874-9781**), or the **Comfort Inn,** 180 Gunnison River Dr. (☎ **800-228-5150** or 970-874-1000).

Lathrop House Bed & Breakfast

$ Montrose

Cindy Crosman took 11 years — one year less than she stayed on as Montrose County Commissioner — to renovate this 1903 home. Lathrop House had been abandoned during the 1980s, but Crosman's hard work has turned it into something special. It's now luxurious, creatively decorated, and inexpensive, especially for single people, who get $10 off the regular rate. Three of the five rooms have fairly standard Victorian decor, the other two are much bolder. My favorite, the J.V. Lathrop room, looks like something you'd find in an Elks Club. The head of a trophy buck is mounted on one wall, above a carved lion's face. The shimmering purple-and-gold drapery and bedspread look like something a wizard might wear. If you're traveling without kids, this would be my first choice in Montrose.

718 E. Main St., Montrose. ☎ *970-240-6075. Fax:970-240-6075. Internet:* www.lathrophouse.com. *Rack rates: $65–$85. Rates include breakfast. DC, DISC, MC, V.*

Country Lodge

$ Montrose

This motel, built in 1950 but clean and full of character, is perfect for families. In each room, a sliding-glass rear door opens onto a courtyard with gardens and an outdoor swimming pool. The rooms have knotty pine walls and quilts on the beds, and some have kitchenettes. Located at the west end of town, the motel is convenient to both Black Canyon of the Gunnison National Park and to the restaurants on Montrose's Main Street.

1624 E. Main St., Montrose. ☎ *970-249-4567. Fax: 970-240-3082. Internet:* www.countryldg.com. *Rack rates: Summer $62–$78; spring and fall $48–$75; winter $48–$55. AE, DC, MC, V.*

Where to dine

Montrose and Delta have always been meat-and-potatoes towns, where the restaurants stick to the basics and the food sticks to the ribs. This seems to be changing as more newcomers relocate here, but you still won't have problems finding some beef. If you're not a fan of the red stuff, your dining choices will be limited, though Cazwella's (reviewed in this section) does offer some lighter fare.

Camp Robber Café
$-$$ **Montrose AMERICAN/NEW MEXICAN**

My server at the Camp Robber Cafe swore that she'd worked there a year without fielding a complaint. I forgot my polygraph that night, but she seemed to be telling the truth. There was other evidence that the place was okay: word of mouth around town, a crowd on an otherwise slow night, prompt service, and tasty food. In all, this seemed like the type of place where every meal scores a 7 on a scale of 1 to 10 — no small feat when you have a gargantuan menu of salads, pastas, New Mexican fare, sandwiches, burgers, ribs, fish, and steaks.

Corner of Main Street and Townsend Avenue. ☎ *970-240-1590. Reservations accepted. Main courses: $7–$16. Open Tues–Fri lunch and dinner, Sat dinner only, Sunday brunch only. AE, MC, V.*

Cazwellas
$$ **Montrose MEXICAN**

Transplanted from Telluride, Caswellas looks and feels like a trendy ski-town eatery. Instead of the wagon wheels you'd expect in this town, it has Oaxacan masks fashioned from coconuts, hung on a wall painted "Enchilada red." And its food qualifies as downright exotic. The chef learned traditional recipes in Oaxaca and uses four different mole sauces in the menu. At least a few locals love the *hen con mole Negro* — a guinea hen grilled and served over roasted mashers, basted with mole Negro and toasted sesame seeds.

320 E. Main St., Montrose. ☎ *970-252-9200. Reservations accepted. Main courses: $8–$22. Open: Mon–Sat lunch and dinner. AE, DISC, MC, V.*

Delta Fireside Food & Spirits
$-$$ **Delta AMERICAN**

This place serves the All-American fare you'd expect in western Colorado: Three cuts of prime rib and cut-to-order New York strip steaks, ribeyes, filet mignon, and sirloins. If you don't want a steak — or, for that matter, veal, chicken, pork, or fish — you can always opt for unlimited trips to the soup-and-salad bar. Pictures of local 4H Club winners are mounted on the walls, reminding you of where your meal came from.

820 Hwy. 92. ☎ *970-874-4413. Reservations accepted. Dinner: $7.50–$19. Open: Dinner daily; Sun brunch. AE, DISC, MC, V.*

Mad Dog Ranch Fountain Café
$-$$ **Crawford AMERICAN**

The rock singer Joe Cocker lives in a 17,000-square-foot mansion in Crawford and owns this cafe on the town's sleepy main drag. All proceeds from his restaurant go to the Cocker Kids' Foundation, which helps needy kids. Although Cocker wants a little help from his friends, a meal here won't make you unchain your, um, wallet. The food tastes fine and the prices are fair. What's more, the hardwood floors, hand-blown glass lamps, marble counters, and stools with animal hides were all (so) beautiful to me. You can leave your fat on by ordering a milkshake, French fries, pizza, burger, sandwich, steak, or ribs. When you're done eating, check out Cocker's gold and platinum records in the banquet room.

Highway 92 in the heart of Crawford. ☎ *970-921-SODA. Reservations accepted. Breakfasts $4–$5; lunches $4.50–$9; dinners $4.50–$22. Open: Breakfast, lunch, and dinner daily. MC, V.*

Exploring Montrose and Delta

This is flat-out beautiful country, and the most stunning sight is the Black Canyon of the Gunnison. After experiencing the park, you can enjoy these low-key towns and the other natural wonders in the area.

The best things to see and do

Black Canyon of the Gunnison rates high on the pecking order in these parts. Go there first and then explore Montrose and Delta.

Black Canyon of the Gunnison National Park

In the Black Canyon, the Gunnison River falls farther over the course of 48 miles than the Mississippi does over 1,500. Because it had gravity working in its favor, the water was able to saw downward through some of the earth's basement rocks — including incredibly hard gneiss. Because this rock is so hard, rainfall has caused little erosion around the river, and few side canyons have formed. The result is a gorge that's much narrower (as little as 1,300 feet) than it is deep (up to 3,000 feet). Along the river, far below the rims, ponderosa pines cling to rocky shores above the steep, thundering river, but in many places the canyon walls are too steep to hold much vegetation.

Black Canyon of the Gunnison National Park encompasses 15 of the most spectacular miles of the Black Canyon. During late spring, summer, and fall, you can visit either canyon rim. During the warm-weather months, I recommend doing the extra driving, including a few miles on dirt roads, to reach the North Rim. Far fewer people go there, and because the canyon walls are nearly vertical on that side, you can look almost straight down at the river. Being just 7 miles north of U.S. 50 via paved roads, the South Rim can be a quick hit, but it's more crowded and slightly less spectacular.

Here are a few ways to enjoy either rim:

✔ **Visit the rangers.** On the South Rim, you can easily spend a half-hour perusing the displays at the modern, full-service Visitor Center (open daily 8 a.m. to 5 p.m. June through September; 8:30 a.m. to 4:00 p.m., rest of year). The Rangers there can answer your questions about the park. On the North Rim, the Ranger Station is the closest thing to a Visitor Center. Sometimes there's even a ranger around.

✔ **Take a scenic drive.** This is an enjoyable activity on either rim and should take only about an hour. As noted earlier, the five over-looks on the North Rim are more stunning (some might say scary) than the 12 South Rim viewpoints. However, the road on the South Rim is paved; the North Rim has gravel roads.

✔ **Hike on the rim.** On the North Rim, you can choose between two scenic rim trails. Near the North Rim Campground, there's a short, easy ⅓-mile loop known as the **Cedar Point Nature Trail.** If you're inclined to exercise, I'd skip the Cedar Point Trail and instead walk 3½ miles (round-trip) to and from Exclamation Point on the **North Vista Trail.** The North Vista Trail drifts through a forest of juniper and pine en route to remote Exclamation Point, where you can look far upstream in the canyon. The North Vista trailhead is right next to the Ranger Station. On the South Rim, your best choice is the 1½-mile (round-trip) **Warner Point Nature Trail.** Located at High Point (the terminus of the South Rim Road), the trail follows a ridgeline with panoramic views south into the Uncompahgre Valley and north into the canyon.

✔ **Hike to the river.** The Park Service doesn't advertise the fact that you can hike deep into the canyon, and with good reason — these descents are really nasty. You'll need to obtain an inner-canyon permit before going, even if you're only day-hiking. (On the North Rim, you can simply sign the message board at the ranger station.) The routes — not to be confused with trails — are very steep and covered with loose rock, so it's hard to get traction. If you insist on hiking into the canyon, start with the **Gunnison Route,** which drops 1,800 feet over 1 mile from its trailhead near the South Rim Visitor Center. There are backcountry campsites along the river, for which free permits are issued on a first-come, first-served basis. I wouldn't take a heavy pack down any inner-canyon route, but when you reach the river, you may relish having the chance to spend the night. So take minimal gear when you head into the canyon.

✔ **Camp on the rim.** There are first-come, first-served campgrounds (cost: $10) on both rims. Both have water and toilets, but some differences exist. The North Rim has a smaller, prettier camp-ground, with a few sites that have partial views of the gorge. It sometimes fills up during spring and fall, when rock climbers flock there to take advantage of the temperate weather and big walls. The South Rim campground is larger and set back farther from the rim. It seldom fills up.

The South Rim is open year round. The North Rim is open from mid-April through mid-November, weather permitting. To reach the south entrance, drive 8 miles east of Montrose on U.S. 50, and then go 7 miles north on Colorado 347. The north entrance to the park is 11 miles south of Crawford via Colorado 92 and the North Rim Road. Admission, good for seven days, is $7 per car, $4 for individuals on foot, bicycle, or motorcycle. For more information call ☎ **970-641-2337** or surf the Internet to www.nps.gov/blca.

Other things to see and do

Black Canyon of the Gunnison National Park isn't the only area attraction. In Montrose, you can

- ✔ **Experience Ute art.** Prior to the arrival of Western settlers, many members of the Ute tribe wintered in Montrose then hunted on the Uncompahgre Plateau during summer. Since 1956, the **Ute Indian Museum,** U.S. Hwy. 550 at Chipeta Road in Montrose (☎ **970-249-3098**), has preserved artifacts of the tribe. It's worth coming here just to see the beadwork, headdresses, and ceremonial attire. The museum is open Monday through Saturday from 9:00 a.m. to 4:30 p.m., and Sunday 11:00 a.m. to 4:30 p.m. Admission is $3 for adults, $2.50 for seniors, and $1.50 for kids ages 6 to 10.

- ✔ Located in the former Denver and Rio Grande Railroad depot at the corner of Main and Rio Grande, the **Montrose County Historical Museum** (☎ **970-249-2085**), has exhibits on railroads, Victorian life, and a rail yard's worth of antique tools. Its most unique displays include a collection of teapots and cast-iron still banks (mainly piggy banks). It's open mid-May through September Monday through Saturday from 9 a.m. to 5 p.m. Admission is $2.50 adults, $2 seniors over 55, $1 students 12 to 18, and 50¢ for kids 5 to 12.

Staying active

After hiking alongside Black Canyon, you may need to wind down over a round of golf in Montrose. The centerpiece of a new 445-acre planned community, **Cobble Creek Community Golf Course,** 699 Cobble Dr. (☎ **970-240-9542**), opened 9 holes for play in 1999. Another 9 holes are set to open in September 2003. Greens fees for nine holes are currently $18. The **Montrose Golf Club,** 1350 Birch St. (☎ **970-249-GOLF**), has an 18-hole course, practice greens, a driving range, and a restaurant. You can play 9 holes for $15, 18 holes for $25. In **Delta,** the 18-hole **Devil's Thumb Golf Club,** 968 1560 Drive (☎ **970-874-6262**), affords views of Grand Mesa and the San Juan and Big Elk ranges. Greens fees for 18 holes are $38.

Shopping

Montrose gets my award for the most down-to-earth Main Street in Colorado. Among the businesses, it has pawnshops, two bookstores, and a medical supply store. Its most unique shop may be **Mr. Detector 1545 Sneffels St. (☎ 970-252-0429)**, which specializes in metal detecting and prospecting supplies. **Colorado Cat House and Dogs Too,** 300 Main St. (☎ **970-253-7373**), isn't so much a store for cats as about them. It's full of clothes, cards, and gifts that celebrate felines. **Coffee Trader,** 845 Main St. (☎ **970-249-6295**), serves java inside a Victorian home and outside the home in carefully manicured gardens. Not on Main Street, but also worth visiting, is **Corks Fine Wines and Spirits,** 16420 S. Townsend Ave. (☎ **970-249-5565**), which has one of the largest selections of wine in western Colorado.

Fast Facts: Montrose and Delta

Hospital

Montrose Memorial Hospital (☎ 970-249-2211), 800 S. Third St., in Montrose, offers 24-hour emergency care. So does Delta County Memorial Hospital, 100 Stafford Lane (☎ 970-874-7681), in Delta.

Information

Make your way to the Delta County Tourism Council, 310 Main St., in Delta (☎ 970-874-1616); or the Montrose Visitors Center, 1519 E. Main St., in Montrose (☎ 800-873-0244 or 970-240-1413; Internet: www.visit montrose.net).

Post Office

The Montrose Post Office is at 321 S. First St. (☎ 970-249-6654). In Delta, go to 360 Meeker St. (☎ 970-874-4721).

Weather

For recorded information, dial ☎ 970-243-0914.

Gunnison, Crested Butte, and Lake City

Home to Western States College, Gunnison is a low-slung ranching town with a historic Main Street and, around its perimeter, a sprawl of gun stores, liquor stores, motels, and restaurants. It sits in a broad ranching valley at the confluence of the Gunnison River and Tomichi Creek. If you travel more than a few miles to the north or south of town, the scenery gets even better. Eight federally designated wilderness areas are within easy driving distance. Much of the wilderness is inside two geologically similar, volcanic mountain ranges: the Elks to the north and the San Juans to the south. In each range, a historic mining town has endured and flourished high above Gunnison. In the Elk range, Crested Butte boasts world-class mountain biking, a famously steep ski area, and colorful high-alpine basins. In the San Juan range, Lake City's few year-round residents live quietly just downstream of Lake San Cristobal, the second largest natural body of water in Colorado.

Getting there

During winter, **Gunnison Crested Butte Airport** (☎ **970-641-2304**) has nonstop service to and from Houston on **Continental Airlines.** You can fly to and from Denver year-round on **United Airlines. Avis, Budget,** and **Hertz** all have desks at the airport. For information on contacting individual airlines and car-rental agencies, see the Appendix.

Alpine Express Shuttle Service (☎ **800-822-4844** or 970-641-5074) provides round-trip transportation between the airport and Crested Butte for $44 per person. There's no taxi service in Gunnison, but some lodges will pick you up at the airport.

The main highway through this area is U.S. 50, which extends all the way from Pueblo, 161 miles east of Gunnison, to Grand Junction, 126 miles to Gunnison's northwest. To reach **Crested Butte,** take Colorado 135 north from Gunnison for 28 miles. Keep going another 3 miles north to reach the ski area, in an area known as **Mount Crested Butte. Lake City** is 55 miles southwest of Gunnison. To reach Lake City from Gunnison, take U.S. 50 west for 9 miles and then go 46 miles south on Colorado 149. If you continue southeast past Lake City on Colorado 149, you'll cross the continental divide and then follow the course of the Rio Grande River down to Creede (46 miles from Lake City) and, beyond that, the San Luis Valley (via U.S. 160 east).

Getting around

If you plan on visiting all three towns, you'll need a car. If you don't want to rent a car and only want to see one town, Crested Butte is the best place to be car-less. Crested Butte's free **Mountain Express** (☎ **970-349-7318**) shuttles link downtown **Crested Butte** with **Mount Crested Butte,** 3 miles to the north. During summer and winter, the buses run from around 7:30 a.m. until 11:30 p.m., with service at least every 20 minutes during peak hours. **Mountain Express** observes a more relaxed schedule in spring and fall. The shuttles can accommodate both bicycles and wheelchairs. Call **Crested Butte Town Taxi** (☎ **970-349-5543**) if you still need a ride.

All three towns are small enough to negotiate on foot, and each has a main street that's worth exploring. In Crested Butte, **Colorado 135** enters town from the south, becomes **Sixth Street** and continues to Mount Crested Butte as **Gothic Road. Elk Avenue,** the main road through the Crested Butte historic district, intersects Sixth Street in the heart of the downtown area. In Gunnison, **U.S. 50** travels east and west through town as **Tomichi Avenue.** Dozens of businesses are on Tomichi Avenue, but the heart of the downtown is **Main Street** (Colorado 135), which goes north off Tomichi as Colorado 135. In **Lake City,** Colorado 149 runs north and south through town as **Gunnison Avenue,** the town's main road.

Where to stay

When booking a room, remember that Crested Butte and Lake City are more than 80 miles apart. You can sleep in Gunnison when skiing Crested Butte, but Lake City won't work as your base. The most expensive rooms in this area, during winter at least, are at Mount Crested Butte, at the base of Crested Butte Mountain Resort. The town of Crested Butte costs a few dollars less than Mount Crested Butte, and Gunnison costs much less. Lake City can be expensive during July and August, but it's a bargain for most of the rest of the year.

Cristiana Guesthaus
$–$$ Crested Butte

Completed in 1962, this was the first lodge built expressly for skiers coming to Crested Butte. Today, its low rates still tend to attract avid mountain athletes. The guests usually rise early; consume the strong coffee, cereals, and homemade pastries included with their room rate; and then leave for the day. When, hours later, they finally return to this Swiss-style lodge, they gather and socialize by the fireplace, on the large sundeck, in the television area (there are no TVs in the rooms), or in the hot tub. All told, the place has a communal spirit that you seldom find at a lodge. The only drawbacks are the small rooms and a few spots where the building shows its age.

621 Maroon Ave., Crested Butte. ☎ *800-824-7899 or 970-349-5326. Fax: 970-349-1962. Internet:* www.crestedbuttechamber.com/cristiana. *Rack rates: Spring, summer, and fall $57–$68 double; winter $71–$95 double. Rates include breakfast. AE, DISC, MC, V.*

Matterhorn Mountain Motel
$ Lake City

You can tell this motel is a half-century old by looking at its vintage neon sign — it was "grandfathered in" when Lake City banned other, similar signs. Inside, the rooms have showers instead of tubs, but everything else is modern. Fully remodeled in 2000, all have barn-wood furniture and large windows, and they're inviting. The rooms have either a queen-size bed and full kitchen or two queens and no kitchen. If you're here for a romantic getaway, spend the extra $5 per night for a cottage. They're roomy and private, and sleep two people comfortably — not counting Fido, who's also welcome here. The motel sits on a hillside just above dusty, sleepy, downtown Lake City.

409 Bluff St., Lake City. ☎ **970-944-2210**. *Fax: 970-944-2267. Internet:* www.coloradodirectory.com/matterhornlodge. *Rack rates: June–Sept. $79 double, $85 cottages (four-night minimum); Oct.–April $60 double, cottages closed. MC, V.*

Sheraton Crested Butte Resort

$$–$$$$ Mount Crested Butte

This hotel's solidity, height (five stories), shops, and attentive employees call to mind a big-city hotel that caters to business travelers. One look out the window, however, and you'll happily remember that you're at the base of Crested Butte Mountain Resort, with the chairlifts just a few yards away. Though the hotel has a restaurant, a coffee shop, and room service, its rooms also have in-room refrigerators, coffeemakers, and microwaves (in the suites only), so you won't feel locked into paying for expensive services. This is one of my favorite luxury hotels near a ski area. It's all business, and the business is skiing.

6 Emmons Road, Mount Crested Butte. ☎ **970-349-8000** *or 888-223-2469 (reservations only). Fax: 970-349-8050. Internet:* www.sheraton.com. *Rack rates: May–Nov $65–$175, Dec–April $95–$265. AE, DC, DISC, MC, V.*

Wildwood Motel

$ Gunnison

To really experience Gunnison (and perhaps Crested Butte) on the cheap, stay at this 1928 motel, located in a parklike setting just outside downtown Gunnison. The rates here top out at $64 during summer; in winter, you can often get a room with full kitchen for three days for $100. The winter prices make this place a steal if you want to ski for cheap. The rooms are worn around the edges but clean, and they're individually decorated, sometimes in vintage furnishings. Outside, cottonwood trees shade the spacious dirt parking lot and grassy barbeque areas. You can also rent an RV site here, at rates ranging from $17 to $22 per day.

1312 W. Tomichi, Gunnison. ☎ **970-641-1663**. *Fax: 970-641-7044. Internet:* www.wildwoodmotel.net. *Rack rates $35–$64 double. DISC, MC, V.*

Where to dine

Most of the tourist money in this area flows to Crested Butte, and that's where the bulk of the fine dining is. But you can also eat well in Gunnison and Lake City. Gunnison is a beef-eating town that's also blessed with a fine Italian restaurant. Lake City's beauty lures a few skilled chefs who try to cash in on a very short tourist season. All three towns also offer moderately priced, family fare.

Charlie P's

$ **Lake City** **AMERICAN/TEX-MEX**

Charlie P's is in a building that has been a morgue, cigar factory, and bakery. Nowadays it produces barbeque, burgers, five different chicken dishes, and some tasty Tex-Mex fare, among other offerings. The food is consistently palatable, and the low prices attract a stream of (living) locals. The restaurant has a large patio where you can watch the occasional car or pedestrian pass by on Lake City's main drag.

951 N. Hwy. 149., Lake City. ☎ *970-944-2332. Reservations accepted. Main courses: $5–$17. Open: Mon–Tues and Thurs–Sat for breakfast lunch and dinner; Sun lunch only. Closed Wed. DISC, MC, V.*

The Crystal Inn

$$$ **Lake City** **FRENCH**

Chef Bruno, who runs this place, once served as banquet chef at New York City's famous Tavern on the Green. In the twilight of Bruno's career, a friend invited him to cook at this small country inn 2 miles south of Lake City, and, fortunately for us, he's still here. Chef Bruno keeps the menu small. Most nights, he cooks a single veal, pork, fish, and beef dish, each with a classic French sauce. He hopes you'll have some wine, too. You can tell he loves the fermented grape juice — the place overflows with magnums and wine bottles, empty and full, including a few that hold candles. It's a pretty romantic spot.

2175 Hwy. 149 South, Lake City. ☎ *877-465-6343 or 970-944-2201. Reservations encouraged. Main courses: $20–$30. Brunch: $9–$13. Open: Ssummer dinner daily and Sun brunch; rest of year Wed–Mon dinner and Sun brunch. MC, V.*

Garlic Mike's

$$ **Gunnison** **ITALIAN**

Michael Busse's credentials as a chef of Italian food are impeccable: New Jersey native, Italian heritage, and culinary school in Atlantic City. Factor in his warm demeanor, and you have a big reason why this was voted the best restaurant in Gunnison by readers of a local publication you've probably never heard of. Look for Mike's specialties, marked by the little garlic-bulb icons on the menu. The best may be the veal with prosciutto, mozzarella, and Madeira wine. During summer, you can dine on a large deck overlooking the Gunnison River.

2674 N. Hwy. 35 (2 miles north of Gunnison). ☎ *970-641-2493. Reservations accepted. Main courses: $9–$22. Open: Daily for dinner. AE, MC, V.*

Pitas in Paradise

$ Crested Butte   MEDITERRANEAN

The folks behind the counter at Pitas in Paradise dish up cheap, healthy, tasty food faster than you can get through the first article in the town's tabloid newspaper. For under $7, you can get a wrap or pita sandwich crammed with vegetables, rice, and sometimes meat. The choices are mostly Greek, but a Thai wrap (vegetables in a blend of curry and coconut) and a Bombay wrap (creamy spinach sauce with Indian flavors, tofu, vegetables, and ginger) number among the popular offerings. For dessert, have a milkshake or a smoothie. Free Internet access is provided for customers.

214 Elk Ave., Crested Butte. ☎ 970-349-0897. No reservations. Main courses: $4.95–$7.95. Open: Daily for breakfast, lunch, and dinner. MC, V.

The Slogar Bar & Restaurant

$$ Crested Butte Plain   OLD AMERICAN

At the Slogar, your only choices are the best skillet-fried chicken you've ever tasted or a 10-ounce rib-eye steak. Along with your entree, you'll receive relishes, tomato chutney, sweet-and-sour cole slaw, mashed potatoes, creamed corn, and baking-powder biscuits with honey butter. The servers even throw in some home-style ice cream. One of the owners says the staff needed three years to get the menu down, but for the past 14 years or so everything has run smoothly.

Corner of Second and Whiterock. ☎ 970-349-5765. Reservations recommended. Set meals $13.45 adults; $7.45 children 2–12. Open: June–Sept and Dec–mid-April daily for dinner. MC, V.

Soupçon

$$$ Crested Butte   FRENCH

Soupçon occupies a tiny 1916 Miner's Cabin, holds only 30 people, and has just two seatings nightly — at 6:00 and 8:15 p.m. The menu is about as small as the building: six starters and seven main courses, plus a few dessert choices scratched onto a chalkboard in the dining room. What's huge is the flavor. You'd be hard pressed to find more tender meats than the sashimi tuna, Hudson Valley foie gras, and double-cut grilled lamb chops. And the chef prepares them perfectly. Don't miss this restaurant.

127 Elk Ave. (in the alley behind Kochevar's bar). ☎ 970-349-5448. Reservations requested. Main courses: $19–$36. Open: June 1–Sept 30, Dec 1–mid-April daily for dinner. AE, MC, V.

Exploring Crested Butte, Gunnison, and Lake City

Most of the best things in this area are outside in the mountains, but there's also a lot of human history in each town. Even if you're not a mountain person, you'll find plenty to do.

The best things to see and do

When you're not in the wilderness surrounding the Gunnison Valley, you can

✔ **Visit a museum.** In summer 2003, the **Crested Butte Mountain Heritage Museum and Mountain Bike Hall of Fame** (☎ 970-349-1880) will open in its new, permanent location inside an old gas station at 331 Elk Ave. Supplementing the obligatory silver-mining exhibits are displays on more recent local industries such as coal mining and skiing. The Mountain Bike Hall of Fame has trend-setting mountain bikes and the racing jerseys, bikes, and bios of the sport's legends. A $2 donation is suggested; call for hours of operation. The smallish **Hinsdale County Museum,** 130 Silver St., in Lake City (☎ 970-944-2050), introduces visitors to the story of Alferd Packer, who was convicted of killing and cannibalizing five men near Lake San Cristobal in 1874. It's open from 10 a.m. to 5 p.m daily, Memorial Day through Labor Day. Admission is $2 adults, $1 children. And the **Gunnison Pioneer Museum,** on East Highway 50 in Gunnison (☎ 970-641-4530), has artifacts and memorabilia scattered through eight buildings, including a 1905 schoolhouse and an 1876 post office. A longstanding institution, this museum costs $7 for adults, $1 for children 6 to 12. It's open Memorial Day through mid-September, Monday through Saturday from 9 a.m. to 5 p.m. and Sundays noon to 4 p.m.

✔ **Spring a lake. Lake San Cristobal,** 3 miles north of Lake City, is dammed like most other "lakes" in Colorado — only in this case the dam is natural. About 700 years ago, a huge earthflow of partly decomposed volcanic rock slumped into the Lake Fork of the Gunnison River, stalling enough water to create the second largest natural body of water in Colorado (behind Lake George). Come here to camp, picnic, and savor the forested hills around still water. **Wupperman Campground** offers first-come, first-served camping (cost: $10 per car) on County Road 33 on the lake's southeast side. **Lakeview Resort** (☎ 800-456-0170 or 970-944-2401), also on County Road 33 on the lake's east side, rents fishing boats (cost: $45/half-day), pontoon boats ($80/half-day), and sea kayaks ($45/half-day). Personal watercraft (such as jet skis) are forbidden here, because the lake is very small.

✔ **Shop.** All three towns have lively shopping districts. Crested Butte is more artsy (think: matted, framed wilderness photographs).

Lake City is folksy (think: chainsaw art and quilted wall-hangings). Gunnison's downtown caters to college students, tourists, and cowboys alike (think: skateboards, T-shirts and sidearms).

✔ **Drive a Jeep.** Lake City is one of those places where people who don't mountain bike should rent a Jeep and spend a day bouncing up into the stratosphere. Leaving from the downtown, you can rumble over **12,800-foot Engineer Pass** to Ouray, meander up the San Juan Skyway (U.S. 550) to Silverton, and lurch your way back to Lake City via **12,600-foot Cimarron Pass.** Except for U.S. 550, these roads are part of the **Alpine Loop Backcountry Byway,** which travels 65 miles through the San Juan high country, passing ghost towns and mines but never departing breathtaking scenery. The **Lake City Chamber of Commerce Visitor Information Center** (☎ 800-569-1874 or 970-944-2527) on Silver Street has information on the loop, open most years from early summer to early October. **Pleasant View Resort,** 549 S. Gunnison Ave. in Lake City (☎ 970-944-2262), rents Jeeps for $95 per day (gas not included).

Staying active

The immense mountains around Crested Butte and Lake City naturally challenge visitors. This is the place to bike longer trails, ski steeper runs, and catch bigger fish than you ever have. Just don't stretch yourself too far when you're:

✔ **Boating and sailing:** Just west of Gunnison along U.S. 50, the Gunnison River has been dammed three times inside the **Curecanti National Recreation Area** (☎ 970-641-2337). If you like water sports, get off the highway near **Blue Mesa Reservoir,** the largest and most user-friendly of the three reservoirs — and, incidentally, the largest body of water in Colorado. Blue Mesa Reservoir stretches for 20 miles along the road and has three breezy main basins that are perfect for sailing and windsurfing. Marinas are located at **Elk Creek** (☎ 970-641-0707), along U.S. 50 midway between the reservoir's west and east ends; and at **Lake Fork** (☎ 970-641-3048), off U.S. 50 at the west end of the reservoir. The **visitor center** is also at Elk Creek. Before launching a motorboat or a Colorado State–registered boat, you'll need to pay $4 for a two-day user fee. As for swimming, it's the usual reservoir fare: cold water, rocky shores, and no beaches. The recreation area has numerous first-come, first-served campgrounds, with most sites costing $10.

✔ **Fishing:** Near Gunnison you can fish from a raft, rowboat, lakeshore, or streambed. In the **Curecanti National Recreation Area,** federal and state hatcheries stock over 3,000,000 fish every year. Along with brown trout, **Blue Mesa Reservoir** has Kokanee salmon and some immense lake trout. It's a good place for trolling. On the **Gunnison River,** you can spin-fish from a raft for some formidable trout. There's also premier fly-fishing in the **Gunnison, East,** and

Taylor rivers, among others. A one-day Colorado fishing license costs $5.25, a five-day license goes for $18.25. To find the best fly-fishing in this area or to get a fishing license, contact **High Mountain Outdoors,** 115 S. Wisconsin St., in Gunnison (☎ 800-793-4243 or 970-641-4243).

✔ **Golfing: The Club at Crested Butte,** 385 Country Club Dr. (☎ 800-628-5496 or 970-349-6131), is one of Colorado's top mountain courses. Greens fees for this 18-hole, Robert Trent Jones course range from $65 to $120, depending on the time of year and the time of day.

✔ **Hiking:** Waterfalls, flower-flecked alpine basins, and immense, craggy cirques surround the trails in the mountains above Crested Butte and Lake City. Some of these trails remain snow-covered until mid-summer. During peak snowmelt periods, they may require dangerous (or at least very cold) creek crossings. But what exciting places to get your feet wet! The visitor centers in all three towns can identify popular hikes. For topographical maps and updates on trail conditions, stop at the **Gunnison National Forest Gunnison Ranger District** office, 216 N. Colorado St. in Gunnison (☎ 970-641-0471). The office can tell you about eight wilderness areas, including ones near both Crested Butte and Lake City.

✔ **Mountain biking:** Like Durango, Crested Butte has some of the most acclaimed mountain biking in North America. Besides the quick and easy rides next to town, you can pedal on an extensive network of single track and forest roads high in the Elk Mountains.

One legendary ride, **The 401 Trail** via Gothic Road, has a long, snaking single track descent through hip-high vegetation and flowers — but first, you have to climb to Schofield pass. Before embarking on this 24-mile, advanced ride, stop at **The Alpineer,** 419 Sixth St. (☎ 970-349-5210), for a detailed trail description and, if needed, a rental bike. When it's too snowy to ride near Crested Butte, you can sometimes pedal on 40 miles of trails at **Hartsman's Rock,** near Gunnison. This arid area has a mixed bag of surfaces, including slickrock, sand, and some craggy, technical stretches. **Tomichi Cycles,** 104 N. Main St., in Gunnison (☎ 970-641-9069), can tell you more about it and rent you a bike.

Hitting the slopes

Crested Butte Mountain Resort sits on the flanks of Mount Crested Butte, an ominous, 12,162-foot shark's tooth that would look right at home in either of two Steven Spielberg movies (*Jaws* or *Close Encounters of the Third Kind*). The mountain appears no less forgiving up close. Its north side has some of the scariest lift-served terrain in the country, including steep glades, steeper chutes, and jagged cliffs. If you want to test your mettle in areas that require you to pass through gates, consult a ski patroller first or else sign up for one of the ski school's guided **North Face Tours** (cost: $20). The upshot for everyone else is that this terrain is safely removed from the rest of the runs. While experts tangle with the likes of **The Headwall, Banana Funnel,** and the **North Face,** beginners can tackle **Peanut** and **Yellow Brick Road.** Intermediates can glide down the long groomed slopes and forgiving mogul runs on the mountain's northwest side. Anyone who likes to ski or snowboard will have fun here, but, for talented riders, this is a special mountain. Check out Table 20-2 for more on the resort.

Table 20-2   Ski Report: Crested Butte Mountain Resort

Location: 3 miles north of Crested Butte, 30 miles north of Gunnison, 230 miles southwest of Denver
Trails: 85
14% beginner
32% intermediate
54% advanced/expert
Lift-served vertical: 2,787 feet
Base elevation: 9,375 feet
Uppermost lift: 12,162 feet
Skiable terrain: 1,058 acres
Average snowfall: 298 inches
Lifts: 14
Snow phone: ☎ 888-442-8883
Central reservations: ☎ 800-544-8448
Internet: www.crestedbutteresort.com
2002–2003 high-season adult all-day lift ticket: $58

Nightlife

Being a ski town, Crested Butte has a vigorous party scene during winter. Start your journey on Elk Avenue between Second and Third streets.

- ✔ **Crested Butte Brewery,** 226 Elk Ave. (☎ **970-349-5026**), serves handcrafted beers, including the award-winning Red Lady Ale.

- ✔ At **The Eldo,** 215 Elk Ave., (☎ **970-349-9958**), you can look out the windows while dancing to live music (a sure-fire way to please your date).

✔ Go to **The Last Steep,** 208 Elk Ave. (☎ **970-349-7007**), for late-night munchies.

✔ For more subdued socializing (not to mention single-malt scotches), head for **The Historic Princess Wine Bar (☎ 970-641-1491)** at 218 Elk Ave.

Fast Facts: Gunnison, Crested Butte, and Lake City

Hospitals

For 24-hour emergency care, go to Gunnison Valley Hospital (☎ 970-641-1456), 711 North Taylor in Gunnison. The Crested Butte Medical Center (☎ 970-349-0321) operates smaller clinics in Crested Butte, at the Ore Bucket Building ½ block north of the Visitors Center on Sixth Street, and in Mount Crested Butte, in the Axtel Building, at the base of the Silver Queen Chairlift.

Information

In Crested Butte, call or write the Crested Butte/Mount Crested Butte Chamber of Commerce, P.O. Box 1288, Crested Butte, CO 81224 (☎ 800-545-4505 or 970-349-6438; Internet: www.crestedbuttechamber.com). Or visit the Information Center at the corner of Sixth Street and Elk Avenue

or at the Town Center Bus Stop in Mount Crested Butte. In Gunnison, visit the Gunnison Country Chamber of Commerce, 500 E. Tomichi Ave. (☎ 800-274-7580 or 970-641-1501). The Lake City/Hinsdale County Chamber of Commerce Visitor Information Center, 800 S. Gunnison Ave. (☎ 800-569-1874 or 970-944-2527), can tell you about goings-on in that community.

Post Office

In Gunnison, the post office is at 200 N. Wisconsin (☎ 970-641-1884). In Crested Butte, go to 215 Elk Ave. (☎ 970-349-5568). And in Lake City, well, you can't miss it on North Highway 149 (☎ 970-944-2560).

Road Conditions

Call ☎ 877-315-7623.

Chapter 21

Southwest Colorado

• •

In This Chapter

▶ To-Hell-U-Ride no more: Telluride embraces families

▶ Digging archeology in Cortez

▶ Train-ing in Durango

▶ The sleepy San Juans: Silverton, Ridgway, and Ouray

• •

*I*f you could design a perfect landscape, you'd have a hard time topping Southwest Colorado, where the spiky, volcanic peaks of the San
Juan Mountains give way to the desert mesas of the Four Corners Area.
Thundering rivers drain the mountains of snow, careen downhill, and
then carve deep canyons into the colorful layers of sedimentary rock
in the desert.

Besides being scenic, Southwest Colorado has a rich human history,
too. Alpine towns such as Telluride and Silverton boomed with silver
mining in the 1880s and again with gold mining in the 1890s. Historic
mines still dot the hills around them. Not far away, 800-year-old cliff
dwellings left by once-thriving Ancestral Puebloan communities fill the
openings in canyon walls south of Cortez and Mancos. You can go to
this region to explore remnants of the past or forget the past and go
just for the recreation, excitement, and beauty.

Located where the mountains meet the mesas, Durango is the largest
and busiest town in the area, and it's central to both the mines of
Silverton and the pueblo dwellings of Mesa Verde. If you stay here, you
can take the historic Durango and Silverton Narrow Gauge Railroad one
day and tour multistory cliff dwellings the next. Telluride is less central, but it's one of the most stunning spots in North America. Though
trendier than it used to be, it still combines soothing surroundings with
an abundance of lodging, recreation, dining, and entertainment. Cortez,
Mancos, and Dolores are all down-to-earth communities where you can
stay for cheap while you get serious about exploring the world of the
Ancestral Puebloans. And if you want to stop exploring and soak your
weary muscles in hot springs, you should head for Pagosa Springs.

What's Where?: Southwest Colorado and Its Major Attractions

Don't let nicknames like Derange-O and To-Hell-U-Ride scare you away from Southwest Colorado. Though the mountains are still rugged, the towns have been more or less scrubbed clean for visitors.

Telluride

This 1880s mining town saw its fortunes rise again when Telluride Ski Area opened in 1972. The ski area attracted hippies who saw the beauty here and made the mistake of talking about it. Today the town is far wealthier than it was 20 years ago, but the residents still pride themselves on being relaxed and fun-loving. Make sure to check out the following while you're around:

- **Telluride Ski Resort,** a mogul-studded ski area that recently developed a family-friendly side.

- **Bridal Veil Falls,** 300-foot falls that form the headwaters of the San Miguel River, which flows right through town.

- **Downtown Telluride,** which offers great shops, restaurants, and bars.

Silverton, Ridgway, and Ouray

These three distinct mountain communities have a few things in common. They all have year-round populations under 800, and, nestled between craggy peaks and crossed by rivers, they're all stunning places with rich histories either as mining or rail towns. Their attractions include

- **Ouray County Historical Museum,** an old hospital where former patient rooms now house displays on the town's history.

- **Hikes around Ouray,** on forested hillsides with few roads.

- The **Old Hundred Gold Mine Tour,** near Silverton, worth visiting because much of the machinery still works.

Cortez, Dolores, and Mancos

The Ancestral Puebloans left behind thousands of dwellings and artifacts in this area during the years A.D. 300 to 1300. Today, people come here to explore the distant past, but the towns are fun, too. During your visit don't miss

Southwestern Colorado

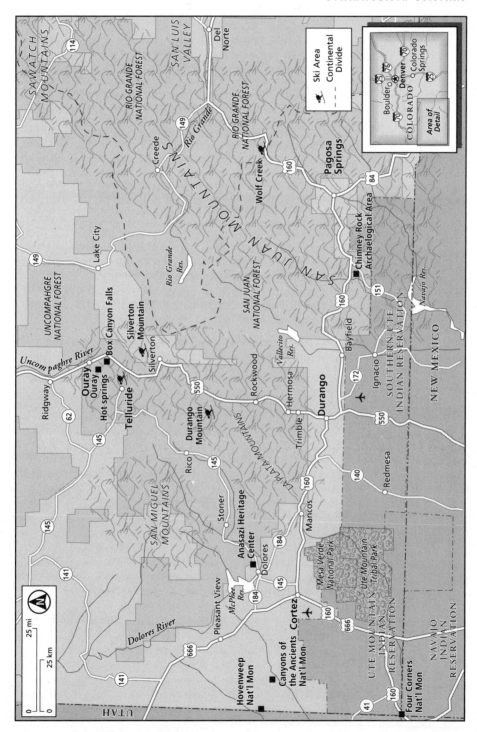

SAWATCH MOUNTAINS

114

RIO GRANDE NATIONAL FOREST

SAN LUIS VALLEY

Del Norte

149

Rio Grande

RIO GRANDE NATIONAL FOREST

Creede

SAN JUAN MOUNTAINS

Wolf Creek

160

Pagosa Springs

84

Ski Area   Continental Divide

Area of Detail

Boulder 76 Denver 70 Colorado Springs

25

COLORADO

70

25

Lake City

149

Rio Grande Res.

SAN JUAN NATIONAL FOREST

Chimney Rock Archaeological Area

151

Navajo Res.

UNCOMPAHGRE NATIONAL FOREST

Box Canyon Falls

Silverton Mountain

Silverton

Vallecito Res.

Bayfield

160

SOUTHERN UTE INDIAN RESERVATION

NEW MEXICO

Uncompahgre River

Ouray
Ouray
Hot springs

Telluride

Ridgway

62

550

Rockwood

Hermosa

Durango

172

Ignacio

145

Durango Mountain

Trimble

550

Rico

145

LA PLATA MOUNTAINS

Redmesa

SAN MIGUEL MOUNTAINS

Stoner

140

141

160

Mancos

145

Anasazi Heritage Center

184

Mesa Verde National Park

Ute Mountain Tribal Park

Dolores

Pleasant View

McPhee Res.

184

145

Cortez

160

666

UTE MOUNTAIN INDIAN RESERVATION

141

Dolores River

666

Canyons of the Ancients Nat'l Mon.

Hovenweep Nat'l Mon

160

Four Corners Nat'l Mon

41

NAVAJO INDIAN RESERVATION

UTAH

25 mi

25 km

0

0

- ✔ **Anasazi Heritage Center** and **Crow Canyon Archeological Center,** two great places to learn about the world of the Ancestral Puebloans.

- ✔ **Mesa Verde National Park,** the largest archeological preserve in the nation, packed with pit houses, mesa-top pueblos, *kivas* (circular, partly subterranean ceremonial chambers), and cliff dwellings.

- ✔ **Ute Mountain Ute Tribal Park,** where you can experience amazing cliff dwellings and archeological sites while traveling in small groups accompanied by Native American guides.

- ✔ **Nighttime programs at Cortez Cultural Center,** including Native American dancing, music, and even plays.

Durango

Built as a rail town to serve the mines in Silverton, Durango sits in a horseshoe-shaped gap in the foothills of the San Juans. Partly because it has a college, a popular railroad line, and abundant recreation, this city of 14,000 stays busy year-round. Highlights include

- ✔ **Durango and Silverton Narrow Gauge Railroad,** a historic rail line that chugs backward in time and upward in elevation.

- ✔ **The Strater Hotel,** where you can catch a show, have a meal or a cocktail, or simply admire the ornate woodwork.

- ✔ **Durango Mountain Resort,** that rare ski area that may be more fun in summer.

Telluride

Telluride locals often use the word *funky* to describe their town, and somehow it manages to live up to its billing, even though it's hard to be funky 24/7. This may be the only place where you can hear the reggae artist Burning Spear playing over the stereo inside the grocery store; where businesses have cheerful (if corny) names such as "Sunshine Pharmacy," "Baked in Telluride," and "The Magic Market"; and where dogs wander about town with little interference. Old mining shacks and sheds still clutter the town's muddy back alleys, remnants of the days when Telluride boomed with immigrants seeking silver.

Still, Telluride is more than just funky. Cradled in a glacier-carved box canyon with the San Miguel River at its heart, this is one of the most majestic places in North America. It's also remote. It's not exactly at earth's edge — commercial air service reaches the town's airstrip, as well as the airport at Montrose, 65 miles to the north — but it does take extra effort to get here, which helps keep it peaceful. If Telluride weren't so expensive, most of us would probably be living there right now, and the town wouldn't feel half as funky, majestic, remote, or peaceful anymore.

Getting there

Telluride is situated 4 miles down a 6-mile spur of Colorado 145. It's 73 miles northeast of Cortez on Colorado 145 and 68 miles south of Montrose. To reach Telluride from Montrose, follow U.S. 550 21 miles south to Ridgway, go south (right) for 25 miles on Colorado 62. In Placerville, go left on Colorado 145 and then continue for 17 miles to Telluride, bypassing a turnoff where Colorado 145 turns right (south) toward Cortez.

If you'd like to avoid the 335-mile drive from Denver, you can fly directly to **Telluride Regional Airport** (☎ 971-728-5313), 6 miles north of town, either from Phoenix (on America West Express) or Denver (on United Express). In winter, **Montrose Regional Airport** (☎ 970-249-3203) offers daily service to and from Dallas/Fort Worth (on American) and Houston (on Continental); frequent service to and from Denver (United Express) and Phoenix (America West Express); and Saturday-only service to and from Newark (Continental) and Chicago (American).

Budget and **National** have car-rental offices at Telluride Regional Airport. At Montrose Airport, you can choose between **Budget, Dollar, Thrifty,** and **National.** For information on contacting individual airlines and car-rental agencies, see the Appendix.

Telluride Express (☎ 888-212-TAXI or 970-728-6000) offers taxi service between Telluride and both airports. Rides to and from Telluride airport cost $8. Service to Montrose costs $32 per person between 7 a.m. and 7 p.m., and $50 per person other times.

Getting around

In Telluride, you'll want to travel on foot as much as possible, if only so you can see the mountains towering above you.

By car

Driving around town and just outside of town is pretty easy. You can't get lost; Telluride's tiny and surrounded by natural barriers. About 3 miles west of town, Highway 145 becomes Colorado Avenue, Telluride's main thoroughfare. Colorado Avenue travels east and west through the downtown. Most of the cross streets, which run north and south, are named for trees. Continuing east out of town on Colorado Avenue, you'll pass Town Park — site of numerous music festivals and, in winter, the Nordic center and ice rink. Two miles later you'll reach Bridal Veil Falls, at the head of the box canyon occupied by Telluride. Bridal Veil and other, threadlike falls become the headwaters of the San Miguel River, which curves along the base of Telluride Ski Resort and borders the north side of town.

By shuttle

During peak periods, parking costs 50¢ an hour on Colorado Avenue and the roads to its south. Look for a spot north of Colorado Avenue. Negotiating the downtown area on foot or by using the free **Galloping Goose** shuttles, which run every 20 minutes during summer and winter, is easier than driving everywhere. During summer, the shuttles only operate on weekdays. Call ☎ **970-728-5700** for 24-hour shuttle information.

A free gondola, which runs from 7 a.m. to midnight daily, links Telluride's downtown with the luxurious Mountain Village development. The gondola makes the trip between Telluride and Mountain Village faster than it is in a car. What's more, you can easily load your bike on it and get off at mid-mountain on the ski area, where some of the best trails are. (You can ride at low elevations even in winter, if there's a warm dry spell while you're visiting.) To reach Mountain Village by car, follow Colorado 145 for 1 mile south from the Telluride turnoff, then go left on Mountain Village Boulevard.

Where to stay

Staying in Telluride isn't cheap. You can choose between historic hotels that have lots of character and new hotels that have every imaginable luxury. What you won't find here are a lot of economical lodges that cater to tired skiers on a budget.

The top hotels

Hotel Telluride
$$$$ **Telluride**

Like many other new luxury hotels in Colorado ski towns, the Hotel Telluride has a turreted exterior reminiscent of a European castle, a faux-rustic Western lobby with antler lamps, a flagstone fireplace and leather sofas; and guest rooms that blend European and Western elements. Even if the formula isn't original, it works well here, mostly because the ownership has enough bucks to create some bang. The plush rooms, for example, feature feather bedding, down comforters, and monogrammed sheets on the beds, as well as Aveda spa products in the bathrooms. All rooms offer mountain views. If you want personal pampering, the hotel's full-service spa offers an array of deluxe treatments.

199 Cornet St., Telluride. ☎ 866-HOTEL-01 or 970-369-1188. Fax: 970-369-1292. Internet: www.thehoteltelluride.com. *Rack rates: Dec 1–April 15, $219–$329; Christmas week, Presidents week, and major festivals $429–$479; rest of year $179–$229. AE, DC, DISC, MC, V.*

The Ice House

$$$–$$$$ Telluride

This 1990 lodge feels snug and efficient like a dormitory, but its rooms are luxurious and its location is among the best in town. It's 100 yards from the Oak Street Ski Lift, 2 blocks from Telluride's lively Colorado Avenue, and flush on the bank of the San Miguel River. The rooms, which are decorated in a Southwestern motif, have private balconies. The deluxe rooms are roughly twice the size of the lodge rooms, and many have balconies right above the river. If you value space, they're probably worth the extra $30 to $50.

310 S. Fir St., Telluride. ☎ *800-544-3436 or 970-728-6300. Fax: 970-728-6358. Internet:* www.icehouselodge.com. *Rack rates: Lodge rooms Nov 27–Dec 20 and Jan 4–31, $195; Dec 21–Jan 3, $325; Feb 1–April 6, $225; summer $145; festivals $215–$285. Add $30–$50 for deluxe rooms. AE, DC, DISC, MC, V.*

New Sheridan Hotel

$$$ Telluride

Built in 1895 after the (old) Sheridan Hotel burned down, the (comparatively) New Sheridan combines the solidity of a bygone era with the comforts of modern living. The property has the façade of a classic Old West hotel, which recently served as the backdrop for an annoying Chevy truck commercial. Guest rooms boast Victorian furnishings and amenities such as bathrobes and teddy bears. Ask for a room with a view. The Sheridan also rents out pleasant two-bedroom condominium-style suites a few blocks away. A fine restaurant and a delightful historic bar are on the premises.

231 W. Colorado Ave., Telluride. ☎ *800-200-1891 (reservations only) or 970-728-4351. Fax: 970-728-5024. Internet:* www.newsheridan.com. *Rack rates: April 1–Dec 20 $90–220; Dec 21–Jan 1 $150–$400; Jan 2–March 31 $100–$275; during music and film festivals $150–$400. AE, DISC, MC, V.*

The Victorian Inn

$$–$$$ Telluride

The year 1976 is carved on the side of the Victorian Inn, as if the building were an architectural landmark that would endure for generations. Truth be told, this inn is still here because it's clean, well maintained, and, above all, among the cheapest in town. Your pocketbook will take a small hit if you stay here, but this is still Telluride's best option for travelers on a budget. For $10 extra, you can get a room with a kitchenette and do a little cooking on your own.

The Victorian's "Honeymoon Suite" is an extra-large room with superlative mountain views. If you're the first to ask for it, you'll get it for the same rate as for the other rooms.

401 W. Pacific Ave. ☎ *800-611-9893 or 970-728-6601. Fax: 970-728-3233. Internet:* www.tellurideinn.com. *Rack rates: Winter, $138; rest of year, $98. AE, DC, DISC, MC, V.*

Wyndham Peaks Resort and Golden Door Spa

$$$$$ **Telluride**

Gone are the days when bone-weary skiers gladly settled for a stein of beer, a few bites of summer sausage, and a bug-free bed. Completed in 1992, this six-story, ski-in, ski-out hotel has nearly everything a mortal could want — except maybe character. It has a 42,000-square-foot spa with 44 treatment rooms, a climbing wall, racquetball courts, swimming pools, a water slide, an immense exercise room, a golf course, two restaurants, and a spacious bar. Located in Telluride's tony Mountain Village community, the hotel, easily the largest in town, observes what it calls "seasonality." In mortal-speak, that means it's closed from mid-April to late May and again for a time in late fall.

136 Country Club Dr., Telluride. ☎ *970-728-6800 or 800-WYNDHAM (reservations only). Fax: 970-728-6175. Internet:* www.wyndham.com. *Rack rates: Low-season, $180–$280; high season, $250–$400. AE, DC, DISC, MC, V.*

Camping

If you're not averse to pitching a tent, you can camp in the **Town Park Campground** (☎ **970-728-2173**) from mid-May to mid-October. It's a scenic, wooded campground within easy walking distance of town. During music festivals, campsites are sold as part of festival packages, and the place can be noisy. The rest of the season, campsites are available on a first-come, first-served basis, at a cost of $12 per site, or $10 for primitive (meaning no nearby parking) sites. The campground has no hookups and can only accommodate vehicles under 30 feet long.

Where to dine

Telluride's food compares with the best on the coasts, probably because some of the best chefs from the coasts have fled to Telluride. Far from being cloistered, they return home periodically to check on the latest trends in the industry, and then bring back what they've learned.

Baked in Telluride

$ **Telluride   BAKERY**

During winter, dogs always seem to be fixating on the door of this 26-year-old Telluride landmark, a place that seems to bake nearly everything possible. Lined up in its glass display cases are bagels, donuts, pizzas, breakfast pastries, calzones, and puff pastries. As for the dogs, they fare best during summer, when the many outdoorsy patrons of Baked in

Telluride while away hours on the restaurant's deck, making calls on the pay phones and passing crusts to the canines. If you're only drinking coffee, you can deposit your money in an "honor box" on the counter — or not!

127 S. Fir St., Telluride. ☎ *970-728-4775. No reservations. Sandwiches $4.95–$6.95, medium pizzas $13.95–$19.95, pastas $5.95–$8.95. Open: Breakfast, lunch, and dinner daily. AE, DISC, MC, V.*

The Cosmopolitan
$$–$$$ **Telluride   AMERICAN**

Located in a sunny room right next to the gondola terminal in downtown Telluride, this is the place to splurge on a first-rate meal with friends. Chef Chad Scothern, who recently did a stint at the James Beard House in New York, keeps his prices lower than other establishments of this caliber, and the place stays full even during the off-season. Lately, Scothern has been tweaking traditional American favorites such as roast duck and pork roast and getting great results. To cap off your meal, try one of the restaurant's homemade sorbets and ice creams.

300 W. San Juan Ave., Telluride. ☎ *970-728-1292. Reservations recommended. Main courses: spring and fall, $15; ski season and summer, $19–$28. Open: Dinner daily. Closed mid-April–Memorial Day and for one week in November. AE, MC, V.*

Fat Alley
$ **Telluride   BARBEQUE**

"Bourbon, beer, and barbeque" is the motto of this casual eatery, which lacks table service but dishes up hearty, inexpensive fare that makes it a favorite among locals. Its staples are meaty Southern dishes such as barbeque ribs, fried chicken, and chicken fried steak, but the restaurant also throws a few non-bones to vegetarians, including a tasty ziti-and-black-bean plate. Side dishes, ordered à la carte, include fried okra; red beans and rice; and sweet potato fries. For your beverage, you're free to order a top-shelf bourbon and take it back to your picnic bench, but if pure trailer-park chic is your goal, throw down $1 for a can of Schlitz.

122 South Oak St. (below Elk's Park), Telluride. ☎ *970-728-3985. No reservations. Main courses: $5.95–$15.95. Open: Lunch and dinner daily. AE, MC, V.*

La Cocina de Luz
$ **Telluride   MEXICAN**

If you don't get to this tiny restaurant before the locals do, they'll take all five tables and linger all night over the fresh — and, by Telluride standards, cheap — fare. If you can't get the other customers to go, get the food to go instead. The restaurant's owner, Lucas Price, does everything possible to support local farmers and to acquire recently harvested ingredients, and the staff rolls tortillas and roasts chiles daily. The freshness permeates a menu that includes *posole* (traditional hominy stew in roasted tomato, guajillo chile broth, with chicken beef or veggies) and garlic roasted veggie burritos. If you want beer or wine, stop at the liquor store next door and bring your own.

123 Colorado St. (behind Telluride Liquors), Telluride. ☎ 970-728-9355. No reservations. Main courses: $4.75–$9. Open: Breakfast, lunch, and dinner Mon–Sat. MC, V.

Rustico Ristorante
$$–$$$ **Telluride** **ITALIAN**

Brush up on your Italian before visiting this restaurant, because it's the real deal. The owners are from the northern Italian town of Bormio, and some of the servers hail from the boot (as well as other far-flung locales). You'll need to utter a word or two of Italian just to order. Your options include pizzas, zuppas, insalatas, and rizotte. Even if you can't pronounce all the words, you'll be glad you tried, especially if you wash down this fare with any of the 300 Italian wines available here.

114 E. Colorado Ave., Telluride. ☎ 970-728-4046. Reservations recommended. Main courses: $13–$35. Open: Summer lunch and dinner daily; rest of year lunch Mon–Tues and Thurs–Fri, dinner daily. MC, V.

Exploring Telluride

If you want to do Telluride like a local on his or her day off, you should party late, sleep in, exhaust yourself on the slopes or trails, seriously relax for a few hours, and then do it all over again. Below are a few things you may want to pencil into your schedule.

The best things to see and do

When you get up in the morning and start moving around, you can

- ✔ **Find out about the guy who cut out his own appendix.** The **Telluride Historical Museum,** 201 W. Gregory Ave. (☎ 970-728-3344), was the town's hospital from 1888 to 1964. The best exhibits at this newly renovated museum link Telluride's history to the building's past as a hospital. There are displays on mining accidents, causes of death among miners (mostly lung disease and accidents), and the building's onetime claim to fame — the doctor who anesthetized himself and then removed his own, perfectly healthy appendix. It's open Tuesday through Saturday from noon to 5 p.m. and is closed from mid-April through mid-May. Admission is $5 for adults, $3 children ages 5 to 17 and seniors over 64.

- ✔ **Walk the historic downtown.** Telluride may look a little more spiffy than neighboring towns, but its history is just as, uh,

unusual. Telluride's *Official Visitor's Guide,* available throughout
town, outlines a 14-stop historic walking tour and explains each
stop along the way. If you want to hear an audio narration, you
can rent a tape and headphones for $7 at the historical museum.
During summer, the museum can also arrange 90-minute guided
group walking tours, for which a minimum of $40 total is charged.

✔ **Visit Bridal Veil Falls.** To reach the general area of this 300-foot
falls, continue east out of town on Colorado Avenue and keep
going for 1.2 miles past where the pavement ends. A Jeep road
goes to the top of the falls. If you have four-wheel-drive and high
clearance, you can drive to the top, but there's little room to
maneuver or park after you're up there. You're better off parking
at the bottom and walking the mile or so to the top. If you're walking or pedaling, you can pass the power plant building at the top
of the falls and go into the high-alpine **Bridal Veil Basin,** which is a
great place to see wildflowers during summer.

✔ **Skate around.** Telluride has a free skateboard ramp in Town Park,
open daily from 10 a.m. to 10 p.m. If your kids don't skate and
need a place to hang out, they can go to the **Telluride Youth
Center,** 233 E. Pacific St. (☎ 970-728-0140), which has a basketball court, games, a big screen TV, and a VCR.

Staying active

No matter what your sport, you can probably do it in Telluride's **Town
Park** (☎ 970-728-3711), along the San Miguel River at the east end of
town. There's a skate park, swimming pool, tennis courts, volleyball
courts, and a softball diamond, not to mention a campground. In winter,
you can ice skate or Nordic ski here.

Here is a small selection of the many other options you can choose
from:

✔ **Climbing:** Just a short drive (or walk) east of Telluride, is Falls
Walls, home to more than 100 climbable pitches. You can also
boulder along Bear Creek. The staff at **Telluride Mountaineer,** 219
E. Colorado Ave. (☎ 970-728-6736), can equip you for climbing,
mountaineering, and backpacking. If you'd feel more comfortable
climbing with a guide, call **Fantasy Ridge Alpinism** (☎ 970-728-
3546).

✔ **Fishing:** Kids under 12 can fish for free, without a permit, all summer long at the **Kid's Fishin' Pond** at Town Park. Everyone else
has to find a spot on the San Miguel or on one of a half dozen or so
nearby alpine lakes. For advice and Colorado fishing licenses, call
or visit **Telluride Outside and Telluride Angler,** 121 W. Colorado
Ave. (☎ 970-728-3895).

✔ **Golf:** Located at the Wyndham Peaks Resort in the Mountain
Village community, **Telluride Golf Club** (☎ 970-728-3458) opens

its 18-hole, par-71 course soon after the snow melts. Greens fees are $145 July through Labor Day; $125 the rest of the season.

✔ **Hiking:** Hiking trails go into the mountains all around Telluride. The free *Official Visitors Guide,* available throughout town, has information on 15 area trails. If you're looking for one that's rewarding and easy to find, walk to the end of South Pine Street, cross the bridge, and walk 2 miles up the **Bear Creek Canyon Trail.** This easy-to-follow trail ascends 1,040 vertical feet to its terminus at a waterfall. If you want to keep going, you can pick up the more challenging **Wasatch Trail** just below the falls.

✔ **Mountain biking:** The mountain biking around Telluride ranges from gradual, wide railroad grades to white-knuckle single track. Beginners often pick up the **San Miguel River Trail** near Town Park and follow it west for 2½ miles. More advanced riders load their bikes onto the free gondola, unload at Station St. Sophia, and then ride trails beginning at mid-mountain at the Telluride Ski Area. For information, maps, and rentals, contact **Telluride Sports,** 150 W. Colorado Ave. (☎ **970-728-4477**).

✔ **Nordic skiing:** The **Telluride Nordic Center** (☎ **970-728-1144**), located at the east end of Town Park, has 3 kilometers of groomed cross-country trails. There's no charge for using the track, and rentals are available. There are also six groomed kilometers on the golf course at Mountain Village, as well as a number of other great places a short drive from town.

Hitting the slopes

In 2002, **Telluride Ski Resort** added three new chairlifts, virtually doubling the amount of lift-served terrain within the ski area, to 1,700 acres. Suddenly what had been a mogul-studded, mid-sized mountain had much more to offer. The mountain now has beginner terrain spanning much of its 3,535 vertical feet. It has several new intermediate runs to supplement the likes of See Forever, which meanders 3.1 miles from summit to base. And it has some exciting new steep terrain around the new Gold Hill chairlift. Telluride still deserves its reputation for being challenging; the mountain's south side, which plummets into the downtown area, continues to sprout Humvee-sized moguls during dry spells. But the resort's new Gorrono Basin area will please skiers for whom bumps are a jarring experience.

The "new" Telluride also prides itself on its family-friendly services. Telluride ski instructors will videotape and critique your skiing for free. Its mountain hosts provide free tours daily. And if your kids have questions about Telluride, they can go straight to a Web site for kids: www. telluridekids.com. Best of all, Telluride almost never has lift lines. For more on the resort, see Table 21-1.

Table 21-1	Ski Report: Telluride Ski Resort

Location: 65 miles south of Montrose; 125 miles north of Durango; 335 miles southwest of Denver; 45 miles from the nearest stop light

Trails: 85

	22% beginner
	38% intermediate
	40% advanced/expert

Vertical drop: 3,535 feet

Base elevation: 8,725 feet

Summit elevation: 12,260 feet

Skiable terrain: 1,700 acres

Average snowfall: 309 inches

Lifts: 15 (includes 2 gondolas)

Snow phone: ☎ 970-728-7425

Telluride Central Reservations: ☎ 866-287-5016

Internet: www.telluride-ski.com; www.telluridekids.com

2002–2003 high-season adult all-day lift ticket: $65

Nightlife

Telluride may be a puny little town but it can easily out-party the flashiest big city. Here are a few options for Telluride nightlife:

✔ When I first visited the **Last Dollar Saloon,** 100 E. Colorado Ave. (☎ **970-728-4800**), a dozen or so women started dancing on the bartop, including one who was dangerously close to my beer. Concerned friends had warned me about Telluride's vigorous nightlife, but the display still surprised me. It surprised me even more when someone took one of my dollars off the bartop and stuffed it into the blue jeans pocket of a dancer (as if I needed help). The women turned out to be the Telluride women's hockey team out for their season-ending party. I learned that because this bar is popular with locals, and because the locals are a festive sort, this type of spectacle can happen anytime at "The Buck," as the bar is known around town. If you don't feel like dancing on the bar, you can play pool and throw darts. As for decor, you'll find everything from a stuffed, hanging catfish to a Dollar Rent-A-Car sign.

✔ Please don't dance on the counter at **Allred's** (☎ **970-728-7474**), a posh bar and restaurant perched inside the 10,535-foot-high Gondola Station Saint Sophia, but go here anyway to absorb the views from the restaurant nearly straight down 1,800 vertical feet into Telluride.

Even if you can't afford dinner here (the food is delicious — and *pricey*), order a beverage at sunset and watch the alpenglow illuminate the surrounding peaks. You can ride the gondola to the restaurant for free between 7 a.m. and 11 p.m. A private club at lunchtime, the restaurant opens to the public for après-ski (beginning at 3:30 p.m.) and stays open for dinner.

✔ The **New Sheridan Bar,** 231 W. Colorado Ave. (☎ **970-728-3911**), has changed little since opening in 1885. It still boasts a large mahogany bar, chandeliers, and room dividers with lead-glass panels, all of which date back to the days when miners cut loose at the bar. It's also a friendly place, popular with both tourists and locals.

✔ For live music, the hotspot is the **Fly Me to the Moon Saloon,** 132 E. Colorado Ave. (☎ **970-728-6666**). Pick any musician who can pick a guitar, mandolin, or banjo, and they've probably played here.

Festivals

Telluride hosts music, art, and film festivals of world renown. The music festivals are held primarily in Town Park. The best known one is the Folk and Bluegrass Festival. Held in mid-June, it draws some of the world's top pickers as well as singer/songwriters who play acoustic music. Call ☎ **800-624-2422** for details. Other notable festivals include MountainFilm, which screens films celebrating mountain life and environmental issues (call ☎ **970-728-4123** for tickets and information); Brews and Blues; Jazz; and the Telluride Film Festival, showcasing mostly independent films. For more on upcoming festivals, surf the Internet to www.visittelluride.com.

Fast Facts: Telluride

Emergency

Dial ☎ **911.**

Hospital

Telluride Medical Center (☎ 970-728-3848), 500 Pacific Ave., provides 24-hour emergency care.

Information

The Telluride and Mountain Village Visitor Information Center

(☎ 970-728-3041) is located at 600 W. Colorado Ave.

Pharmacy

Sunshine Pharmacy (☎ 970-728-3601), 236 W. Colorado Ave, can fill your prescriptions.

Post Office

The Telluride post office (☎ 970-728-3900) is at 150 S. Willow St.

Ridgway, Ouray, and Silverton

This is my favorite part of the state: three tiny towns, each with year-round populations under 800, surrounded by jagged mountains. The most remote of these towns, Silverton still has a respectable business district of false-fronted stone and wood buildings, as well as the notorious Blair Street, where warped wooden shacks date back to its days as the town's red-light district. Around it are 13,000-foot peaks streaked with avalanche paths and littered with mine debris. For a few hours every day from May through October, the Durango and Silverton Narrow Gauge Railroad deposits hundreds of oxygen-deprived tourists in this 9,318-foot-high town, but when they're gone, Silverton seems to absorb silence from the surrounding forests.

Ouray fittingly bills itself as the Switzerland of America — it's pinched between cliffs nearly as foreboding as those found in places like Chamonix. Ice climbers love the town's frozen waterfalls, both man-made and natural. Come evening, they thaw themselves in the town's geothermal hot springs, which bubble out of the earth mere yards from the Uncompahgre River.

In Ridgway, the mountains draw back and reveal a lush (during summer) valley floor, home to some of the most expensive ranches in the country. The town has its own hot springs and an ultra-mellow population that seems to have just finished soaking.

Getting there

Ouray, Ridgway, and Silverton are strung along **U.S. 550,** which links Durango and Montrose. Silverton, 47 miles north of Durango on U.S. 550, is the farthest south and most remote of the three. Ouray is a harrowing 26-mile drive north of Silverton, via the 11,008-foot-high Red Mountain Pass on a stretch of Highway 550 known as The Million Dollar Highway (it was once used to move lots of precious minerals out of Silverton). Ridgway is a comparatively quick 11-mile jaunt north of Ouray. Ridgway is 26 miles south of Montrose and 86 miles southeast of Grand Junction.

During winter, **Montrose Regional Airport** (☎ 970-249-3203), has daily service to and from Dallas/Fort Worth (on American) and Houston (on Continental), frequent service to and from Denver (United Express) and Phoenix (on America West Express), and Saturday-only service to and from Newark (Continental). Upon landing, you can rent a car at Montrose Airport from **Budget, Dollar, Thrifty,** and **National.**

America West Airlines, American Airlines (winter only), **Continental,** and **United Express** all serve **Durango/La Plata County Airport** (☎ 970-247-8143), 14 miles southeast of Durango on Colorado 172. There, you can rent cars through **Hertz, Avis, National, Budget,** and

Dollar. For information on contacting individual airlines and car-rental agencies, see the Appendix.

During spring, summer, and fall, you can also reach Silverton on the **Durango and Silverton Narrow Gauge Railroad (☎ 970-247-2733;** Internet: www.durangotrain.com). For more on the railroad, skip ahead to my review of it later in this chapter.

Getting around

All three of these towns are tiny, so you shouldn't have much trouble getting around. Just park your car in the business district (there is free on-street parking) and start walking. In Ridgway, U.S. 550 passes near the east end of town. Most of the town's businesses are on Colorado 62 a few blocks west of U.S. 550. In Ouray, U.S. 550 becomes Main Street and passes right through the heart of town. To locate Silverton's main drag, take Colorado 110 east from U.S. 550. Colorado 110 immediately becomes Greene Street, which is Silverton's main road.

Where to stay

These towns are fun places to sleep. Ouray and Silverton have historic hotels and bed-and-breakfasts in a variety of price ranges. Some have every conceivable luxury; at the other extreme is one hotel whose staff names "running water" as an amenity. Options are fewer in Ridgway, but the town does have an airy, luxurious lodge. Here are some good choices.

Box Canyon Lodge
$–$$ **Ouray**

Hot sulfur-free springs feed four private tubs on the hills above this lodge, where you can soak until you keel. What's more, the guest rooms are clean and comfy. The lodge's management cautions that their place is "not suitable for noisy, shouting adults or children," but you can still have fun. The Ouray Ice Park, Box Canyon Falls, and trailheads for great hikes are all within walking distance, and Ouray's main drag is only a block or so away.

45 Third Ave., Ouray. ☎ *800-327-5080 or 970-325-4981. Fax: 970-325-0223. Internet:* www.boxcanyonouray.com. *Rack rates: Low-season, $65; mid-season, $75; high-season, $100. AE, DISC, MC, V.*

Chipeta Sun Lodge and Spa
$$$ **Ridgway**

This pueblo-style lodge in a stubbly field at the edge of Ridgway lets you dabble in New Age enlightenment without feeling, well, unenlightened.

Inside, it has lots of windows, potted trees, splashing fountains, and panoramic views of the Uncompahgre Valley and Cimarron Mountains. If you want the room with the largest view, go for Canyon de Chelly, a nearly circular room with 270 degrees worth of glass. The room also has peeled log beams, a bed on a sandstone pedestal, hand-painted sinks, and a private deck. You can get healthy here by using the spa, exercise room, lap pool, and hot tub. The staff is around, but mellow and unobtrusive. Rates include a hearty buffet breakfast.

304 S. Lena, Ridgway. ☎ *800-633-5868 or 970-626-3737. Fax: 970-626-3715. Internet:* www.chipeta.com. *Rack rates: Lodge rooms $95–$145; suites and deluxe rooms $135–$215. Rates include buffet breakfast. DISC, MC, V.*

The Historic Western Hotel
$ **Ouray**

Some Victorian hotels just don't seem all that Victorian. Maybe it's the large-screen TV in your room, or the jetted hot tub, or the steam shower. Well, you won't have any doubts about the authenticity of the 1891 Historic Western, that rare Victorian hotel with historic *plumbing,* few modern amenities, and a traditional floor plan. Fourteen guest rooms are in snug miners' quarters with shared baths down the hall. The floors creak; the doors catch on the doorjambs, and at least one room has its original wallpaper. It feels as if the miners may arrive any minute. Historic Western does have two suites with private baths, but even these aren't what you'd expect. In one, the clawfoot bathtub sits in the middle of the room, mere feet from the bed. I love this place.

210 Seventh Ave., Ouray. ☎ *888-624-8403 or 970-325-4645. Internet:* www.ouray colorado.com-histwest.html. *Rack rates: Standard rooms $30–$45, suites $70–$85. DISC, MC, V.*

Riverside Inn and Cabins
$ **Ouray**

This motel is popular with climbers spending time in Ouray. One look at the rooms and you'll know that climbers aren't slumming as much as they used to. Accommodations are decorated in rich earth tones and downright luxurious, with large TVs, peeled log furniture, and, best of all, the soothing whitewater thrum of the Uncompahgre River. If you still want to rough it, you can rent a riverside cabin with a double bed and two bunk beds (but no linens or private toilet) on a nightly, weekly, or monthly basis. The two owners can tell you about the boating, fishing, skiing, and climbing in the area.

1805 N. Main St., Ouray. ☎ *800-432-4170 or 970-325-4061. Fax: 970-325-7302. Internet:* www.ourayriversideinn.com. *Rack rates: Cabins $30–$50, rooms $50–$100, suites $65–$160. Rates include gourmet coffee. Minimum stay usually required during holidays. AE, DISC, MC, V.*

St. Elmo Hotel

$$ **Ouray**

This 1898 hotel has sumptuous suite rooms, red carpeting, Victorian-replica wallpaper, perfect antiques, and a sunny breakfast area. It's all a little too perfect for me, but you may like it. Right now this is the most luxurious historic hotel in Ouray. However, the Beaumont Hotel, once the town's jewel, will soon reopen after being shuttered for years so the St. Elmo may lose its place in the pecking order.

426 Main St., Ouray. ☎ *970-325-4951. Fax 970-325-0348. Internet:* www.stelmo hotel.com. *Rack rates: $85–$125. No guests under 10 years old. AE, DC, DISC, MC, V.*

Villa Dallavalle Inn

$–$$ **Silverton**

The Dallavalle/Swanson family has owned this building for over 100 years, and the inn reflects their long history in Silverton. Seven cozy and comfortable rooms are crammed with photos and heirlooms. A narrow upstairs hallway is further constricted by trunks, sculptures, bookcases, and display cases full of memorabilia — not to mention plastic flowers. The innkeepers seem to have set aside a special little corner for everything, including the guests.

1257 Blair St., Silverton. ☎ *970-387-5555. Fax: 970-387-5965. Internet:* www.villa dallavalle.com. *Rack rates: May 25–Oct 14, $80–$90 double; rest of year, $65 double. Summer rates include breakfast. AE, DISC, MC, V.*

The Wyman Hotel and Inn

$$ **Silverton**

This luxurious 1902 B&B is best known for its "Elevator Room." Inside it, a two-person whirlpool tub has been nestled into the framework of the building's old elevator. (No, you can't go up and down while you soak.) There's also a lavishly decorated guest room inside a caboose next to the hotel. Even if you can't reserve the elevator or the caboose, you can still enjoy the European antiques, mountain views, and a staircase wide enough to accommodate turn-of-the-century ball-goers. Rooms range in size from cozy to cavernous, the largest being a three-room suite that sleeps six comfortably.

1371 Greene St., Silverton. ☎ *800-609-7845 or 970-387-5372. Fax: 970-387-5745. Internet:* www.thewymancom. *Rack rates: Standard rooms, $100–$120; suites $145–$175. Rates include breakfast. AE, DISC, MC, V.*

Where to dine

Of the three towns, Ouray has the best food and the most variety, with a half-dozen or so quality restaurants scattered along Main Street. The options are fewer in Silverton and Ridgway, but you can still find a hearty meal at a reasonable price.

Bon Ton Restaurant
$$ **Ouray   ITALIAN**

Because Bon Ton stays open during winter, its food and service are more consistent than at other area eateries. In this case, consistency is a plus. Located in a rathskeller-style basement, this restaurant dishes up rich Italian fare such as chicken Parmesan and veal Piccata. It also boasts one of the largest wine lists in southwest Colorado.

426 Main St. ☎ *970-325-4951. Reservations recommended. Main courses: $9.50–$25. Open: June–Oct dinner daily and Sunday Brunch. Closed Tues–Wed Nov–May. AE, DISC, MC, V.*

Buen Tiempo Restaurant
$–$$ **Ouray   MEXICAN**

Buen Tiempo charges muchos pesos for burritos, tacos, fajitas and the like, but at least the food is fresh and zippy. You'll dine in a high-ceilinged room that's divided by booths, on the sides of which are colorful carvings of cacti. Once seated, you can crane your neck to see what may be the world's highest television screen. Give your server a dollar bill to stick on the ceiling. It's a stunt worth seeing, and your buck will eventually be taken down and donated to charity.

515 Main St., Ouray. ☎ *970-325-4544. No reservations. Main courses: $9.50–$15.50. Open: Dinner daily. AE, DISC, MC, V.*

Coachlight Restaurant and Tavern
$$ **Ouray   AMERICAN**

Come to the Coachlight when you want a big steak, fish, or chicken dinner with all the fixings, served by a low-key staff. Every dinner comes with salad or soup, choice of potato or wild rice, and fresh brown bread. The most popular dish is the Miner's Filet, a lean steak that's been served here since the 1960s. The dining room has stained-glass windows from a condemned church and some of the most striking historic photos in town. There's also an upstairs tavern with a large deck.

118 W. Seventh Ave., Ouray. ☎ *970-325-4361. Reservations accepted. Main courses: $8–$26. Open: May–Oct dinner daily. AE, DISC, MC, V.*

Drakes Restaurant

$$ **Ridgway** **ECLECTIC**

This is the place to dine in Ridgway. The owner and chef, whose name happens to be Drake, doesn't limit himself in his cooking any more than he does in his decorations, which range from the fanciful drawings by Ralph Steadman to traditional Western paintings of cowboys. Along with straightforward steak and fish dishes, Drakes offers entrees inspired by Cajun, Greek, Italian, Thai, and Indian cuisine. The restaurant gets lots of sun and has two decks, so you won't feel shut in.

220 S. Lena, Ridgway. ☎ 970-626-3113. Reservations accepted. Main courses $13–$22. Open: Tues–Sat dinner. Closed Nov and late May. AE, DISC, MC, V.

The Pickle Barrel

$–$$ **Silverton** **AMERICAN**

Passengers on the Durango and Silverton Railway flock here at lunchtime when they get off the train. Once inside, they have to let their eyes adjust before they can make out see the dark stone walls, hardwood floors, and six-stool backroom bar that has surely witnessed volumes of history. The lunch menu is geared for people who have a train to catch: sandwiches, burgers, and salads. You can still get sandwiches and burgers at dinner, as well as heartier entrees such as top sirloin steak and a black bean burrito with beans, rice, and chicken.

1304 Greene St., Silverton. ☎ 970-387-5713. Reservations accepted. Main courses: $7–$15. Open: Mid-May–mid-Oct lunch daily; summer Thurs–Mon dinner. AE, DISC, MC, V.

Trail's End Public House

$–$$ **Silverton** **ECLECTIC**

Trail's End looks like a barroom, but the food tastes nothing like bar fare. The chef churns out rich, heart-warming entrees such as Jamaican jerk-seared chicken and bacon-wrapped salmon as easily as other bars hand out potato chips. If you just want an appetizer, you won't be disappointed. Among the selections are cheddar-potato-stuffed Anaheim chili rellenos, sweet potato fries, Creole wings, and, yes, pretzels.

1323 Greene St., Silverton. ☎ 970-387-5117. Reservations not accepted. Main courses: $9–$18. Open: Lunch and dinner daily. Closed Nov–April. DISC, MC, V.

Exploring Ouray, Silverton, and Ridgway

In these towns, make sure to immerse yourself in their history — and hot springs. After spending a few hours visiting the mines and museums, unwind in the geothermal springs in Ridgway or Ouray.

The best things to see and do

Old Hundred Gold Mine Tour

The Old Hundred didn't produce many precious minerals, but today it's one of the best mine tours in the state. The mine operated from 1967 to 1972 without turning a profit. Because it's newer than most other area mines, the guides here can fire up and demonstrate fully operational equipment, such as pneumatic drills, slushers, and mucking machines. It's really loud. While learning about mining techniques, you can look around at the tunnels, drifts, and rises, as well as veins of mineral-bearing white quartz. Each tour, or "shift," rides a narrow gauge train into the mountainside and spends about 40 minutes underground, in air that's around 48 degrees. Dress warmly!

Five miles northeast of Silverton on County Road 4-A. ☎ *800-872-3009 or 970-387-5444. Internet:* www.minetour.com. *Tours depart on the hour from 10 a.m.–4 p.m., May 10–Oct 13. Cost: $13.95 adults, $6.95 kids ages 5–12, $12.95 seniors 60 and over.*

Orvis Hot Springs

After paying your $10 entrance fee and showering at Orvis Hot Springs, you don your towel ($1 if rented) and walk a few yards to a 103-degree outdoor pond that's 4 feet deep and about 40 feet across. Once there, you can lose that towel and your worries, too. Wearing a bathing suit here is a little like sporting a tux at Woodstock. Besides, your shape is no worse than the other whales in the pod. Later, you can relax in an indoor tub, broil in the small outdoor pool known as the "lobster pot" (temperature: about 110 degrees), or unwind further with a massage.

You can camp at Orvis for $20 per person, or check into one of six guest rooms available for $75 each (the cost includes soaking for two for two days). The rooms are spare but comfortable, and they share a bath. In each room, you'll find a queen-size bed, a water tank, and plenty of towels, which should remind you where you're supposed to be spending your time.

On U.S. 550, 1½ miles south of Highway 62. ☎ *970-626-5324. Open: Daily 9 a.m.–10 p.m. Soaking cost: $10 per person, $5 for kids 4–12.*

Ouray County Museum

Rooms that once housed patients in an 1886 hospital now serve as windows into Ouray's past. From the looks of the place, Ouray not only had a lot of sick and injured people at one time, it also had a lot going on. Today the museum has an old jail cell, a simulated mine, an assay office, a mineral room (illuminated by fluorescent lights), a hospital kitchen, a railroad room, an antique dentist's office, and a huge collection of vintage toys, to name just a few exhibits. Even the hallways brim with memorabilia from Ouray's past, including captivating photographs from the town's mining heyday. If you only go to one county museum in the course of your travels, make it this one.

420 Sixth Ave., Ouray. ☎ *970-325-4075. Summer hours: Daily 10 a.m. to noon, 2–6 p.m. Call for hours, rest of year. Admission: $4 adults, $1 kids ages 6–12.*

Ouray Hot Springs Pool

The Ouray Hots Springs Pool holds more than a million gallons of geothermally heated, but non-sulfuric, water. A lot of those gallons are in a lap pool and a deep area with a diving board. The swimming areas are usually heated to the 80-degree range, but there are other, hotter sections where you can sit back and poach yourself, including one that runs 102 to 106 degrees. For an extra $2.50, you can also use the cardiovascular machines and free weights in the fitness center.

Located on the west side of U.S. 550 at the north end of Ouray. ☎ *970-325-4638. Open: June–Aug daily 10 a.m.–10 p.m; rest of year daily noon to 9 p.m. Admission: $7.50 adults, $6 seniors 65 and over, $5 students 7–17, and $3 children 3–6.*

Other things to see and do

If you start getting water-logged, you can dry off and:

- ✔ **Go for a walking tour of Silverton or Ouray.** Both these towns have dozens of unspoiled turn-of-the-century Victorian buildings. Ouray's *Visitor's Guide,* available at the visitor center next to the Ouray Hot Springs Pool, maps out a 20-stop walking tour centered around Main Street between Fourth and Eighth avenues. Silverton's walking tour is described in *Silverton Magazine,* available at the visitor center and in businesses around town. There are about 50 stops on the tour, each described in detail that falls just short of providing actual family trees.

- ✔ **Visit Ridgway State Park and Reservoir.** Ridgway State Park and Reservoir (☎ 970-626-5822) has a 1,000-acre lake, a sandy beach, two campgrounds (☎ 800-678-CAMP or 303-470-1144; Internet: www.coloradoparks.org), a marina, picnic areas, a playground, 14 miles of hiking trails, and a visitor center. Camping costs $10 for tent sites, $16 for electric hook-ups. It's located 2 miles north of Ridgway on S.R. 550. A vehicle day-use pass is $5. Campgrounds and facilities are open May through October.

- ✔ **Check out the San Juan County Museum.** The museum (☎ 970-387-5838) in Silverton isn't as absorbing as the museum in Ouray, but it does occupy an old jail, so you can wander the cells and mug for photos. The museum displays Derringer guns, minerals, and old mining equipment, among other items. It's behind the San Juan County Courthouse, at the corner of 15th and Greene streets. The museum is open from 9 a.m to 5.p.m. daily from Memorial Day through mid-September, 10 a.m. to 3 p.m. daily through mid-October. Admission is $2.50 for adults, free for children 12 and under.

✔ **Watch water fall.** It's hard to justify paying to see a waterfall when so many nearby waterfalls are free. But the **Box Canyon Falls Park** (☎ 970-325-4500), located on Oak Street above Third Avenue at the southwest corner of Ouray, is convenient to town and has two hiking trails near a powerful falls, so it may be worth the price. Plan on hiking both trails if you come here. One trail is a 500-foot-long route that crosses ledges dynamited into quartzite walls and goes straight to the falls, which thunder through a slot in a rock wall. The other, less crowded trail climbs 175 rocky feet over the course of ¼ mile (one-way) to a bridge that crosses the canyon directly above the falls. It's open from May to mid-October, from 8 a.m. to dusk. Admission is $2.50 adults, $2 seniors, $1 kids 5 to 12.

Taking Jeep tours

Over 500 miles of Jeep trails thread across the mountainsides surrounding Silverton and Ouray. Many lead to historic mines, and some eventually connect with other mining towns such as Ophir, Telluride, and Lake City. **Switzerland of America,** 226 Seventh Ave. in Ouray (☎ 800-432-JEEPk or 970-325-4484), offers ten different half- and full-day Jeep tours on the roads around Ouray. The best time to go is in late July or early August, when the wildflowers in the high-alpine basins are in bloom. Tours range in cost from $45 to $95. Switzerland of America also rents late-model Jeeps for a half-day (cost: $85) or full day (cost: $120).

Staying active

You can find a lot to do in the mountains near Ouray, Silverton, and Ridgway. Just make sure you have a detailed map, especially if you're traveling on the Jeep roads or backcountry trails. Here are some options:

✔ **Fishing:** All three of these towns have rivers nearby, and all offer premium fishing. In Silverton, some great holes are located along the Animas River above town. Stop at **Outdoor World,** 1234 Greene St. (☎ 970-387-5628), for licenses and information In Ridgway, the brown trout bite often and hard in Ridgway State Park. Near Ouray, there's good fishing along the Uncompahgre River, as well as in countless mountain streams and lakes, some of which require hiking. Call the **Riverside Inn and Cabins,** 1805 N. Main St. (☎ 800-432-4170 or 970-325-4061), if you need flies or advice on Ouray-area fishing.

✔ **Hiking:** On two sides of Ouray, trails climb steeply into forest and up to tree line. These trails are fairly challenging, but mellower options do exist. If you hike uphill from Main Street on Eighth Avenue in Ouray, it's only four blocks to **Lower Cascade Falls,** which are just as pretty as the nearby Box Canyon Falls and cost nothing. (Unfortunately, they sometimes dry up during late summer and early fall, so this may be another case of getting what you pay for.) There's also a wide, gentle, ½-mile trail alongside the

Uncompahgre River on the north end of town. Consult the *Ouray County Trail Guide,* available at the visitor center, for more-detailed information on area trails. In Ridgway, families enjoy the easy walk on the **Uncompahgre Riverway Trail,** a paved multi-use trail that starts in the town park (by the tennis courts) and goes 2 miles to Ridgway State Park, where it links up with 14 miles of paved and gravel trails.

✔ **Ice climbing:** A few years ago, a leaky penstock on a canyon wall above the Uncompahgre River south of Ouray became a frozen waterfall — and a popular ice climbing spot. Savvy climbers theorized that more leaks would create more routes, so they built a network of pipes and spigots along the cliffs bordering the Uncompahgre. During cold weather months, the **Ouray Ice Park** (☎ 970-325-0345) now offers 150 routes for climbers of all skill levels. There's no charge to climb, but you have to have a helmet and crampons to be on the ice. All guiding in the area is done through the ice park's concessionaire, **San Juan Mountain Guides** (☎ 970-325-4562). The park starts at the junction of Third Avenue and Box Canyon Falls Road and follows the river south to County Road 361. Even if you're not a climber yourself, it's worth driving up there to watch.

✔ **Ice skating:** Ouray has an outdoor hockey rink that has free skating during winter. The rink is at the north end of town alongside U.S. 550. For information on open skating hours and to rent skates, contact the **Ouray Hots Springs Pool** (☎ 970-325-4638). In Silverton, you can skate at **Kendall Mountain Community Center** (☎ 970-387-5522).

Hitting the slopes

Fashioned after a black-on-yellow highway sign, the logo for **Silverton Mountain** (☎ 970-387-5706, Internet: www.silvertonmountain.com) shows the silhouette of a skier somersaulting down a mountainside. Like any effective highway sign, it's both an accurate description and a warning. The slopes at Silverton Mountain plummet at angles ranging from 33 degrees (an expert slope) to 50 degrees (bordering on extreme). Partly because of the challenging terrain, the owners require that all customers be guided. Yet the price is surprisingly reasonable: For $99, you can sign up for a day of guided, lift-served skiing on snow that compares in quality to the seldom-skied fluff in the backcountry. The mountain's staff uses explosives to reduce the likelihood of avalanches, but you'll also need to carry an avalanche beacon, shovel, and probe (available for rent for a modest fee), just in case. The chairlift operates Thursday through Sunday, and reservations are strongly recommended. If you don't ski often and well, this probably isn't the right place for you. Just look at the sign.

Shopping

During summer, Ouray's Main Street is a bustling shopping area. When you're there, don't miss the **Salsa Trade Company** (☎ 970-325-4562) at 640 Main Street. It has a wall's worth of little-known hot sauces with names like "Third-Degree Burn," "Nuclear Waste," and "See Spot in Heat." At 520 Main St., you'll find **Mouse's Handmade Truffles** (☎ 877-7WE-SHIP), a store that fills two critical needs for travelers — gourmet chocolate and inexpensive ($5 per hour) Internet access.

Silverton really has two shopping districts — one on Greene Street, which used to be the respectable part of town, and the other a block away on Blair Street, which was where the brothels, dance halls, and opium dens used to be. To this day, the structures on Blair Street are more ramshackle than on Greene Street, but some intriguing shops and galleries are located there. My favorite shop in Silverton, though, is **Weathertop Wovens,** 1335 Greene St. (☎ 970-387-5257), where two artists weave jackets, pullovers, and other clothing while they look after the store.

Nightlife

No bar will acquaint you with local culture like the **Miner's Tavern/American Legion Post 14** at 1069 Greene St. in Silverton (☎ 970-387-5560). The bar has operated for 54 years, and some of the patrons look like they've been along for the whole ride. Sit down, order an American pilsner, and start playing pull-tabs. If you get bored, you can shoot pool, play darts or shuffleboard, or spin some tunes on the jukebox. Cap it all off with a cup of dangerously black coffee.

Fast Facts: Ouray, Silverton, and Ridgway

Information

Visit the Ouray Visitor Center (☎ 800-228-1876 or 970-325-4746; Internet: www.ouraycolorado.com), next to the Ouray Hot Springs Pool. In Ridgway, contact the Ridgway Area Chamber of Commerce (☎ 970-626-5181), or stop by their office at the County Fairgrounds (on Colorado 62 west of the traffic light). The Silverton Chamber of Commerce (☎ 800-752-4494 or 970-387-5654; Internet:

www.silverton.org) has a visitor center at 414 Greene St. (Colorado 110).

Medical Care

The nearest medical clinic is the Mountain Medical Center, 295 Colorado 62 in Ridgway (☎ 970-626-5123). The nearest hospital to Ridgway and Ouray is Montrose Memorial Hospital, 800 S. Third St. (☎ 970-249-2211). The nearest hospital to Silverton is Mercy Medical Center at 375 E. Park Ave., in Durango (☎ 970-247-4311).

Post Office

The Ouray Post Office (☎ 970-325-4302) is at 620 Main St. The Ridgway Post Office (☎ 970-626-5576) is at 485 W. Clinton. And the Silverton Post Office (☎ 970-387-5402) is at 128 W. 12th St.

Cortez, Dolores, and Mancos

Years ago, the Ancestral Puebloans — ancestors of the modern-day Pueblo people — lived throughout the Four Corners area, including the current location of Cortez. When they departed the area around A.D. 1300, the Puebloans left behind countless ruins and artifacts, the most famous being the cliff dwellings inside Mesa Verde National Park, a few miles southeast of town. Besides being a hotbed for archeologists, Cortez also serves as a trading hub for the Navajo and Ute peoples, many of whom live on reservations south of town. Dolores, once a railway stop, today serves as a gateway between the agricultural valleys to the south and the San Juan Mountains to the north. Mancos, a dusty ranching community, makes for a peaceful break on the road between Cortez and Durango.

Getting there

The best way to get here from the east or west is via U.S. 160, which spans all the way from I-25 in the east to the Grand Canyon area to the southwest. If you're traveling from the west on I-70, you can take U.S. 191 south to Monticello, Utah, then pick up U.S. 666 to Cortez. If you're coming from the east on I-70, you can pinball south on U.S. 50, U.S. 550, Colorado 62, and Colorado 145. If you're coming from the south, take U.S. 666 north to Cortez from Gallup, New Mexico.

Great Lake Airlines (☎ 800-554-5111) offers service between Denver and **Cortez-Montezuma County Airport** (☎ 970-565-9510), 1½ miles southwest of town on County Road G (via U.S. 160/666). Upon arriving in Cortez, you can rent a car from **Budget** (☎800-527-0700), **American Auto Rentals** (☎970-565-9168), or **Enterprise** (☎800-736-8222).

Getting around

You'll need to drive to travel between these communities. Most of the activity in Cortez is on the east-west **U.S. 160,** which runs through town as Main Street. At the west end of Cortez, U.S. 160 merges with north-south **U.S. 666,** or Broadway Avenue, and heads south as U.S. 160/666. On the east side of town, U.S. 160 crosses Colorado 145, which heads 11 miles north to Dolores and then continues on to Telluride and

Montrose. The entrance to Mesa Verde National Park is 10 miles east of Cortez on U.S. 160. The small town of Mancos is another 6 miles east of Mesa Verde on U.S. 160. Mancos is situated just south of the highway. A business loop of U.S. 160 curves off the main highway and goes through downtown Mancos.

Where to stay

Cortez has a strip of chain hotels a few miles west of the entrance to Mesa Verde. The area also has guest ranches, bed-and-breakfasts and historic hotels. Some lodgings are in the towns; others are in the high desert countryside, and one is deep inside Mesa Verde National Park.

Bauer House Bed & Breakfast

$$ **Mancos**

At this 1890s Victorian mansion, you'll have a hard time deciding whether to spend time inside or out. On the B&B's 1.5 grassy acres, you'll find a putting green, a gazebo, and areas for bocce ball and croquet. Inside are four guest rooms, each decorated with different styles of antiques. I like the Wicker Room, full of antique wicker furniture. If you want to feel like you're outside when you're in your room, rent the third-floor "penthouse." Because of its wood paneling and 360-degree views of the Mancos Valley, one recent guest called it a "cabin in the sky."

100 Bauer Ave., Mancos. ☎ *800-733-9707 or 970-533-9707. Internet:* www.bauer-house.com. *Rack rates: $75–$125. Open: April–Oct. MC, V.*

Enchanted Mesa Motel

$ **Mancos**

The name of this motel sounds nice and the owners are, too. They've put out a grill for guests and will even let you use their computer to get your e-mail. Some of the guest rooms have themes, including cappuccino (lots of brown stripes) and cowboy (cowboys and barbed wire stenciled on the walls). Most rooms have refrigerators and microwaves, and all have coffeemakers and cable television.

862 Grand Ave., Mancos. ☎ *866-533-MESA or 970-533-7729. Fax: 970-533-7758. E-mail:* enchantedmotel@aol.com. *Rack rates: $30–$40. AE, DC, DISC, MC, V.*

Far View Lodge

$$ **Mesa Verde**

The rooms at this motor lodge are old and smallish. Perched on a 9,100-foot hilltop deep inside Mesa Verde National Park, they have private balconies and large windows opening onto views of the surrounding mesas, canyons, and mountains. The views alone make a stay here worthwhile, but there are other advantages to staying inside the national park. If you stay here, you can conveniently drive the Mesa Top Loop Drive right before sunset, when the lighting is perfect and few people are around. You can stargaze at Mesa Verde's crystalline night sky and watch deer and wild horses browse on the vegetation outside your room at dawn. Then, you can take the first — and least crowded — ruins tours of the day.

Mesa Verde National Park, Mancos. ☎ *800-449-2288 or 970-533-1944. Fax: 970-533-7831. Internet:* www.visitmesaverde.com. *Rack rates: Standard rooms $72–$101, deluxe rooms $82–$113. Closed Nov–March. AE, DISC, MC, V.*

Holiday Inn Express
$$ Cortez

This may be my favorite chain hotel in the Four Corners area. It's colorful, clean, quiet, and chock-full of amenities. It has an indoor pool, laundry room, sauna, hot tub, and an exercise room that's short on medicine balls and long on state-of-the-art equipment. Everywhere you turn, you'll find signs that the staff cares: over 6,000 flowers planted outside every year, rock-art images on the floor tiles, and family suites with bunk beds that look like Western forts.

2121 E. Main, Cortez. ☎ *800-626-5652 or 970-565-6000. Fax: 970-565-3438. Internet:* www.coloradoholiday.com. *Rack rates: Standard rooms $79–$109, suites $149. AE, DISC, MC, V.*

Where to dine

A few restaurants in Cortez have borrowed a trick or two from the restaurants a few miles to the southwest in Arizona. In one or two, you may even find a green chili cheese steak. But heartburn is by no means mandatory. You can eat well in this area without spending too much — or paying later.

Dusty Rose Cafe
$ Mancos   NORTHERN ITALIAN

This restaurant serves creative Italian fare in a sun-splashed dining room on a quiet (and sometimes dusty) street corner. The offerings include pastas in a variety of sauces, as well as veal, chicken, beef, and shrimp dishes. The best choice may be the Veal Dijon, but you really can't go wrong here.

200 West Grand, Mancos. ☎ *970-533-9042. Reservations accepted. Main courses: $8–$18. Open: Wed–Sat lunch and dinner; Sun brunch only. MC, V.*

Main Street Brewery and Restaurant
$ Cortez   ECLECTIC

The owners of this microbrewery hope to improve public health through beer consumption. Their motto is "Avoid heart attacks — drink beer." Their dinner menu equates beer with "life itself." And their dessert menu proposes an "amber bock or mild stout" as a "delicious and healthy" substitute for sins such as ice cream. Brewed by a real Bavarian brewmeister, the medicine is hardly bitter; in fact, I recommend an extra dose of the Schnozenboomer Amber Bock. The brewery also has some beer-worthy food, including pasta, fish, steaks, burgers, and salads.

21 E. Main, Cortez. ☎ *970-564-9112. Reservations for large parties only. Main courses: $6–$20. Open: Dinner daily. AE, MC, V.*

Metate Room (at Far View Lodge)
$$ Mesa Verde   REGIONAL/AMERICAN

This isn't the only restaurant inside Mesa Verde National Park, but it's the best, hands-down. Unlike the park's cafeterias, where the food brings to mind the stuff you get on airplanes, the fare at Far View tastes gourmet. Even if it didn't, you'd still need to get here to absorb the expansive views out the restaurant windows. The offerings consist of traditional American dishes highlighted by fresh regional ingredients. One winner is the Turkey Roulade, a turkey breast stuffed with mushrooms and pine nuts.

Mesa Verde National Park, Mancos. ☎ *800-449-2288 or 970-533-1944. Reservations not accepted. Main courses: $12–$26. Open: April–Oct dinner only. AE, DISC, MC, V.*

Nero's
$–$$ Cortez   ITALIAN

If you like Italian food and Southwestern decor, this restaurant will seem like paradise. In a room jammed with Native American art, you can feast on Sicilian-style dishes such as linguini with pesto sauce, veal Marsala, and mushroom ravioli. While listening to Native American flute music and staring at turquoise walls, you can sip red wine and nibble off an antipasto plate. It's as if the chef has never peered into the dining room, and the owners have never sampled the food. Fortunately, this food would taste fine anywhere.

303 W. Main St., Cortez. ☎ *970-565-7366. Reservations accepted. Main courses: $8.95–$20.95. Open: Dinner daily. Closed Jan. AE, MC, V.*

Old Germany Restaurant
$$ Dolores   GERMAN

This restaurant's name doesn't exactly represent a flight of fancy, and neither does its food. Come here when you're hungry for solid, hearty, traditional German dishes such as *Jaeger schnitzel* (grilled pork loin steak covered with mushroom sauce), pork roast with purple cabbage, *spatzle* (noodles), and potato dumplings. Desserts include apple strudel, Bavarian cream, and a cake of the day.

On Highway 145, Dolores. ☎ *970-882-7549. Reservations accepted. Main courses: $10.95–$16.95. MC, V. Open: Tues–Sat dinner.*

Exploring the world of the Ancestral Puebloans

Most of the ruins in this area were left by the Ancestral Puebloan (or Anasazi) people, who lived in the Four Corners region from around A.D.300 to 1300. The Ancestral Puebloans may have lived long ago, but they weren't primitive. They built multistory stone dwellings out in the open and, later, under overhangs in cliffs. Plastered in bright colors, the cliff dwellings were shaded in summer and sun-warmed in winter. In addition to being capable architects, the Ancestral Puebloans domesticated animals, hunted for game, foraged for nuts, berries, and other foods; and farmed corn, beans, and squash using sophisticated irrigation systems that gathered water and conserved soils. They even used astronomy. If you're curious about their world, you'll probably enjoy a few days in and near Mesa Verde.

Getting started

Exploring Mesa Verde is more fun if you know a little about the Ancestral Puebloans first. The spots listed here can help you get started:

✔ The **Anasazi Heritage Center,** 27501 Colorado 184 (☎ **970-882-4811**), 2 miles south of Dolores, has more than 3,000,000 curated artifacts inside. Some of the most intriguing ones are displayed in a timeline that explains how the culture of the Ancestral Puebloans evolved. The Heritage Center also has a pit house replica; interactive computer programs summing up the findings of different archeological digs; and hands-on activities such as weaving, corn-grinding, and using a microscope.

The Heritage Center serves as headquarters for the newly created **Canyons of the Ancients National Monument.** If you're planning on visiting the monument, make sure to get information and maps while you're here. It's open daily from 9 a.m to 5 p.m. March through October, and 9 a.m. to 4 p.m. November through February. Admission is $3 adults 17 and over, and free for youths under 17.

✔ After you're done inside the Anasazi Heritage Center, you can hike a paved, ½-mile trail from the parking lot to **Escalante Pueblo,** a 12-room dwelling with panoramic views. There's always something special about the places where the Puebloans built. Escalante Pueblo is a perfect example of this.

✔ If you want to find out even more about the Ancestral Puebloans (and about archeology) before going to Mesa Verde, take a one-day class at the **Crow Canyon Archeological Center,** 23390 Road K, Cortez (☎ **800-422-8975,** Internet: www.crowcanyon.org). On Wednesdays and Thursdays during the summer, you can take one-day courses (cost: $50 for adults, $25 for 18 and under) in which you handle and interpret artifacts, tour the center's laboratory, and visit a real dig. You'll need to reserve a spot ahead of time. When not offering classes, the center is not geared for visitors.

✔ The **Cortez Cultural Center,** 25 N. Market St. (☎ **970-565-1151**), in downtown Cortez, has a museum, a gift shop, and a gallery with rotating displays. The best time to visit is on summer evenings, when cultural programs are offered in an outdoor amphitheater. These include Native American dances, music, and even dramas. From June through August it's open daily from 10:00 a.m. to 9:30 p.m.; from September through May, it's open Monday through Saturday from 10 a.m. to 5 p.m. Admission is free.

Mesa Verde National Park

Simply put, this is the best place to view Ancestral Pueblo archeological sites. It's the largest archeological preserve in the country, with 4,000 sites ranging from pit houses to stunning, multistoried cliff dwellings with towers, *kivas* (round, subterranean ceremonial chambers), and terraces. These dwellings, which appear almost as an outgrowth of the earth, justify a special trip to southwest Colorado. The largest and best known of them, Cliff Palace, has 217 rooms, 23 kivas, and a four-story tower. Situated on a relatively pristine 9,000-foot-high mesa, Mesa Verde also lets you absorb some of the natural splendor of the Southwest.

Mesa Verde isn't a quick hit. It takes 45 minutes to get from the park entrance to the **Far View Visitor Center.** The entrance road climbs steadily for 14 miles and has corners too sharp for vehicles longer than 25 feet. From the visitor center, you'll need to drive another half-hour to reach the park's most popular archeological sites, Balcony House and Cliff Palace, and an hour to reach Wetherill Mesa. Allow a full day to see the park, more if you have time.

Here's how to see the park efficiently:

✔ The only way you can get close to the largest cliff dwellings is by going on a ranger-guided tour. Your first stop should be at the **Far View Visitor Center** to buy tickets (cost: $2.25 per person). Try to get there before noon, because the tours do sometimes sell out. During spring, summer, and fall, you can go on a guided tour of either **Cliff Palace** or **Balcony House,** but not both on the same day. During summer only, you can also buy tickets for a tour of **Long House,** which is on Wetherill Mesa (a very slow 12-mile drive from the visitor center). All the tours involve walking and climbing. The Balcony House tour is the most strenuous and — some would say — most exciting. On it, you'll climb 90 vertical feet of stairs, 32- and 20-foot long ladders, and slip through a narrow 10-foot long crawl space.

✔ After buying your tickets, visit the **Chapin Mesa Archeological Museum.** This place is so old, it's a historic building itself. It has an impressive collection of artifacts as well as dioramas showing life in Ancestral Puebloan communities. The museum also has an information desk, and it serves as the park's visitor center during winter. While you're in this area, take a short walk to **Spruce Tree House.** This is the only large cliff dwelling you can visit without going on a guided tour. (During winter, it's the only cliff dwelling you can visit, period.) Then, drive to the more remote ruins.

✔ If you have tickets to a tour of Balcony House or Cliff Palace, you'll want to drive the **Mesa Top Loop Drive,** which consists of two 6-mile-long lasso-shaped loops. Along these loops are ten parking areas. From each parking area, you can take a short walk to mesa-top ruins or to overlooks of the surrounding canyons. Cliff dwellings and granaries are tucked into opcnings in the canyon walls, and you can see them if you look carefully. If you have tickets for a tour of Cliff Palace or Balcony House, try to time your drive so that you show up at the tour's meeting place at least ten minutes early. Along the way, don't miss **Square Tower Overlook,** where you can scan the canyon walls for archeological sites, and the mysterious **Sun Temple,** a windowless structure that may have been a prayer to the gods.

✔ If you have a ticket for a Long House tour, you'll need to head out to **Wetherill Mesa.** When you're on the mesa, you'll need to park your car and walk or take a shuttle to the different dwellings and overlooks, including Long House.

If you have extra time, do the following:

✔ Go to places you haven't yet visited. If you've been on the Mesa Top Loop Drive, go to Wetherill Mesa, and vice versa.

✔ Go for a longer hike near Spruce Tree House. Two hiking loops begin at Spruce Tree House: the 2.1-mile **Spruce Canyon Trail,** which drops 500 feet to the bottom of Spruce Canyon, and the 2.3-mile **Petroglyph Point Trail,** which has some rock art alongside it. Before going, you'll need to register at the trailhead. If you only have time for one, do the Petroglyph Point Trail.

Mesa Verde's entrance is on U.S. 160, 10 miles east of Cortez. For park information call ☎ **970-529-4465** or surf the Internet to www.nps.gov/meve. The park entrance is always open, but you aren't allowed to visit

Beating the crowds at Mesa Verde

It's hard to contemplate life 1,000 years ago when 21st-century people surround you. Mesa Verde can get crowded, but you can do a few things to give yourself a little time alone with the past:

✓ **Visit during May, June, or, best of all, October.** During these months, you can still see most of the ruins, but with fewer people around.

✓ **If you come during summer, drive to Wetherill Mesa.** Most park visitors don't make this trip, and it's a beautiful area.

✓ **Drive the Mesa Top Loop Drive right before sunset, after most visitors have departed.**

✓ **Go on a guided tour of Cliff Palace or Balcony House first thing in the morning.** The first tours, at 9:00 and 9:30 a.m., seldom fill up. If you get to the Far View Visitor Center soon after 8 a.m., you should be able to buy tickets and make it to the tour's meeting area on time.

archeological sites after dusk. The Far View Visitor Center is open from 8 a.m. to 5 p.m. from May through September. Chapin Mesa Museum is open from 8:00 a.m. to 6:30 p.m. in summer, 8 a.m. to 5 p.m. the rest of the year. Admission costs $10 per car.

Ute Mountain Tribal Park

If you want to see amazing cliff dwellings with fewer people around than at Mesa Verde, go to the Ute Mountain Tribal Park (☎ 800-847-5485 or 970-565-9653), a 125,000-acre area bordering Mesa Verde. Located on the Ute Mountain Ute reservation, the park has dwellings that are nearly as large as the grandest ones in Mesa Verde. You can choose between half-day and full-day trips. The half-day trip goes mostly to unexcavated sites littered with thousands of potsherds (pieces of broken pottery). It's much less strenuous than the full-day trip, which goes to the same unexcavated sites and then continues on to at least four well-preserved cliff dwellings.

The full-day tour is the only way to see the most spectacular cliff dwellings, so be sure to take it if you visit the tribal park. The most stunning cliff dwelling, Eagles Nest, is on a 75-foot-high ledge underneath a large overhang. To get there, you need to climb a 30-foot ladder, among other challenges.

Throughout the tour, the Ute guides discuss the Puebloans (who were not related to the Utes) and the history of their tribe. A lot of driving is involved — if you can, try to ride in the same vehicle with the guide, so you can converse while you ride. And bring plenty of sunscreen and water.

Tours meet at Ute Mountain Museum, 20 miles south of Cortez, at the southernmost junction of U.S. 666 and U.S. 160. Tours are offered April through October. The museum is open daily from 7:30 a.m. to 3:30 p.m., from April through October. Half-day tours cost $18 per person; full day tours cost $30 per person. Transportation provided by guide costs $6 extra per person. Reservations are required.

Remote sites

Mesa Verde and the Ute Mountain Tribal Park aren't the only places in southwest Colorado where you can visit archeological sites. There are thousands of other dwellings and artifacts scattered through the area. Many are unexcavated mounds barely recognizable as past dwellings. At least a few excavated sites are worth seeing if you don't mind taking long, dusty drives in the sticks. Here are two options:

✔ **Hovenweep National Monument** is best known for the remains of towers that the Ancestral Puebloans built in this area between A.D. 1100 and A.D. 1300. These towers may have been used for cere- monies, signaling, storage, defense, living quarters, or observato- ries. No one knows for certain, and part of the fun is coming up with your own theories. Today, all the towers at Hovenweep have either partly or entirely collapsed, but structures as high as 20 feet remain. Eight obvious ones flank a 1½-mile trail that travels along the rim of **Little Ruin Canyon.** The trail takes one to two hours to hike and has one short, steep stretch where it drops into, and then climbs out of, Little Ruin Canyon. A less strenuous option is the ½-mile **Tower Point Loop,** which takes about 30 min- utes and doesn't require much climbing. To reach Hovenweep, take U.S. 160 south 2 miles to County Road G (where the airport is located), and follow the signs. It takes about an hour to get there from Cortez. If you go this way, you'll be on paved roads all the way. Admission is $6 per vehicle. For more information, call the monument at ☎ **970-562-4282** or surf the Internet to www.nps. gov/hove.

✔ You can also visit widely scattered sites in the new **Canyons of the Ancients National Monument.** Established in 2000, the 164,000- acre monument has more than 5,000 documented archeological sites, and the highest density of sites in the nation. One of the most interesting is **Lowry Pueblo,** the remains of a pueblo-style dwelling that had 40 rooms and 9 kivas. Nearby is a Great Kiva spanning more than 54 feet in diameter — one of the largest ones in this area. Toilets and picnic tables are nearby. Lowry Pueblo is on County Road CC, 9 miles west of Pleasant View, a small commu- nity 20 miles northeast of Cortez on U.S. 666. For information on Lowry Pueblo and other sites inside Canyons of the Ancients National Monument, contact or visit the **Anasazi Heritage Center** (☎ **970-882-4811**) at 27501 Colorado 184.

Guided tours of Mesa Verde National Park

Not everyone wants to zoom off into the desert Southwest in search of far-flung archeological sites. For those who prefer extra guidance, **Aramark** offers half-day and full-day motor coach tours of Mesa Verde National Park. The tours stop at some of the most intriguing sites and overlooks, save you from parking hassles, and include a ranger-guided walking tour of a cliff dwelling. Morning half-day tours go to Spruce Tree House, afternoon half-day tours go to Balcony House, and full-day tours go to Cliff Palace.

If you're choosing between the two half-day tours, go for the afternoon affair, because Balcony House is more fun to tour than Spruce Tree House. (Besides, you can always do Spruce Tree House on your own.) The motor-coach tours, which run from May to October, leave from Far View Lodge. You can sign up at the lodge or by calling ☎ **800-449-2288** or 970-529-4421. The morning tour costs $34 for adults, $23 for kids 5 to 17. The afternoon tour costs $36.25 for adults, $25.25 for kids 5 to 17. The full-day tour is $55.25 for adults, $43.25 for kids 5 to 17.

Other things to see and do

The offerings in this area aren't limited to archeological sites. When you're done seeing the ruins, you can

- ✔ **Relive the pioneer days, and then eat steak. Bartels' Mancos Valley Stage Line** (☎ **800-365-3530** or 970-533-9857; Internet: www.thestagecoach.com) will take you for a ride on a replica of the horse-drawn mud coaches used throughout the West in the 1800s. Just like in the old days, the ride is dusty and, despite the leather straps under the coach that serve as shock absorbers, on the bumpy side. Three different tours are offered: The one-hour rides will give you a taste of stagecoach travel but not much more. You're better off taking the lunch or dinner tour. Each lasts about three and a half hours and includes a meal at a peaceful old homestead deep inside a canyon near Mesa Verde. The dinner tour costs a little more, but the meal consists of steaks instead of sandwiches, the air is cooler, and you can catch the sunset on the ride home. The rides start and finish at 4550 County Rd. 41, and reservations are required. To get there, continue south on Main Street for 5 miles past Mancos. The rides operate May through September. Prices for the one-hour tour are $25 adults, $12.50 kids 3 to 12; for the lunch tour it's $55 adults, $27.50 kids 3 to 12; and for the dinner tour it's $65 adults, $32.50 kids 3 to 12.

- ✔ **Go for broke. Ute Mountain Casino** (☎ **800-258-8007** or 970-565-8800; Internet: www.utemountaincasino.com) offers slot, keno, and video poker machines, as well as blackjack and poker tables. The casino is in Towaoc, Colorado, 11 miles south of Cortez on U.S. 160/666, on the Ute Mountain Ute reservation.

✔ **Soak your feet. McPhee Reservoir,** near Dolores, has 4,470 acres of water and more than 50 miles of shoreline at average water levels. Below the dam is an 11-mile stretch of Gold Medal catch-and-release fly fishing (you'll need a license). Admission is free. You can float your boat and camp at McPhee Campground (☎ **970-882-2294** or 877-444-6777 for reservations), off Colorado 184 just east of Colorado 145. Camping costs $12 for regular sites, $15 for hookups.

Shopping

Go to Cortez to shop for Native American arts, crafts, and jewelry.

✔ Open since 1961, **Notah Dineh,** 345 W. Main St. (☎ **800-444-2024** or 970-565-9607), carries roughly 250,000 works of art by the Hopi, Navajo, Ute, and Zuni tribes. The store is best known for its rugs, both antique and new, which range in price from $50 to $25,000.

✔ **Mesa Verde Pottery** (☎ **800-441-9908** or 970-565-4492) makes its own line of molded, decorated pottery, which sells for $12 to $200. It also has traditional Native American wares. It's at 27601 Hwy. 160, 1 mile east of Cortez.

✔ The **Cortez Cultural Center,** 25 N. Market St. (☎ **970-565-1151**), has a small but pleasing selection of Native American jewelry at reasonable prices.

Fast Facts: Cortez, Dolores, and Mancos

Hospital

Southwest Memorial Hospital, 1311 N. Mildred Rd, Cortez. (☎ 970-565-6666), has a 24-hour emergency room.

Information

For information on the Cortez area, contact the Mesa Verde Country Visitor Information Bureau, P.O. Box HH, Cortez, CO 81321 (☎ 800-253-1616; Internet: www.mesaverdecountry.com). Upon arriving, visit the Colorado Welcome Center at Cortez 928 E. Main St. (☎ 970-565-4048).

Post Office

The Cortez Post Office (☎ 970-565-3181) is at 35 S. Beech St.

Durango

Nestled in the sun-drenched foothills of the San Juan mountains, Durango flourished in the late 19th century as a railroad town that helped move minerals mined in Silverton. Today, the same 1881 rail line ferries more than 200,000 tourists a year. The railroad long ago helped

pay for the many architectural landmarks in Durango's historic downtown, and today it helps support a bustling row of restaurants, bars,
shops, and hotels. A community of 14,000 people also thrives in this
active town. Sinewy cyclists careen across mountain bike trails in the
pinyon-juniper and ponderosa-pine forests around town. Kayakers
splash through the whitewater of the Animas River, which flows through
the community. And, come winter, skiers search for powder on slopes of
the nearby Durango Mountain Resort. During the school year, students
from Fort Lewis College flood the downtown area on weekends. And
ranchers still run cattle on the rangeland south of town. Whether you
come here for the history, the recreation, or merely the sight of the red-
rock cliffs surrounding town, you'll probably enjoy Durango.

Getting there

Durango sits amid some rugged topography, so the trip to town is often
prettier than it is smooth.

By car

Most people who drive through Southwestern Colorado land in
Durango at some point. It's 5 miles from the easternmost junction of
U.S. 160 and **U.S. 550,** which are two major routes through the region.
(The roads join one another for 5 miles, then part ways again in at the
southwest corner of town.) U.S. 160 links Cortez (to the west) and **I-25**
(to the east). U.S. 550 joins Farmington, New Mexico (to the south), and
Grand Junction (to the north).

By plane

America West Airlines, American Airlines (winter only), **Continental,**
and **United Express** all serve **Durango/La Plata County Airport**
(☎ **970-247-8143**), 14 miles southeast of Durango on Colorado 172.
After landing, you can rent cars through **Hertz, Avis, National, Budget,**
and **Dollar.** For information on contacting individual airlines and car-
rental agencies, see the Appendix.

Getting around

Durango's roads can be confusing. The main route through town is U.S.
160/550, which parallels the Animas River and, together with the river,
defines the southern edge of the community. At the southwest corner
of town, highways 160 and 550 part ways, with U.S. 160 continuing west
out of town to Cortez. U.S. 550, meanwhile, curves through town on
Camino Del Rio and Main Avenue and eventually leaves the north side
of Durango en route to Silverton and points beyond.

Durango's downtown area surrounds north-south Main Avenue between
College Drive and 15th Street. To get there, take Camino Del Rio north

from Highway 160 and then go right (east) on College Drive. Most of the shops are right on Main Avenue, but parking can be scarce. Be sure to carry some nickels, dimes, and quarters for the meters; an hour's parking costs 25¢. If you stay in the historic downtown, you can do most of your shopping and dining without getting in the car. Pedestrians always have the right of way in Durango, so be sure to take advantage of it.

If you prefer public transportation, the **Durango Lift** (☎ **970-259-5438**), a local bus system, travels three loops through town, weekdays from 7 a.m. to 7 p.m. year-round. The cost is 50¢ per ride.

Durango's **Main Avenue Trolley Service** goes up and down Main Avenue, hitting stops every 20 minutes or so. It's not a real trolley; rather, it looks like the offspring of a trolley and a bus. When the town is busy, you can park at a lot north of the historic downtown and take the trolley into town. During summer, it operates from 6 a.m. to 10 p.m. During winter, it runs from 7 a.m. to 7 p.m. The cost is 50¢ per ride.

Durango Transportation (☎ **800-626-2066** or 970-259-4818) provides taxi service.

Where to stay

Durango has three of the best-preserved historic hotels in western Colorado. They're brick-and-stone classics, all with hand-carved woodwork and antiques inside, and all situated, naturally enough, in the historic district, where you can hear the whistle of the Durango and Silverton Railway (even when you don't want to). Here's the lowdown on those hotels, as well as on lodging at Durango Mountain Resort.

General Palmer Hotel
$$ **Durango**

Like the nearby Strater Hotel, the General Palmer is an elegant, well preserved 19th-century hotel in downtown Durango, but it's smaller and more subdued than its better-known counterpart. Unlike the Strater, there's no old-time saloon or restaurant on the premises, employees dress as if this were the 21st century, and the furnishings include many reproductions. Yet you'll still sense the history here, and the depot for the Durango and Silverton Narrow Gauge Railroad is only a block away. My favorite relic is the hotel's 1910 Otis elevator, with a door that has to be opened and closed by hand. If you plan to use your room mainly for sleeping, go for one of the windowless "inside" rooms. Cocooned from street noise, they're surprisingly restful — and affordable, too!

*567 Main Ave., Durango. ☎ **800-523-3358** or 970-247-4747. Internet:* www.general palmerhotel.com. *Rack rates: April 1–Oct 15 and Dec 20–Jan 1, $98–$275 double; rest of year, $75–$275 double. AE, DC, DISC, MC, V.*

Leland House and Rochester Hotel

$$–$$$ **Durango**

If you love Westerns, saddle up and ride to the 1892 Rochester Hotel, where each of the 15 guest rooms pays homage to a particular Western. The Viva Zapata room, for instance, holds sombreros and Mexican clay pots; the Butch Cassidy and the Sundance Kid room bears photos of Redford and Newman back when they weren't so long in the tooth. Located across the street, The Leland House — owned by the same company as the Rochester — is a restored 1927 apartment building. Being former apartments, each guest unit has a kitchen, and some have extra rooms and sitting areas. Each unit is named after a different person from Durango's history, someone you've probably never heard of. The kitchens and extra space make Leland House a great place for families, but it's not as much fun as the Rochester Hotel.

Both hotels share the same address and check-in for both hotels is at the Leland House.

721 E. Second Ave., Durango. ☎ *800-664-1920 or 970-385-1920. Fax: 970-385-1967. Internet:* www.rochesterhotel.com, www.leland-house.com. *Leland House rack rates: Double $109–$139; suite $159–$320. Rochester Hotel rack rates: Double $111–$179; suite $150–$199. AE, DC, DISC, MC, V.*

Purgatory Village Condominium Hotel

$$$ **Durango**

At this modern condominium hotel, which offers ski-in, ski-out access at Durango Mountain Resort, your options include compact studios with Murphy beds; one-bedroom, two-bedroom, and three-bedroom condominiums; and standard hotel rooms with king beds. Shop for a package deal and bring your own food — most rooms have either kitchenettes or full kitchens. Ideally, you'll spend most of your time pursuing an active lifestyle here and little time considering the decor, which varies from unit to unit depending on the whims of the owners. The hotel and resort offer a variety of activities, especially during summer. (Skip ahead to the review of the Durango Mountain Resort to see the activities offered there.) And with views of both the ski area and the Twilight and West Needle mountains, the backdrop is hard to beat.

1 Skier Place, Durango. ☎ *800-693-0175. Fax 970-382-2248. Internet:* www.durango mountainresort.com. *Free parking. Rack rates: Studios and standard rooms, $79–$179; condominiums, $169–$1025. AE, DISC, MC, V.*

The Strater Hotel

$$–$$$ **Durango**

This four-story hotel of red brick and ornate white stonework still dominates the Durango skyline, much as it did 100 years ago. Just by looking at it, you can tell that the Strater is *the* place to stay. Thanks to a succession of owners who invested in it even during hard times, it never slipped into disrepair and has always been elegant. Today, the hotel even employs a master woodworker to look after its elaborate woods, including a Mahogany entryway, a front desk of solid pine, and the world's largest collection of Victorian walnut antiques. The hotel celebrates its history, almost to a fault. Employees in turn-of-the-century period clothing show guests to rooms overlooking Durango's thriving downtown. The guest rooms are more antiquey than posh, but they're comfortable. There's also a saloon with live entertainment, a restaurant, and a theater that presents melodramas during summer.

699 Main Ave., Durango. ☎ *970-247-4431. Fax: 970-259-2208. Internet:* www.strater.com. *Rack rates: June 1–Sept 30 $129–$160 standard, $169–$229 deluxe; Sept 30–May 31 $69–$129 standard, $79–$149 deluxe. AE, DC, DISC, MC, V.*

Where to dine

I wouldn't say you *couldn't* find a bad meal in Durango because, with over 60 restaurants in town, some chef somewhere must be cooking a bad meal at this very minute. But I've never had a bad meal here. Because this is a college town that also caters to wealthy tourists, the food choices run the gamut from burrito joints and brewpubs to the finest of fine dining. Here are some choices to get you started as you dine Durango.

Cyprus Café
$$ Durango   WEST COAST/MEDITERRANEAN

At certain times of day, Cyprus Café seems aglow with light emanating from the ceramic masks, castings, and urns, and from the clay-like faux finish on the walls. Consisting largely of organic produce and meats, the food, like the surroundings, blends the earthy and the sublime. You can choose from entrees such as *Salmon sto Fourno* (fresh salmon, goat cheese, grape leaves, and olive caper tapenade, baked in parchment paper) and lamb meatball fettucini, or opt for a creative salad. Cyprus Café is most fun on summer nights when it opens its patio and features live jazz.

725 E. Second Ave., Durango. ☎ *970-385-6884. Internet:* www.cypruscafe.com. *Reservations accepted. Main courses: $12–$18. Open: Summer lunch and dinner daily; rest of year Tues–Sun for lunch and dinner. AE, DISC, MC, V.*

Ken and Sue's Place
$ Durango   AMERICAN BISTRO

This restaurant's owners have won some major awards in recent years, but for some reason they aren't taking it out on their customers. They still serve inexpensive salads and sandwiches at both lunch and dinner, welcome kids, and leave free jelly beans by the door. The dining room resembles a small town cafe that has been gussied up a little, and the prices are reasonable. Despite the casual trappings, you can dine on expertly prepared fish, chicken, and steak dishes, including a pistachio-crusted grouper that stands apart.

If it's dinnertime and this restaurant is full, walk three blocks down Main Avenue to **Ken and Sue's East** (☎ **970-385-1810**), 636 Main Ave. Being farther east, it has similar fare but with an Asian twist, and the dining area is a tad more formal.

937 Main Ave., Durango. ☎ *970-259-2616. Reservations accepted. Main courses: $11–$19. Open: Lunch and dinner daily. AE, DC, DISC, MC, V.*

Seasons Rotisserie and Grill
$$–$$$ Durango NEW AMERICAN

Seasons is a great choice if you're looking for quality upscale dining. You can sit in a yellow dining room with original art, high ceilings, and hardwood floors. Prepared in an open kitchen, the entrees are highlighted by quality meats cooked over an oak-fired, rotisserie grill. The staff here is "99% sure" that they have the largest wine list in town. I'm only 50% sure that they're credible, but the list is certifiably long.

764 Main St., Durango. ☎ *970-382-9790. Reservations recommended. Main courses: $14.50–$29.50. Open: Mon–Fri lunch and dinner, Sat–Sun dinner only. AE, DC, DISC, MC, V.*

Sow's Ear
$$ Near Durango Mountain Resort STEAKS

Hanging from the high ceiling of this dining room is an extravagant mobile, with components that call to mind a three-way-collision between skier, hiker, and duck. There's a mirrored ball, too. Other than that, the place feels like a country club, with mountain views, hardwood floors, great steaks, strong cocktails, and friendly service. Come here for the elk tenderloin medallions with portobello mushroom red wine sauce — and for the mobile.

48475 Highway 550 (about 2 miles south of Durango Mountain Resort), Durango. ☎ *970-259-1438. Reservations accepted. Main courses: $8–$26. Open: Dinner daily. Closed April 1–May 27 and mid-October through Thanksgiving. AE, DISC, MC, V.*

Steamworks
$–$$ Durango PUB FARE

Located in an old automobile showroom, Steamworks sells copious amounts of homemade beer as well as the many foods that go with beer — soups, salads, Mexican fare, burgers, pasta, a Cajun boil (on weekends only), and pizza, among others. After ordering, the kids can scribble with chalk on the old showroom floor, and you can gaze through windows that open onto the kitchen, brewing vats, and the street.

801 E. Second Ave., Durango. ☎ *877-372-9200 or 970-259-9200. Reservations accepted. Main courses: $9–$18. Open: Lunch and dinner daily. AE, DISC, MC, V.*

Exploring Durango

In Durango, you can spend a lot of time train-ing. When you've ridden the Durango and Silverton Narrow Gauge Railroad, you can work out on the trails, on the river, or at the ski area.

The best things to see and do

Durango and Silverton Narrow Guage Railroad

Every morning from mid-May through late October, a 1923 coal-fired steam locomotive pulls Victorian-era coaches out of Durango and uphill 45 miles and 3,000 vertical feet to the historic mining town of Silverton. During much of the three-and-a-half-hour trip, the train follows the Animas River upstream, alternately dipping deep into gorges and traversing narrow ledges high above the river. It stops for two hours in Silverton, where most people shop, eat lunch, and get in the way of locals. Then the train returns to Durango. It's one of the prettiest rides you'll ever take, and the history of the train and its surroundings can really make you feel as if you've stepped back in time.

The full ride, however, takes about ten hours, which can seem like ten years when you get tired. Unless you're rabid for rails, I recommend spending the extra $5 to go either to or from Silverton via motor coach. This shortens the trip by two hours and makes it less taxing.

There are other interesting ways to break up the trip if you have a little extra time. You can make an overnight layover in Silverton, which has historic hotels and a lively shopping district — not to mention beautiful mountains and old mines all around. Or, you can get off the train at Elk Park or Needleton and hike or backpack in remote areas of the San Juan National Forest, including the Weminuche Wilderness, then flag down the train again that afternoon or even a few days later. For more on hiking in this area, contact the **San Juan National Forest,** 15 Burnett Court, Durango (☎ **970-247-4874**). More trains are added as business picks up, so you can usually find a seat even if you don't book ahead. During fall and winter, a shorter, four-and-a-half-hour round-trip to Cascade Canyon is offered.

479 Main Ave., Durango. ☎ *888-872-4607 or 970-247-2733. Internet:* www.durango train.com. *Reservations recommended. Fares: Nonpeak, $55 adults, $27 children 5–11; peak, $60 adults, $30 children 5–11; Cascade Canyon (fall), $60 adults,*

$30 children 5–11; Cascade Canyon (winter), $45 adults, $22 children 5–11. Parking $7 per day for cars, $9 per day for RVs. Ticket includes admission to the Durango and Silverton Narrow Gauge Railroad Museum.

Durango and Silverton Narrow Gauge Museum

Even if you don't take a ride on the historic train, this museum tucked behind the depot for the Durango and Silverton Narrow Gauge Railroad is worth exploring. Under one 12,000-square-foot roof, it has one of the largest collections of historic railroad cars, engines, and memorabilia anywhere. Highlights include a combination engine, personnel mover, and ambulance known as a Casey Jones and a luxurious "Nomad" business car.

479 Main Ave. (in the rail yard for the Durango and Silverton Railroad), Durango. ☎ *970-247-2733. Free for train passengers. Open: Year-round; hours vary seasonally. Cost for non-passengers: $5 adults, $2.50 kids 6–12.*

Other things to see and do

The train isn't the only way to time-travel in Durango. You can step back in history by visiting these area museums:

✔ Located in a three-story, 1904 schoolhouse, the **Animas Museum,** 3065 W. Second Ave., at 31st Street (☎ **970-259-2402**), pays homage to the history of Durango and its precursor, Animas City. Its ground floor still houses a century-old classroom, which, if my experience is typical, may look disturbingly similar to the classrooms of your youth. Upstairs are exhibits on Native Americans, European settlers, and the town itself. Next to the museum is a restored, furnished 1876 cabin. Summer hours run Monday through Saturday from 10 a.m to 6 p.m. Winter hours are Wednesday through Saturday from 10 a.m. to 4 p.m. Admission is $2.50 adults, free for kids under 12.

✔ *Time* magazine is said to have rated the **Diamond Circle Melodrama** (☎ **970-247-3400**) production as "one of the top three melodramas in the U.S." When or why *Time* magazine began rating melodramas, I'm not sure. At any rate, this is fun stuff, and everyone gets to hiss at the villain. It's located at the corner of Seventh and Main streets inside the Strater Hotel. Shows are Monday through Saturday nights from June through August. Admission is $17 for adults, $12 for children under 12.

Staying active

With mountains above, desert below, and a river through town, Durango is perfect of year-round recreation. Visitors here often end up doing one or more of the following:

- ✔ **Golfing: Hillcrest Golf Course,** 2300 Rim Dr. (☎ **970247-1499**), next to Fort Lewis College, is Durango's 18-hole municipal course. This is a good public course with reasonable rates: $20 for 18 holes, $10 for 9. There's also a driving range and putting green on the premises.

- ✔ **Hiking:** For information on hiking in and around Durango, including some more remote spots, call the **Animas Ranger District** (☎ **970-247-4874**).

- ✔ **Mountain biking:** This sport may not have been invented in Durango, but it came of age here. And **Mountain Bike Specialists**, 949 Main Ave. (☎ **970-247-4066**), has absorbed a lot of the bumps along the way. The Mountain Bike Hall of Fame is in Crested Butte, Colorado, but this store is sort of a satellite version, with bikes and jerseys of famous riders such as Juli Furtado, John Tomac, and Ned Overend mounted across the upper walls. The shop can prepare you — mentally, at least — for the challenging single-track trails surrounding town. It sells trail guides and has maps available for either perusal or purchase. You can rent a full suspension bike for $40 per day.

- ✔ **Taking river trips:** During years when it snows (or rains), Durango has great rafting right in the heart of town. Some of the top-flight kayakers train on the Animas River right next to the town's visitor center. Above town, the Animas makes for extra-challenging boating, with class IV and V rapids. Below town, it's mellow enough to float on an inflatable kayak. **Durango Rivertrippers,** 720 Main Ave. (☎ **800-292-2885;** Internet: www.durangorivertrippers.com), offers two-hour ($20) and half-day ($30) trips on the Animas.

- ✔ **Soaking and swimming:** Located 9 miles north of town, **Trimble Hot Springs,** 6475 County Rd. 203 (☎ **800-275-8777** or 970-247-0111), has a large, warm swimming pool and even warmer pools for soaking. The cost for soaking is $8.50 for adults, $6 for kids 12 and under.

Hitting the slopes

Durango Mountain Resort's 10,822-foot summit isn't particularly high for a ski area so far south on the map. So the snowfall can be hit or miss, even more so than at other areas. Nor is the mountain enormous. It boasts a respectable 2,029-foot vertical drop, but the thrust of the 1,200 skiable acres is more horizontal than vertical. But if you like lots of warm sunshine, a resort where the bottom of the hill isn't a lifetime away, and rolling intermediate terrain, DMR makes a fine choice. You'll enjoy the relaxed, open people. And if you're a lukewarm skier but a full-blown hedonist, you'll love the resort's Total Adventure Ticket, a program that allows guests holding four- or more day lift-tickets to exchange a day of lift-served skiing for activities such as cross-country skiing, snowshoeing, star-viewing, hot springs, and even massages. See Table 21-2 for more information on DMR.

Table 21-2	Ski Report: Durango Mountain Resort
Location: 25 miles north of Durango on Highway 550	
Trails: 75	
	23% beginner
	51% intermediate
	26% advanced
Vertical drop: 2,029 feet	
Base elevation: 8793 feet	
Summit elevation: 10,882 feet	
Skiable terrain: 1,200 acres	
Average snowfall: 260 inches	
Lifts: 11	
Snow phone: ☎ 970-247-9000	
Central reservations: ☎ 800-525-0892	
Internet: www.durangomountainresort.com	
2002–2003 peak-season adult all-day lift ticket: $55	

Shopping

If you want to tour Durango's many art galleries, start at the **Durango Art Center**, 802 E. Second Ave. (☎ **970-259-2606**). Open Tuesday through Saturday from 10 a.m. to 5 p.m., it has a large exhibit space that houses traveling shows as well as group shows highlighting local and regional artists. There's also a small gift shop selling local art. When you're done browsing, the art center's staff can help you identify local galleries that have the type of art you like most.

Nightlife

With over 100 bottled beers and an additional 20 beers on tap, **Lady Falconburgh's Barley Exchange,** 640 Main Ave. (☎ **970-382-9664**), boasts one of the largest beer selections in the Southwest. The restaurant also has single-malt scotches and other premium liquors, and it serves a popular Philly cheese steak sandwich. **Scoot 'n' Blues,** 900 Main Ave. (☎ **970-259-1400**), books rock 'n' roll, blues, and jazz acts and even has a weekly karaoke night. The hot pickers and jam bands often perform at **Haggard's Black Dog Tavern,** 13544 County Rd. 240 (☎ **970-259-5657**).

Springing off on a side-trip to Pagosa Springs

In the past few years, folks have been flooding into Pagosa Springs — just 59 miles east of Durango — to live. Archuleta County, where Pagosa Springs is located, ranks among the fastest growing counties in America. I recommend going there as a day-trip to soak. Mineral-rich hot springs, rumored to have magical healing powers, bubble out of the earth right across the San Juan River from downtown Pagosa Springs.

Soaking in Pagosa Springs

Besides having therapeutic effects, the geothermal pools have heated many of the buildings on Pagosa's Main Street for almost a century.

To fully appreciate **The Springs at Pagosa,** 165 Hot Springs Blvd. (☎ 970-264-BATH), you'll have to soak in most of the 15 outdoor pools, each with its own name and temperature. If you overheat in the 114-degree Lobster Pot, you can immediately cool off by dunking in the San Juan River, which flows right past the springs. While you soak, you can savor the sound of the river and the sight of the landscaped ter-races all around you. It's open daily from 5 a.m to 1 a.m. (24 hours for guests of the Spring Inn). Admission is $12 adults, free for children under 7 with a paying adult.

Where to stay and dine

If all that bathing makes you hungry, **Isabel's,** 20 Village Dr. (☎ 970-731-5448), serves excellent fish, meat, pasta, and vegetarian dishes, but the herb-crusted lamb chops are best of all. Main courses at din-nertime cost $12.50 to $35.

If you order from the "early supper" menu (available until 6:30 p.m.), you can eat in style for under $10.

If you want to spend more than a day soaking up Pagosa's atmosphere, many of the rooms at the **Springs Inn,** 165 Hot Springs Blvd. (☎ 800-225-0934 or 970-264-4168) offer views of the so-called "mother spring," which spouts 142-degree water into a pool behind the lodge. Everything around here smells a bit sulphurous, but you won't mind when you start soaking in the adjacent hot springs, included with the room rate. If you tire of the healing waters, you can have your skin moisturized at the spa or take a yoga class. As for the rooms themselves, they're bright, pleas-ant and restful. Rates at the inn range from $95 to $169 for a double.

Fast Facts: Durango

Emergency

Dial ☎ **911.**

Information

Contact the Durango Area Chamber Resort Association, 111 S. Camino del Rio (P.O. Box 2587), Durango, CO 81302 (☎ 800-525-8855 or 970-247-0312; Internet: www.durango.org). It's located just south of downton on U.S. 160/550.

Hospital

Mercy Medical Center, 375 E. Park Ave. (☎ 970/247-4311), has a 24-hour emergency room.

Pharmacy

The Rite-Aid (☎ 970-247-5057) at 28 Town Plaza has a full-service pharmacy.

Post Office

The Durango Post Office (☎ 970-247-3434) is at 222 W. Eighth St.

Road Report

Call ☎ 970-247-3355.

Weather and Ski Conditions

Call ☎ 970-247-0930.

Part VI
The Part of Tens

The 5th Wave   By Rich Tennant

In this part . . .

Other parts of this book cover essential Colorado information; this one provides inessential but fun answers to the two questions that I wish more people would ask about the state: "How do I know I'm in a Colorado mountain town?" and "What is a signature Colorado experience?" The answers won't help you save money or find the best hotels. They will, however, tell you more about the state's unique spirit and the best ways to enjoy it.

Chapter 22

Ten (or So) Signs You're in a Colorado Mountain Town

• •

In This Chapter

▶ Listening to native music

▶ Craving a coffee

▶ Enjoying the beauty of the mountains

• •

*T*here's more to a Colorado mountain town than the surrounding mountains. Colorado mountain towns all share a few quirky attributes. When you discover what these quirky attributes are, you'll be able to spot a Colorado mountain town even if the mountains are nowhere to be seen. You'll also know what to expect when you do roll into one of these towns, and you can plan accordingly. For example, allow an extra hour for the coffee shop to prepare your double latte. Expect to see dozens and dozens of white men in baseball caps and T-shirts — and not a lot of women. Budget your time and money accordingly. And set aside an hour or so for a lecture about "the good old days" from an authentic Colorado native. Below are some ways you can identify a Colorado mountain town.

Jamming the Night Away

If you don't know what a jam band is, then you probably haven't spent enough time in one of Colorado's funky mountain towns. To put it simply, jam bands are rock bands that go on and on — not their careers necessarily, but their largely improvisational songs. The longer the song goes on, the better it's usually received. If a song lasts three days, you can be sure that a few jam band fans will dance the whole time. Many jam-band songs are about feeling good — euphoric even — so the music is perfect for mountain settings where people, by and large, are happy about life.

The Grateful Dead started the whole jam wave and then spawned many lesser bands, much as Led Zeppelin spawned countless second-rate heavy-metal bands. The surviving jam bands seem to spend a disproportionate amount of time in Colorado's mountain regions. So if you want a truly hip, local experience, you owe it to yourself to dip into the tequila and see whether you can feel good enough to groove with a jam band when you're in Colorado.

Sporting Caps

Men arriving in the mountains during winter often complain that there aren't enough women around. Award them points for their keen powers of observation! In most Colorado towns, especially during winter, men outnumber women by roughly the same amount that they did during Colorado's mining heyday. I've walked into bars where every single person looked like me — in other words, the places were chock-full of white guys in jeans, T-shirts, and baseball caps. It was Hell On Earth. Men seeking women should vacation in the tropics. Women who like white guys in jeans, T-shirts, and baseball caps — well, you'll love Colorado.

Racking Up the Equipment

I read in a magazine that you can tell the quality of a mountain-person by the number of toys on the roof rack or his or her SUV. I strongly disagree. You can tell the *income* of a mountain-person by the number of toys on the roof rack or his or her SUV. Some of the best mountain-people I know still hitchhike or drive crummy little rack-less sedans, always jammed chock-full of gear. However, the presence of elaborate SUV roof racks festooned with kayaks, bikes, surfboards, skis, and snowboards does indicate that you've hit one of Colorado's more fashionable mountain towns.

Saluting Raptors

Real estate plays a critical economic role in Colorado's mountain towns. The prettier a town is, the more realtors it has. And local realtors and developers like to name neighborhoods after the species they have displaced. So, if you're surrounded by developments named after deer, elk, beavers, moose, and — above all — any species of raptor, it's probably safe to say that you're within spitting distance of one of the state's hipper spots.

Clocking the Caffeine

I don't mean to act pushy, but it shouldn't take 45 minutes to make a double-latte. Due to a mysterious statewide phenomenon, something intergalactic happens at espresso bars in Colorado's swankier towns that renders the clock meaningless. If you've waited more than ten minutes for your gourmet coffee, it's a sure sign you're in a Colorado mountain town.

Basking in Beauty

If there is one thing a mountain town has plenty of, it is beauty (no, not those emaciated cover girls). These spots really do have it all: thundering rivers, immense peaks, bright sunlight, and clear blue skies. Sometimes I can't help but wish that the whole world looked like one of the state's mountain towns! If you're walking down the sidewalk and suddenly want to sit down just to absorb the sights, it's almost a sure bet you're in one of Colorado's magnificent mountain communities.

Calling all Curmudgeons

In Colorado's barrooms, you'll occasionally meet people who moved to town five years before everyone else and who resent the people who arrived after them to enjoy the high life. In most parts of the country, these people would be known as *curmudgeons*. Here, they prefer to be called *Colorado Natives*. If you see lots of "Colorado Native" bumper stickers attached to pickup trucks, you're probably closing in on a funky Colorado mountain town.

Celebrating One's Hipness

When a cool mountain town in Colorado becomes conspicuously wealthy, it reflexively emphasizes its own undiminished hipness. Of course, by that point, it's no longer *tres chic* to visit, and people begin moving on to the next "in" spot, which most likely doesn't even know that it's hip yet. If there's one final gold rush left in the Colorado hills, it's for the up-and-coming funky town, the one that isn't wise to its own appeal. Good luck finding it. If you do manage to locate it, let me know. I'll be right behind you, ready to crowd that place, too.

Chapter 23

Ten Signature Colorado Experiences

In This Chapter

▶ Soaking au naturel

▶ Witnessing bizarre fall football fan rituals

▶ Tossing back a beer

So you're looking for that distinctive Colorado experience? You've come to the right chapter. Here I describe ten signature experiences that help reveal Colorado's true character — and orange color. These are experiences, mind you, not destinations. You can enjoy them throughout much of the state. If you work your way through all the signature experiences described in these pages, you'll have a pretty good idea what it's like to be a Coloradoan, except for the work part. For now, just pretend that it doesn't exist.

Dropping Trou and Soaking in a Hot Spring

Not all of us have spent a lot of time naked around strangers. So you may need to take a minute or two to get used to the idea of being sans clothing at one of Colorado's clothing-optional hot springs. Take that minute or two, then remove your garments — if necessary, do it in a dressing room or tipi when no one's looking — grab a towel, and make your way towards the blissful pool of your choice. Trust me, soaking in the buff is not going to start you down a slippery slope leading to biker rallies, Steppenwolf medleys, and rowdy sex. When you climb into a natural hot spring au naturel, you'll realize that there's nothing left to protect you and, better yet, no need to be protected. The springs are there to warm and comfort you, the crystalline air hangs above, and there's nothing to get in between you and your own personal bliss.

Getting Scared (Preferably Not to Death) in the Backcountry

As advertised, the Colorado Rockies really are huge, intimidating, and dangerous. That's all the more reason to get out on foot and enjoy them. Don't be overtly dumb — make sure you have map and compass, warm clothing, and food and water — but don't be mortified by the mountains either. If you go out in the backcountry and frighten or challenge yourself, it's no sin — it's called living. The important thing is to get out there and get after it. Just use a little common sense. Pay close attention to where you are, take the aforementioned equipment, tell a friend where you're going and when you expect to be back, and allow yourself lots of time to return to your car or campsite.

Taking Your Rental Car down the Jeep Road from Hell

Rental-car insurance doesn't always cover damage or breakdowns that happen off paved roads. If you reach 12,000 feet on a precipitous Jeep road in your rented Geo Prism, you're definitely taking a risk. From my point of view, it's an admirable one. If it were up to me, the annual Pikes Peak Auto Hill Climb would be open only to tourists in uninsured rental cars — that way, the suspense would stem not only from the danger of catastrophic injury, but also from the lack of comprehensive coverage. To really enjoy Colorado, take your rental car down the Jeep road from hell. See the old mines, lurch across the alpine cirques, and bounce past the burned-out hulks of abandoned vehicles. Make a 20-point turn on a road so narrow and exposed, you could spit out the window and it would land a thousand feet downhill. You won't forget it. If you really want to play it safe, you can rent a Jeep instead.

Freaking Out at a Jam Band Show

Let's say you're on vacation and at a bar where a Colorado jam band is playing. The song they're playing goes on and on. You could go back to your motel room and watch TV, you could stay seated at the bar, drinking, or you could get up and dance. If no one seems to be looking, I suggest dancing as strangely as you can. If the song keeps going, dance more strangely. If you keep dancing, the worst thing that can happen is that you sober up and get a workout. The best thing? You may have some small epiphany or moment of bliss. It's worth a try. After all, you're on vacation.

Conversing with Your Horse

Everyone should ride a horse at some point during his or her Colorado vacation. When you get on your mount, you'll probably want to demonstrate that you, unlike other tourists, have a special connection with horses, much as Robert Redford had in *The Horse Whisperer.* Unfortunately, relationships with hooved mammals don't always pan out as hoped for. You may soon find out that your steed behaves as unpredictably as a giant, stupid cat. When no one is looking, you'll need to have a hushed conversation with your horse. Ask it what its thoughts are and why it doesn't do what you suggest. Finally, tell it that its days as a loafing piece of aged Jell-O are done, and give it a swift kick with your river sandal. When you do, you'll definitely be having a traditional Colorado moment.

Sampling a Colorado Microbrew (or Two)

Colorado has more microbreweries than any other state, and if you're an adult who likes beer, you should make sure to visit at least one during your trip. Nearly every town has a brewpub, and each brewpub has its own style, be it German, Scottish, Belgian, or all of the above. Be forewarned, however: Colorado brewpub beer is not your father's Old Style lager. Although they do make some lighter beers, most brewpubs pride themselves on their darker, stronger brews, including stouts, porters, and amber ales. The alcohol content usually runs a little higher than in regular beer, and your body won't burn it off as fast, either, when you're high above sea level. So don't be surprised if you find yourself talking a little funny after one or two. Don't worry if you do — you've just picked up a Colorado accent.

Riding and Sliding on That Slippery White Stuff

Colorado's high country is usually under snow from November through May, and the state's many "snow riders" take advantage of the long winter season. If you visit Colorado during the cooler months, you'll need to choose the kind of snow rider you want to be. There are skiers, who slide around on two extremely expensive, colorfully painted, hourglass-shaped, boards; snowboarders, who surf the great white on something akin to a surfboard; sliders and tubers, who careen downhill on sleds and inner tubes in the state's many "snow play" areas; and careless drivers, who skid their SUVs into ditches, bury them to the axles, and get stuck. Colorado's snow riders spend a lot of money on equipment and medical bills, but don't let that stop you. Just pull your goggles down and go!

Watching Broncos Fans in Frenzied Celebration

If you're traveling in Colorado during fall, you'll have the chance to experience one of the most bizarre, intense, animal activities on the planet. No, I'm not talking about the courtship rituals of elk; I'm referring to the behavior of fans of the Denver Broncos football team. From September through December of most years, the coats of Broncos fans turn orange and blue, and their behavior becomes more temperamental and volatile. On Sundays, Broncos fans have been known to do impromptu, celebratory dances, or, in their more aggressive moments, hurl objects and invectives at televised images of football players. You can see these bizarre fall rituals by visiting one of the state's many sports bars on a fall Sunday. The truly adventurous should try to visit the fans in their native habitat at Invesco Field. If you're interested in wildlife watching during springtime, time your visit to coincide with a playoff game for the Colorado Avalanche hockey team.

Dining on Native Game

As of 2002, Colorado's gourmet restaurants generally sport one of two favorite themes. One is French/Asian/American fusion, which consists of fare that's rich, tasty, and as confusing as international relations. You can get this cuisine in nearly all the fancy Colorado towns, usually for about $30 a plate. But if you want to experience traditional Colorado fare, go for the second option: Native game. *Native game* refers to those animals you saw in and around Rocky Mountain National Park, only, in this case, they've been cooked, diced, seasoned, and put on a plate with side dishes. Throughout the state, you can dine on Colorado species such as elk, venison, trout, grouse, pheasant, and even rattlesnake. Most of these animals are really tasty. Give them a shot — that is, a try.

Holding Hands and Soaking Up the Scenery

The color and light in the Colorado Rockies will fill your soul. Sometimes the mountains can seem like a terrestrial version of love. If you're lucky enough to be in the mountains with someone you love, you can multiply the beauty by holding hands or touching. If there's no one around, hold on tighter.

Appendix

Quick Concierge

● ●

*T*his handy section condenses all the practical and pertinent information — from crucial phone numbers to ATM locations — you may need to have a successful and stress-free vacation. And if you believe there is no such thing as being too prepared, I list a bunch of additional information sources for you to consult. And, best of all, you won't need to tip this concierge — although I won't refuse if you insist.

Colorado A to Z: Facts at Your Fingertips

AAA

Members of the American Automobile Association can call ☎800-AAA-HELP for 24-hour emergency road service anywhere in the U.S. AAA has offices in a half-dozen Colorado cities east of the continental divide. Offices in Durango and Grand Junction serve western Colorado. To get exact addresses, log on to www.aaa.com.

American Express

American Express has a full-service office in downtown Denver at 555 17th Street (☎ 303-383-5050). Additional locations in Denver, Boulder, Centennial, Longmont, Wheat Ridge, and Steamboat Springs offer select American Express services. For cardholder services and exact office locations, call ☎ 800-528-4800. To report lost or stolen checks, dial ☎ 800-221-7282.

ATMs

Most Colorado banks and large food stores have automated teller machines connected to the major ATM networks; so do many convenience stores. To locate an ATM nearest your location, contact MasterCard/Cirrus (☎ 800-424-7787; Internet: www.mastercard.com) or Visa/Plus (☎ 800-843-7587; Internet: www.visa.com). Note that if you withdraw money in Colorado from an ATM not affiliated with your bank, you'll generally be charged a service fee of about $1.50.

Business Hours

In Denver, most small retail stores open by 9 a.m. and operate until 5 or 6 p.m. Stores in Colorado's resort communities start and finish their business day an hour or two later, allowing proprietors to capitalize on the dinner crowd. You can expect large department stores such as Wal-Mart to greet customers from about 9 a.m. to 10 p.m.

Most Colorado banks do business on weekdays from at least 9 a.m. to 5 p.m.; the branches in cities often tack on evening and weekend hours. Similarly, the supermarkets in cities often stay open for 24 hours; small-town grocers generally close around 10 p.m. and don't reopen until 7 or 8 a.m. Small-town restaurants close by 10 p.m. — or five minutes before you get there, whichever comes first.

Credit Cards

If your credit card is lost or stolen, call the issuer of your card immediately. To contact American Express, call ☎ 800-528-4800. For MasterCard, dial ☎ 800-307-7309. And the number for Visa is ☎ 800-847-2911.

Doctors

Don't assume that the medical care will be inferior just because you're in the sticks. Colorado's beauty has attracted top-flight physicians to some surprisingly far-flung locales. If you need to see a physician in a non-emergency situation, check with your insurer about your conditions of coverage. If your hotel has a concierge, he or she may be able to recommend a local physician if you become ill. If the *quality* of care still worries you, go to www.bestdoctors. com. For $35 per year, Best Doctors provides subscribers with referrals to physicians who score high in peer evaluations.

Drugstores

Two chain drugstores — Walgreens (☎ 800 WALGREENS or 800-289-2273; Internet: www.walgreens.com) and Longs (☎ 800-865-6647; Internet: www.longs.com) — have a strong presence in Colorado. There's a 24-hour Walgreens pharmacy in Denver at 3000 East Colfax Ave. (☎ 303-331-0815).

Large food stores such as Albertsons (☎ 888-746-7252; Internet: www.albertsons. com) and King Soopers (☎ 801-974-1400; Internet: www.smithsfoodanddrug. com) often have their own pharmacies. And you can still find some independent pharmacies in the state as well.

Emergencies

For fire department, police, or ambulance assistance, call ☎ 911. From hotels and motels, you may need to dial ☎ 9-911.

Fishing

Before you can legally start casting for any of Colorado's 80 fish species, you'll need to obtain a fishing permit from the Colorado Division of Wildlife. An annual permit costs $40.25 for nonresidents, $20.25 for residents. Five-day and one-day permits cost $18.25 and $5.25, respectively, for residents and non-residents alike. Permits are available at local sporting goods stores and at Colorado Division of Wildlife (www.wildlife. state.co.us) offices.

Health

If you don't protect yourself in the mountains, you can become sunburned, dehydrated, and hypothermic — sometimes even in the same day. Exposure to the sun's burning rays increases with elevation. When spending time in the mountains, wear sunblock and sunglasses, even when it seems cloudy.

Hydration helps prevent heat-related illness, hypothermia, and altitude sickness alike. In the dry air, you may not realize how much water you're losing, so drink up! If you're coming from sea level, allow yourself a few days (at least) to rest and acclimate before you start exerting yourself in the mountains. Try starting your trip somewhere — Denver's a good choice — that's a little lower in elevation. To avoid hypothermia, wear multiple layers of synthetic fabrics such as polar fleece and polypropylene, plus a water-resistant outer layer, and, of course, take shelter from wind and rain if you do begin shivering.

Information

For Colorado information, start by contacting the Colorado Tourism Office (☎ 800 COLORADO; Internet: www.colorado.com). See "Where to Get More Information" at the end of this chapter for more details.

Liquor Laws

You must be 21 to consume alcoholic beverages in Colorado. If you do imbibe, don't drive. Colorado has some of the nation's strictest standards for drunk driving. If your blood alcohol content tops 0.05%, you can be charged with driving while intoxicated; if it passes 0.10%, the more serious charge of driving under the influence applies.

Colorado law allows bars to stay open from 7 a.m. until 2 a.m. daily; liquor stores can do business from 7 a.m. to midnight, Monday through Saturday. Liquor stores are the only retail outlets for full-strength beer, wine, and liquor. Grocery stores, gas stations, and convenience stores do sell beer and wine coolers, but the alcohol content of these beverages cannot legally exceed 3.2% by weight.

Mail

You can call ☎ 800-275-8777 to find the location of the post office nearest you, but first you'll need to know which zip code you're in. You can receive mail by having it addressed to your name and "General Delivery," care of the post office of your choice. You will have one month from the date the post office receives it to claim General Delivery mail.

Maps

For driving directions, go to www.mapquest.com or, if you're a member of the American Automobile Association (☎ 800-541-9902; Internet: www.aaa.com), stop by the nearest AAA office.

If you're planning to explore the backcountry, United States Geological Survey (USGS) topographical map can be a lifesaver. You can sometimes find these maps (cost: $6 per map, plus $5 handling per order) at local Forest Service offices and sporting goods stores. Or, you can order directly from the USGS by calling ☎ 888-ASK-USGS or surfing the Internet to www.usgs.gov.

Newspapers

The two major metropolitan daily newspapers in Colorado are the *Denver Post* and *Rocky Mountain News.* Both offer comprehensive coverage of local, state, and national news. Another 18 daily and 31 weekly newspapers report news in smaller cities and towns throughout Colorado. For arts and entertainment coverage, however,

you can often do better by picking up an alternative newspaper such as *Boulder Weekly* (Internet: www.boulderweekly.com) and *Denver Westword* (Internet: www.westword.com).

Safety

Allow extra time to travel on mountain roads, especially during storms. If you plan on hiking in the mountains, make sure to carry extra clothing, food, water, and a topographical map of the area. As you walk, memorize landmarks and terrain features, including the ones behind you, so that you can find your way back if you get confused. During winter, people unfamiliar with avalanche conditions and terrain should hire a guide before venturing into the backcountry.

Smoking

Despite Colorado's reputation for having an active lifestyle (and despite its relative lack of oxygen), over 20% of Colorado adults smoke, just 1% under the national average. Colorado's state government encourages restaurants to develop separate nonsmoking areas, but doesn't mandate these areas. Many cities and towns, however, have passed ordinances that limit smoking. Denver prohibits smoking in restaurants that don't have separate, well-ventilated areas for puffing, and it limits smoking to designated areas in venues such as sports stadiums and museums. Boulder has banned smoking in all restaurants. Because ordinances vary from town to town, smokers should look for ashtrays before lighting up. And if you want to buy tobacco, you must be 18 years old to do so in Colorado.

Taxes

In addition to Colorado's 2.9% state sales tax, you may be asked to pay city sales taxes of up to 4% and county sales taxes of up to 5%. In most Colorado locales, the total sales tax is between 6 and 9%. Some areas levy an additional tax (usually around 2%) on hotel rooms. Cars rented at Denver International Airport are subject to a $2.98

per-day usage fee and a 10% tax designed to recoup the cost of building the airport.

Time Zone

Colorado is located in the Mountain standard time zone, two hours behind New York City and one hour ahead of Los Angeles. From the first Sunday in April through the last Saturday in October, it observes daylight saving time by moving its clocks one hour ahead along with the rest of the United States (except Arizona and parts of Indiana).

Weather Updates

The National Weather Service Web site (www.wrh.noaa.gov) provides current weather forecasts and information for every part of America. You need only type in the zip code of the area that interests you.

During winter, the Colorado Avalanche Information Center (☎ 303-275-5360; Internet: www.geosurvey.state.co.us/avalanche) provides recorded information on current avalanche conditions and mountain weather. The Colorado Department of Transportation (☎ 303-639-1111) provides recorded updates on road conditions throughout the state.

Toll-Free Numbers and Web Sites

Major Airlines

Air Canada
☎ 888-247-2262
www.aircanada.ca

America West Airlines
☎ 800-235-9292
www.americawest.com

American Airlines
☎ 800-433-7300
www.aa.com

American Trans Air
☎ 800-225-2995
www.ata.com

British Airways
☎ 800-247-9297 in U.S.
☎ 0345-222-111 in Britain
www.british-airways.com

Continental Airlines
☎ 800-525-0280
www.continental.com

Delta Air Lines
☎ 800-221-1212
www.delta.com

Frontier Airlines
☎ 800-432-1359
www.frontierairlines.com

JetBlue Airways
☎ 800-538-2583
www.jetblue.com

Mexicana
☎ 800-531-7921
www.mexicana.com

Midwest Express
☎ 800-452-2022
www.midwestexpress.com

Northwest Airlines
☎ 800-225-2525
www.nwa.com

Southwest Airlines
☎ 800-435-9792
www.southwest.com

United Airlines
☎ 800-241-6522
www.united.com

USAirways
☎ 800-428-4322
www.usairways.com

Major car-rental agencies

Advantage
☎ 800-777-5500
www.advantagerentacar.com

Alamo
☎ 800-327-9633
www.goalamo.com

Avis
☎ 800-331-1212 in the Continental U.S.
☎ 800-879-2847 in Canada
www.avis.com

Budget
☎ 800-527-0700
https://rent.drivebudget.com

Dollar
☎ 800-800-4000
www.dollar.com

Enterprise
☎ 800-325-8007
www.enterprise.com

Hertz
☎ 800-654-3131
www.hertz.com

National
☎ 800-227-7368
www.nationalcar.com

Payless
☎ 800-729-5377
www.paylesscarrental.com

Rent-A-Wreck
☎ 800-535-1391
www.rentawreck.com

Thrifty
☎ 800-367-2277
www.thrifty.com

Major hotel and motel chains

Best Western International
☎ 800-528-1234
www.bestwestern.com

Clarion Hotels
☎ 800-252-7466
www.clarion.com

Comfort Inns
☎ 800-228-5150
www.choicehotels.com

Courtyard by Marriott
☎ 800-321-2211
www.courtyard.com

Days Inn
☎ 800-325-2525
www.daysinn.com

Doubletree Hotels
☎ 800-222-8733
www.doubletree.com

Econo Lodges
☎ 800-553-2666
www.choicehotels.com

Fairfield Inn by Marriott
☎ 800-228-2800
www.fairfieldinn.com

Hampton Inn
☎ 800-426-7866
www.hampton-inn.com

Hilton Hotels
☎ 800-774-1500
www.hilton.com

Holiday Inn
☎ 800-465-4329
www.basshotels.com

Howard Johnson
☎ 800-654-2000
www.hojo.com

Hyatt Hotels and Resorts
☎ 800-228-9000
www.hyatt.com

ITT Sheraton
☎ 800-325-3535
www.starwood.com/sheraton

La Quinta Motor Inns
☎ 800-531-5900
www.laquinta.com

Marriott Hotels
☎ 800-228-9290
www.marriott.com

Motel 6
☎ 800-466-8536
www.motel6.com

Quality Inns
☎ 800-228-5151
www.choicehotels.com

Radisson Hotels International
☎ 800-333-3333
www.radisson.com

Ramada Inns
☎ 800-272-6232
www.ramada.com

Red Carpet Inns
☎ 800-251-1962
www.reservahost.com

Red Lion Hotels and Inns
☎ 800-547-8010
www.hilton.com

Residence Inn by Marriott
☎ 800-331-3131
www.residenceinn.com

Rodeway Inns
☎ 800-228-2000
www.choicehotels.com

Travelodge
☎ 800-255-3050
www.travelodge.com

Westin Hotels and Resorts
☎ 800-937-8461
www.westin.com

Wyndham Hotels and Resorts
☎ 800-822-4200
www.wyndham.com

Finding More Information

I packed this book with a lot of information, but if you still want more, you can consult the following resources to get more advice and tips on planning your vacation to Colorado.

Tourist information

For planning information, start by contacting the **Colorado Tourism Office,** 1127 Pennsylvania St., Denver CO 80203 (☎ **800 COLORADO;** Internet: www.colorado.com). The office answers questions and mails out free *Colorado Ski Country* and *Official State Vacation* guides.

For a free *Official Visitors Guide* to Denver, contact the **Denver Metro Convention and Visitors Bureau,** 1668 Larimer St., Denver, CO 80202 (☎ **303-892-1112;** Internet: www.denver.org). The guide has extensive information on hotels, attractions, and dining in and around Denver.

Useful Web sites

The *Rocky Mountain News* keeps past and present stories on its Web site (www.insidedenver.com), as well as links to what it considers the 100 best Web sites in Colorado. Denver's alternative weekly *Westword* (www.westword.com) has an online calendar of upcoming events.

For information on Denver's cultural attractions and events, surf the Internet to www.artstozoo.org. Click "Discounts and Free Tickets" for info on cheap last-minute tickets to performances.

State guides

Frommer's Colorado is an excellent complement to this book. If guidebooks were food, this one would be french fries and *Frommer's Colorado* would be a steak. In other words, *Frommer's Colorado* is a lot more beefy and nourishing, and you can chew on it for a lot longer. Ideally, you'll still want some fries with it, just 'cause they're fun to eat.

Making Dollars and Sense of It

Expense	Daily cost	x	Number of days	=	Total
Airfare					
Local transportation					
Car rental					
Lodging (with tax)					
Parking					
Breakfast					
Lunch					
Dinner					
Snacks					
Entertainment					
Babysitting					
Attractions					
Gifts & souvenirs					
Tips					
Other					
Grand Total					

Fare Game: Choosing an Airline

When looking for the best airfare, you should cover all your bases — 1) consult a trusted travel agent; 2) contact the airline directly, via the airline's toll-free number and/or Web site; 3) check out one of the travel-planning Web sites, such as www.frommers.com.

Travel Agency_____ Phone_____
    Agent's Name_____ Quoted fare_____

Airline 1_____ Quoted fare_____
    Toll-free number/Internet_____

Airline 2_____ Quoted fare_____
    Toll-free number/Internet_____

Web site 1_____ Quoted fare_____

Web site 2_____ Quoted fare_____

Departure Schedule & Flight Information

Airline_____ Flight #_____ Confirmation #_____

Departs_____ Date_____ Time_____ a.m./p.m.

Arrives_____ Date_____ Time_____ a.m./p.m.

Connecting Flight (if any)

Amount of time between flights_____ hours/mins

Airline_____ Flight #_____ Confirmation #_____

Departs_____ Date_____ Time_____ a.m./p.m.

Arrives_____ Date_____ Time_____ a.m./p.m.

Return Trip Schedule & Flight Information

Airline_____ Flight #_____ Confirmation #_____

Departs_____ Date_____ Time_____ a.m./p.m.

Arrives_____ Date_____ Time_____ a.m./p.m.

Connecting Flight (if any)

Amount of time between flights_____ hours/mins

Airline_____ Flight #_____ Confirmation #_____

Departs_____ Date_____ Time_____ a.m./p.m.

Arrives_____ Date_____ Time_____ a.m./p.m.

Fare Game: Choosing an Airline

When looking for the best airfare, you should cover all your bases — 1) consult a trusted travel agent; 2) contact the airline directly, via the airline's toll-free number and/or Web site; 3) check out one of the travel-planning Web sites, such as www.frommers.com.

Travel Agency_____ Phone_____
    Agent's Name_____ Quoted fare_____

Airline 1_____ Quoted fare_____
    Toll-free number/Internet_____

Airline 2_____ Quoted fare_____
    Toll-free number/Internet_____

Web site 1_____ Quoted fare_____

Web site 2_____ Quoted fare_____

Departure Schedule & Flight Information

Airline_____ Flight #_____ Confirmation #_____

Departs_____ Date_____ Time_____ a.m./p.m.

Arrives_____ Date_____ Time_____ a.m./p.m.

Connecting Flight (if any)

Amount of time between flights_____ hours/mins

Airline_____ Flight #_____ Confirmation #_____

Departs_____ Date_____ Time_____ a.m./p.m.

Arrives_____ Date_____ Time_____ a.m./p.m.

Return Trip Schedule & Flight Information

Airline_____ Flight #_____ Confirmation #_____

Departs_____ Date_____ Time_____ a.m./p.m.

Arrives_____ Date_____ Time_____ a.m./p.m.

Connecting Flight (if any)

Amount of time between flights_____ hours/mins

Airline_____ Flight #_____ Confirmation #_____

Departs_____ Date_____ Time_____ a.m./p.m.

Arrives_____ Date_____ Time_____ a.m./p.m.

Sweet Dreams: Choosing Your Hotel

Make a list of all the hotels where you'd like to stay and then check online and call the local and toll-free numbers to get the best price. You should also check with a travel agent, who may be able to get you a better rate.

Hotel & page	Location	Internet	Tel. (local)	Tel. (Toll-free)	Quoted rate

Hotel Checklist

Here's a checklist of things to inquire about when booking your room, depending on your needs and preferences.

- ❏ Smoking/smoke-free room
- ❏ Noise (if you prefer a quiet room, ask about proximity to elevator, bar/restaurant, pool, meeting facilities, renovations, and street)
- ❏ View
- ❏ Facilities for children (crib, roll-away cot, babysitting services)
- ❏ Facilities for travelers with disabilities
- ❏ Number and size of bed(s) (king, queen, double/full-size)
- ❏ Is breakfast included? (buffet, continental, or sit-down?)
- ❏ In-room amenities (hair dryer, iron/board, minibar, etc.)
- ❏ Other_____

Places to Go, People to See, Things to Do

Enter the attractions you would most like to see and decide how they'll fit into your schedule. Next, use the "Going My Way" worksheets that follow to sketch out your itinerary.

Attraction/activity	Page	Amount of time you expect to spend there	Best day and time to go

Places to Go, People to See, Things to Do

Enter the attractions you would most like to see and decide how they'll fit into your schedule. Next, use the "Going My Way" worksheets that follow to sketch out your itinerary.

Attraction/activity	Page	Amount of time you expect to spend there	Best day and time to go

Going "My" Way

Day 1

Hotel _____ Tel. _____

Morning _____

_____

Lunch _____ Tel. _____

Afternoon _____

_____

Dinner _____ Tel. _____

Evening _____

_____

Day 2

Hotel _____ Tel. _____

Morning _____

_____

Lunch _____ Tel. _____

Afternoon _____

_____

Dinner _____ Tel. _____

Evening _____

_____

Day 3

Hotel _____ Tel. _____

Morning _____

_____

Lunch _____ Tel. _____

Afternoon _____

_____

Dinner _____ Tel. _____

Evening _____

_____

Going "My" Way

Day 4
Hotel_____ Tel._____

Morning_____

_____

Lunch_____ Tel._____

Afternoon_____

_____

Dinner_____ Tel._____

Evening_____

_____

Day 5
Hotel_____ Tel._____

Morning_____

_____

Lunch_____ Tel._____

Afternoon_____

_____

Dinner_____ Tel._____

Evening_____

_____

Day 6
Hotel_____ Tel._____

Morning_____

_____

Lunch_____ Tel._____

Afternoon_____

_____

Dinner_____ Tel._____

Evening_____

_____

Index

• **C** •

● **E** ●

● **F** ●

• N •

• O •

• T •

FOR DUMMIES®

The easy way to get more done and have more fun

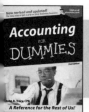

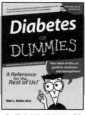

FOR DUMMIES®

A world of resources to help you grow

HOME, GARDEN & HOBBIES

0-7645-5295-3

0-7645-5130-2

0-7645-5106-X

Also available:

Auto Repair For Dummies
(0-7645-5089-6)

Chess For Dummies
(0-7645-5003-9)

Home Maintenance For Dummies
(0-7645-5215-5)

Organizing For Dummies
(0-7645-5300-3)

Piano For Dummies
(0-7645-5105-1)

Poker For Dummies
(0-7645-5232-5)

Quilting For Dummies
(0-7645-5118-3)

Rock Guitar For Dummie
(0-7645-5356-9)

Roses For Dummies
(0-7645-5202-3)

Sewing For Dummies
(0-7645-5137-X)

FOOD & WINE

0-7645-5250-3

0-7645-5390-9

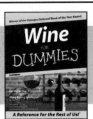
0-7645-5114-0

Also available:

Bartending For Dummies
(0-7645-5051-9)

Chinese Cooking For Dummies
(0-7645-5247-3)

Christmas Cooking For Dummies
(0-7645-5407-7)

Diabetes Cookbook For Dummies
(0-7645-5230-9)

Grilling For Dummies
(0-7645-5076-4)

Low-Fat Cooking For Dummies
(0-7645-5035-7)

Slow Cookers For Dummies
(0-7645-5240-6)

TRAVEL

0-7645-5453-0

0-7645-5438-7

0-7645-5448-4

Also available:

America's National Parks For Dummies
(0-7645-6204-5)

Caribbean For Dummies
(0-7645-5445-X)

Cruise Vacations For Dummies 2003
(0-7645-5459-X)

Europe For Dummies
(0-7645-5456-5)

Ireland For Dummies
(0-7645-6199-5)

France For Dummies
(0-7645-6292-4)

London For Dummies
(0-7645-5416-6)

Mexico's Beach Resorts For Dummies
(0-7645-6262-2)

Paris For Dummies
(0-7645-5494-8)

RV Vacations For Dummies
(0-7645-5443-3)

Walt Disney World & Orlando For Dummies
(0-7645-5444-1)

Available wherever books are sold. Go to www.dummies.com or call 1-877-762-2974 to order direct.

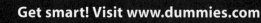

FOR DUMMIES®

Helping you expand your horizons and realize your potential

INTERNET

The Internet For Dummies
0-7645-0894-6

The Internet All-in-One Desk Reference For Dummies
0-7645-1659-0

eBay For Dummies
0-7645-1642-6

Also available:

America Online 7.0 For Dummies
(0-7645-1624-8)

Genealogy Online For Dummies
(0-7645-0807-5)

The Internet All-in-One Desk Reference For Dummies
(0-7645-1659-0)

Internet Explorer 6 For Dummies
(0-7645-1344-3)

The Internet For Dummies Quick Reference
(0-7645-1645-0)

Internet Privacy For Dummies
(0-7645-0846-6)

Researching Online For Dummies
(0-7645-0546-7)

Starting an Online Business For Dummies
(0-7645-1655-8)

DIGITAL MEDIA

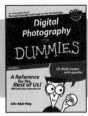

Digital Photography For Dummies
0-7645-1664-7

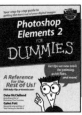

Photoshop Elements 2 For Dummies
0-7645-1675-2

Digital Video For Dummies
0-7645-0806-7

Also available:

CD and DVD Recording For Dummies
(0-7645-1627-2)

Digital Photography All-in-One Desk Reference For Dummies
(0-7645-1800-3)

Digital Photography For Dummies Quick Reference
(0-7645-0750-8)

Home Recording for Musicians For Dummies
(0-7645-1634-5)

MP3 For Dummies
(0-7645-0858-X)

Paint Shop Pro "X" For Dummies
(0-7645-2440-2)

Photo Retouching & Restoration For Dummi
(0-7645-1662-0)

Scanners For Dummies
(0-7645-0783-4)

GRAPHICS

PowerPoint 2002 For Dummies
0-7645-0817-2

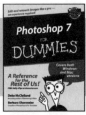

Photoshop 7 For Dummies
0-7645-1651-5

Macromedia Flash MX For Dummies
0-7645-0895-4

Also available:

Adobe Acrobat 5 PDF For Dummies
(0-7645-1652-3)

Fireworks 4 For Dummies
(0-7645-0804-0)

Illustrator 10 For Dummies
(0-7645-3636-2)

QuarkXPress 5 For Dummies
(0-7645-0643-9)

Visio 2000 For Dummi
(0-7645-0635-8)

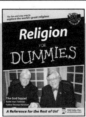

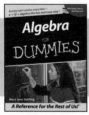
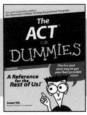